EXCAVATIONS IN CASTLETOWN, ISLE OF MAN 1989–1992

EXCAVATIONS IN CASTLETOWN, ISLE OF MAN 1989–1992

P J Davey, D J Freke and D A Higgins

with contributions from

M M Archibald, G Egan, C T Fisher, R Hurst Vose,
A C C Johnson, N C Johnson, J Lawrence, S B Mc Cartan,
M Mc Carthy, J Roscow, J R Senior, E A Slater and S D White

Liverpool University Press

First published 1996 by
LIVERPOOL UNIVERSITY PRESS
SENATE HOUSE, LIVERPOOL, L69 3BX

British Library Cataloguing-in-Publication Data
A British Library CIP Record is available
ISBN 0–85323–389–6 cased
     0–85323–399–3 paper

Typeset by Wilmaset, Birkenhead, Wirral
Printed and bound in the European Union by
Redwood Books, Trowbridge, UK

CONTENTS

ENVIRONMENTAL EVIDENCE FROM CASTLE RUSHEN AND CASTLE RUSHEN STORES

LIST OF ILLUSTRATIONS

Introduction

Castle Rushen

Bank Street

Castle Rushen Stores

Technical Appendix

LIST OF TABLES

Castle Rushen Stores

Environmental Evidence

LIST OF CONTRIBUTORS

Dr Peter Davey, Department of Archaeology, University of Liverpool

Mr David J Freke, R.P.S. Clouston

Dr David A Higgins, Department of Archaeology, University of Liverpool

Miss Marion Archibald, Department of Coins and Medals, The British Museum

Mr Geoff Egan

Dr Clemency Fisher, Liverpool Museum, National Museums and Galleries on Merseyside

Ruth Hurst Vose, Department of Archaeology, University of Liverpool

Mr Andrew Johnson, Manx National Heritage

Mr Nick Johnson, Department of Archaeology, University of Liverpool

Jane Lawrence, Department of Archaeology, University of Liverpool

Sinéad B Mc Cartan, Department of Archaeology and Ethnography, Ulster Museum

Ms Margaret Mc Carthy, Department of Archaeology, University College Cork

Mr J Roscow

Dr John Senior, Department of Adult and Continuing Education, University of Durham

Professor Elizabeth Slater, Department of Archaeology, University of Liverpool

Susie White, Department of Archaeology, University of Liverpool

ACKNOWLEDGEMENTS

This monograph is the culmination of many months of hard work over the last six years both in the field and during post-excavation; thanks are due to everyone who has worked so hard to make this possible. The work was commissioned and funded by Manx National Heritage, without whose continued interest and support this advance in our understanding of Castletown's past would not have been possible. In particular, the authors would like to thank the Director of Manx National Heritage, Stephen Harrison, and its Deputy Director, Wendy Horn. This publication has been produced jointly by the Centre for Manx Studies and the Field Archaeology Unit, University of Liverpool. Many people have provided valuable support and advice during its production. Special thanks are due to Marshall Cubbon, former director of the Manx Museum, and to Frank Cowin, who have provided a wealth of local knowledge. Particular thanks are due to Susie White, who has been responsible for the compilation of the report, and to Fenella Bazin, Nick Johnson, Philippa Tomlinson and Jenny Woodcock for the long hours which they spent in checking and editing.

Authors who have contributed to the various sections in this monograph would like to make the following acknowledgements.

Castle Rushen

David Freke directed the 1989 excavation and would like to acknowledge the assistance of Andrew Johnson, the Assistant Keeper of Field Archaeology at the Manx Museum, and Betty Southall, who supervised the finds work. The workforce was composed of volunteers, Ian Burrell, Jim Roscow, Robert Farrar, Jerzy Podbereski, Alan Skillan and Edmund Hornby, to whom he is most grateful for giving their time and energy so generously. He is also indebted to Frank Cowin, who made his considerable knowledge of the castle's history freely available, to the custodian Iain MacKinlay, who gave much practical assistance, often in uncomfortable circumstances, and to the contractors, who loaned equipment and gave advice and practical assistance. He would also like to thank Peter Davey for his enthusiasm and assistance in the production of this report.

Susie White is grateful to Dr Rodney Wright from the University of Liverpool and Dr Trevor Ford, retired senior lecturer from the University of Leicester, for helping with the identification of the stone fragments. She also wishes to thank Debra Jaques and Brian Irving of the Environmental Archaeology Unit at the University of York for their identification of the shark vertebrae and the piece of worked bone waste.

Bank Street

Andrew Johnson directed the 1989 excavations and would like to thank the owner, Mr J Smith, for his patience and interest, and also the two volunteers, Mr Alan Skillan and Mr Cyril Renshaw, for their help during the course of the excavation.

Castle Rushen Stores

Jennifer Lewis directed the 1991 trial work and would like to thank all those who gave of their time and energy so freely to assist in the excavation: Margaret Davidson, Fenella Dawson, Robert Farrar, Bill Kissack, Ritchie McNicholl, Jerzy Podbereski, Fred Radcliffe, Alan Skillan and Marjorie Vernon.

David Higgins directed the 1992 excavations and would like to thank the owners, Mr J W Callow and Mr J M Grady, for allowing access to the site and the architects, McLeod Shipley, for providing plans of the buildings. Mr Callow was also most informative about the history of the site and gave practical help with tools and equipment. Thanks are also due to all those who worked so hard with the excavation and finds processing: Andrew Bates, Stuart Beardwell, Ian Burrell, Robert Comber, Chantel Costain, Margaret Davidson, Anna Fargher, Fenella Farrer, Robert Farrer, Andrew Hopwood, Edmund Hornby, Andrew Johnson, Ken Knight, Ritchie McNicholl, Robert Middleton, Sarah Milligan, Jerzy Podbereski ('Buster'), Tim Porter, Alan Skillan, Katie Southall, Neil Southall, Emilia Wilton-Godberfforde, Helen Wilton-Godberfforde and Ruth Wilton-Godberfforde. Particular thanks are due to Nick Johnson and Betty Southall, who helped supervise the excavations and carried out the post-excavation processing of the finds. He would also like to thank Jennifer Lewis for her helpful comments and discussions of the 1991 excavation.

Geoff Egan would like to thank Hazel Forsyth for advice on the knife end-cap and Dr Simon Hillson of the Institute of Archaeology for advice concerning the marked lead shot.

Peter Davey is grateful to the following for their assistance in the identification of the pottery: J G Hurst, M Ponsford and J A Axworthy-Rutter. He also wishes to thank the staff of Manx National Heritage for their help with access to the collections and library, especially Larch Garrad, Andrew Johnson, Hazel Simons and Wendy Thirkettle.

David Higgins would like to express his thanks to Mrs E H Brotherton-Ratcliffe for providing access to the as yet unpublished Cheshire Tile Census, and for much other useful help and advice in identifying the floor tiles; and to Dr Philippa Tomlinson for identifying the plant and fibre remains.

Environmental Evidence

Margaret Mc Carthy would like to thank all those who have contributed towards the production of her report: Dr Peter Davey, Director of the Centre for Manx Studies, for details on the phasing of the deposits at Castle Rushen and for general discussion; Mr Stephen Harrison, Director, and Ms Wendy Horn,

Deputy Director, of the Manx Museum for their assistance during the identification of the Castle Rushen material; Dr Larch Garrad, Assistant Keeper at the Manx Museum, who provided useful information on the natural history of the island; and finally Nick Johnson, at the Centre for Manx Studies, for advice received at the final stages of writing the report. She is grateful to the Department of Archaeology, University College Cork, for allowing access to its skeletal collections.

Clem Fisher is very grateful to Jo Bailey, of the Bird Group of the Natural History Museum, for checking the identities of some of the bones, notably the two fragments of Great Auk. She would also like to thank Effie Warr, Librarian of the N H M Library at Tring, for helping her with references for the report.

Peter Davey wishes to thank Dr Stephen Hawkins and staff of the Port Erin Marine Laboratory for their assistance in the identification of the molluscs, and discussion of part of the limpet collection.

Illustrations

The original Castle Rushen pottery illustrations were prepared by Betty Southall. The medieval floor tiles, clay tobacco pipes and hair curler were drawn by David Higgins. All of the other finished plans and finds illustrations have been drawn by Susie White.

Fig 1   View of Castletown from the air

THE ARCHAEOLOGY OF CASTLETOWN

Introduction

P J Davey

'Towns have some claim to be more representative of the nature of the society of which they formed part than any other type of site. It will be there that we are most likely to find the archaeological evidence of both long-distance and local trade, of specialisation and technological evidence in manufactures, of the exploitation of natural resources, of social differentiation, of the means of political control, and of the religious aspirations of the population' (Schofield, Palliser and Harding 1981, v).

Town and castle

Castletown is situated on a gravel terrace at the mouth of Silver Burn, overlooking a small natural harbour (Fig 1). The castle, which was already in existence in 1265, was placed in a dominant position which could guard both river and sea frontages. The town, as its English and Manx (Balley Cashtal) names imply, appears to have grown up around the castle. The earliest extant list of cottages dated 1506 (Appendix 1) includes a total of 86 properties, which implies a population of around 500—a small town by any standards. The first reliable census figure of 785 was produced some 220 years later in 1726 (Moore 1900, 1, 412). The Collins chart of 1693 shows a small settlement centred on the castle and spread along both river and sea waterfronts (Fig 2).

Although the town lacks a defensive circuit of walls, the appearance of its present-day street system suggests both its antiquity and the dependence of this network on the focus provided by the castle (Fig 2).

The objects of archaeological research

A number of significant questions concerning the history of Castletown can only be seriously approached through archaeological evidence, in particular in the period up to the sixteenth century, before more detailed written records are available.

– Archaeology can clarify chronological issues. When was the first settlement on the site? When does that settlement become truly urban? Does it predate the castle?
– Archaeology can also provide evidence for sequence and change. In what order was the castle built? Are the present standing buildings the earliest defensive structures on the site? How did the town develop over time? Where was its original focus? Is there evidence for change in its location or function? Are episodes of town planning apparent?
– Archaeology can help to understand past activities on the site. In particular, artifactual evidence of productive industrial activity and the consumption of goods and materials should be recovered.
– Archaeology can provide models for economic and political relationships. What was the economic relationship between Castletown and the other towns in the Isle of Man, such as Peel, Ramsey and Douglas? How far were goods and materials derived from overseas and how far locally produced? Is the transfer of the Lordship of Man to the Stanleys in 1406 reflected in the archaeological evidence and, if so, in what ways?

All of these questions are capable of resolution through archaeological excavation.

Previous excavations in Castletown

Although a certain amount of material evidence has come to light over the years as a result of repairs and alterations to the castle, the excavations described in this volume are the first to be carried out with serious archaeological intent.

The most important previous work in the town was carried out by Cubbon at the medieval chapel of St Mary's, later the Castletown Grammar School, in 1960–61 and 1971 (Fig 3, No 9; Cubbon 1971). The excavations recovered artifactual evidence mainly of eighteenth- and nineteenth-century date, including pottery, glass, animal bones and shellfish (Cubbon 1971, 11). Only a handful of pottery sherds dated to the medieval period and none to the actual period of construction of the building which, on architectural grounds, appears to have taken place between 1190 and 1230 (Cubbon 1971, 26). The report provides a useful

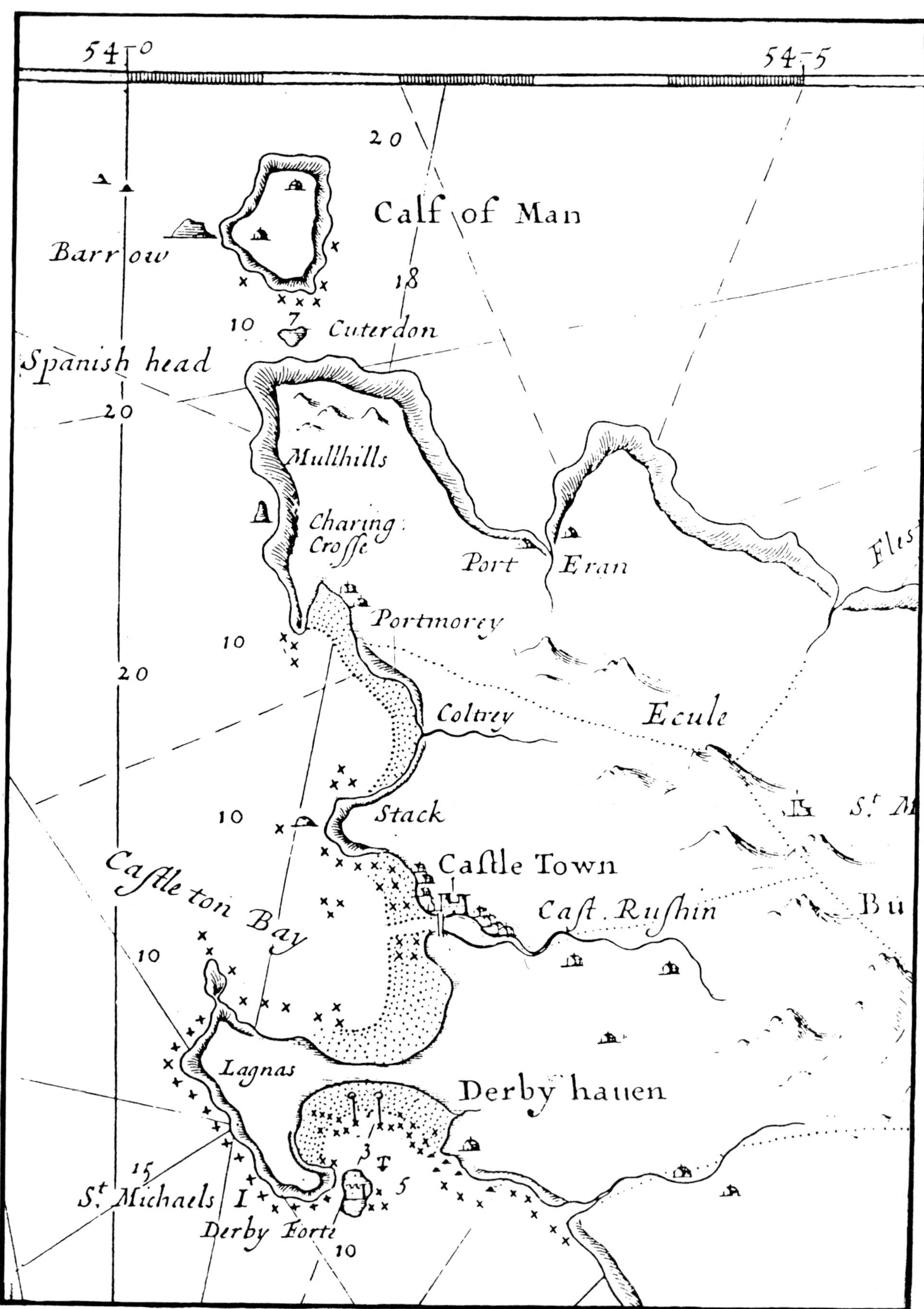

Fig 2   Part of Collins' 1693 chart of the Isle of Man

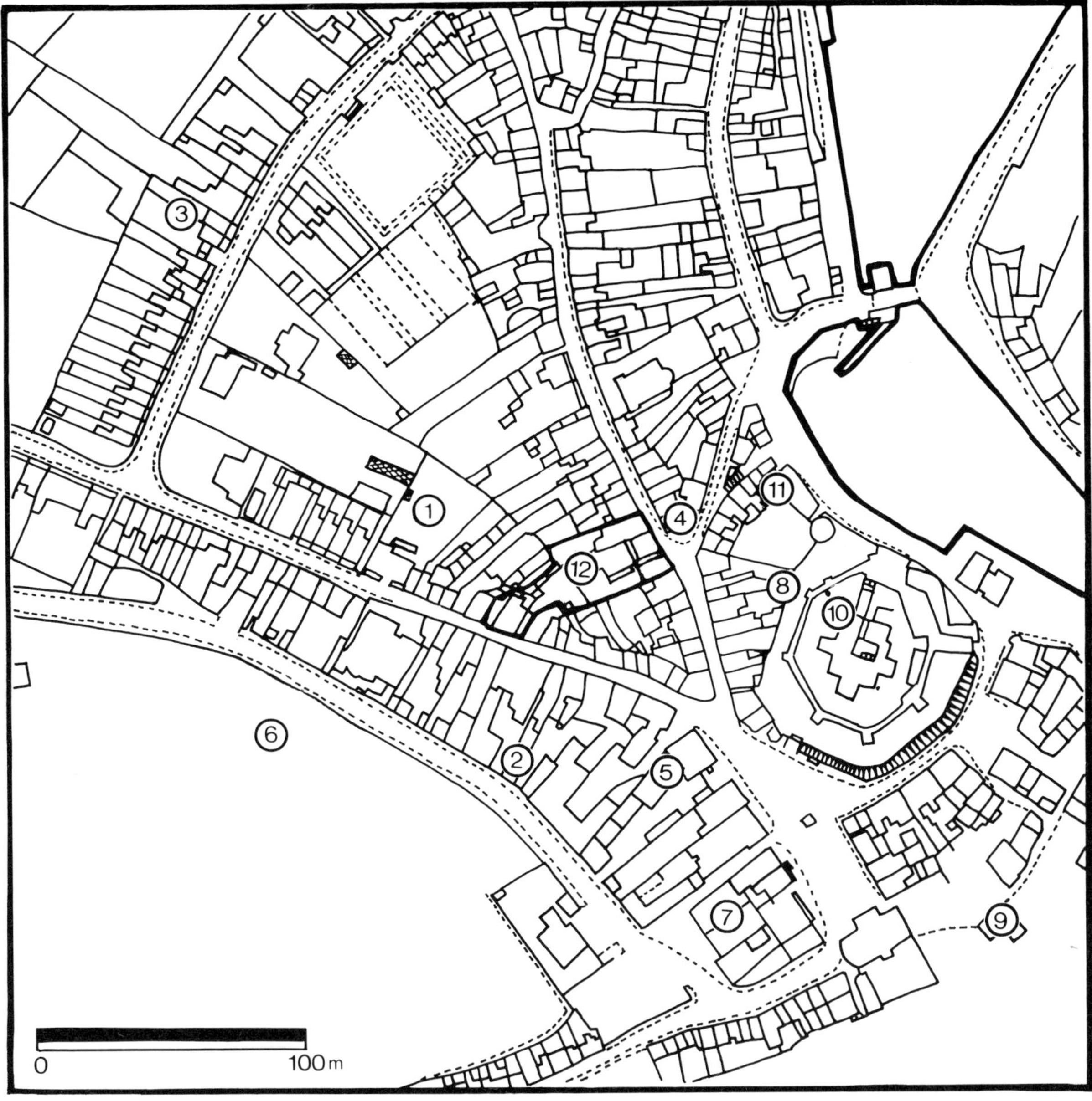

Fig 3   Map of Castletown, showing location of sites mentioned in the text (based on the 1959 Ordnance Survey Map):   1 Bagnio House   2 Croft Cottage   3 18 The Crofts   4 18 Malew Street   5 8 The Parade 6 Farrant's Flat   7 4 The Parade   8 16 Malew Street   9 Grammar School (St Mary's Chapel)   10 Castle Rushen 1989   11 Bank Street 1989   12 Castle Rushen Stores 1991 and 1992

summary of the documentary sources for the history of the chapel and grammar school. In the context of the earlier history of the town, one of its most important points is that the romanesque arches of the chapel, dating from the late twelfth or early thirteenth century, must have been built before any of the extant stone structures of the castle were erected. That a chapel of this size, with a south aisle, should have been needed at this period suggests that contemporary archaeological deposits in both town and castle may still exist.

The most extensive attempt to locate the earlier archaeology of Castletown was made in 1968 by the Isle of Man Natural History and Antiquarian Society, led by Dr L S Garrad (Fig 3, Nos 1–8; Garrad 1969). A number of small trial trenches were excavated in a variety of locations in the town. No structural evidence was located but artifactual material was collected from nine sites (Fig 3). The majority of the 77 pottery sherds recovered were of eighteenth- or nineteenth-century date, with only two certain medieval finds, 12 of sixteenth-century and six of seventeenth-century date. The post-medieval material does exhibit considerable range both in quality and source, suggesting a cosmopolitan centre with a dynamic economy.

Castle and town archaeology elsewhere in the Isle of Man

Peel is the only other urban centre in the island where excavations have been carried out. Between 1982 and 1987 D J Freke undertook extensive excavations at Peel Castle, particularly in the area of the 'Earl of Derby's Quarters' to the north of the Cathedral (Freke forthcoming). These illustrated complex prehistoric and Early Christian phases of occupation before the construction of the first of a series of ramparts in the Norse period, together with a rich, diverse material culture.

Elsewhere in the island, only at Peel, where 16 1 metre square quadrats were excavated in 1985 (Philpott and Davey 1992), has any other archaeological evidence been retrieved from archaeological contexts in a town. The Peel quadrats included a number from the harbour area reclaimed during the 1500s and two at the lower end of Castle Street, which identified medieval structural evidence of floors, post-features and charcoal spreads. The material culture enjoyed in the town was indistinguishable from that recovered from the castle on St Patrick's Isle.

The contents of the monograph

The purpose of this volume is to provide an excavation report with associated finds analyses for each of the three excavations that are included.

The first opportunity to excavate came in 1989 when, in advance of the re-presentation of Castle Rushen to the public, Manx National Heritage decided to investigate the north-western part of the outer courtyard. This was carried out on its behalf between August and October 1989 by the Field Archaeology Unit of Liverpool University under the direction of D J Freke (Fig 3, No 10).

Later in 1989, A C C Johnson of the Manx Museum was able to excavate a small area behind Bank Street, very close to the castle's outer defences (Fig 3, No 11).

In 1991 and 1992 a large area of the town between Malew Street and Arbory Street became available for excavation, in advance of a shopping development. J M Lewis and D A Higgins of the Field Archaeology Unit of Liverpool University dug three test pits, followed by extensive area excavations in three trenches on the site (Fig 3, No 12).

The structural evidence from each site is presented first. This information is followed by a series of specialist finds reports. When all of the site evidence and artifacts have been discussed, there follows a section in which the environmental evidence for both Castle Rushen and Castle Rushen Stores is presented.

There are two substantive appendices: one on the 1506 list of cottagers in Castletown, the other on the thin-sectioning of a number of granite-tempered pottery sherds. There is also a technical appendix, which includes a list of pottery codes and a summary list of the excavated contexts and stratigraphic matrices that should be referred to when any relative chronological question occurs in the main texts.

The excavations between 1989 and 1992 reported on in this volume represent the first sustained effort to locate and excavate archaeological structures both at the castle and in the town, and are the first truly urban excavations in the Isle of Man.

EXCAVATIONS AT CASTLE RUSHEN, 1989

The Excavations

D J Freke

Introduction

Excavations were carried out at Castle Rushen by D J Freke of the University of Liverpool's Field Archaeology Unit, on behalf of the Manx Museum and National Trust, from 9th August to 1st October 1989. In addition, archaeological supervision was provided during the excavation of two narrow cable trenches in July 1989. The area of the main excavation agreed with the Manx Museum was in the north-west part of the outer courtyard (Fig 4) and was intended to examine the sequence of courtyards and any structures and features associated with them. The requirements of the restoration work at the castle had produced a particular interest in the early drainage systems.

Background

The project was a response to discussions with the Director and the Deputy Director of the Manx Museum and National Trust about proposals, submitted at their invitation in February 1989, for an archaeological investigation at Castle Rushen, which would form part of the research required for the new presentation of the castle to the public in 1991. The scope of the proposals was, therefore, limited to the parts of the castle's history which could be researched and reported on during the timetable set for the presentation programme. They were not intended to explore the full research potential of Castle Rushen. Inevitably, further lines of research and new questions have arisen out of results obtained by carrying out the present scheme.

Previous archaeological work

There has been no previous systematic archaeological work carried out at Castle Rushen, although there have been refurbishment programmes aimed at the consolidation and elucidation of the buildings from time to time. As at least some parts of the castle have been in active use continuously, there have been practical schemes to maintain the fabric from early in its history to the present day, and some of these have revealed evidence of the castle's development as well as contributing to it. The most valuable of these programmes, from the point of view of establishing a basic understanding of the structure and its development, was the work of Armitage Rigby in 1910 during the major refurbishment carried out for Lord Raglan (Rigby 1927) and the re-interpretation of Rigby's evidence by O'Neil over 40 years ago (O'Neil 1951). To these can be added the studies of Robert Curphey, who brought together in summary form the documentary evidence for the castle's history (Curphey 1982). O'Neil's interpretive study concentrated on the fabric of the keep and involved no investigative probing of the archaeology. Unpublished research by Frank Cowin has recently added to the picture of the castle's development, and has thrown doubt on some of the previously accepted dates (Cowin pers comm).

Present knowledge

The present interpretation of the castle is based on studies carried out 70 years ago and revised over 40 years ago, with no input from systematic archaeological research, so much remains conjectural or provisional in the following account. The castle keep is generally reckoned to have been commenced in the late twelfth century as a square tower, with projecting towers added in the early thirteenth century and again in the fourteenth century. The keep is assumed to have been surrounded by a bailey and protected by a ditch. There was major rebuilding in the fourteenth century, perhaps to repair the destruction wrought by enemy action, and to up-date the defences. This included the construction of a curtain wall, and in the outer ward thus formed a collection of buildings was erected which by the mid-eighteenth century included courtrooms, two kitchens, three sheds, a mint, a chapel and the Earl of Derby's house. The latter still stands, albeit much modified, and the sites of several of the other buildings were revealed in the work of 1910, although their mid-eighteenth century functions are probably not the same as those of several centuries earlier. Corbels visible on the internal face of the curtain wall indicate that such structures were nonetheless envisaged by the builders of the outer defences in the fourteenth

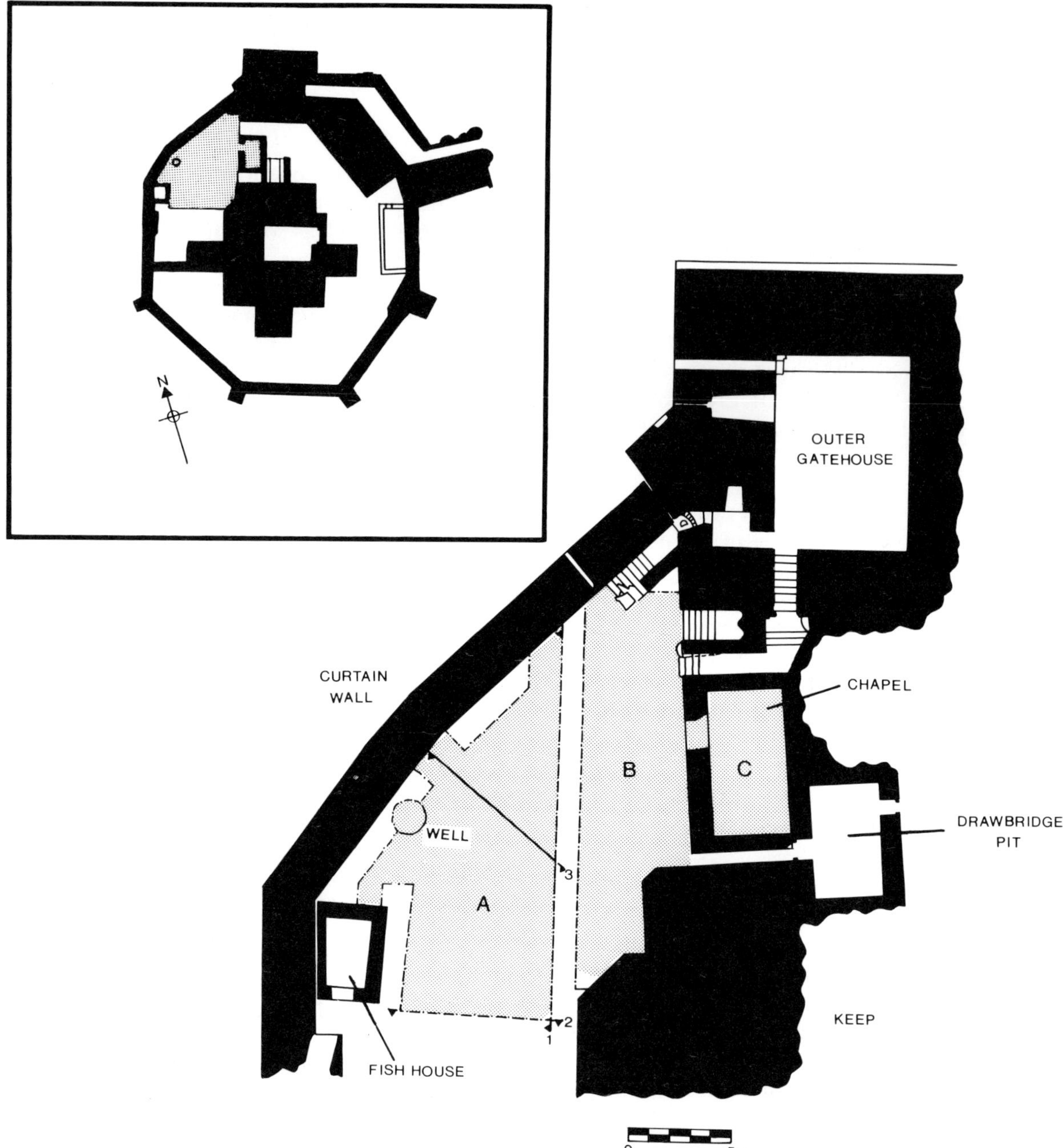

Fig 4   Castle Rushen, Trench and Section Location Plan

century. The ditch was filled and a glacis was built around it in the sixteenth century to counter the introduction of cannon. The modification of the castle to house the gaol in 1813 resulted in considerable reconstruction and demolition.

Research possibilities

The critical problems at Castle Rushen which might be amenable to archaeological investigation are as follows.

The existence of structures pre-dating the stone keep

It has been argued that the stone keep is the first building on the site, with the motte at Cronk Mooar near Port Erin being a possible earlier seigneurial castle. This proposition requires testing, which is only possible through archaeological methods. There is also the possibility that the castle is on the site of an earlier settlement, which is not unlikely given the physical advantages of the area. Investigations into both these possibilities would require area excavations beside the walls of the keep in the outer ward and within the courtyard of the keep itself. If any early structures do exist there is a good chance of recovering timber artifacts and structures from the waterlogged layers beneath the castle.

The date of the keep

The present dating of the keep is based on the similarity of the castle layout and construction to Norman castles, such as Trim in Ireland, and Norse castles, such as Cubbie Roo's Castle in Orkney. There is no independent archaeological evidence for such dating and the investigation of this problem would also entail excavations beside the walls of the keep. The modern batter at the foot of the keep's walls will make the investigation of the foundations particularly awkward.

The date of the curtain wall

The date of the curtain wall is conventionally ascribed to the fourteenth century, and on this depends the date of the raising of the keep to enable defenders to fire over it. The traditional date is derived from events in the fourteenth century which might reasonably be supposed to require the rebuilding of the castle, but there is no independent structural or archaeological evidence to support it. A small trench to examine the foundations of the curtain wall would be likely to provide evidence which would confirm or contradict this dating.

The detailed elucidation of the development of the keep

Much recording was done by Rigby, and O'Neil, Curphey and Cowin have produced detailed interpretive material, but a full stone-by-stone survey of the remaining fabric would provide a permanent record of the modifications and allow detailed studies with reference to the recorded masonry to be carried out.

The date and function of ancillary structures in the outer ward

It is probable that the earliest buildings in the outer ward were medieval and contemporary with the curtain wall, on the evidence of corbels apparently built into sections of the wall to support them. The corbels on the northern stretch of wall overlooking the trench may have been inserted. Subsequent re-use and rebuilding over four centuries makes the original dates, functions and layouts of these buildings impossible to assess without archaeological research. Understanding the evolution of this accommodation within the castle precincts would provide evidence for the life of the castle, which is necessary to complement the evidence of the surviving structures. It was considered that area exca-

vation of parts of the outer ward should produce such information without the necessity of excavating to any great depth.

The layout of the outer ward during its use as a prison

The castle was remodelled as a prison in the early nineteenth century and the outer ward divided into exercise areas for the various categories of prisoner. The north-west portion was designated for the use of the female prisoners. A chapel sealed it off from the gatehouse and Derby House area, while a wall divided it from the part of the outer ward to the south-west. This part of the castle's history is not well represented following Rigby's activities in the early twentieth century, but the female exercise yard was considered to be a discrete area which could be investigated, especially as the ruins of the chapel still stand.

These aspects of potential research were considered in the light of the overall presentation project and its practical requirements, and a research strategy was developed.

The research aims of the 1989 excavation

The requirement to provide an information base for the presentation programme indicated that the layout, date and function of the prison and ancillary buildings in the outer ward to the north-west of the gatehouse were given priority. The excavation programme was particularly directed to the use of the area as a prison in the early nineteenth century. This was intended to make the most effective use of the visible remains, as well as provide evidence for an important aspect of the castle's history not apparent elsewhere. Also built into the programme was an intention to investigate the date of the curtain wall, upon which depends both the dating of the earliest ancillary buildings and the dating of the raising of the keep.

The only visible remains of the nineteenth-century prison period of the castle's history in the area west of the gatehouse are the low walls and flagged floor of the chapel. The steps up to the wall walk do not appear in their present position on a plan showing the layout of the castle during its prison phase. The area was designated as the female prisoners' exercise yard and on the plan it was separated from the adjacent area by a wall, of which no trace survives above ground. It was proposed that the line and construction details of this feature should be investigated. Access from the exercise yard to the interior of the castle was through a door in the north-west corner of the tower, and some evidence for this should also survive in the layout of the yard surface.

The intention of the excavation was therefore to establish the layout of the female exercise yard and associated buildings at the time of the castle's use as a prison, and to examine the foundations of the curtain wall. It was expected that the excavation would recover artifacts related to the use of the area and evidence of the development of the castle as a prison. Rigby reported three layers of cobbles in the courtyard, but it was not clear if these all related to the prison period or earlier. The excavation was intended to relocate the yard surfaces and examine their structure and inter-relationships.

Method

The area indicated in Figure 4 was excavated to ascertain the presence, date and functions of buildings constructed there and the layers associated with them. The depth of the deposits was not expected to be very great, given the evidence of the water-table in the well and Rigby's report of water-logging at the present level when he removed the overburden in 1910. In addition, the two cable trenches dug under archaeological supervision in July 1989 showed apparently natural clay at a depth of approximately 200mm. It was thought likely that features would be revealed which would merit display and consolidation. Because of the practical difficulty of its bulk and the uncertainty about the level at which the site should be restored until the results of the excavation were assessed, spoil was kept on site in a dump to the south of the trench.

Recording

A grid reference system was established, with its notional origin outside the curtain wall. This was to enable any future work which might be carried out in the courtyard to be related to the same grid. The site was given a Manx Museum accession code of 89.159 and contexts were numbered in a single numerical series in the order of their discovery. A single context recording system was adopted and, for the convenience of on-site references and planning, the site was divided into three areas designated A, B and C (eg, see Fig 4). General finds were recorded under context numbers and finds of particular interest by virtue of their value, fragility, significance or location were assigned a two-letter special find code and grid reference in addition to their context number identification. The stratigra-

phic position of each of the contexts referred to in the following report is shown on the Site Matrix diagram (Figs 65, 66 and 67).

Results

The early ditch or moat

The earliest feature was a large ditch (78) which was sectioned in two places and detected in a third (Figs 5 and 6, Section 2). It survived as a feature 4m wide and 1.2m deep, steep sided and flat bottomed. It was probably originally deeper and wider, having lost its upper portion through later levelling operations. In the oblique section recorded in Area A (Fig 8, Section 3), its fill was clean clay in its lower levels, and coarse gravels and small stone chips in its upper levels. There were thin smears of organic material near the bottom and two lenses of gravelly material in the clay fill, the only characteristics which distinguished it from the clay the ditch was dug into here. In the section recorded at the southern edge of the site in Area A, however, the ditch was filled with layers of coarse gravel. Thirteenth- or early fourteenth-century pottery recovered from within its fill suggests that it is medieval in origin.

The plan of the ditch or moat was not fully recovered, although the western edge of the top of the gravel fill was traceable for 12m. At the bottom of this feature was a well-made stone box drain with an incline down to the north (Drain O). This had been laid in a trench cut through the bottom layer of clayey silt and into the natural clay at the bottom of the ditch. The ditch showed no signs of recutting except to insert the drain.

A second early feature was a short stretch of masonry (194) underlying both the outer gatehouse and the curtain wall at the extreme north end of the site (Fig 6, Section 1). It was massively constructed of mortared limestone blocks and the fragment revealed in the trench must represent only a small portion of a major structure. This structure survived at least up to four courses and 0.8m high above a wide offset of large rough limestone blocks, interpreted as the ground level at the time of its construction. The masonry could not be investigated below this offset within the confines of the trench. The upstanding face appeared to be faceted, or possibly roughly curved, but there was not enough of the structure visible in the restricted area of the trench to establish which. The masonry courses of the foundations of the curtain wall butt up to and run over the top of this truncated structure. The foundations of the outer gatehouse similarly run over this structure. It could not be dated except relatively, its relationship with the gatehouse and curtain wall demonstrating that it was earlier than

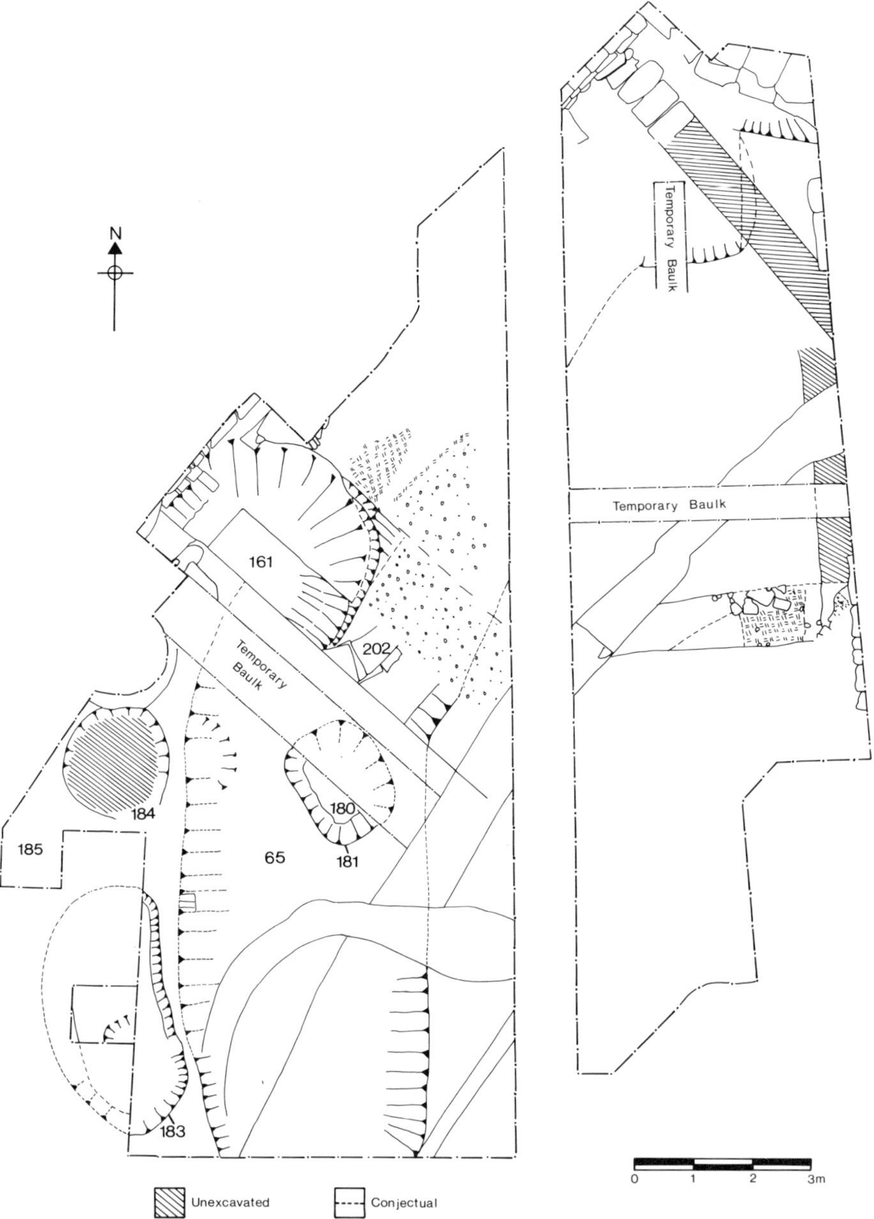

Fig 5   Castle Rushen, Trench Plan 1—Pits and Ditches

both. Its relationship with the ditch described above could not be determined. A box drain built through the curtain wall which lies higher than the foundation offset of the masonry may be the same one which was revealed in the ditch. The masonry may represent an outwork associated with the keep, which was swept away by the curtain wall.

The curtain wall

The inner face of the curtain wall (195) was examined at three points in an attempt to date it and determine its method of construction (Figs 6 and 8, Sections 1, 2 and 3). Each of the three attempts to examine the foundations thoroughly was frustrated by either a factor in the stratigraphy or by the timetable of the project.

The stratigraphy at the initial location at the north end of the site, east of the main baulk (Fig 6, Section 1), was confused by later drains and steps and by restricted access. The proximity of standing structures and their foundations also limited the scope of the investigations. The second attempt to establish a section against the inside of the curtain wall north of the well (Fig 8, Section 3) encountered a deep waterlogged late-medieval pit (161) which had totally removed earlier deposits. There was no time to pursue the third option at the north end of the site to the west of the main baulk, where there were apparently none of the later disturbances which complicated the adjacent section. The investigations did, however, locate an offset approximately 0.9m to 1.2m below present court-

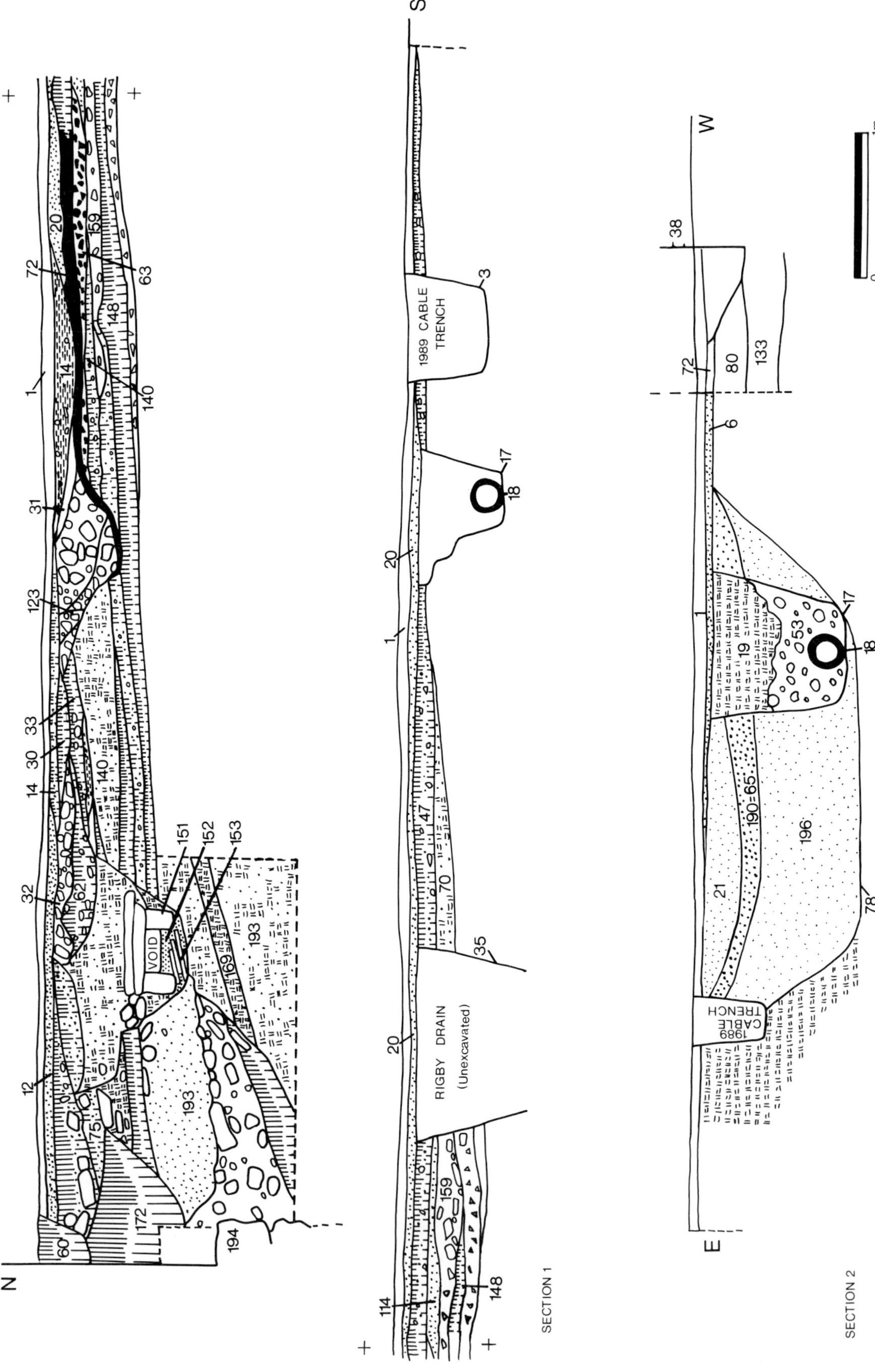

Fig 6   Castle Rushen, Sections 1 and 2. For key to contexts see Figure 8

yard ground level. It was found at all three locations and consists of a two-stage thickening of the wall over two courses. The upper of the two courses projects from the upper face of the wall by about 200mm and the lower by another 100mm. Above these offsets the limestone blocks of the wall face are finely finished, whereas below they are only roughly dressed so the offsets probably mark the level of the courtyard at the period of the construction of the wall. The offset is approximately level, although there is an unexplained rise of about 200mm in Section 3.

The excavation of the fills of the later pit north of the well (Section 3) showed that the curtain wall has deep internal foundations which were followed for over 3m below present ground level (2m below the offset). The excavation did not establish the full depth of the foundations, as waterlogging and considerations of safety overruled further exploration. The clay and masonry foundations are concreted together by lime redeposited from water seeping from the limestone curtain wall above, making a monolithic mass which spreads outwards from the offset. The natural clay must have been cut back to accommodate the construction of the foundations, but the later pit had removed all evidence of the original construction trench.

The curtain wall above the offset is 2.3m thick. External ground level presently rises from north to south. It is approximately 1.5m below the level of the internal offset at the point where the small outlet of Drain M (see below) discharges at external ground level, and is therefore 2.5m below present internal ground level at this point. There is no clear indication that this was the original external ground level, and indeed the openings of the sluice and privy shaft in the west wall of the outer gatehouse only 8m away are roughly 1m lower. It is likely that there was originally a wide ditch around the curtain wall but this was not investigated in these excavations.

Drains and privies

The construction of the curtain wall was the beginning of the castle's long term drainage problems (Fig 7). The numerous drains and the features directly associated with them have been identified by letters. Site matrices and a summary of the excavated contents can be found in the Technical Appendix (Figs 65, 66 and 67). The only outlet through the curtain wall located by the excavation was at the north end of the site in Area B (Drain M). The top of the capping stone of the associated drain was approximately 1.2m below the offset on the curtain wall. It was constructed at its junction with the curtain wall foundations with massive limestone blocks laid in clay. It was not possible to

establish the original run of this drain, although it may link up with Drain O revealed at the bottom of the ditch (the fall between the two is about 0.95m).

The privy shaft built into the wall of the north-west angle of the inner gatehouse discharges through the batter at the base of the wall into an underground covered stone-built cess-pit, which occupies the angle between the inner gatehouse and the keep proper. Another privy shaft attached to the outside of the same angle also discharges into the cess-pit (198). The pit is internally 2.5m north to south and 1.5m east to west, 0.9m deep below ground level, and is covered by long slate slabs. It has been repaired using concrete and its southern wall appears to have been cut down in the past, indicating that it may once have been deeper.

The masonry of the batter overruns the top of the south and east walls of the pit. The cess-pit has a stone floor and an outlet with a shallow lip in its north wall. This leads to a well-constructed stone drain (92), wide and high (0.5m by 0.5m) enough for a man to crawl along (Drain D). There was little silt or debris in the length of this drain until it reached the outer gatehouse wall. It was traced underneath the chapel, in the middle of which it is joined by Drain E. Under the north wall of the chapel it is joined by Rigby's 1910 drain (B). Under the narrow passage to the outer gatehouse cellar it is fed by a modern ceramic drain (L), after which it bends to the west and slopes steeply down under the outer gatehouse wall, where it is choked with rubble.

Tests with dye show that the drain connects with the privy in the cellar of the outer gatehouse. The site of its eventual discharge outside the castle is still unknown. There was a complex of drains leading to the area where Drain M cut through the wall, and probably the surface drainage of the courtyard as well as sewage was discharged here.

The sequence of drains could be established by the junctions where earlier drains were cut off or incorporated in later runs. The earliest was Drain K, a stone box drain which survived only as a group of five narrow capping stones and associated side walls and drain floor (201), cut off by Drain F. The capping stones are worn and are likely to have been at courtyard level at the time of its use. The source of this stretch of drain could only be conjectured and, although the whole area was not excavated to any great depth, a section across the projected line of the drain did not reveal it. It is assumed that the original sloping courtyard surface has been levelled at some point in the past, removing all other traces of the drain. A straight run would bring it to the angle between the inner gatehouse and the keep now occupied by the cess-pit described above, suggesting that it was the original sewer.

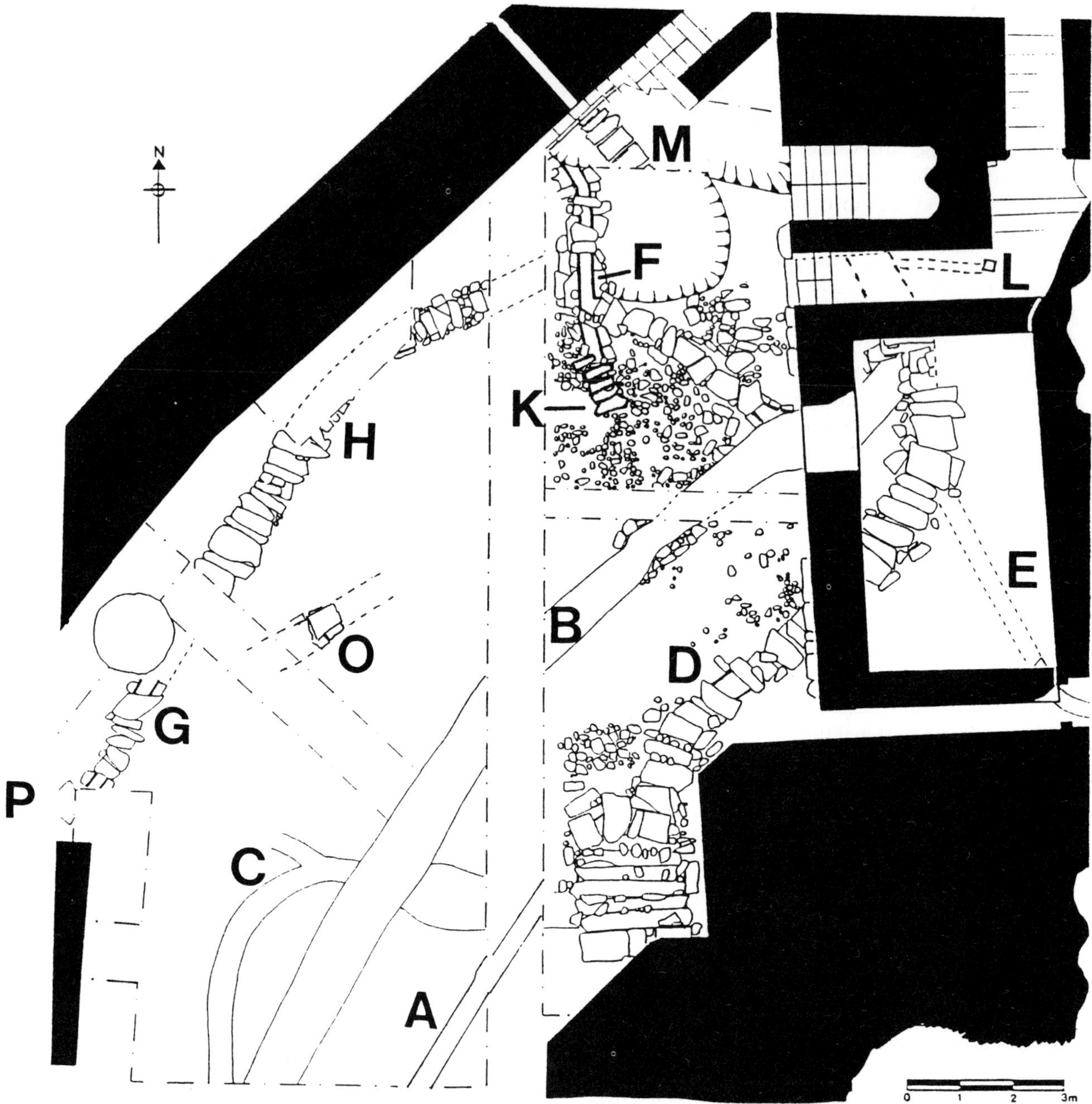

Fig 7   Castle Rushen, Trench Plan 2—Drains

It is probable that Drain K originally continued in a straight line before its lower portion was appropriated by Drain F, as it is similar in dimensions and structure. Its lowest part has been removed by previous excavations at the northern end of the courtyard, probably earlier attempts to sort out the drainage at this point. This meant that its precise relationship with the tunnel through the wall and Drain M could not be established, but there were the remains of a feature which is interpreted as a soakaway or trap embedded in the baulk here. This consisted of a curved, roughly built dry-stone wall extending from the level of the drain down to the

stones which covered the inlet to the tunnel through the curtain wall.

Drain F, which cut off and blocked the upper part of Drain K, was a box drain capped by large limestone and slate slabs (126). It was 0.25m wide and 0.25m deep. The top slabs were part of a roughly cobbled surface, which overran the top slabs of Drain K. The source of this drain was destroyed by Rigby's 1910 French drain (B) which cut through the door of the chapel here. There is a slight indication that Drain F may also have run under this door, as there is a clear bend in its eastern wall just before it is cut off by Drain B. An interpretive puzzle is posed by the fact that several bricks have been used only at this point in the drain. It is possible that this was the result of a realignment of the drain at the time of the construction of the chapel. It is difficult to be certain where the source of this drain can have been. There is the drain from the drawbridge pit, Drain E, now discharging into the box Drain D at a junction in the middle of the chapel. Drain E may have been the original upper portion of Drain F, but this can only be conjectural, and there must have been realignments, first of Drains E and F to lead them through the door of the chapel, then of E to enable it to feed into D.

There was a stone box drain (85) running close to, and roughly parallel with, the curtain wall. Its various sections were labelled G, H and P, but they constitute a single drain, albeit broken by a later well. It was larger than Drains E, F and K with an average internal width and height of 0.35m. Its side walls were not made as neatly as those of the other drains, however, often being re-used lumps of building stone. The top slabs were large slates. The lower end of the drain originally joined the lower part of Drain K but it was sealed off, possibly when Drain F took over this part of it. The source was the north wall of the 'fish-house' (174), where a single sandstone block with a hole 100mm in diameter built into the foundations presumably drained the interior. The fish-house was not excavated, so its internal arrangements are unknown. It is possible that the drain continued to the south before the fish-house was built because there is a marked bend in it, suggesting that the drain from the fish-house was joined to an existing length.

Deep pit against the curtain wall

A large, almost circular pit (161), with a diameter of 3.5m, was revealed just north of the stone well-head. It had been dug against the foundations of the curtain wall to a depth of over 3m below present ground level. The sides were steep and the bottom sloped sharply down towards the curtain wall (Fig 8). The pit cut through the wide ditch and clipped the edge of the drain laid in its bottom. It had been filled in with layers of clay and peat, possibly fuel, and was waterlogged in its lower parts. Drain H from the adjacent fish-house, and the random cobbles and stones in which the drain is laid, both ran over the top of it. In a document of 1788 this location is identified as being occupied by a storehouse with a well-head (Cowin pers comm), and it may be that this steep-sided waterlogged circular pit is the remains of this well. There was no other archaeological evidence for this storehouse except for the scars of corbels on the curtain wall.

The corbels on this stretch of curtain wall were probably inserted into the wall after it was built, as they occupy the sockets of large blocks, with the leftover spaces being filled up with smaller packing stones. The buildings which stood in the courtyard are listed in several post-medieval inventories

A pit under the fish-house

A second large pit (183), although not so deep, was found under the east wall of the fish-house (38), a lean-to building against the curtain wall at the south-west corner of the site. The pit was steep sided, 1.3m deep, oval and measured 4m north-south by 1.5m east-west. The pit pre-dated the fish-house. Its lowest fill consisted of a thick layer of rubble with mortar under a layer of clay mixed with mortar. The pottery from these layers, though sparse, appears to be fifteenth-century in date. There was no evidence of the original function of the pit. It was sealed by a thick layer of tumbled cobblestones, not laid as a surface but part of the spread of random cobbles and stones which stretched almost from the southern edge of the site for 14m north-east, roughly parallel to the curtain wall.

An area of gravel and limestone chips appeared to be set parallel to the curtain wall about 4m into the courtyard. Initially it seemed possible to interpret this area as evidence of a freestanding building, but there was no corroborative evidence in the form of post-holes, walls, drains or surviving floor material. Between this area and the curtain wall was the zone of large cobblestones described above. The box Drain P, G, H from the fish-house was laid into this zone, which may have been deposited in order to improve drainage.

The fish-house

This structure was identified from inventories as the small stone building at the south-west edge of the trench, built against the curtain wall. It survived as low walls up to 0.5m high with an entrance in the south. Against the curtain wall was a narrow (0.4m wide) wall which may represent a bench, as a load-bearing wall is unnecessary here. The fish-house was not excavated internally, but sections were cut up to the outer faces of the east and north walls. The section against its northern wall revealed the drain-hole from the interior 0.45m below present ground level. Both sections revealed that the foundations were shallow. The foundations of the north wall extend to 0.55m below present ground level at the point of the drain, and the east wall foundations are shallower, at only 0.3m below ground level. There was an external construction trench visible in the eastern section, which was filled with gravel. The construction trench was dug from a high level, and although there was no dating evidence from it, the

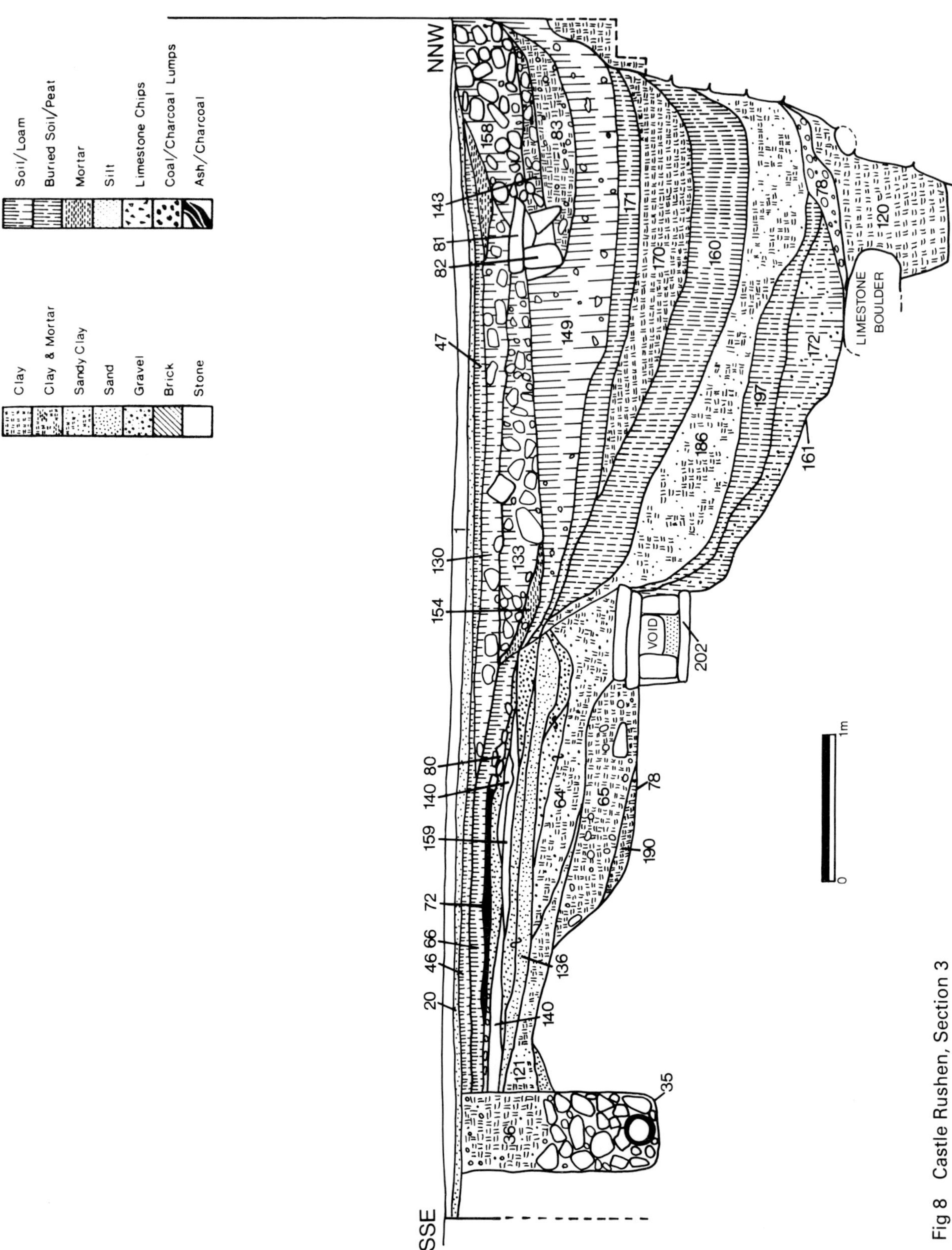

Fig 8   Castle Rushen, Section 3

fish-house is stratigraphically the latest surviving structure in the courtyard, with the possible exception of the chapel.

The surface which survived as a battered area of cobblestones to the east of the main baulk was tentatively interpreted as the remains of an early courtyard, but it was so patched and repaired and so close to the present surface that a precise date was not obtainable (Fig 9). The level of the flagstones used as drain covers for Drains F and K suggests that in the period of their use this was ground level in the northern part of the site. The truncated southern end of Drain K and the cut-down sides of the cess-pit strongly imply that the slope up to the south was more marked than at present, and that the present level of the cover slabs of Drain D marks a levelling operation in the southern part of the site.

The chapel

The building adjacent to the drawbridge pit, the 'chapel' (95–97), was examined and it was found that the walls of its southern half were founded directly on natural clay, and the northern half over a wide feature filled with clay. It is possible that this feature is the continuation of the large ditch to the west, but further work would be required to estab-lish the validity of this suggestion. The walls of the chapel butt against the walls of the drawbridge pit (99) and are built over the cover slabs of Drains D and E. The Rigby Drain B is directed through the door of the room and then joined to Drain D under the north wall with much brick patching, including a brick course inserted under the wall itself. The masonry above this junction shows signs of con-siderable repair. The flagged floor of the room was randomly laid and butted up against a row of large upright blocks, approximately 0.5m inside the southern wall. The flagstones did not continue between the blocks and the wall. The function of this feature is unknown, but it served as a flower bed until recently, as did a 1m square feature free of flagstones in the north-east corner.

In about 1910, as part of his attempt to restore the castle to its medieval form, the architect Armitage

Fig 9 Castle Rushen, Trench Plan 3—Courtyard Layout

Rigby stripped out the nineteenth-century prison accretions, leaving only a few ceramic sewer pipes of that era *in situ*. He seems to have removed as much as 2m of overburden in places, removing not only nineteenth-century structures but also earlier surfaces and features, seriously truncating the stratigraphy, particularly to the south of the site where the original ground level seems to have risen and his levelling was therefore more destructive. His work did not appear to penetrate to medieval levels near the curtain wall, however, as present ground level is approximately 1m above the offset in the wall at medieval ground level. In addition, a number of post-medieval pits of sixteenth- and seventeenth-century date appear to have survived at the north-eastern end of the site.

The nineteenth-century prison yard and its associated features have been totally destroyed, leaving graffiti of this period 2m and more above present ground level on the masonry of the covered well, just to the south-west of the trench. A vestigial line of pitch or tar on the curtain wall, about a metre above present ground level at the southern end of the site, rises to almost 1.6m towards the steps to the rampart walkway at the north end of the site, probably marking the ground level of the prison period. The 'French drain' attributable to Rigby traverses the site and connects to Drain D.

Finds from the site comprise principally post-medieval animal bones and fragments of medieval and post-medieval pottery. Individual finds include a fragment of a medieval gargoyle made of non-Manx sandstone, coins and military objects such as lead shot. The detailed analysis of these materials is contained in the specialist reports which follow this survey of the structural evidence. Despite the limited nature of the excavations and the degree of disturbance to which the site had been subjected, the material evidence which was recovered provides a significant contribution to the understanding of the economy of the castle and its relationship with the outside world.

Conclusion

Rigby's destruction of nineteenth-century prison features is virtually total and the presence of post-medieval levels is patchy. Medieval structures survive near the curtain wall. Dating evidence for the early features was stratigraphic and imprecise, and more excavation would be necessary to recover the artifactual evidence for more precise dating of the keep, curtain wall and outer gatehouse. The possible moat in particular would be an important resource for the understanding of the early castle, if any part of it contains waterlogged organic material.

Future archaeological research at Castle Rushen

The 1989 excavations have suggested a number of lines of research which might be followed in future investigations of the same area of the castle. These particularly concern the new evidence for early structures at the site and the dating of the standing structures.

More information on the line and date of the medieval ditch or moat is important to establish its significance in the early history of the castle. The continued excavation of the northern part of the 1989 trench would establish these aspects of the feature. The 1989 excavation showed that the lower levels within the curtain wall are likely to be waterlogged and the same is probably true outside the wall. This will present the opportunity for detailed environmental study and the recovery of organic cultural remains, to provide a more complete picture of life within the castle. The services of a specialist environmentalist and a conservator would be essential.

The medieval sewer must emerge from under the west wall of the outer gatehouse tower, and a continuation of the trench outside the curtain wall should reveal it. This would also assist the understanding of the modern drainage system. The early structural evidence from the 1989 excavations suggests that this feature should continue to the west underneath the curtain wall. Any trench proposed for the location of the medieval sewer should also reveal any surviving remains of this structure.

The dating of the curtain wall remains a problem. This may best be pursued through a section which meets the curtain wall at the north end of the 1989 trench, where the previous excavation revealed no obvious late disturbances, and continues on the outside of the wall, to produce a notional straight section through the wall. The purpose of this would be to find the internal construction trench and recover artifacts from its fill which would date it. The 1989 work demonstrated that the excavation will need to be at least 3m below present ground level in the courtyard, and probably another metre again.

Pottery

P J Davey and N C Johnson

Introduction

A total of 3011 sherds from 81 contexts, representing at least 399 vessels, was recovered from the excavations. When the pottery is divided into broad chronological groups covering a century each, and these are tabulated by site phase, it is quite clear that many of the contexts are disturbed with a high degree of residuality. Others show evidence of contamination. This is almost certainly due to the extensive nature of the reorganisation which occurred in the area excavated in the eighteenth, nineteenth and early twentieth centuries. It is also a function of the fact that many of the contexts represent damaged surfaces with many voids, or drain fills, where finds post-date the structures often by many centuries. In consequence, it is difficult to use the pottery as a means of precise dating for features and contexts on the site.

The following is an attempt to reconcile the pottery dating evidence with the site stratigraphy. The sequence has been divided into four phases which appear to be related to the surviving structures. The first phase consists of the group of contexts associated with the early moat feature, which pre-dates all of the existing standing buildings on the site. The second is a pit sequence, just inside the curtain wall and north-east of the well, together with a series of drains (D, F, K) and cobbled surfaces, all of which are later than the curtain wall. The third is a large pit sequence north of the well which post-dates both these early drains and the curtain wall. The fourth consists of complex and far reaching reorganisations of the site in the nineteenth and early twentieth centuries. Numbers in brackets refer throughout to contexts.

Method

On site, the pottery was collected in context groups and its presence was noted in the site archive. It was then cleaned, marked with the relevant Manx Museum accession number and context number, boxed and stored in context groups. All the material was subsequently identified to type, and listed on computer by trench and in context number order. For ease of handling, the ware types have been allocated a three-letter code which is given in square brackets at the first mention in the following text (*cf* Appendix 3). This information was then re-ordered, initially according to phase and then in ware groups.

The pottery in context

Phase 1
There is very little pottery directly associated with the early moat and its associated structures. Four sherds from the fills of the moat, including one of

Ham Green Ware [HGT] (65) and one granite-tempered jar rim [GTW] (65; Fig 10.5) are of thirteenth- or fourteenth-century date. A fine white ware sherd [WHW] (190) and a small green-glazed fragment (65) are also probably contemporary. A sherd of mottled ware [MOT] was found in the fill of Drain F (168); this suggests that it was still in use in the eighteenth century. Two sherds of coarse purpleware [CPW] which cannot reasonably be dated earlier than 1500 were found in the mixed lower fill of the moat (134). As this layer is stratigraphically below the curtain wall, chapel and drawbridge pit, these finds must be considered intrusive. This must also be the case with the sherd of nineteenth-century white ware found in an upper fill of the moat (121).

Phase 2
Stratigraphically the next earliest group of 13 sherds derives from a large pit in Area B which is later than both the moat and construction of the curtain wall. A sherd of unglazed Saintonge [UGS] (172), ten sherds of granite-tempered ware (160, 172), one indeterminate medieval sherd [MED] (172) and part of a red-bodied Martincamp flask [MAR] (154) were found within the steep-sided pit north-east of the well (161). Whilst the material from contexts 160 and 172 is firmly fifteenth-century in date, the Martincamp find, which should date to the sixteenth or seventeenth century, may represent contamination from a drain cut (147) belonging to a later phase.

The succeeding series of layers produced a total of 41 sherds. These include 28 sherds of granite-tempered ware of fifteenth-century type, nine earlier medieval fragments, including a sherd of Saintonge polychrome [SPY] (171; Fig 10.1), which are probably residual, and a base sherd from a fifteenth-century Surrey White ware cup (138; Fig 10.9). Two contexts, 80 and 133, include three later sherds of sixteenth- to eighteenth-century date. These layers consisted of a series of cobbled surfaces which were described by the excavator as being 'very battered' and having 'many voids'. The later finds are almost certainly contamination from the upper levels of the site.

Phase 3
Nineteenth-century 'restoration' of the castle seems to have destroyed all of the prison structures and most earlier post-medieval contexts. A small series of pits and layers appears to have survived this activity in Area C. The pottery from these is predominantly of sixteenth-century date. The upper layer of the sequence (103) includes two complete profiles of Midlands Yellow jars [MYW] (Fig 11.11), one of which has been distributed

upwards through a further five nineteenth-century contexts (16, 60, 68, 74, 75). The five sherds from the other jar, derived from a series of soil layers (63, 129, 137, 157) associated with the later cobbled surfaces (80), also appear to be of this period or slightly later. Five sherds of sixteenth-century type dark-glazed wares [DRB], including pieces from two tygs, were recovered from the pit sequence (103, 104, 157).

Phase 4

The final phase of activity on the site can be divided into three: contexts associated with the construction of the fish-house in the eighteenth century (4A), surviving nineteenth-century surfaces and drains (4B) and the massive clearance brought about by the 'restorations' of Rigby in 1910 (4C).

The 81 sherds from the general layers which immediately precede the fish-house, and the single dark-glazed sherd from its construction trench, suggest a date of 1760–80 for its construction. There are a few residual medieval and post-medieval sherds.

The nineteenth-century activity on the site which survived Rigby's clearances consists mainly of scrappy soil spreads (21, 22, 46, 47, 57, 108, 142), cobbled layers (33, 41, 43, 44, 45) and drains (B and C). The 321 sherds from these 12 contexts include a good deal of eighteenth-century and earlier material and seem to span the whole of the nineteenth century. Given the extensive nature of the area which was excavated in 1989, the very small proportions of individual vessels which were actually recovered gives some indication of the quantity of archaeological deposits lost through removal by Rigby.

The final, almost overwhelming, phase of activity which appears to be associated with Rigby's 'restoration' in 1910 produced almost 95% of all the pottery from the excavations, including much earlier material (Fig 10). Five contexts, consisting of superficial layers, individually exceeded all previous finds from Phases 1 to 3 (4, 5, 7, 8, 15).

The pottery itself

The text which follows provides a brief over-view of the ceramic types which were recovered from Castle Rushen. As detailed discussions of a majority of these, including lists of all previous occurrences on Man, are contained in the Peel Castle report (Davey forthcoming), only new types or forms are discussed here in detail. The pottery is described in three groups: medieval; post-medieval, that is sixteenth- and seventeenth-century; and modern.

MEDIEVAL POTTERY (*c*1250–1500) [Fig 10]

Imported medieval pottery

A total of 43 sherds of non-Manx medieval pottery from 22 contexts, representing a minimum of 24 vessels, was recovered.

The material is very fragmentary and a majority of the finds are residual. They are of interest in providing an excavated medieval group from a Manx medieval castle to contrast with and complement the much larger assemblage from Peel.

The continental wares

Ten sherds from at least six vessels derive from the Saintonge region of south-western France. These include examples of Saintonge polychrome [SPY], Saintonge mottled green [SMG], pink Saintonge [SPI] and unglazed Saintonge [UGS] (Hurst, Neale & Van Beuningen 1986, 76–99). The earliest are the three sherds from a polychrome jug, which probably date to the late thirteenth or early fourteenth century (7, 36, 171; Figs 10.1 and 2). This ware occurs regularly at the Welsh Edwardian castles built from the late 1270s and in the richer quarters of towns such as Chester (Davey and Rutter 1977) and Southampton (Platt and Coleman-Smith 1975, Vol 2, 123–52). The mottled green wares are rather more common and widespread in the British Isles, similarly on high-status sites. Their date range is somewhat wider, from the mid-thirteenth century to the end of the fourteenth. The two sherds from Castle Rushen are also from a jug (108, 113). Unglazed Saintonge has an even longer date range, covering most of the later medieval period from the thirteenth century. The three sherds from Castle Rushen are from different vessels, a body sherd and handle from two different jugs (57, 172; Fig 10.4) and a small bottle-like vessel (104). Pink Saintonge is a rare find in Britain, having been identified only at Southampton. The two sherds found in 1989 are probably from a jug (36, 47).

The British wares

Thirty sherds of medieval pottery deriving from a range of probable and possible sources in Britain, and representing at least 15 vessels, were recovered from the excavations. The most diagnostic are the seven sherds of a green-glazed, reduced ware jug with applied strip and rouletted decoration which is a Bristol Redcliffe product [BGE] (37; Fig 10.3, *cf* Good and Russett 1987). Also from the Bristol area are two large body sherds from different jugs or pitchers which are of Ham Green type, probably dating from the thirteenth century (7, 65, *cf* Ponsford 1983, 81–103). A base sherd from a small

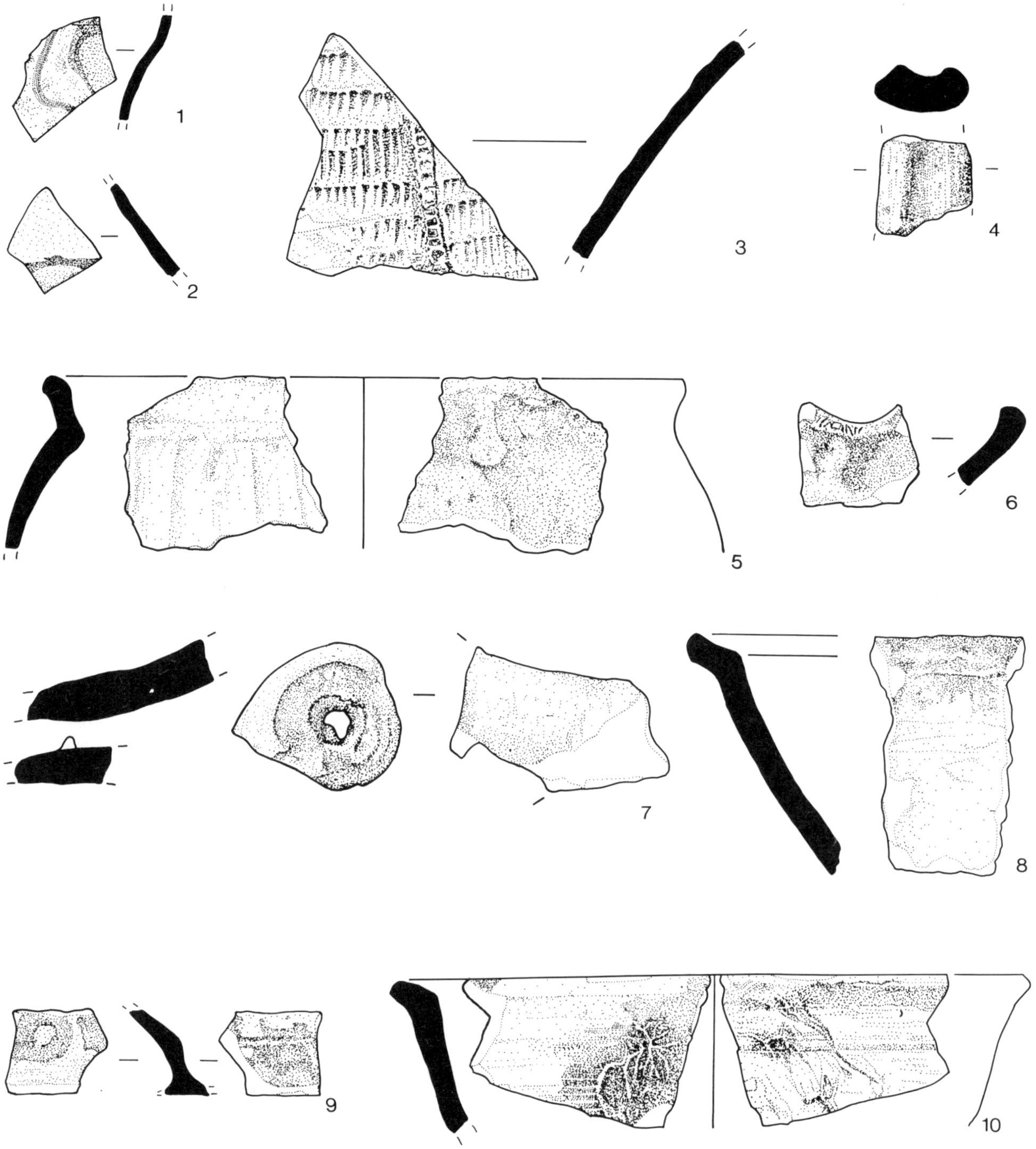

Fig 10   Castle Rushen, Pottery; Nos 1–10 (Scale 1:2)

fifteenth-century Surrey ware cup (Holling 1977, 61–66) and two sherds from a Cheshire-type red-ware jug (170, 172, *cf* Rutter 1977, 86 Fabric B) are the only others which can be assigned to source with any real confidence. A further very small body sherd may be a Bristol product (114). Two joining sherds and a further sherd in a buff-bodied gritty ware (u/s, 57, 190) with dark brown glaze are similar to elements in the type series created for Cocker-mouth in Cumbria (a copy of which is held in the Department of Archaeology in the University of Liverpool). Much further research in the Irish Sea area is required before it will be possible to identify and date the remaining sherds from Castle Rushen.

The Manx products

A total of 79 sherds in Manx granite-tempered ware [GTW] (Garrad 1977, 1978; Parkes 1992), repre-senting at least 13 vessels, and two sherds from different vessels in granite-free or 'smooth' ware [MSM] (Davey 1992a, 63), were recovered from a total of 32 contexts, of which 21 are post-medieval in date. Only four sherds from two vessels are unglazed. The remaining finds include glazed oxidised and reduced wares. The uneven firing of most of the products of this industry makes it difficult to estimate minimum vessels, particularly when the material is so fragmentary.

The thin-section analysis of five sherds of this ware type from the Castletown area by J R Senior (Appendix 2) has confirmed that the filler used in its manufacture is freshly crushed granite, most likely from the Foxdale source. Insufficient work has so far been carried out to determine whether the pottery was made at one centre in the island or was perhaps acquired at extended family level. A programme of sampling finds from other areas of the island, particularly the north, where a range of erratic granites are freely available in the drift, might determine whether the ware was centrally or locally produced.

The forms which can be identified at Castle Rushen include open jars or cooking pots (65; Fig 10.5), closed jar forms (106; Fig 10.6), bung-hole pitchers (110; Fig 10.7) and bowls (108; Fig 10.8). The two sherds from granite-free wares, both of which are from nineteenth-century contexts (19, 47), probably represent jug forms.

This excavation has not greatly assisted the dating of these wares. There are no unglazed, reduced wares with everted rims, such as were recovered by Bersu from Peel Castle (Wright 1980–82, 40–41, Fig 6, 1–5). These are likely to date from the thirteenth century and possibly earlier. At Castle Rushen a single jar rim sherd formed part of the moat sequence and, therefore, probably dates to the fourteenth century (65; Fig 10.5). It is not possible to distinguish between the finds from fifteenth- and sixteenth-century sealed contexts and those from the post-medieval layers on the basis of fabric or form. With the evidence of its occurrence in sixteenth-century groups in Peel Town and Castle Rushen Stores, some of the fully oxidized wares from Castle Rushen may be of sixteenth-century date. The majority appear to belong to the fifteenth century.

POST-MEDIEVAL WARES
(*c*1500–1750) [Fig 11]

Continental imports (cf *Hurst, Neale and Van Beuningen 1986*)

These are rare in this period and consist of a sherd from a red-bodied Type III Martincamp flask [MAR] (154), part of an appliqué mask from a Frechen *Bartmann* [FSW] (6; Fig 11.14) and five sherds of Westerwald stoneware [WES] from at least two vessels (5, 15, 28, 108; Fig 11.15). The site

stratigraphy does not assist the interpretation of these finds. The Frechen and Westerwald sherds are in nineteenth-century contexts and must be considered residual. The Martincamp piece is from a clay layer (154) which may represent either a seventeenth-century capping of the fifteenth-century pit north-east of the well-head, or contamination from one of the upper layers.

British products (cf *Davey forthcoming*)

These consist of reduced wares from Cumbria or south-west Scotland, yellow wares from the English Midlands and a range of coarse dark green-glazed reduced wares, purple wares, yellow, speckled and dark wares from north-west England.

Northern reduced greenware [NRG] (cf *White 1977*)

A single sherd, including a bung-hole from a pitcher and probably of sixteenth-century date, was recovered from a nineteenth-century context (33).

Midlands Yellow Ware [MYW] (cf *Woodfield 1966*)

Thirty-six sherds from six contexts and a minimum of three vessels were recovered from the site. One, a small straight-sided bowl, was found in six contexts in 28 pieces, 18 of which join (16, 60, 68, 74, 75, 103). The other is a larger bowl, in five joining pieces (103; Fig 11.11). These two pots derive from contexts which on other grounds appear to date from the sixteenth century. The third vessel, probably sixteenth-century and consisting of a single rim sherd (7), is from a nineteenth-century context.

Coarse dark green-glazed reduced wares [CEW] (cf *Bearpark and Johnson 1977*)

Fifteen sherds from at least five vessels were recovered from nine contexts, one of which (162) securely belongs to the sixteenth-century pit sequence in Area C. The ware is likely to derive from north-west England.

Coarse purplewares [CPW]

This highly fired purple-bodied ware with thin external glaze was probably made in South Lancashire. Three vessels are represented in the Castle Rushen collection. One was a bung-hole pitcher of which 16 sherds joined together from a total of ten contexts. One of these, a single base sherd, was recovered from the sixteenth-century pit sequence in Area A (122) which also produced a rim sherd of a highly fired strap handled pitcher (106; Fig 11.12). These wares appear to be the north-western equivalent of 'Midlands Purple' and probably date from

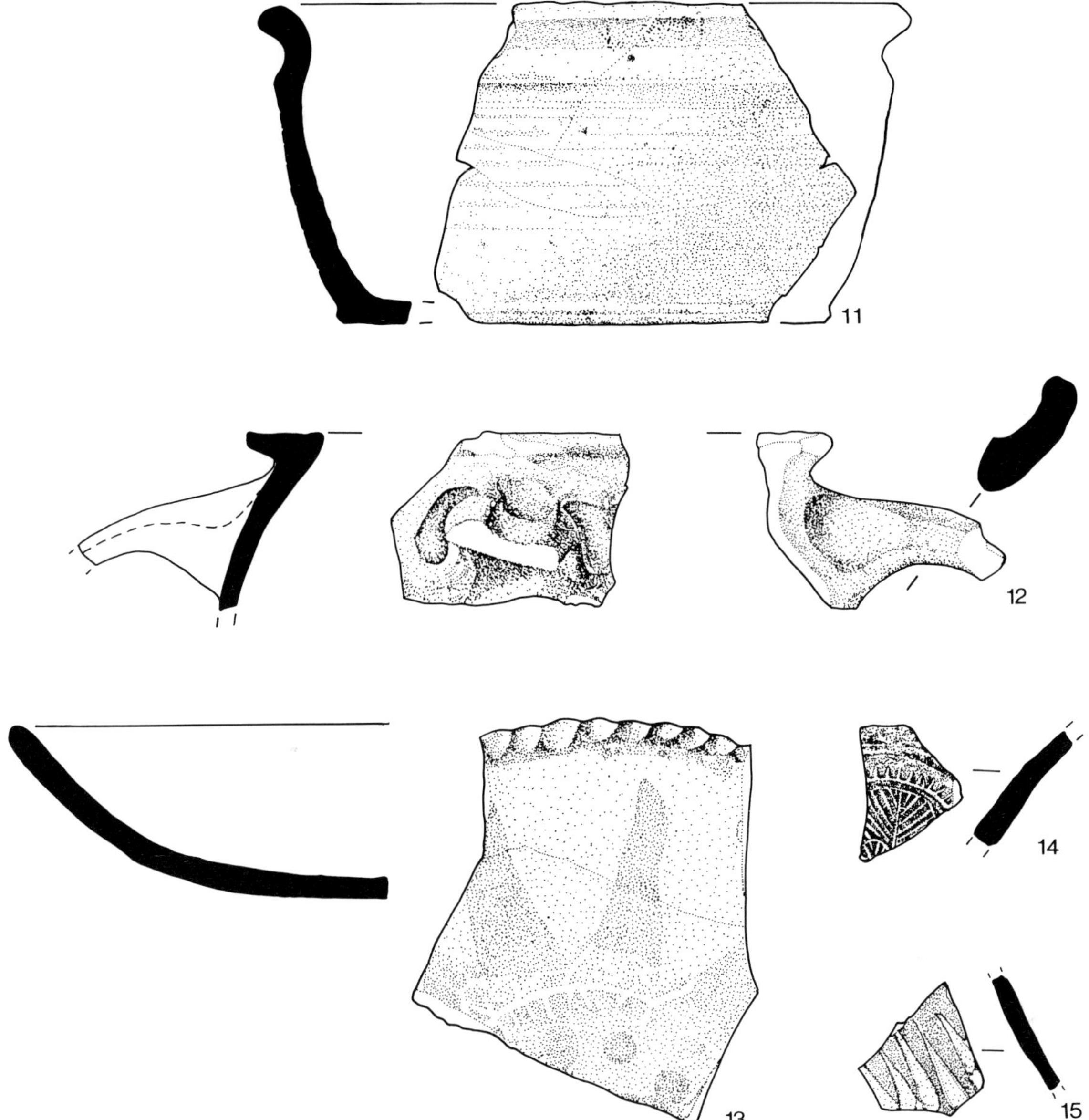

Fig 11   Castle Rushen, Pottery; Nos 11–15 (Scale 1:2)

the later fifteenth to the early seventeenth centuries.

Dark-glazed wares [DRB] (Moorhouse and Roberts 1992; Philpott 1985a; 1989)

A total of 83 sherds from a minimum of 22 vessels were found during the excavations. They consist of a range of small storage vessels and at least nine tygs. Only five sherds, from four vessels, derive from sixteenth-century deposits; the rest are residual in nineteenth- and early twentieth-century disturbed contexts. The wares are typical of those produced in the north-west of England, and, given the economic and political connections between the island and the South Lancashire base of the Derbys, are most likely to have been made in the Rainford/ Prescot area (Davey 1989; 1991, 127).

Rainford-type yellow wares [RYW] (Davey 1991, 127–8, Fig 5, Nos 4, 5, 7, 8 and 10)

Lead-glazed, buff or pink-bodied earthenwares with no added minerals in the glaze were produced in the mid-seventeenth-century Rainford kilns. They have a characteristic wiped gloss on the external surfaces. Four small sherds, all from different vessels and contexts, were found at Castle Rushen (12, 44, 47, 80). These were either made in Rainford or somewhere on the South Lancashire coalfield.

Rainford-type speckled wares [RSP] (Davey 1991, 127–8, Fig 5, No 1)

Four speckled ware vessels are represented by 14 sherds in eight contexts. Three of the vessels are shallow bowls (5, 6, 37, 66, 73, 129), the third is a straight-sided jar (7, 66). They were all probably made in South Lancashire in the seventeenth century. With the exception of one of the bowls (Fig 10.10), which occurs in a Phase 3 context (129) and is typologically early, all of the finds appear to be residual in nineteenth-century contexts.

Manx products

With the exception of some probable sixteenth-century granite-tempered ware, there is no evidence that any of the pottery of this period was made in the Isle of Man.

MODERN POTTERY (*c*1750–1910)

Although the majority of all the ceramic finds from the site are of late nineteenth- or early twentieth-century date, a number of eighteenth-century types were recovered and are worthy of mention here. A wide range of dark-glazed wares form the biggest group. These include large storage vessels, bowls and some tableware. An important sub-group is the 31 sherds of 'Jackfield Black' [JBW] which probably date to the third quarter of the eighteenth century. Mottled wares [MOT] are very common. One hundred and thirty-four sherds of the ware from at least 42 vessels were found, the vast majority from tankards. The specific technologies employed in the production of this material suggest importation to the island from a range of sources in England.

Slipwares are another significant component of the assemblage. These include 77 sherds of hollow-wares [HBS] from at least 12 vessels, including nine 'posset pots' and three small jugs, together with 18 sherds from at least nine press-moulded plates [PMS] (Fig 11.13). There is a single sherd of agate bodied ware [AGB]. Sixteen sherds of tin-glazed earthenware [TGE] or 'Delft' from six vessels and one wall tile were found. These included plates, a punch bowl foot-ring and small fragments of hollow-ware, all probably made in Liverpool. Thirty-four sherds of white salt-glazed stoneware [WSS] from at least nine vessels were recovered, together with six sherds from different vessels in the much rarer transitional white dipped stoneware [WDS]. This ware type dates from the first two decades of the eighteenth century, whilst the true white-bodied ware is a little later. The site also produced evidence for stoneware use during the second half of the century in the form of brown stoneware types usually associated with production in Nottingham and Derby [NDS]. Twenty-one sherds from at least eight vessels were recovered, almost all tankards.

Most of these products are typical of the material circulating in England at the time; although a majority were probably made in the South Lancashire potteries or Liverpool, individual examples from Buckley and Staffordshire and elsewhere in the English Midlands are discernible.

Discussion

Owing to the loss of much of the medieval and post-medieval stratigraphy during Rigby's 'restorations', the ceramic evidence for the site is extremely fragmentary and partial. The small quantity of certainly medieval pottery reflects a similar situation to that established at Peel Castle. A quarter of the group is French; almost all of the remainder derive from a variety of sources in England, including the Bristol Channel area, Cumbria and Cheshire, with a small group of Manx granite-tempered ware and granite-free ware. This is too small a collection for any firm conclusions to be drawn about the status or economic connections of the inhabitants.

The early post-medieval finds are dominated by types which were probably made in the north-west of England, in South Lancashire. Given the importance of this area as the home territory of the Stanleys and the number of apparently Lancastrian names in the list of cottagers in the early sixteenth-century Manorial Rolls, this is not surprising (see Appendix 1). Manx granite-tempered wares form a significant group at this period and appear widespread in the island. There remains a small continental element within the assemblage.

The eighteenth-century finds from the castle demonstrate the kind of range which would be normal in a medieval town in north-west England. They include finewares such as hand-painted creamware, white salt-glazed stonewares and good quality tablewares in brown stoneware, mottled ware and dark-glazed ware. The more expensive of these items probably derive from the occupants of Derby House during this period.

Clay Tobacco Pipes
D A Higgins

The 1989 excavations at Castle Rushen produced 162 fragments of clay tobacco pipe from 32 excavated contexts. A total of 27 bowl, 128 stem and seven mouthpiece fragments were recovered.

Treatment of the material

Each pipe fragment was examined and a detailed record made using a standard recording sheet which has been developed at the University of Liverpool. After the individual pieces had been assessed, an overall date range was attributed to the pipes from each context. These date ranges were then entered onto a context matrix. Examples of the bowl forms, marks and decorated pipes were selected for illustration (Fig 12). Copies of the record sheets and pipe matrix have been deposited in the site archive.

The main problem encountered in examining the material was that some of the context numbers actually written on the pipes did not tally with the context numbers of the bags which contained them. It was considered that the numbers on the pipes were more likely to be reliable than the numbers on the bags into which they had been placed and they were resorted accordingly. The nature of the finds often supported this rationale; for example, this resulted in the removal of an eighteenth-century piece from the predominantly nineteenth-century group from Context 36. It also added another nineteenth-century piece to Context 36 from Context 72, leaving Context 72 as a purely seventeenth-century group. Six pieces were moved in this way. Each piece moved has been marked with a pencil cross so that it can be recognised again. The pieces which have been moved are:

1 piece of stem from Context 5 to Context 36.
1 piece of bowl from Context 36 to Context 37.
1 piece of bowl from Context 37 to Context 72.
1 piece of bowl from Context 72 to Context 36.
2 pieces of stem from Context 74 to Context 52.

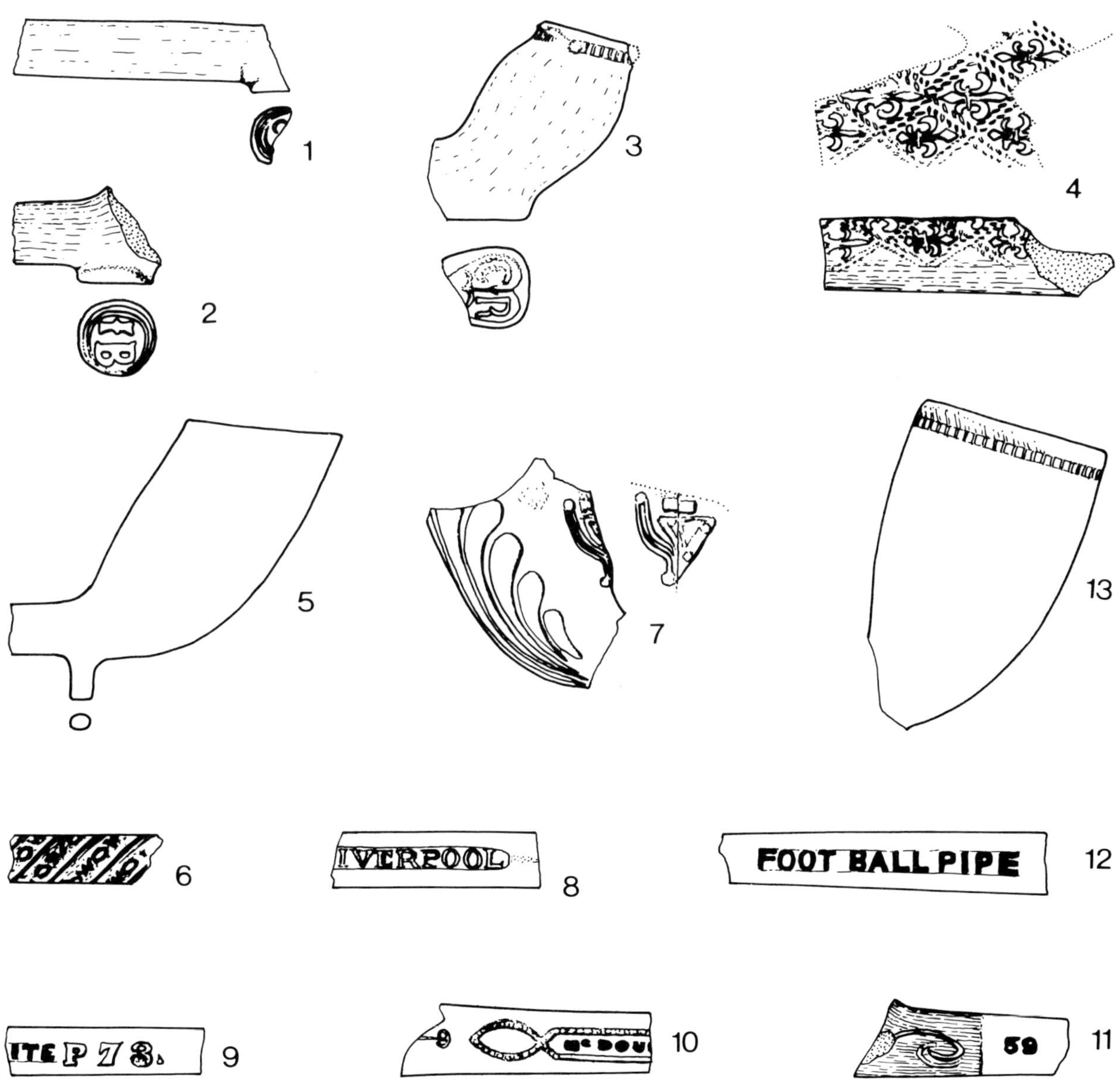

Fig 12   Castle Rushen, Clay Tobacco Pipes (Scale 1:1)

The pipes

The context groups are all small, the largest containing only 17 fragments, and almost all contain material of mixed date. The pipes are generally rather fragmentary, with only two or three relatively intact bowls from the whole excavation. No joins were noticed either within or between the context groups. These factors suggest that most, if not all, of the groups consist of disturbed or re-deposited material. The presence of nineteenth-century fragments in almost all of the pipe-bearing contexts suggests that the majority of the post-medieval deposits on the site have been affected by nineteenth-century or later activity. Despite this, fragments covering a 300-year span are present and provide a valuable addition to the corpus of information available for the Isle of Man.

Seventeenth-century pipes
The earliest bowl seems to be the fragment from Context 72 and probably dates from between 1610 and 1640. It has a fine, hard fired fabric but insufficient of the form survives to suggest an origin for this piece. From the mid-seventeenth century there are two pipes which can be attributed to the South Lancashire industry, which was centred on Rainford. Both are made of an off-white, rather gritty fabric and have typical South Lancashire styles of mark. The first (Fig 12.1) has part of a double border which would have surrounded the maker's initials, now missing, while the second (Fig 12.2) has a single border around the initials IB. This is the most common set of initials amongst the Rainford makers and it is not yet possible to identify any of the numerous IB marks with a specific maker. South Lancashire pipes have been found in seventeenth-century contexts from excavations at both Peel Castle and at Castle Rushen Stores (see report in this volume). It would appear that South Lancashire provided the principal supply of pipes to the island during the seventeenth century.

A third mid-seventeenth-century pipe was recovered which does not come from South Lancashire (Fig 12.3). The bowl form and large heel, which would probably have had a tail originally, are not found in that area, and the use of a heart-shaped mark is extremely rare there. What is interesting is that an almost identical bowl stamped with a similar heart-shaped CR mark (but from a different die) has been found at Peel Castle (86.53, Context 17). The CR mark has not been found amongst the substantial body of material excavated at Chester (Rutter and Davey 1980), and must be regarded as an import to the region.

Another pipe that is certainly an import is the stem from Context 75, which is decorated with a relief moulded pattern of *fleur-de-lys* (Fig 12.4). Duco, in his paper on pipes from the Netherlands, illustrates an almost identical example which he dates from between 1640 and 1660 (Duco 1981, Fig 131). Dutch pipes are not often found in the north-west and this piece may well reflect the shipping connections of the island.

Eighteenth- and nineteenth-century pipes
Although there are a number of plain fragments which probably date from the later seventeenth and eighteenth centuries, there are no more complete bowls, makers' marks or decorated pieces amongst the finds until the later eighteenth and nineteenth centuries. There is a plain bowl from Context 50 which probably dates from the later eighteenth or early nineteenth century (Fig 12.5). This is a period which has produced very few well-dated pipe groups and so it is very difficult to be more precise about the dating. A similar problem is posed by the decorated stem from Context 5 (Fig 12.6). Although it bears comparison with the later stem borders of the Chester series, which may have been produced as late as 1790 or 1800 (Rutter and Davey 1980), it is most similar to an example from excavations at Speke Hall in Merseyside (Higgins 1992). This was recovered from a deposit datable to a refitting of 1867–68, which points to a much later date for this particular type. There are illustrations of what appear to be similarly decorated stems in the Davidson of Glasgow catalogue of around 1880 (Gallagher and Price 1987). This example can, therefore, be regarded as a late survival of decorative stem stamping, dating from between 1850 and 1900.

A piece which can be much more securely placed in the period 1770 to 1820 is the decorated bowl from Context 108 (Fig 12.7). The scalloped decoration is typical of this period, although not necessarily of this area. There are some possible kiln wasters of this type from the Grove Suspension Bridge site in Chester, but this style of decoration is not otherwise found in Cheshire or Merseyside. It is much more common in the Midlands and the east of England and this piece may have travelled from some distance to the island. The decorative device facing the smoker is unusual but cannot be identified with certainty. It is possibly intended to be an Irish harp. There is also a bowl fragment from Context 28 with traces of fluted decoration and a device facing the smoker. This probably dates from the first half of the nineteenth century. There is a long, single line stamp on the top of a stem from Context 60, which probably dates from the later eighteenth or early nineteenth century (Fig 12.8). This style of marking was principally used in the West Midlands and north-west England. Examples are known to have been made in Worcester, Birmingham, Chester, Liverpool and Rainford.

Later nineteenth-century pipes

The remaining marked and decorated pieces probably all date from the mid-nineteenth century or later. There are three pieces made by Whites of Glasgow, who were operating until 1955 (Anon 1987). All three have the maker's name moulded in incuse, *sans serif* lettering. Two of the pieces, both from the same mould, also have 'P73' moulded in relief on the left hand side of the stem (Fig 12.9). This may be the pattern number for the pipe, although these do not usually have any letter before the number. In Whites' 1900 list, 73 is simply given as, 'Plain and Carved Cutties' (Gallagher 1987, 148). There is also one piece from Context 113 which was made by McDougalls of Glasgow (Fig 12.10), who were working until 1967 (Anon 1987). This has the relief mould number 9 on the stem, although it is not clear whether this was the whole number or whether part of it is missing. In the 1900 list McDougalls give number 9 as a Masonic or Scotch Cutty (Gallagher 1987, 144). There is another stem from Context 113 (not illustrated) which has traces of a relief beaded border for a name, none of which is legible. Another pipe with a pattern number, probably 59, from Context 12 (Fig 12.11) and a pipe with 'WIGAN & DISTRICT/ FOOT BALL PIPE' on the stem from Context 36 (Fig 12.12) were also found. The latter type of pipe, which would probably have portrayed footballers on the bowl, was popular at the end of the nineteenth century and early in the twentieth century. It was, presumably, made somewhere in the Wigan area.

The nineteenth-century bowls are very fragmentary but it is possible to recognise a number of different types which were in use. There are a number of plain 'Irish' style bowls, (for example, Fig 12.13). These generally have moulded milling at the rim and were made at numerous centres in both England and Ireland. There are fragments of thick- (Fig 12.13), medium- and thin-walled versions amongst the excavated fragments. There is also a fragment from Context 36 of a similar style, but with a harp and shamrock moulded on the side of the bowl. This, too, was a common pattern. The only other decorated pieces have the Legs of Man moulded on the bowl sides. Three such fragments were recovered, one each from Contexts 8, 28 and 36. All three are from different moulds and demonstrate the obvious popularity that this design would have had on the island. Like the Irish patterns,

these were produced by English makers, as well as those on Man itself.

The final point to note is the occurrence of three glazed mouthpiece fragments and one glazed stem fragment from near a mouthpiece. These were all found in Context 2 and are all glazed with a thin, light green glaze. The mouthpiece fragments all have simple cut ends and probably come from long-stemmed pipes. All the fragments are about 20mm long, and completely covered in glaze over this length. Glazing of the mouthpiece is not a particularly common feature, although it was locally used during the nineteenth century. The similarity of these pieces suggests that they came from a common source.

Site interpretation

As would be expected, the pipes cluster in the upper layers of the site. The earliest deposit, stratigraphically, in which a pipe occurs is Context 149. This piece is just a very small chip of stem of eighteenth- or nineteenth-century date. The context is well below other pipe-bearing horizons and it is quite possible that this pipe fragment is intrusive. Amongst the rest of the deposits there is no discernible chronological gradation, with the lowest pipe-bearing deposits (21, 50, 108, 127) all containing nineteenth-century material. This suggests that most of the post-medieval layers on the site have been disturbed or re-deposited since 1800. The material in Contexts 50 and 72 may be predominantly early in date, since they include a high proportion of seventeenth-century pipes (six pieces) with just one later piece. This piece is the complete bowl (Fig 12.5), which is probably of later eighteenth- or early nineteenth-century date.

Summary

Although the excavation did not produce any particularly large or well-dated groups, the fragments recovered do add significantly to our knowledge of pipes from the Isle of Man. Further weight has been given to the suggestion that South Lancashire was the island's main supply source during the seventeenth century, while Glasgow appears to have supplied a significant number of the later nineteenth-century pipes. In addition, imports from Liverpool and the Netherlands have been identified. There are a few pieces which cannot be matched with known products from the north-west.

These are likely to have come from outside the region and reflect the island's shipping connections.

The illustrated pipes [Fig 12]

1   Hard fired, off-white fabric with poor burnish. Part of a Rainford-type double-bordered stamp of 1630–60 survives on the heel. Stem bore 8/64″ (7).
2   Off-white local fabric with burnished surface and stamped IB mark. Probably Rainford, 1640–80. Stem bore 7/64″ (28).
3   Light buff-coloured fabric, fully milled rim, stamped mark CR, 1640–60. The bowl appears to have been lightly burnished. Stem bore 7/64″ (7).
4   Stem with relief moulded pattern of *fleur-de-lys* in beaded borders. The lower part of the stem has a good burnish on it. This is a Dutch stem, 1640–60. Stem bore 8/64″ (75).
5   Plain, thin-walled bowl; 1760–1810. Stem bore 5/64″ (50).
6   Stem fragment with incuse roll-stamped stem decoration; 1850–1900. Stem bore 6/64″ (5).
7   Bowl fragment with moulded decoration consisting of scallops with a device facing the smoker; 1770–1820. Stem bore 5/64″ (108).
8   Stem fragment with part of a Liverpool maker's mark stamped on the top of it; 1780–1830. Stem bore 6/64″ (60).
9   Composite drawing of two overlapping stem fragments from the same mould. The maker's name (WHITE/GLASGOW) is incuse, the pattern number (P73) is in relief. Neat round stems with a bore of 6/64″ (2). Whites were working from 1806 to 1955, but these pieces are likely to date from the later nineteenth or early twentieth century.
10 Stem fragment with relief moulded beaded border and incuse lettering which would have read McDOUGALL/GLASGOW. This firm was working from 1846 to 1967. The bowl would have been decorated; traces of this survive on the stem. Stem bore 4/64″ (113).
11 Scroll each side, incuse moulded number 59 on left hand side of stem only; 1850–1920. Stem bore 5/64″ (12).
12 Incuse lettering on stem WIGAN & DISTRICT/FOOT BALL PIPE; 1860–1920. Stem bore 6/64″ (36).
13 Thick-walled 'Irish' style bowl with moulded milling; 1850–1920. Stem bore 6/64″ (2).

Glass

J Lawrence
with a note on Fine Glass by
R Hurst Vose

A total of 570 sherds of glass were recovered at Castle Rushen from 50 different contexts. Nearly 70% (398) of the sherds were bottle glass and 24% (135) flat window glass. There was very little evidence of fine vessels, only 22 sherds (less than 4%) falling into this category. Miscellaneous items numbered 15.

Wine bottles

The thick dark olive-green metal which predominates over the olive-brown is of a fair quality with heavy patination. Very much in evidence is the broad base with a pronounced kick of up to 50mm in height. A complete wine bottle shape could not be reconstructed but a very few base sherds are possibly consistent with late seventeenth-century and early eighteenth-century forms: a squat body and broad base up to 180mm in diameter. Rather more show the straighter side and narrower base of the later eighteenth century. There are four bases and various necks of nineteenth-century moulded wine bottles of good quality, pale green metal, and one has a manufacturer's mark.

Analysis of the base diameters showed that two-thirds lie within the range 70mm to about 100mm. There are 11 examples of base diameters of 120mm or more, one-fifth of the total; one, possibly two, of these were multifaceted and can be compared with a dated example of 1769. Only five base sherds were less than 70mm in diameter (see Figs 13 and 14).

Beer bottles

About 20 very good quality brown beer bottle sherds were found, some with a distinctive cheese-grater pattern and lettering.

Mineral and medicine bottles

Forty-five sherds were thought to be from mineral or medicine bottles, of which two could be partially reconstructed. The good quality metal ranges from colourless, pale green, pale blue to a bright mauve. The latter provides an example of a parallel 'rig and furrow' design. Writing was evident on several, with one hailing from a limited company in Castletown.

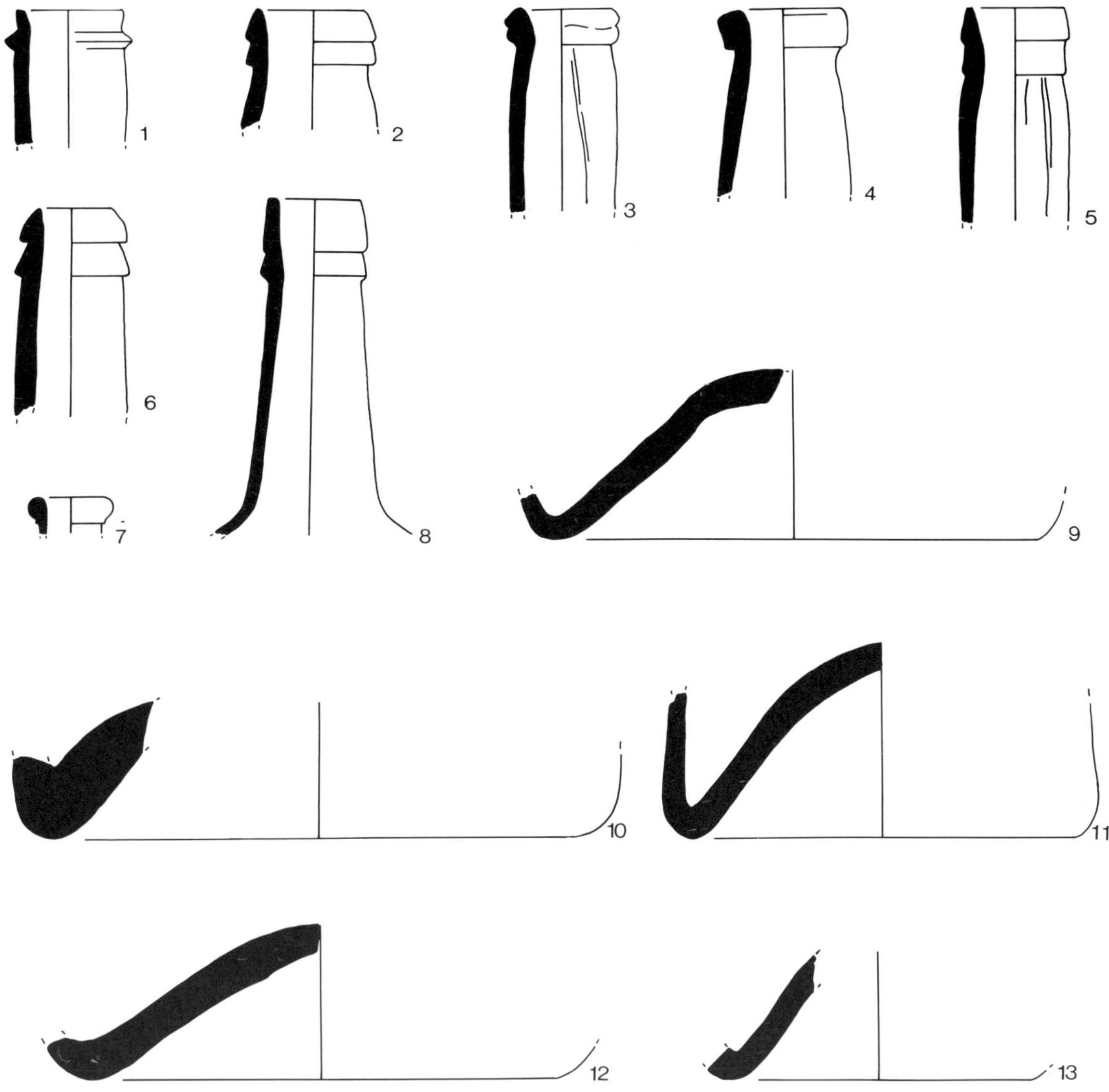

Fig 13   Castle Rushen, Glass; Nos 1–13 (Scale 1:2)

Of the seven examples of multifaceted bottles in this group, one with 13 sides was particularly striking. Another bears the Manx three-legged symbol encircled by a Latin motto: QUOCUN-QUE JECERIS ST[AB]IT (whichever way you throw it, it will stand).

Mineral bottles—Hamilton (Codd's?)

A few very thick base sherds of round-bottomed Hamilton bottles were recovered.

Miscellaneous bottles and jars

A Kilner jar stopper, bearing the words '. . . NER BROTHERS LONDON', and two base fragments are of the same very pale green metal with a frosted (or crackled) surface.

Other miscellaneous items include the quarter fragment of a foot approximately 65mm in diameter, in a thick good quality colourless metal, cut underneath with eight straight-sided petals of a radial design.

Fine vessel glass

Though the metal quality is good, no recognisable forms could be identified from the sparse number of fine vessel glass sherds. Olive-green, very pale green, white/opaque and colourless glass was found varying in thickness up to about 2mm, with slight patination. One drinking glass rim was identified, with a diameter of approximately 70mm.

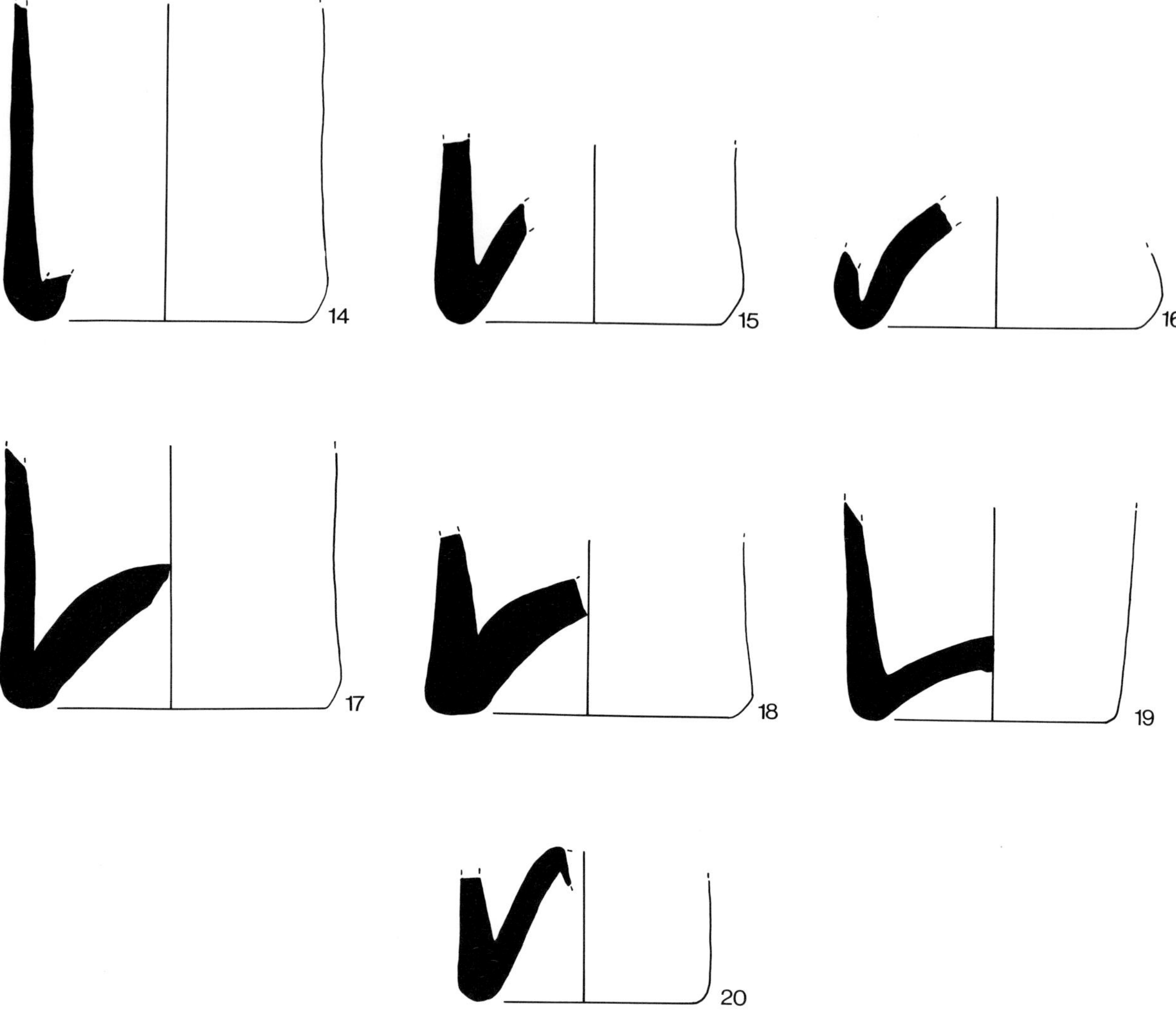

Fig 14   Castle Rushen, Glass; Nos 14–20 (Scale 1:2)

Flat (window) glass

Of the 135 sherds found, fewer than ten pieces were 4mm thick or more. At least 90% of the flat glass was between 1mm and 3mm thick, with just three pieces thinner than 1mm. The glass is largely cylinder or crown, with one clear example of a bullion.

Cut edges could be found on less than a quarter of the material. Quite a number of fragments had indications of diamond cutting and there was one particularly clear example, and two other possible examples, of a grozed edge and two examples of a muff edge. The greatest proportion of the metal was good quality, and pale green or colourless with a tint. There is only one striking piece of cobalt blue. At least two sherds have corners cut at 75 and 80 degrees, both of which also show traces of window-frame marking.

Fine Glass
R Hurst Vose

Eight pieces of small finds glass were recovered and are as follows.

Flat glass
A fragment of flat glass in clear metal with a pale green tint. The glass is 2mm thick, with one smooth rounded edge 5mm thick. The surfaces are slightly weathered, but both have a good fire polish, indicating that the fragment was produced by the crown method, and is from the rim of the crown (5). The introduction of the sash window directly led to crown glass superseding cylinder glass for the best windows because of its better quality, from around 1720 to about 1850; the fragment probably dates from this period (Cable unpublished).

A fragment of flat glass in clear metal with a green

tint. The glass is 1.75mm thick, widening to a rounded edge or rim on one side 4mm thick. There is good fire finish on one side, the other side being dull, perhaps because of weathering, or possibly from slight contamination on the side where it rested on the sand during manufacture (8). Cylinder and crown glass coexisted in separate glasshouses in the eighteenth century, crown being much preferred for the best work (Charleston 1984, 195).

Three fragments of flat glass in clear glass, two green tinted, one colourless, all similar to the above. The fragments were from the rims of glass crowns, probably eighteenth/early nineteenth-century (52, 55 and 66).

Glass paste

A small, round, faceted glass paste jewel in clear blue metal, 3mm diameter. Eighteenth-century to modern in date (7).

Window glass

A fragment from a diamond quarry, 2mm thick, totally weathered so the original metal colour has gone. Two edges have been trimmed with a grozing iron. This piece is probably potash glass and of medieval date (63).

Vessel glass

Part of a pushed-in foot rim, 70mm in diameter, probably from a wine glass in heavily weathered metal 1.5–2mm thick. This fragment is perhaps sixteenth to early seventeenth century in date (145).

Ironwork

N C Johnson

The ironwork from Castle Rushen was recovered from 74 contexts, spread widely over the site. A large proportion of the material is nineteenth century or later in origin. Given the highly disturbed nature of the contexts of this period on the site, and the highly corroded state of the finds, their value was not considered great, and they were not studied in detail. The material from earlier contexts is also highly corroded, but it proved possible to identify about 60 nail heads and shafts. In addition, a small quantity of fragments of iron sheet were present, two small but incomplete shackles in Contexts 145 and 196, and a small hook in Context 160.

The following items were identified by Geoff Egan.

Blade

1   Fragment of a small blade, width 14mm, with ?whittle tang. Possibly from a pair of scissors rather than a knife (145).

Miscellaneous

2   Rusted ?sheet lozenge 25mm × 15mm, with D-shaped cut-out at one end; seventeenth to eighteenth century (57).
3   Rectangular-section rod, length 42mm. Possibly part of a nail shaft (182).

Non-Ferrous Metal

G Egan

There is little contextual evidence to provide close dating, though some items are attributable on typological grounds. Only copper-alloy buckle plates (Figs 15.1 and 15.2) appear to be of late medieval date; the strap end (Fig 15.3) may be from the sixteenth century, while the majority of other items are probably from the seventeenth to nineteenth centuries.

The assemblage is dominated by the 26 pieces of shot, many of them apparently used. There are several dress accessories, none of them particularly distinctive apart from a *repoussé* buckle plate (Fig 15.2). All four of the belt fittings have iron rivets, suggesting they may have been reset on new straps when the old ones wore out. This is a far greater proportion than appears common on the mainland, perhaps a hint that islanders in the sixteenth and early seventeenth centuries found it less easy to acquire completely new accessories than most people in towns on the mainland. The unstratified buckle (Fig 15.2) is paralleled amongst manufacturer's waste in London, indicating its possible origin. The three possible furnishing studs are of forms common elsewhere. The vessel fragment (Fig 15.7) may well be from a tripod cauldron for cooking.

Metalworking is attested by several cut fragments of sheeting, with a fragment from Context 50 being particularly roughly cut. One, at least, of the three folded-sheet rivets for repairing sheet vessels is unused, as is the last of the three rolled-sheet rivets for holding together composite items. There is also a fair amount of casting waste, especially of copper and lead.

The lead/tin items include a plain button (Fig

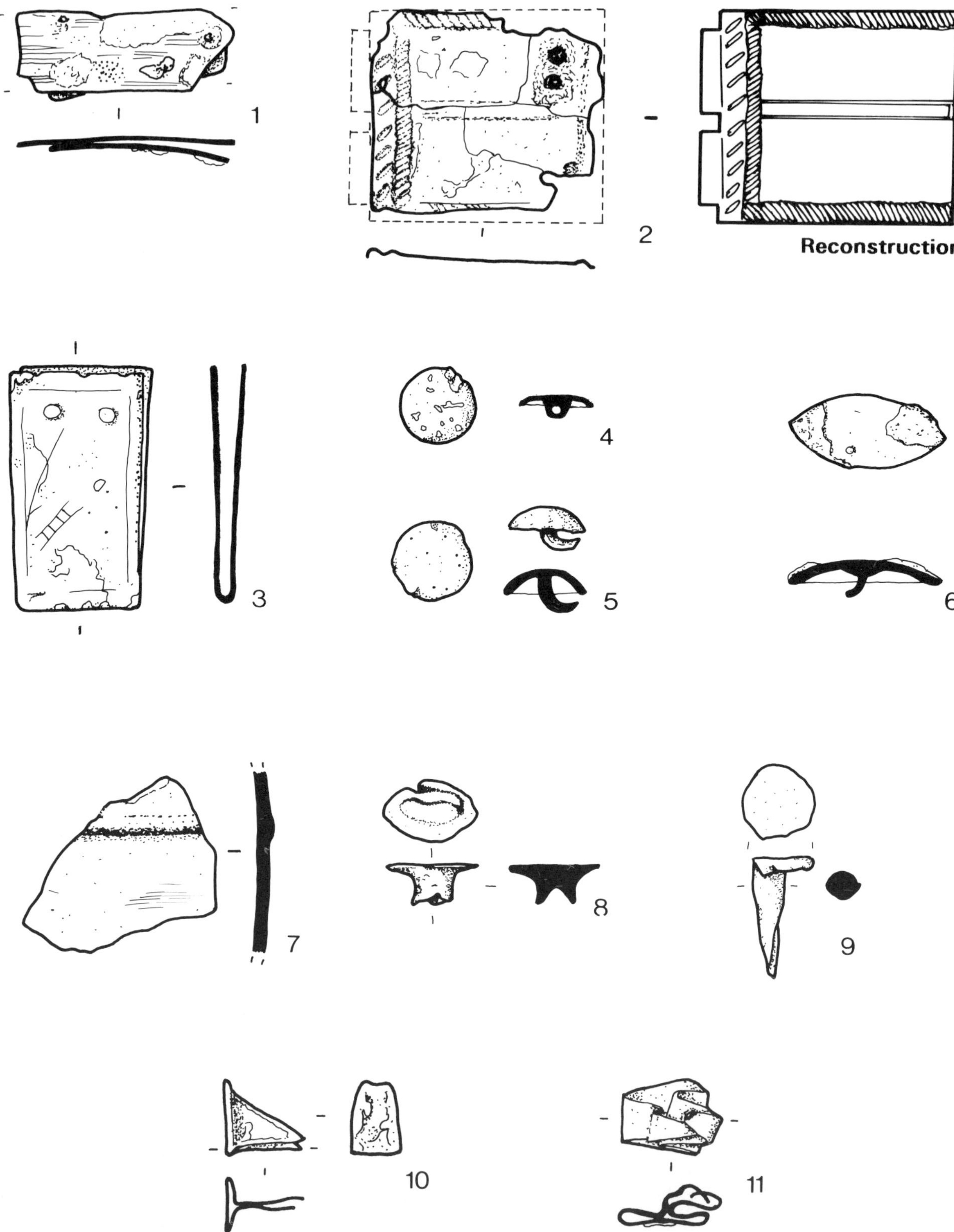

Fig 15   Castle Rushen, Non-Ferrous Metal; Nos 1–11 (Scale 1:1)

16.13), probably of seventeenth-century date, and an eighteenth-century shoe buckle with simple decoration (Fig 16.12). The plumb bob (Fig 16.17) is rough, and not closely datable. The window lead includes cast cames (Fig 16.14 and 15) and relatively unusual evidence for milling (Fig 16.16), all indicating that this basic building component was being finished on the island.

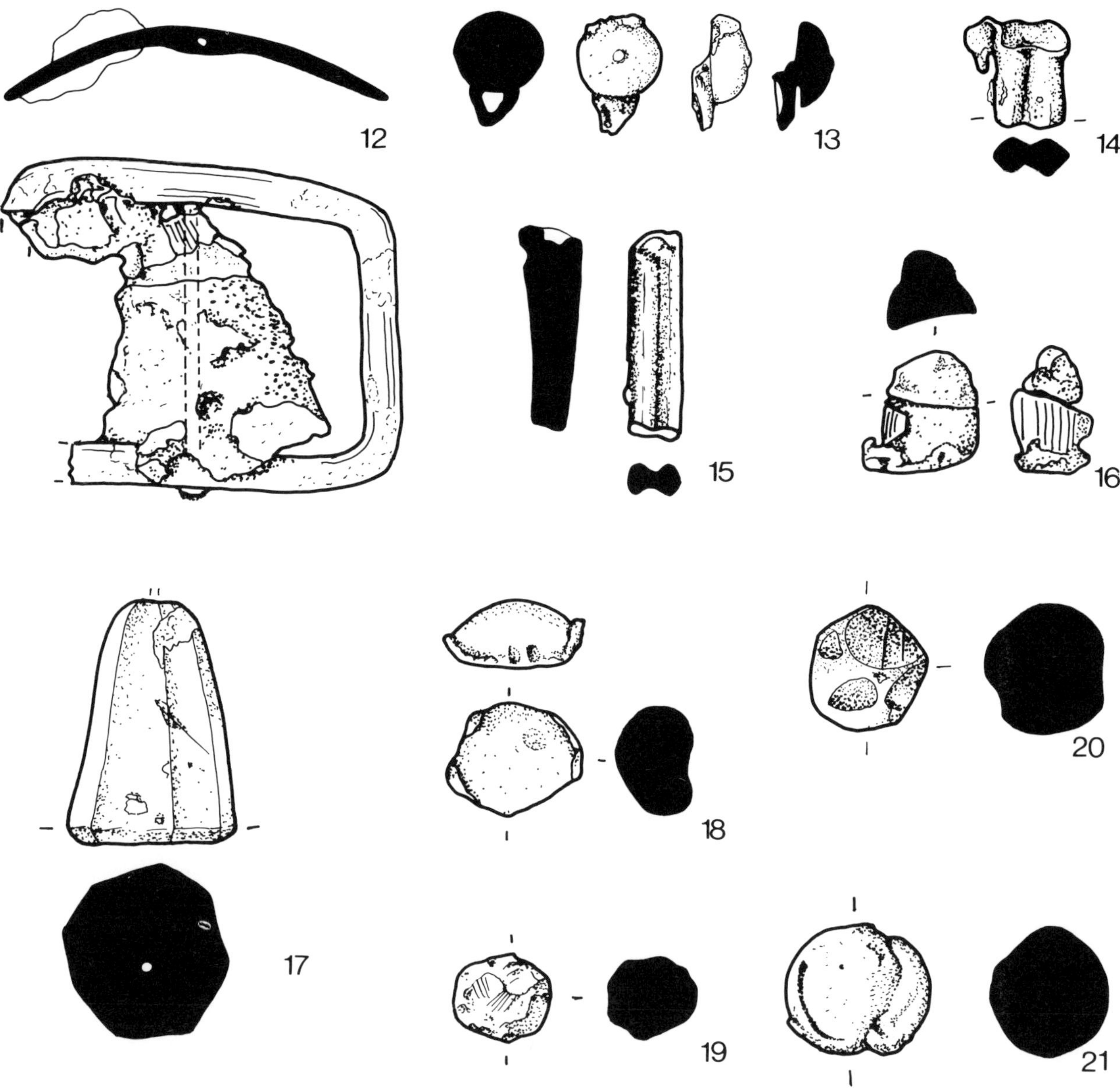

Fig 16   Castle Rushen, Non-Ferrous Metal; Nos 12–21 (Scale 1:1)

CATALOGUE (Figs 15 and 16)

NI = Not illustrated

Copper alloy

Probable buckles (Fig 15.1 and 2)

1   Sheet strip broken off at both ends, 33+mm × 13mm; engraved parallel strokes lengthways; rusted iron sheet on back, held by one or possibly two iron rivets; from a seventeenth- to nineteenth-century context (33).
Presumably part of a buckle plate or a strap end; the former is more likely to have needed the iron repair. Probably medieval to seventeenth-century.

2   Incomplete; four fragments, originally (?)36mm × 33mm; *repoussé* corded border (double at folded edge); two parallel ridges lengthways in middle; two iron rivets. Probably fifteenth- to sixteenth-century (U/S).
Paralleled amongst manufacturer's waste found in London (Margeson 1993, 25 pl IX upper left), perhaps an indication of the source of the present item. The iron rivets probably indicate resetting.

Strap ends (Fig 15.3)

3   Folded-sheet plate, 40mm × 22mm, with folded sides and engrailed top; engrailed design (obscured by corrosion) defined by a line border; two iron rivets; probably six-

teenth-century. The rivets in a different metal are probably from a resetting. (47).

NI   Incomplete, 31+mm × 34mm; hint of coating; two iron rivets. Presumably a strap end; the iron rivets probably indicate resetting (159).

Lacechape
NI   Length 30mm, diameter 1–2mm (end obscured). Seventeenth- to nineteenth-century (52).

Button (Fig 15.4)
Four buttons were recovered as follows:

NI   Button, diameter 16mm; oval conical centre with beaded surround and two holes. Probably seventeenth- to nineteenth-century (19).

NI   Convex button, diameter 17mm; separate wire loop. Seventeenth- to nineteenth-century (33).

4   Convex head, diameter 13mm; semi-circular tab with drilled attachment hole; (?)tin coating (now black). Seventeenth- to twentieth-century (36).
Buttons of similar form date from the early eighteenth century and probably later; some in London have the head of Queen Anne (Noël Hume 1970, 89 Fig 22).

NI   Button, diameter 17mm; concave centre with four holes; maker's name . . . S LTD BHAM (ie Birmingham). Eighteenth- to twentieth-century; (possibly non-ferrous white metal) (112).

Pins
NI   Length 22mm, spherical head; tin coating. Seventeenth- to nineteenth-century (33).

NI   Pin, broken off at looped end. Eighteenth- to twentieth-century. ?Incomplete safety pin (112).

Studs (Fig 15.5 and 6)
Probably from furniture rather than belts.
NI   Domed, circular head, diameter 10mm. Seventeenth- to twentieth-century (36).

5   Domed, circular head, diameter 12mm (127).

6   Domed, lentoid head, 25mm × 12mm (47).

Tack
NI   Irregular-shaped head, length 18mm (143).

Possible roves
NI   Irregular, conical form, maximum diameter 34mm; hammered around perimeter. Probably seventeenth- to nineteenth-century (60).

NI   Fragment of similar item to preceding. Seventeenth- to nineteenth-century (37).

Vessel (Fig 15.7)
7   Wall fragment from cast vessel, diameter approx 200mm; horizontal ridge. Probably from a tripod cauldron or similar cooking vessel. Probably fifteenth- to sixteenth-century (140).

Sheeting
NI   Squarish fragment 12mm × 11mm, cut on three sides, torn off at the other. Seventeenth- to nineteenth-century (33).

NI   Corroded; roughly cut rectangle 31mm × 16mm; with possible folded rivet. Possibly a repair patch (U/S).

NI   Lozenge 41mm × 22mm; (thicker sheeting than for folded rivets). Eighteenth- to twentieth-century (112).

NI   Folded fragment with right-angled cut-out at one end of cut edge (remainder of perimeter is torn). Seventeenth- to nineteenth-century (37).

NI   Irregular fragment (114).

NI   Fragment (159).

NI   Fragment. Seventeenth- to nineteenth-century (50).

NI   Irregular, jagged offcut. Seventeenth- to twentieth-century (36).

NI   Corroded; irregular, very uneven possible sheeting, 37mm × 34mm, with a series of uneven, parallel ridges. Seventeenth- to nineteenth-century. Possibly skimming from a melting pot (72).

Rolled-sheet rivets (Fig 15.8 and 9)
Lozenge-shaped pieces of sheeting rolled into cones and used as rivets. These were used for joining parts of composite copper-alloy items, probably from the sixteenth to eighteenth centuries and possibly later (*cf* Stone 1974, 189 and 192, Fig 108).

The presence of an unused rivet from Context 14 suggests some kind of metalworking in the locality.

8 15mm × 10mm lentoid head at one end, broken off at other. Seventeenth- to nineteenth-century (41).

NI Subround head, diameter 14mm; possibly used (113).

9 Length 20mm, subround head, diameter 22mm; unused (14).

Folded-sheet repair rivets (Fig 15.10 and 11)

For holding sheet patches to repair tears and larger holes in sheet vessels, etc. These simple repairs date back to the medieval period (Egan forthcoming b, Nos 488–94) and probably continued in use until recently. The presence of unused, as well as possibly used, rivets indicates low-technology repairing was going on in the area. All are lozenge-shaped, with subrectangular/hexagonal heads after folding.

10 12mm × 19mm, part-folded, unused. Seventeenth- to nineteenth-century (33).

NI 13mm × 10mm, folded, rust adhering, possibly used. Seventeenth- to twentieth-century (36).

11 14mm × 12mm, folded, possibly used. Seventeenth- to nineteenth-century (72).

Casting waste

All are from deposits of seventeenth-century date or later, unless otherwise indicated.

Thirteen fragments of casting waste as follows:

NI Runnels. Probably eighteenth- or nineteenth-century (4, 6, 7 and two from 21).

NI Runnels. Fifteenth to seventeenth-century (113 and 135); and several fragments (33, 48, two from 37 and two from 72).

Possible casting waste

NI Partly melted fragment. Between 1610 and nineteenth-century (7).

NI Fragment with broken-off end and transverse grooves (?tool marks). Seventeenth- to twentieth-century (36).

Miscellaneous

NI Incomplete rod/strip, length 55mm, with spatulate end; three right-angled tabs with holes. Seventeenth- to nineteenth-century (6).

NI Sheet oval 34mm × 20mm; two holes for attachment. Seventeenth- to nineteenth-century (6).

NI Badge with royal arms of Britain. Eighteenth- to twentieth-century. Possibly police or military in origin (11).

NI Fragment of bone stained green — not copper alloy (37)

Lead/tin and other non-ferrous white metals

Shoe buckle (Fig 16.12)

12 Incomplete, estimated originally 65mm × 45mm; decoration of (?)multiple parallel lines along frame; rusted-iron bar and complex pin. Eighteenth-century object from a seventeenth- to nineteenth-century context (50).

Button (Fig 16.13)

13 Plano-convex, diameter 12mm; central knop; loop on right-angled stem. Seventeenth-century object from a seventeenth- to nineteenth-century context (16).

Window lead

Lead for windows was cast into relatively heavy cames and then turned through a hand mill to draw out the metal so that it would cover a greater length of glass. The wheels of the mill were transversely grooved, so the leads were produced with reeding (*cf* Egan *et al* 1986). The presence of waste pieces indicates window leads were not in this case imported ready for use onto the island, but that the final stage of preparation was carried out locally. Unmilled cames are widespread and similar finishing evidence from milling is known at Winchester (Biddle 1990, 173–4, No 30, Fig 38, dated to the late fifteenth-century) and Salisbury (Salisbury and South Wiltshire Museum collection).

Milled leads

NI Reeded (U/S).

NI Heart (ie the central part in which any reeding would be visible) obscured. Seventeenth- to nineteenth-century (7).

NI   Reeded. Seventeenth- to nineteenth-century (36).

NI   Heart obscured. Seventeenth- to nineteenth-century (41).

NI   Reeded. Seventeenth- to nineteenth-century (72).

Milling waste (Fig 16.14–16)

14   Cut-off end of cast came (47).

15   Cut-off end of cast came (47).

16   Irregular fragment with reeding. Seventeenth- to twentieth-century; probably a version of the two preceding items but distorted by the mill (36).

Plumb bob (Fig 16.17)

17   Slightly irregular; tapered, height 33mm, basal diameter 23mm; nine facets; vertical, slightly off-central hole. *c*1610 to nineteenth-century. A similar object found at Eltham Palace is dated to the mid-sixteenth-century (Woods 1982, 259 and 263, Fig 30, No 5) (66).

Shot (Fig 16.18–21)

Twenty-six pieces of shot were recovered as follows:

NI   Diameter 17mm. Seventeenth- to nineteenth-century (5).

NI   Diameter 17mm, impact marks. Seventeenth- to nineteenth-century (5).

NI   Diameter 17mm. From 1610 to nineteenth century (7).

NI   Diameter 18mm, impact marks. From 1610 to nineteenth century (7).

NI   Diameter 10.5mm, impact marks. From 1610 to nineteenth century (7).

18   Diameter approximately 14mm, impact marks. Seventeenth- to nineteenth-century (73).

19   Diameter approximately 16mm, impact marks, very flat. Seventeenth-to nineteenth-century (73).

20   Diameter 17mm, multiple impact marks. Seventeenth- to nineteenth-century (33).

NI   Diameter approximately 9mm. Seventeenth- to nineteenth-century (33).

NI   Diameter 18mm, impact marks. Seventeenth- to twentieth-century (36).

NI   Diameter 11mm, impact marks. Seventeenth- to twentieth-century (36).

NI   Diameter 17mm. Seventeenth- to twentieth-century (36).

21   Diameter approximately 17mm, mould slightly misaligned, with sprue. Seventeenth- to twentieth-century (36).

NI   Diameter 13mm, impact marks. Seventeenth- to twentieth-century (36).

NI   Diameter approximately 13mm, with sprue, impact marks. Seventeenth- to twentieth-century (36).

NI   Diameter approximately 17mm, possible impact marks. Seventeenth- to nineteenth-century (37).

NI   Diameter 13mm, impact marks. Seventeenth- to nineteenth-century (37).

NI   Probably shot, diameter approximately 13mm, possibly flattened from impact (37).

NI   Diameter 16mm, impact marks. Seventeenth/ eighteenth-century (57).

NI   Diameter 11mm, impact marks. Seventeenth- to nineteenth-century (41).

NI   Diameter 12mm. Seventeenth- to nineteenth-century (47).

NI   Diameter 9mm, impact marks. Seventeenth/ eighteenth-century (57).

NI   Diameter 12mm. Seventeenth- to nineteenth-century (72).

NI   Diameter 17mm, with sprue. Eighteenth- to twentieth-century (112).

NI   Diameter 11mm, possible impact marks. Sixteenth- to seventeenth-century (121).

NI   Diameter 23mm, impact marks. Seventeenth- to nineteenth-century (127).

Miscellaneous

NI   Rough, lentoid knob, diameter 28mm, on (?broken) iron shaft. Between 1610 and the nineteenth-century (7).

NI   Rough-cast, lozenge-section rod, length approximately 55mm; folded in two. Seventeenth/eighteenth-century (57).

NI   Piece of type. Seventeenth- to nineteenth-century (5).

Sheeting

NI   Folded fragment, now 30mm × 20mm, with two straight edges meeting at an acute angle; other side torn off; pinhole near corner (U/S).

NI   Strip, width 6mm, roughly multiple-folded into a ball. Nineteenth/twentieth-century (11).

NI   Folded strip, width 10mm, length approximately 55mm; one cut, one broken end. Eighteenth/nineteenth-century (74).

NI   Thin sheet fragment, 17mm × 9mm (182).

NI   Fragment of strip (185).

Runnels

NI   Possibly incorporating glassy material (154 and 182).

Coins

M M Archibald

Three coins were recovered from the excavations at Castle Rushen and are as follows.

1   England. John, cut-halfpenny, Short Cross issue class 5bii, London mint (off flan here), moneyer Willelm L, between 1205 and 1210. Wt 0.62g (North 1980, No 970 (b)) (184).

This coin could have been lost at any time until the Short Cross issue was superseded by the Long Cross in 1247. It is, however, not much worn and was possibly deposited earlier rather than later within the date bracket, but the date must remain uncertain.

2   England. Elizabeth I, half of a sixpence, initial marked uncertain, dated 1[5 – –]. Issue uncertain. Wt 0.98g (112).

This coin is a halved sixpence twisted into a close curl, reverse outside. It is not possible to quote a reference as the diagnostic details are not visible. In view of the uncertainty of issue date in a long reign, it is difficult to suggest a narrow deposition bracket, but this coin was probably lost by, say, 1625. It is hard to believe that the coin achieved its present appearance accidentally. It was possibly votive or a love token.

3   Ireland. Elizabeth I, silver penny. Third coinage, 1601–2, initial mark trefoil; dated 1601. Wt 1.55g (Seaby 1984, No 6510) (37).

This coin is hardly worn and was probably lost within a short time of issue.

Flint (Fig 17)

S B Mc Cartan

The assemblage contains 12 artifacts of flaked stone and five natural fragments. All the flaked stone artifacts are made of flint which is known to occur on the nearby beaches.

The evidence for primary knapping technology is meagre, but it appears that both hard and soft hammer percussion were employed. Platform preparation is present on some of the pieces (Fig 17.2 and 4). Two artifacts exhibit secondary working with an edge-retouched flake and a leaf-shaped arrowhead (Fig 17.1 and 3). The majority of the artifacts show signs of edge damage, but it is difficult to discern if this occurred during use or more recently.

All the flaked stone artifacts were recovered from the medieval phases. One patinated secondary flake was recovered from the fourteenth-century Phase A deposits, and a secondary blade from fifteenth- to seventeenth-century Phase B deposits. The majority of the artifacts, however, were recovered from the Phase C nineteenth-century deposits, including the leaf-shaped arrowhead. The level of disturbance within the castle walls owing to repeated phases of building, habitation and clearance makes it difficult to determine if the recovered artifacts actually represent previous prehistoric activity in the locality. The fresh condition of the leaf-shaped arrowhead suggests it may have come from elsewhere and was possibly lost by a nineteenth-century worker or visitor to the castle.

Notes to catalogue

1   All pieces are flint unless otherwise stated.
2   During analysis all pieces are held with the dorsal face uppermost and the proximal ends towards the observer.
3   Patination refers to the discolouration of the flint. Due to problems with current terminology no distinction has been made between patination and cortication.

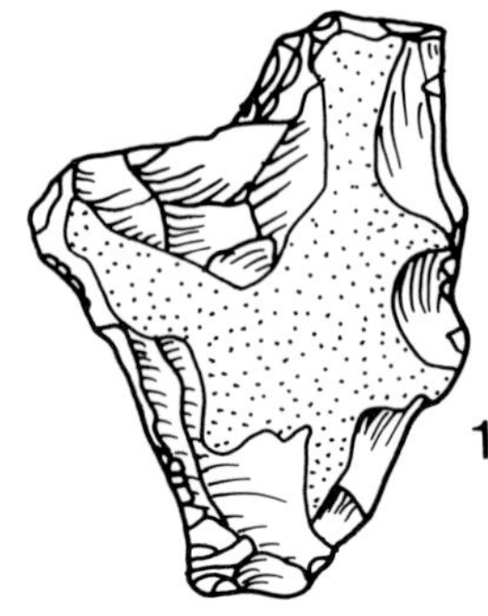

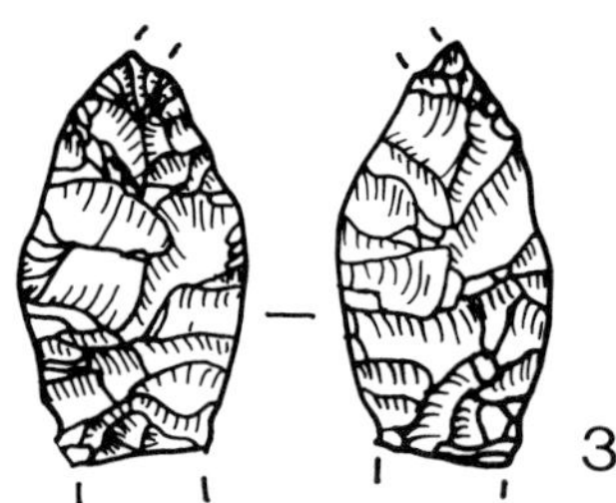

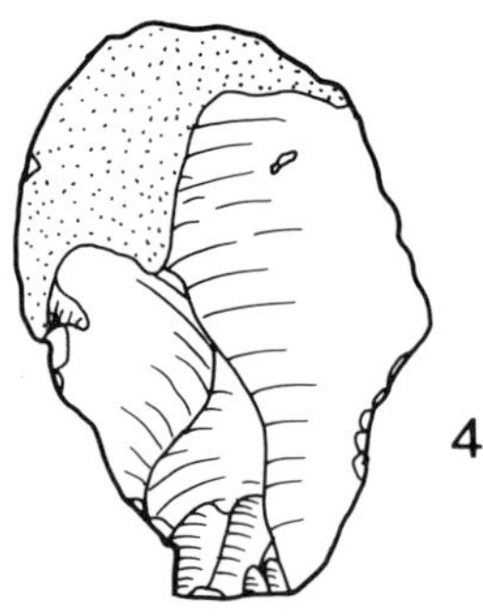

Fig 17   Castle Rushen, Flint (Scale 1:1)

4   Edge damage refers to the removal of small flakes from the pieces. Without the use of a highpowered microscope it is not clear if the damage is due to use or post-depositional processes.

5   Dimensions are given in millimetres in the order: length: width: thickness.

CATALOGUE (Fig 17)

1   Secondary flake; dark grey; distal end surviving; edge damage; 40:40:22 (5).

2   Secondary flake; pale grey; abraded; extensive edge damage; retouch on dorsal right and left laterals; edge-retouched flake; 32:32:12 (6). (Fig 17.1)

3   Inner flake; dark grey; proximal end surviving; slight edge damage; 29:25:15 (6).

4   Inner flake; dark grey; slightly abraded; extensive edge damage; 23:18:07 (6).

5   Inner flake; mottled grey; small fragment missing from distal end; edge damage; 23:32:04 (7). (Fig 17.2)

6   Natural (8).

7   Secondary flake; pale toffee/yellow; slightly abraded; proximal end surviving; 17:35:12 (14).

8   Inner flake; pale grey/toffee; right lateral missing; slight edge damage; 24:15:09 (50).

9   Natural (50).

10   Natural (50).

11   Primary flake; pale grey/yellow; small fragment missing at distal end; edge damage; 45:22:11 (75).

12   Secondary flake; white/pale grey; segment surviving; patinated; abraded; minor edge damage; 33:35:15 (75).

13   Inner flake; small fragments missing from proximal and distal ends; edge damage; bifacial retouch; leaf-shaped arrowhead; 27:15:03 (127). (Fig 17.3)

14   Natural (134)

15   Secondary blade; dark grey; abraded; minor edge damage; 37:16:09 (156).

16 Secondary flake; white/pale grey; patinated; abraded; edge damage; 40:26:06 (172). (Fig 17.4)

17 Natural (177).

Stone and Plaster

S D White

Twelve fragments of stone or plaster were recovered from the excavations at Castle Rushen.

The upper levels of the site were greatly disturbed when the nineteenth-century prison was stripped out and the majority of the contexts that yielded stone fragments are, therefore, undatable. The dates given are based on ceramic evidence.

Stone balls

Three stone balls were recovered, two of sandstone and one of granite. All three could have been naturally produced; spheres of this type can be formed in pot holes in river beds. The force of water in the cavity causes a trapped stone fragment to spin, thereby creating a roughly spherical form. Similar results can be obtained in certain coastal conditions.

The sandstone objects may have been deliberately shaped, but the granite sphere would have taken considerable time and effort to produce. It is possible that a natural supply of these balls was exploited and that they were used as marbles or shot.

1 Sandstone ball, diameter 22mm (U/S).

2 Sandstone ball, diameter 29mm, from a seventeenth- to nineteenth-century deposit (28).

3 Granite ball, diameter 21mm; possibly from the boulder clay, from a fifteenth- to seventeenth-century deposit (170).

Whetstones (Fig 18)

Five objects were collected as possible whetstones, of these only one is certainly a whetstone (Fig 18.2). Whetstones were used to sharpen knives and similar tools, and the size will vary depending on use. A variety of stone types could be used, but the most effective are those which are of an even grain with an abrasive texture. Some whetstones may have had a perforation at one end for suspension, possibly from a belt. None of the Castle Rushen examples is pierced.

All the possible whetstones recovered from Castle Rushen are of a fine black micaceous siltstone from the Manx Series. In two examples veins of a coarser sandstone are clearly visible (Fig 18.3 and 5). Only one stone gives clear indications of use as a sharpening tool (Fig 18.2). The texture of the stone in this example is much coarser and all faces have been ground down to produce four flat surfaces. The remaining four objects all have rounded edges that could have been caused by water action or weathering.

1 Possible whetstone, 38mm × 9mm × 6.5mm; from a seventeenth- to nineteenth-century deposit (57).

2 Whetstone, 39mm × 11mm × 9mm; from an eighteenth- or nineteenth-century deposit (108).

3 Possible whetstone, 79.5mm × 17mm × 8mm; from an eighteenth- or nineteenth-century deposit (108).

4 Possible whetstone, 37.5mm × 10.5mm tapering to 3mm × 8mm; from an eighteenth- or nineteenth-century deposit (108).

5 Possible whetstone, 122mm × 19mm × 12mm; from a fourteenth-century deposit (197).

Miscellaneous

In addition to the stone balls and whetstones, two other pieces of stone were recovered. The first piece, from Context 168 (Fig 18.6), is a piece of fine micaceous red sandstone, possibly Carboniferous or Peel sandstone, measuring 59mm × 36mm × 26mm. One side of the stone has been obliquely cut to produce a wedge shape, which may suggest it was part of a window sill. The stone is broken on one side but the remaining five sides have been neatly shaped.

The second piece of stone (Fig 18.7) is from Context 197, which is a fourteenth-century deposit. It is a roughly rectangular piece of fine black siltstone measuring 81.5mm × 60mm × 20mm. Both the upper and lower surfaces of the stone are slightly convex. This shaping has produced an edge around the stone that is too sharp to have been produced by water action or natural wear and therefore must be deliberate. The stone is very soft. Any attempt to use it as a tool would result in

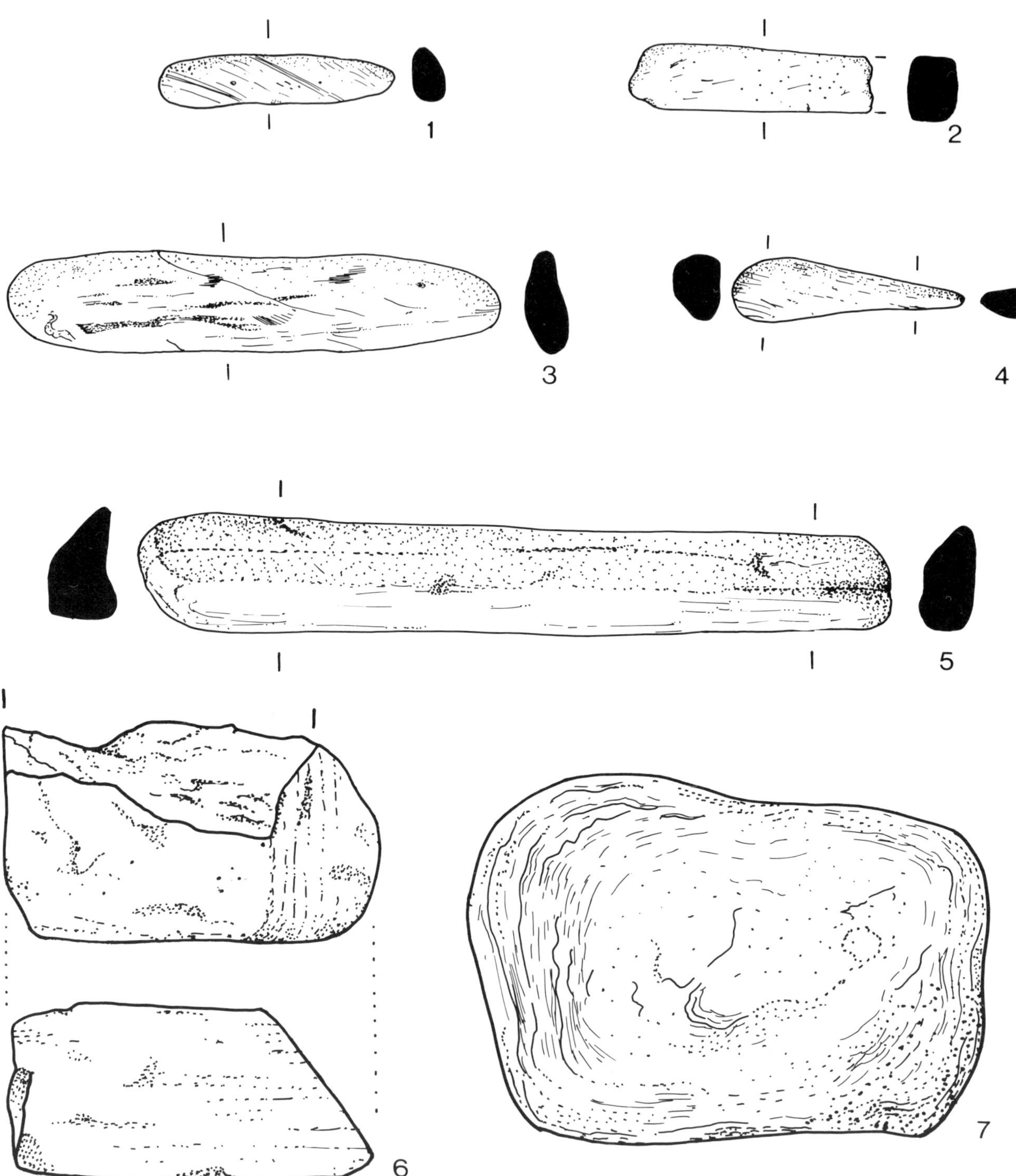

Fig 18   Castle Rushen, Stone (Scale 1:1)

flaking and splitting: its possible use is, therefore, uncertain.

Plaster

Two pieces of painted plaster were recovered. The first comes from Context 6, a nineteenth-century deposit, and measures 37mm × 32mm × 16mm. A smooth plaster surface, approximately 1mm thick, has been applied to a thicker layer of coarser plaster. The outer surface shows signs of red paint on all but a small area approximately 12mm × 5mm in the top, left-hand corner. Just below this area two parallel lines can be seen running across the fragment. The upper line is 1mm thick and the lower line is slightly narrower, being approximately 1/2mm thick, fading out on the left-hand edge.

The second piece of plaster comes from Context 154, a pit against the castle wall containing finds

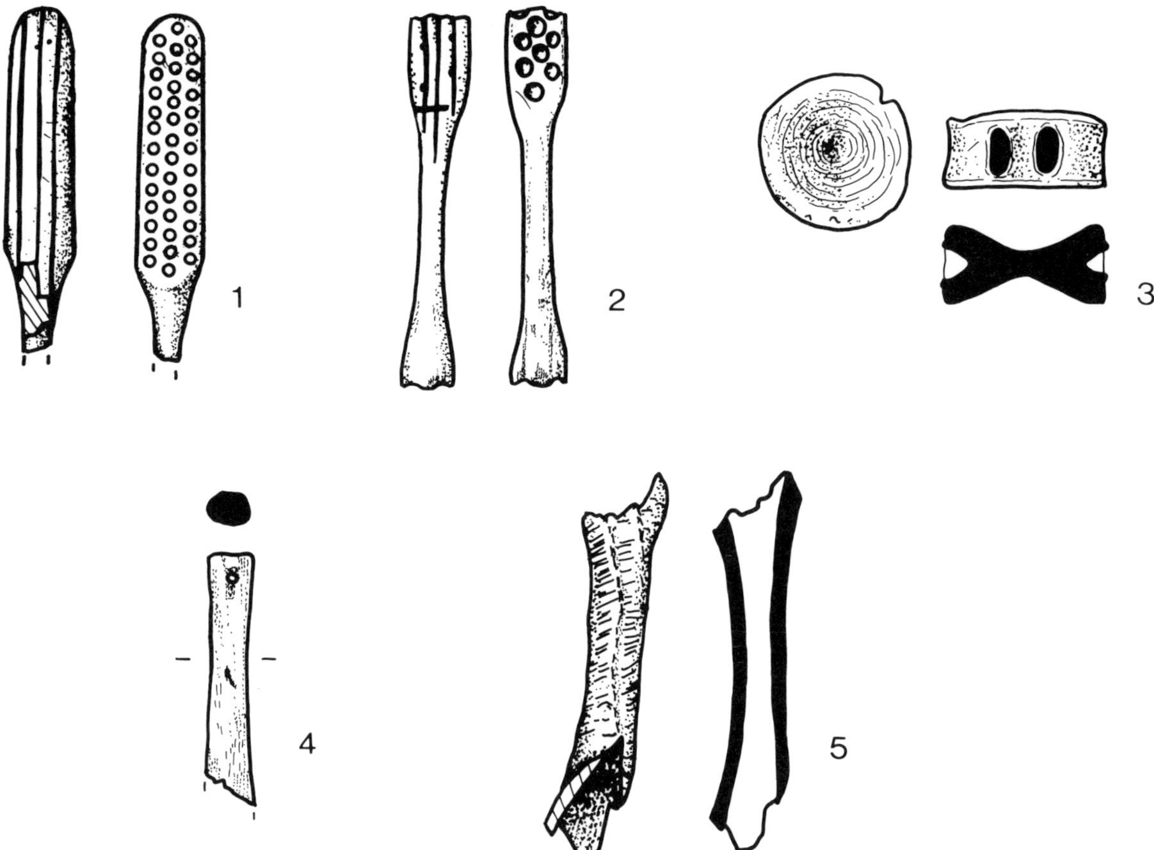

Fig 19   Castle Rushen, Worked Bone (Scale 1:1)

dating from the thirteenth to fifteenth centuries. This piece is very gritty with a roughly smoothed surface, and is decorated with traces of two red lines running parallel to one another across the fragment. The lower line is 3mm thick and this fades out approximately 8mm from the edge.

Worked Bone

S D White

From the excavations at Castle Rushen 12 pieces of worked bone were recovered. This total includes four vertebrae, which may be counters or gaming pieces.

Because of the disturbed nature of the site, dating of the contexts containing the pieces of worked bone is difficult. The dates that are given are based upon pottery or clay pipes found in those contexts.

Brushes (Fig 19)

The heads of two toothbrushes were recovered, both showing signs of green staining on the reverse.

1   Part of the head and handle of a small brush measuring 46mm × 9mm × 5mm. Three parallel grooves have been incised into the full length of the head. The underside has 40 holes arranged in three rows (U/S) (Fig 19.1).

2   Head of a small brush measuring 51mm × 9mm × 5mm. Three parallel grooves have been cut into the back of the head, two of which are crossed by a shorter groove cut at right angles. The rest of the head shows nine holes arranged in three rows. The head tapers to a short handle which then splays out again. Two semi-circles have been cut into the very end of the handle and two parallel grooves incised into the underside of the handle (Fig 19.2). The brush is from a seventeenth-century deposit (72).

Buttons

A total of three buttons were recovered. None is illustrated.

1   A possible button; diameter 14mm, pierced at the centre. From a seventeenth- to nineteenth-century deposit (5).

2   A button; diameter 14mm, pierced four times. From a seventeenth- to nineteenth-century deposit (6).

3   A button; diameter 20mm diameter, pierced at the centre with a strip of metal to form a loop. From a seventeenth-century deposit (50).

Counters (Fig 19)

Four shark vertebrae were recovered from Context 4, a deposit dating from the seventeenth-century to approximately 1900. These vertebrae are of an appropriate size and shape to have been used as gaming pieces. Their form does not appear to have been altered in any way, although they are slightly worn from use as counters. All the counters are of a similar size (see Fig 19.3); their measurements are as follows:

1   Diameter 21mm × height 11mm
2   Diameter 21mm × height 10mm
3   Diameter 20mm × height 11mm
4   Diameter 20mm × height 9mm

The vertebrae were examined at the Environmental Archaeology Unit at the University of York, where they were identified as belonging to one of two species of shark, either the blue shark (*Pronace glauca*) or the thresher shark (*Alopias vulpinus*), both of which are edible. A more precise identifi-cation was not possible as the Unit does not hold either of these species in its reference collection.

Miscellaneous (Fig 19)

NI = Not illustrated

Three pieces of miscellaneous bone were recovered, one of which appears to be a piece of worked bone waste.

4   A piece of shaped bone measuring 33mm × 6mm diameter. It appears to be broken at one end and pierced at the other end (Fig 19.4) (182).

5   A piece of worked bone measuring 51mm × 9mm diameter, flaring slightly at both ends. The bone is hollow, with a maximum thickness of 1.5mm. The outer surface shows signs of working, with vertical cuts running around the shaft (Fig 19.5). This object was recovered from a seventeenth- to nineteenth-century deposit (28).

NI Fragment of co-distal humerus (the lower part of the shaft, anterior section), measuring 87mm × 38mm × 22mm, which has been sawn in several places. These saw marks do not look like normal butchery marks but appear to indicate that this is an example of worked bone waste. From a deposit dating to around 1800 (11).

EXCAVATIONS AT BANK STREET, 1989

The Excavations

A C C Johnson

Introduction

In 1989 a small-scale rescue excavation was undertaken by the Manx Museum and National Trust (now Manx National Heritage) at Castle Cottage in Bank Street. The work was carried out as a planning condition prior to the construction of a two-storey extension to the rear of the cottage (Fig 3.11).

The excavation produced important evidence about the archaeology of Castletown, including a significant corpus of pottery dating from the sixteenth to the early twentieth centuries as well as animal bones and metalworking waste. Within the small area available for excavation, evidence was also recovered for two structures and an early drain.

Location

The site lies at the rear of a plot opening on to the now-pedestrianised easterly arm of Bank Street. The ground here slopes gradually down towards the harbour, which lies just to the north-east. The harbour formerly lay closer to the site, but was pushed back when the present frontage wall was built during the nineteenth century. The site lies just 40 metres to the north-west of the outer works of Castle Rushen. Seventeenth- and eighteenth-century illustrations show the town crowding up against the castle, providing workspace and habitation for those serving its needs.

The area of the proposed extension clearly lay within a former building, since the site was partly covered with rough stone flags which had formed a floor to it. These were related to a surviving gable wall which had been incorporated into the south-

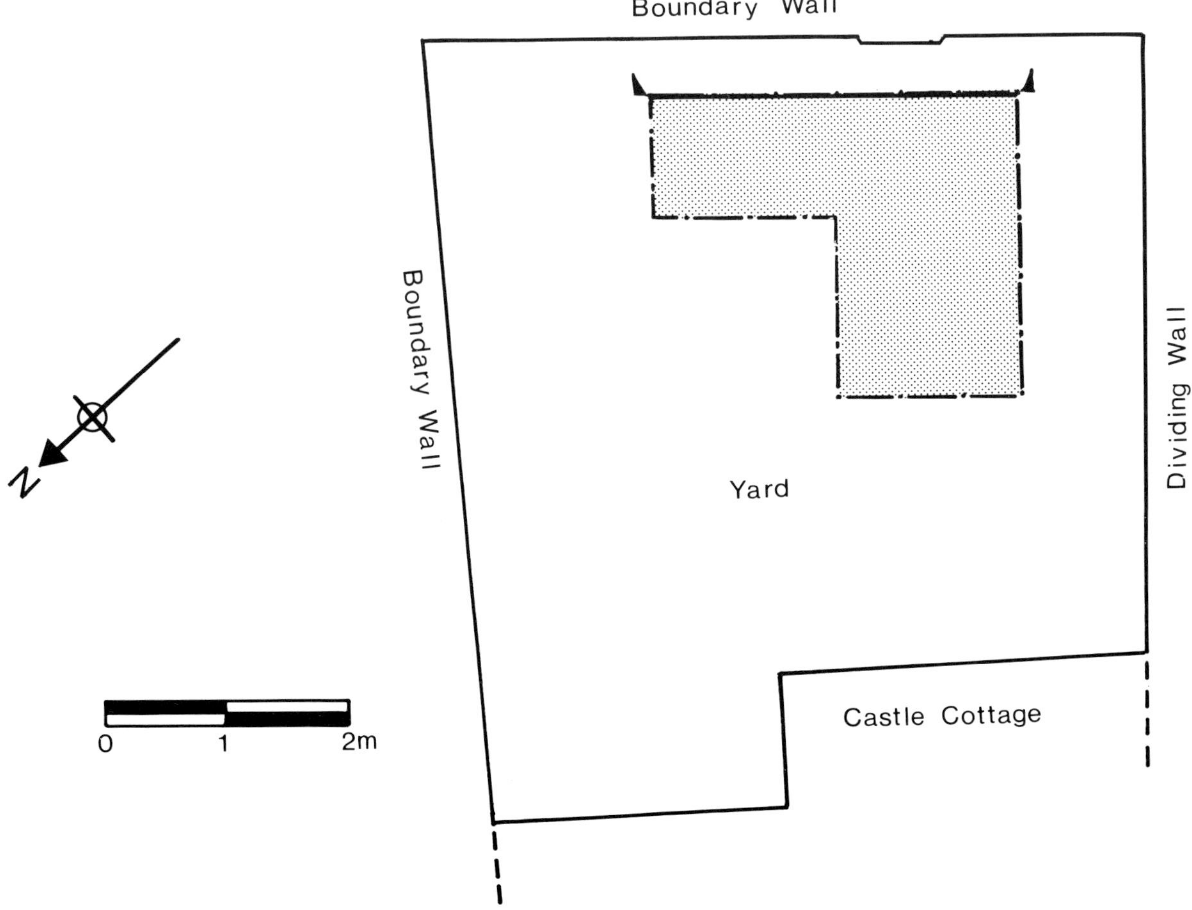

Fig 20 Bank Street, Trench and Section Location Plan

east boundary of the property. The presence of a flue in this gable indicates that the structure was a dwelling.

The excavation itself

The excavation was carried out entirely by hand. There was no turf or hard surface on the site and excavation proceeded directly into the topsoil (Layer 1). This soil was extremely mixed, being interspersed with cinders and ash from household fires. It contained household rubbish, such as pottery, iron objects and some animal bone of nineteenth- and twentieth-century date. The topsoil was thinnest, and discontinuous, over a rectangular platform of rough stone flags in the southern corner of the site. This area clearly related to the gable wall built into the south-east property boundary. The south-west boundary was not, however, related to this flagged floor, being a later insertion that divided a property of which Castle Cottage now

forms half. There was evidence for a long wall along the edge of the platform, corroborated by signs of its removal from the gable. The northerly extent of the structure could not be ascertained due to the limited working area. The flags along the edge of the paved area were all of roughly squared limestone and measured 250–300mm in depth. The thickness of these flags may indicate that they were prepared as large foundation blocks on which a now-demolished wall could be built. Such an interpretation requires the foundations to have been minimal apart from this measure. There is, however, ample evidence on the Isle of Man for houses with stone gable walls and daub, turf or cobble and clay side walls. Such a superstructure would require little or no solid foundation.

An arbitrary spit (Layer 2), 100mm deep, was removed from the remainder of the trench northeast of the flagged area. This spit removed any remaining traces of the mixed topsoil (Layer 1) which might have contaminated earlier features. The removal of this layer cut into the upper surface

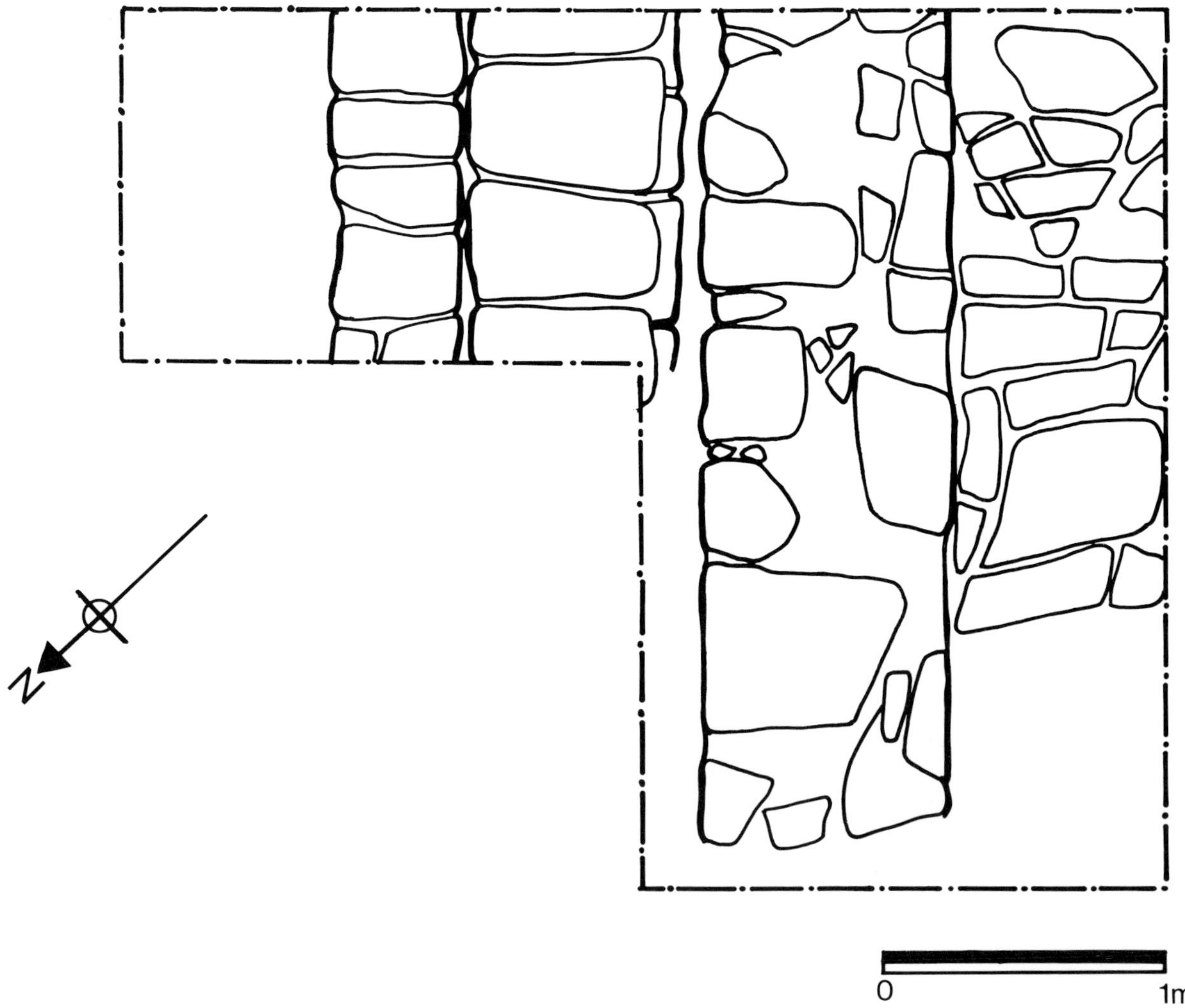

Fig 21   Bank Street, Trench Plan

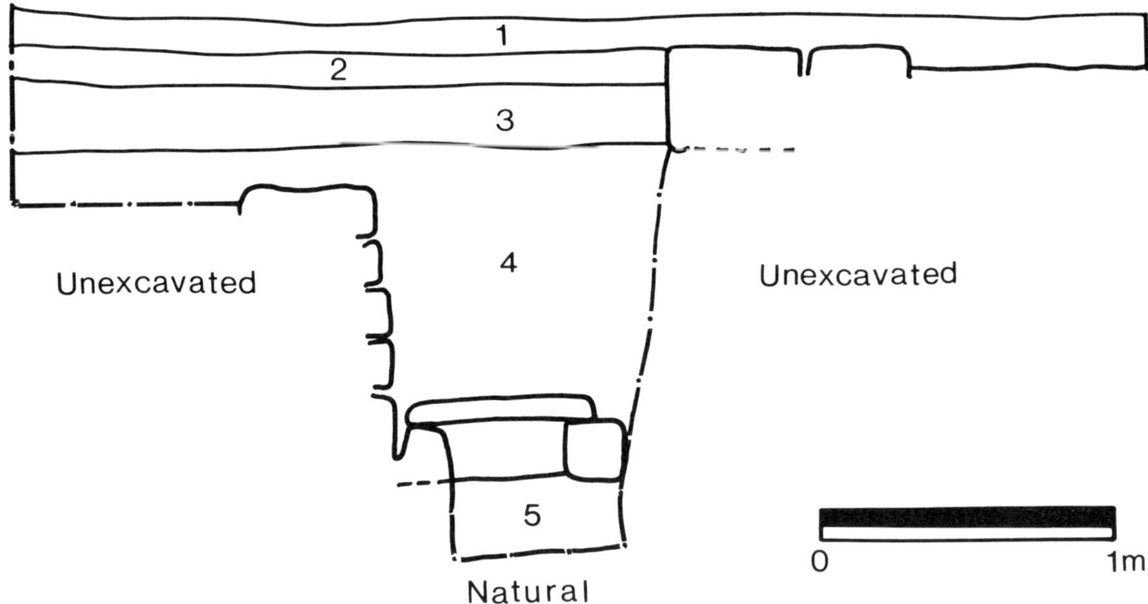

Fig 22   Bank Street, Section

of Layer 3, which accounts for the few earlier finds contained within it.

Layer 3 abutted the flagged floor, and comprised a soft, sandy clay deposit containing occasional small stones and few finds. No construction trench could be identified for the edge of the flagged floor. It is, however, inherently unlikely that these slabs would have stood proud of the surrounding ground.

The boundary between Layer 3 and Layer 4 proved difficult to discern, the differentiation depending largely on consistency. Layer 4 was marginally stonier and more compacted. This layer sealed a low stone wall with an apparent face on the south-west side, at the foot of which was a stone box drain. The wall was constructed from a mixture of slightly rounded and squared slabs of limestone, and survived to a height of 650–700mm in five courses. Restricted time precluded excavation behind the face of the wall. The stone box drain still functioned and therefore disturbance was kept to a minimum. A short section was removed and a wet, clayey deposit (Layer 5) was excavated from beneath it to a depth of 200mm. Two sherds of sixteenth-century pottery were the only finds from this layer. An extremely hard-packed, clean gravel layer in a silty/clay matrix was revealed below Layer 5, which was taken to be natural. Layer 5 was redeposited and the drain reconstituted.

Discussion

The time available precluded the lifting of the flagged floor and so deeper deposits could only be examined over a small area of the site, making interpretation difficult. Half the trench was occu-

pied by this massive flagged surface, which was directly related to the gable wall still extant in the boundary on the south side of the site. The presence of a flagged surface, rather than the more usual beaten earth, is perhaps indicative of the proximity of the harbour. Wall lines are depicted on the 1870 Ordnance Survey map for Castletown, which show that the building had already gone out of use by this date but that remnants of it were still visible.

The building overlay an earlier wall and drain, which in turn must post-date the two sixteenth-century sherds from Layer 5; clearly there have been at least two major building phases on the site since this date. The excavation offers a tantalising glimpse of the surviving archaeological evidence for the post-medieval development of the areas around the castle and harbour in Castletown.

Pottery

P J Davey

A total of 323 pottery sherds from a minimum of 74 separate vessels was recovered from the Castle Cottage site. They are listed below in context order. In the catalogue each ware type is allocated a unique upper case letter for identification and correlation.

Layer 1—topsoil

A   Dark glaze: deep red, very well prepared pure fabric; very dark irridescent glaze (13 sherds from 1 vessel).

Probably Buckley or Liverpool, but possibly Manx.
Typical of late nineteenth-century.

B   Slipware: internally yellow-glazed bowl; fabric as A (11 sherds; 1 vessel).
Possibly Prescot, but many other production centres.
Late nineteenth/early twentieth-century.

C   Flower pot: unglazed (3 sherds from 2 pots).
Nineteenth- or twentieth-century.

D   Self-coloured ware plate rim; fabric as A (1 sherd).
Nineteenth-century.

E   Brown salt-glazed stoneware flagons: (2 sherds; 2 vessels).

F   Nineteenth- and early twentieth-century 'china', including blue transfer printed earthenware and varieties of bone and stone china (68 sherds from at least 16 vessels).

G   ?English porcelain tea-bowl; fire damaged (1 sherd).
Early nineteenth-century.

H   Nineteenth- and early twentieth-century white stoneware (1 sherd).

I   Clay tobacco pipes: 1 mouthpiece.
Nineteenth-century.

J   Late mottled ware: teapot, including parts of base and spout (8 sherds; 1 vessel).
Nineteenth/early twentieth-century.

Total 109 sherds; a minimum of 27 vessels represented.

Layer 2—subsoil spit

A   Dark glaze:

   1   Tall storage vessel with horizontal strap handle; same vessel as Layer 1 (23 sherds).
   2   Mixed clay 'pancheons' (3 sherds, including 1 base sherd; 2 vessels).
   3   Purple-bodied dark ware (1 body sherd).
       Probably seventeenth-century.

4   Cup, internally and externally glazed (1 body sherd). Eighteenth-century.
5   Thin-walled storage vessel (1 body sherd). Eighteenth-century.

B   Slipware (12 sherds from the same vessel as Layer 1).
Late nineteenth/early twentieth-century.

D   Self-coloured ware (2 body sherds; 2 vessels).

E   Brown stoneware (2 small straight-sided pots, 1 complete).
Nineteenth-century.

F   Nineteenth- and early twentieth-century 'china': much the same range as Layer 1 (89 sherds; at least 14 vessels).

J   Late mottled ware: teapot (5 sherds; 1 vessel).
Late nineteenth/early twentieth-century.

Total 139 sherds; 26 vessels (at least 4 the same as Layer 1).

Layer 3

K   Northern reduced greenware (20 sherds; 3 vessels): parts of 2 or 3 jugs, or possibly two-handled pitchers (20 sherds). Cumbria or south-west Scotland.
Fifteenth- to seventeenth-century. (Fig 23.1–3)

L   Cistercian ware cups (8 sherds; 2 vessels): probably from north-west England (Merseyside/Cheshire).
1550–1600. (Fig 24.5)

M   Cistercian related coarsewares (5 sherds; 4 vessels):

   1   Pancheon rim; red earthenware, patchy purple external glaze.
   2   Small base in purple-bodied ware; highly fired brown, purple glaze.
   3   Base and body sherd of dark-glazed red earthenware; patchy purple/green external glaze.
   4   Rim and joining body sherd of a barrel-shaped 'butter pot'; very dense purple body, rich dark brown glaze (Fig 24.4).

All sixteenth-century types, probably from north-west England.

P   Red granite-tempered ware (3 sherds; 2 vessels):

   1   1 base sherd with granitic external coating.
   2   1 externally sooted flat base with spots of green and orange glaze over a red slip.
   3   1 rim; red slip coated.
       Probably sixteenth-century.

Q   1 body sherd of a Martincamp flask. Sixteenth-century.

Total 37 sherds; at least 12 vessels.

Layer 4—over drain

L   Cistercian ware cups (1 sherd; 1 vessel): 1 body sherd; olive-green glaze (reduced body).

M   Cistercian related coarsewares (3 sherds; 3 vessels): body sherds with bright red body and dull purple internal and external glaze. Sixteenth-century.

N   Fine white earthenware: 1 very small body sherd. Probably medieval.

O   Dark grey-bodied gritty ware, olive-green glaze: 1 body sherd.

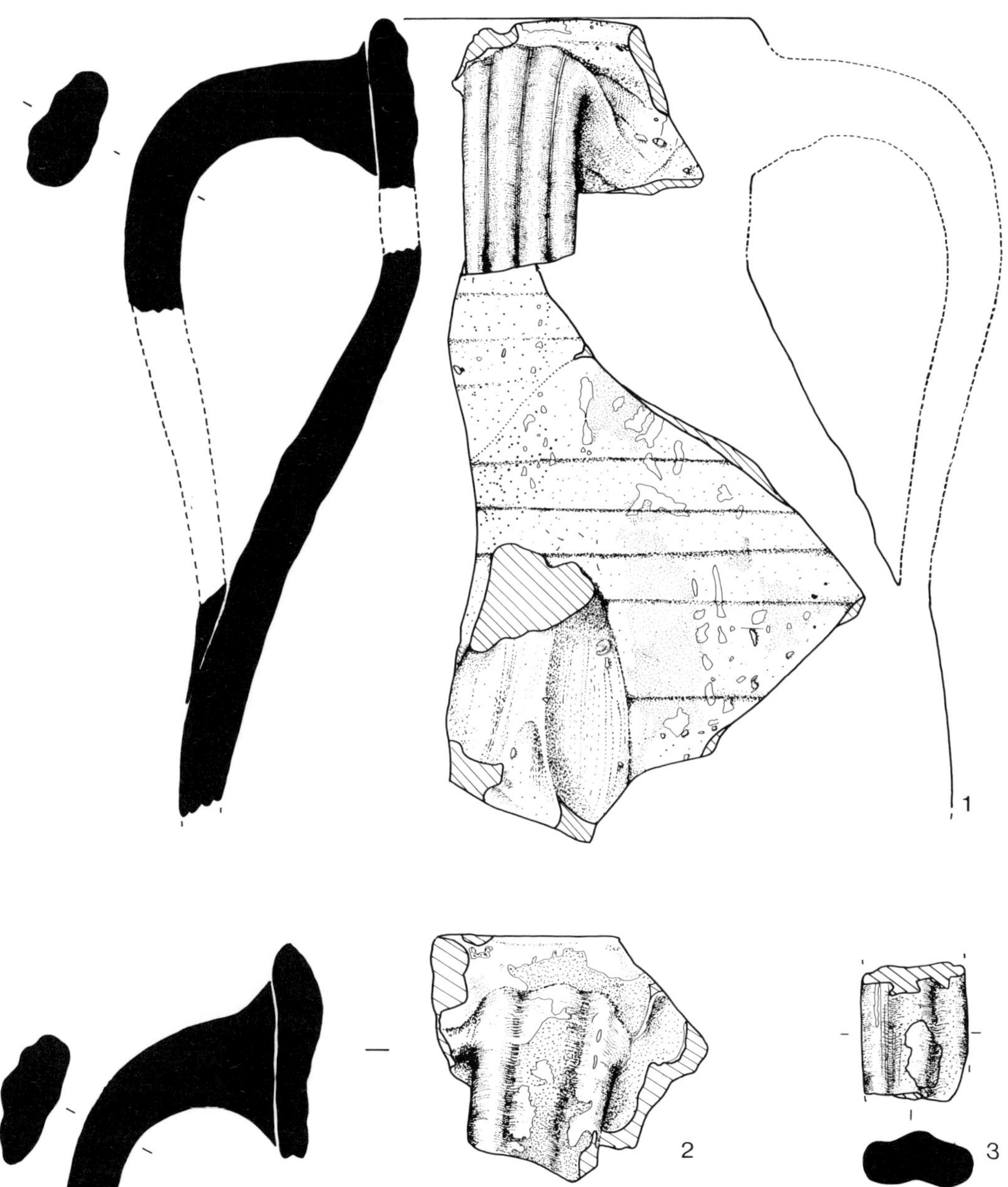

Fig 23   Bank Street, Pottery; Nos 1–3 (Scale 1:2)

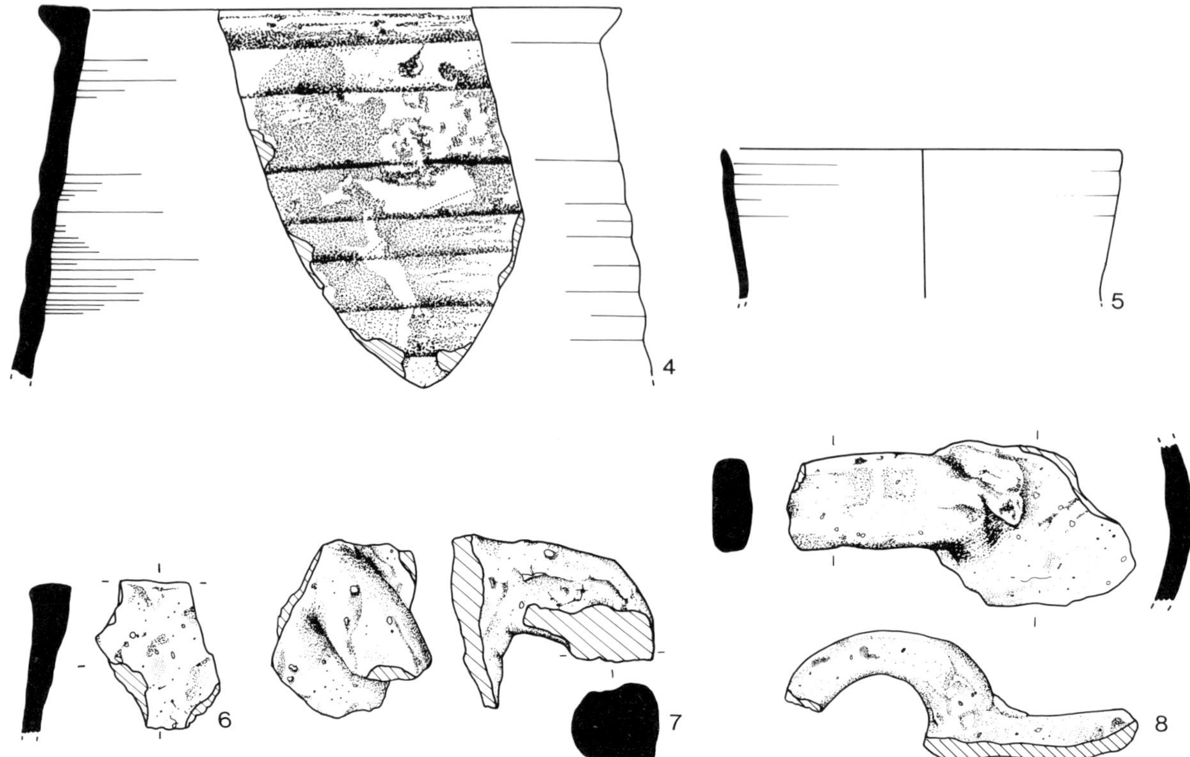

Fig 24   Bank Street, Pottery; Nos 4–8 (Scale 1:2)

Probably north-west England, sixteenth-century.

P   Red granite-tempered ware (30 sherds; 2 vessels): bright red, thoroughly oxidised body with patchy orange and green external glaze; includes a flat-topped ?jug rim and two handles, one very sharply angled; some evidence of internal sooting (30 sherds from at least 2 vessels, both jug forms). All except one rolled sherd appear very fresh and unweathered. They are almost certainly Manx products of the sixteenth century. (Fig 24.6–8)

Total 36 sherds; 8 vessels.

Layer 5—clay below drain, overlying gravel

P   Red granite-tempered ware (2 sherds, including one internally sooted base; possibly the same vessel as one in Layer 4).
Manx; sixteenth century.

Total 2 sherds; 1 vessel.

Discussion

The pottery from Castle Cottage can be divided into two broad groupings. The first, represented by Layers 1 and 2, is a predominantly nineteenth- or early twentieth-century domestic assemblage consisting of table and kitchen wares of rather average quality. Only three small dark-glazed sherds in Layer 2 may be residual from earlier occupation on the site. The second group, comprising Layers 3, 4 and 5, suggest a sharp chronological break in the stratigraphy in that all of the datable finds belong to the sixteenth century and are certainly not later than 1700.

Northern reduced greenware is not common on the Isle of Man, but has been recorded from previous excavations in Castletown (a jug rim, MM 67.56G/47), from Peel Castle (one sherd from the Peel Castle Museum, MM 76.28/d; one sherd from the Cowley Collection, MM 71.195/14; four sherds from the 1982–87 excavations, MM 86.63/17 and 104) and part of a handle from the Ronaldsway smelt site (MM 64.144/16). It was widely produced throughout northern Britain from the fifteenth to the seventeenth century, but was not made or traded in South Lancashire, North Cheshire or North Wales, which was the main source area for pottery supplied to the Isle of Man in the post-medieval period.

Cistercian wares are also quite rare on the island. Peel Castle produced a single sherd from Bersu's excavations (MM 62.18/1) and another in Cubbon's 1966 Trial B (MM 66.32/11). The Half Moon Battery recovered a further eight sherds, a number in late sixteenth-century construction contexts. A further 13 sherds were found on the 1982–87 excavations at the castle and 34 in the quadrats in Peel itself. Elsewhere on Man, a single multi-handled cup base was found in the Castletown excavations (MM67.55/18) and there is a sherd from a fine cup with an unusual face mask in the Manx Museum (MM71.239D). The finds from Castle Cottage, combined with those from the quadrats in Peel, suggest that Cistercian ware provided an important element in the table furniture of sixteenth-century urban dwellers on Man. Its paucity at Peel Castle, given the amount of excavation, may reflect the collecting policy of earlier excavations or merely illustrate a lack of new building and rubbish disposal on St Patrick's Isle during this period. Its absence elsewhere on the Isle of Man is probably due to the lack of excavation of suitable sites. The Castletown Grammar School site, for example, included some interesting late medieval sherds, but was dominated by seventeenth- and eighteenth-century finds, with few from the sixteenth century.

Taking all the Manx finds together, the Cistercian wares seem to be most closely paralleled by those from Cheshire, Merseyside and Greater Manchester and were probably made there. Their presence on Man shows that insular taste had adopted the new table manners of the times, probably following the example of the Earl of Derby and his retinue from England.

The association of locally-produced granite-tempered wares with Cistercian-type fine and coarse-wares probably derived from the Merseyside area, northern reduced greenwares from Cumbria or south-west Scotland and Martincamp flasks from northern France is important in confirming a date in the sixteenth century for this class of native production. Very similar thoroughly oxidised granite-tempered ware was found in the harbour sequence in Peel, where it was also associated with Cistercian fineware and a Martincamp flask, together with a sherd of 'Tudor green', all probably of sixteenth-century date.

In summary, the Castle Cottage finds enlarge considerably the collection of northern reduced greenware and Cistercian ware from the Isle of Man, and provide a very important new association for the latest type of native granite-tempered ware pottery to be found on the island.

Author's note: This report was completed before the much more extensive groups from either Castle Rushen or Castle Rushen Stores became available for study, and does not refer to them.

EXCAVATIONS AT CASTLE RUSHEN STORES, 1991–1992

The Excavations

D A Higgins

Introduction

This report deals with the excavations at 'Castle Rushen Stores' which were carried out during 1991 and 1992. Although these are known as the Castle Rushen Stores excavations they did in fact take place within a number of adjoining properties running between Arbory Street and Malew Street in Castletown (Fig 3). The name 'Castle Rushen Stores' derives from the moulded concrete lettering above the pseudo-medieval gateway giving access to 18 Arbory Street. This was probably erected by T M Dodd in the early years of the twentieth century. Dodd was a prominent grocer and wine and spirit merchant in Castletown, who appears to have operated from three properties which backed onto one another; 18–20 Arbory Street and 19 Malew Street. These three properties, together with the flanking properties of 17 and 21 Malew Street, were all vacant at the time of the excavations (Fig 25). They were in two separate ownerships, but it was proposed to develop them jointly to form a shopping mall linking the two streets.

These five properties cover a substantial part of the historic core of Castletown, which occupies a ridge running parallel to the harbour. The castle was built on a naturally defensive position overlooking the harbour and lies only some 50–100m to the east of the site. The castle is first recorded in 1265 and was probably started earlier in that century (Corlett *c*1974, 3). With the development of the castle the town became the administrative centre of the island, a role which it retained until 1874. The properties in the older part of Castletown occupy long thin plots running back from the frontages in a manner typical of medieval urban townscapes. Although three Roman coins were found during the construction of St Mary's Church in the Market Place (Cumming 1848, 63) and local oral tradition reports the finding of a number of lintel graves during the construction of 'Shoprite' in Arbory Street a few years ago, very little is known of the origins or early development of the town.

There are various documents listing the households in Castletown from the Manorial Roll of 1511 onwards (Talbot 1924), but the first detailed account giving an indication of the nature of the town appears to be the list of Castletown Householders of 1754–55, which is in the Manx Museum. This lists a total of 878 inhabitants, 442 male and 466 female, and gives occupations for 158 of the householders. Whilst this excludes servants and lodgers, it does at least give an idea of the range of occupations and trades which were to be found in mid-eighteenth-century Castletown:

Attorney	1	Glover	2
Butcher	1	Barber	3
Clerk	1	Glazer	3
Comptroller	1	Stone-cutter	3
Deemster	1	Mason	4
Dep:Searcher	1	Merchant	4
Drummer	1	Soldier	4
Farmer	1	Weaver	4
Governor	1	Cooper	5
Hatter	1	Inn-keeper	5
Maltster	1	Shoe-maker	5
Midwife	1	Smith	5
Porter	1	Carpenter	7
Schoolmaster	1	Shop-keeper	7
Slater	1	Gent	8
Sumner	1	Taylor	8
Wheelwright	1	Fisherman	12
Baker	2	Labourer	50

These occupations may be divided into a number of categories; for example, the administrators and soldiers connected with the government of the island, the merchants and shopkeepers connected with trade, and the carpenters and masons connected with building work. The totals are as follows:

Administration	12	Labourers	50
Fishing	12	Shops and trade	53
Building trades	19	Miscellaneous	12

This breakdown suggests that the majority of Castletown's inhabitants were connected with the general retail and building services which would be provided by any small town of the period. Fishing forms a relatively small but presumably significant element of the occupations. Only one farmer is listed, suggesting that Castletown was essentially

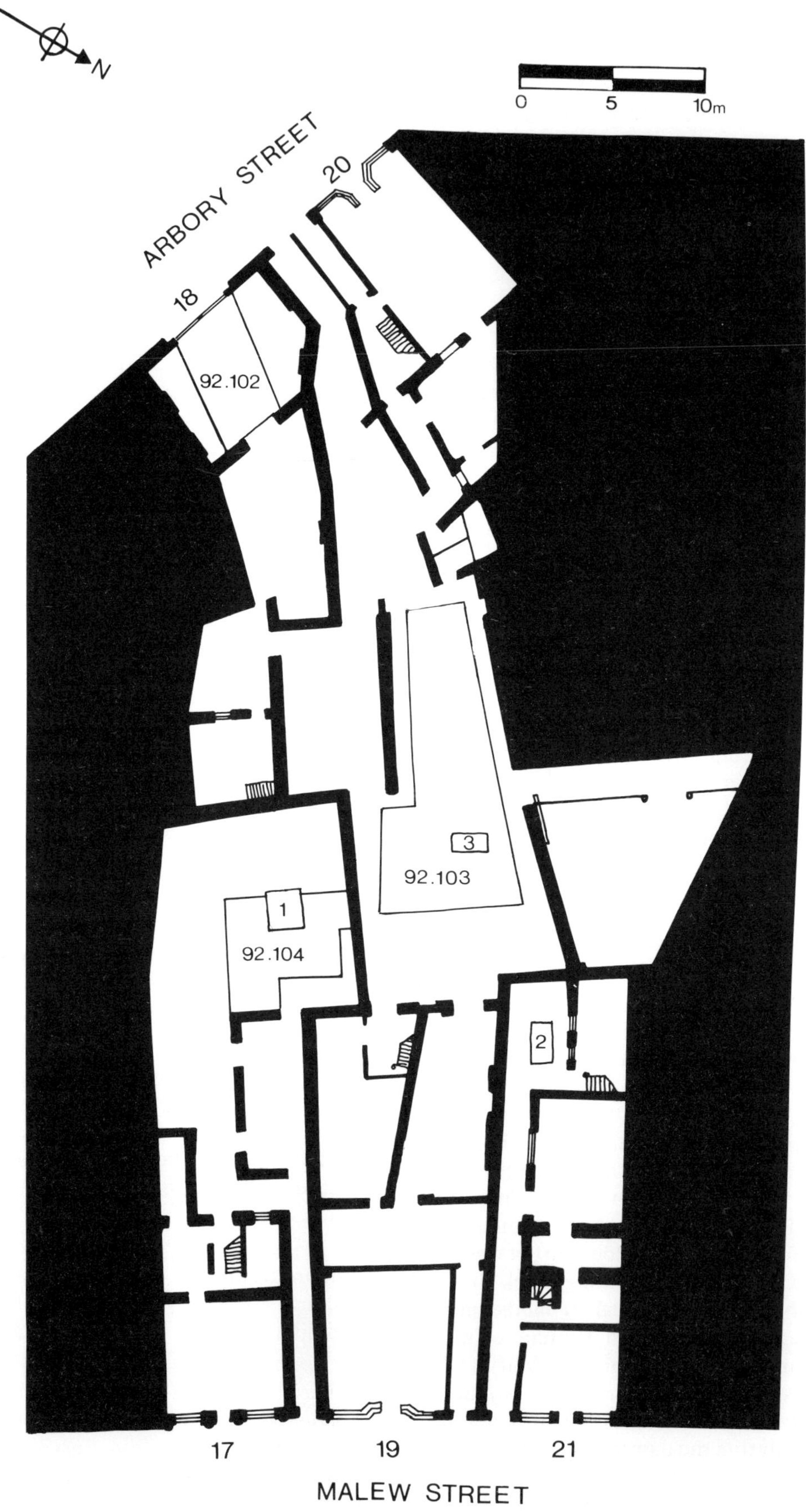

Fig 25   Castle Rushen Stores, Plan Showing Location of Trenches

urban in character, with farm produce being brought in from the surrounding countryside.

The list does not include more specialised trades such as clockmakers, silversmiths or jewellers. It seems likely that, despite being the principal town on the island, the total population was insufficient to support such trades. This in turn implies a reliance on imports for the supply of specialist or luxury goods. If this is the case, it seems surprising that no sailors are listed.

Castletown, with its small harbour, could not compete with the rapid growth of Douglas as a commercial centre and, by 1794, it was said that, 'Castletown, though dignified with the residence of the Governor of the Isle, is in wealth and mercantile importance greatly inferior to Douglas' (Robertson 1794, 63). Castletown continued as the centre of government until 26th November 1874, when The House of Keys finally moved to Douglas. Despite having been eclipsed in importance, Castletown retained a certain style and elegance unmatched by the other settlements on the island.

The excavations

Following proposals to develop the Castle Rushen Stores complex as a shopping mall, trial trenches were excavated to assess the nature and depth of archaeological deposits. This work was directed by Dr Jennifer Lewis from the Department of Archaeology at the University of Liverpool, between 14th and 18th October 1991. Three small trenches were excavated (Fig 25.1–3), the context numbers starting with 100, 200 and 300 respectively. The Manx Museum accession number for all three trenches is 91.129. The trial excavations produced evidence for archaeological deposits dating from the fifteenth or sixteenth centuries through to the modern day. All of the trenches produced evidence for earlier structures and clearly suggested that larger scale excavations would be worthwhile.

The larger area excavations were directed by Dr David Higgins from the Department of Archaeology at the University of Liverpool between 22nd June and 17th July 1992. It was hoped that these would provide information about the origins and development of Castletown, in particular the building sequence on the street frontage, the date and nature of the property boundaries and the use of the backyard areas. It was also hoped that some much-needed domestic finds assemblages could be recovered for the island.

The presence of a complex series of buildings and outbuildings on the site (Fig 25), some of them derelict and unsafe, greatly restricted the areas available for excavation. In the end it proved possible to examine three areas, two of them towards the rear of the properties and one on the Arbory Street frontage. These trenches were each given a unique accession number by the Manx Museum (92.102, 92.103 and 92.104) which was used as a site code to mark the finds. Trial Trenches 1 and 3 were subsumed within the larger area excavation of Trenches 92.104 and 92.103 respectively. For this reason the evidence from these two trial trenches has been incorporated within the description of the larger trenches below, with just Trial Trench 2 being described separately. Site matrices for the main trenches and a summary of the excavated contexts can be found in the Technical Appendix (Figs 68 to 70).

Trial Trench 2

This trial trench could not be extended because it lay in a small yard area behind 21 Malew Street (Fig 25). The trial trench was 2m × 1m in area and showed that only 28cm of deposits survived above the natural gravel. The yard was covered with a tiled and flagged surface, beneath which was a ceramic drain and a lead water pipe serving an outside toilet. These cut across some limestone wall footings which represented an earlier structure in the yard area.

The yard is shown as open space on the 1868 Ordnance Survey map, apparently interconnecting with the open space behind 19 Malew Street. It is not possible to make any sense of the excavated wall fragment or development of the property from this small trench alone. Much larger scale extensive area excavations would be needed to reveal the complex structural history of the backyards of Castletown, and this will not be possible whilst they are still covered with standing buildings.

Trench 92.102

This trench was located immediately behind the 'Castle Rushen Stores' archway fronting onto Arbory Street, the only street frontage which was available for excavation. The area was covered with a concrete floor which had to be broken and lifted. Due to the joint lines in the concrete the resulting trench was in the shape of a parallelogram with sides measuring approximately 6.7m north to south by 4m east to west (Fig 25).

The street frontage consisted of a high stone wall with a crenellated top and contained a large arched

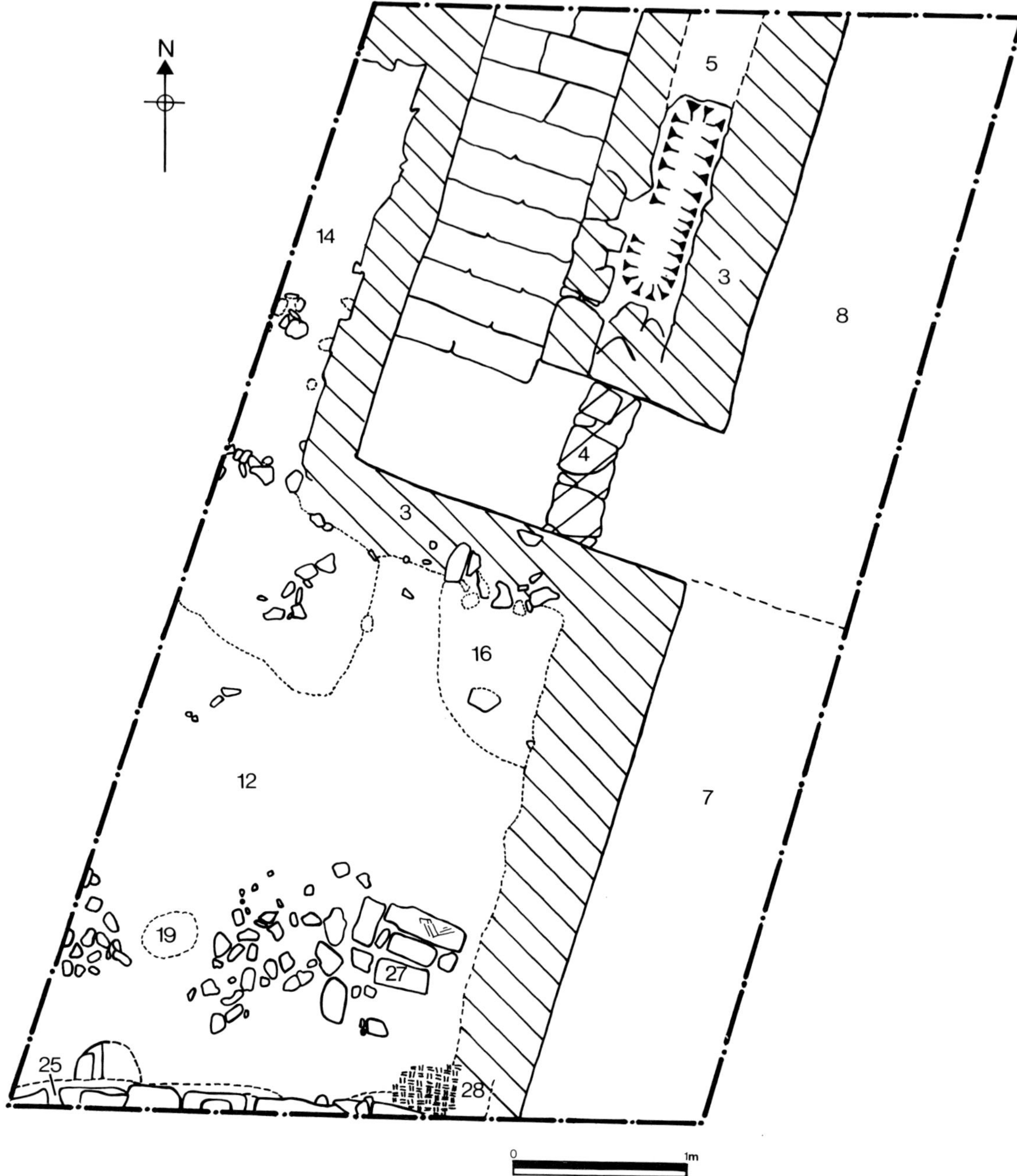

Fig 26   Castle Rushen Stores, Composite Plan Showing Later Features in Trench 92.102

opening with a sliding door. The whole wall had been rendered with concrete externally, with the words 'CASTLE RUSHEN STORES' moulded in relief. The arch gave access to an open yard with a concrete floor. The end walls of the flanking buildings clearly showed that this had formerly been roofed with a single pitch sloping roof at first floor level. Before that the site must have been occupied by a taller building, since the flanking wall to the east contained blocked fireplaces at both ground floor and first floor levels. These properties must also have interconnected, since there was also a blocked doorway at first floor level.

The concrete floor had been cast as three large slabs, the central one of which had grooves in it to provide grip; it may well have been used to back vehicles onto. The covered area to the north-west of the yard had a much higher floor level with a large doorway giving access to it. This may well have been used as a loading bay for vehicles parked on the concrete floor. The concrete (1) contained a number of sea shells, suggesting that gravels from the coast had been used in its construction. It was laid on a bed of stone rubble and demolition debris which proved to be the remains of the previous structure on the site.

The cellar

The demolition rubble overlay and filled the remains of a cellar which occupied most of the northern part and all of the eastern side of the trench. It had been cut into the natural gravels which underlie this area of Castletown and had destroyed any earlier archaeological deposits. The cellar walls (3) had been constructed of local limestone and had a flight of stone steps giving access from the north (Fig 26). The steps showed signs of some wear, although not enough to suggest that the cellar had been used on a very regular basis. There was a build-up of well-packed dark material on the steps and floor of the cellar (10). This contained some coal and charcoal as well as organic remains, possibly straw, and pottery dating from the late eighteenth or early nineteenth centuries. The walls of the cellar had been whitewashed and there were traces of iron fittings for a shelf. The main body of the cellar could not be excavated since the trench was too narrow, but its position to the east of the yard suggests that it might originally have extended under the adjoining building on that side. The cellar walls and steps had been cut into by the foundations of the covered building immediately to the north of the yard, indicating that this post-dates the cellar's demolition.

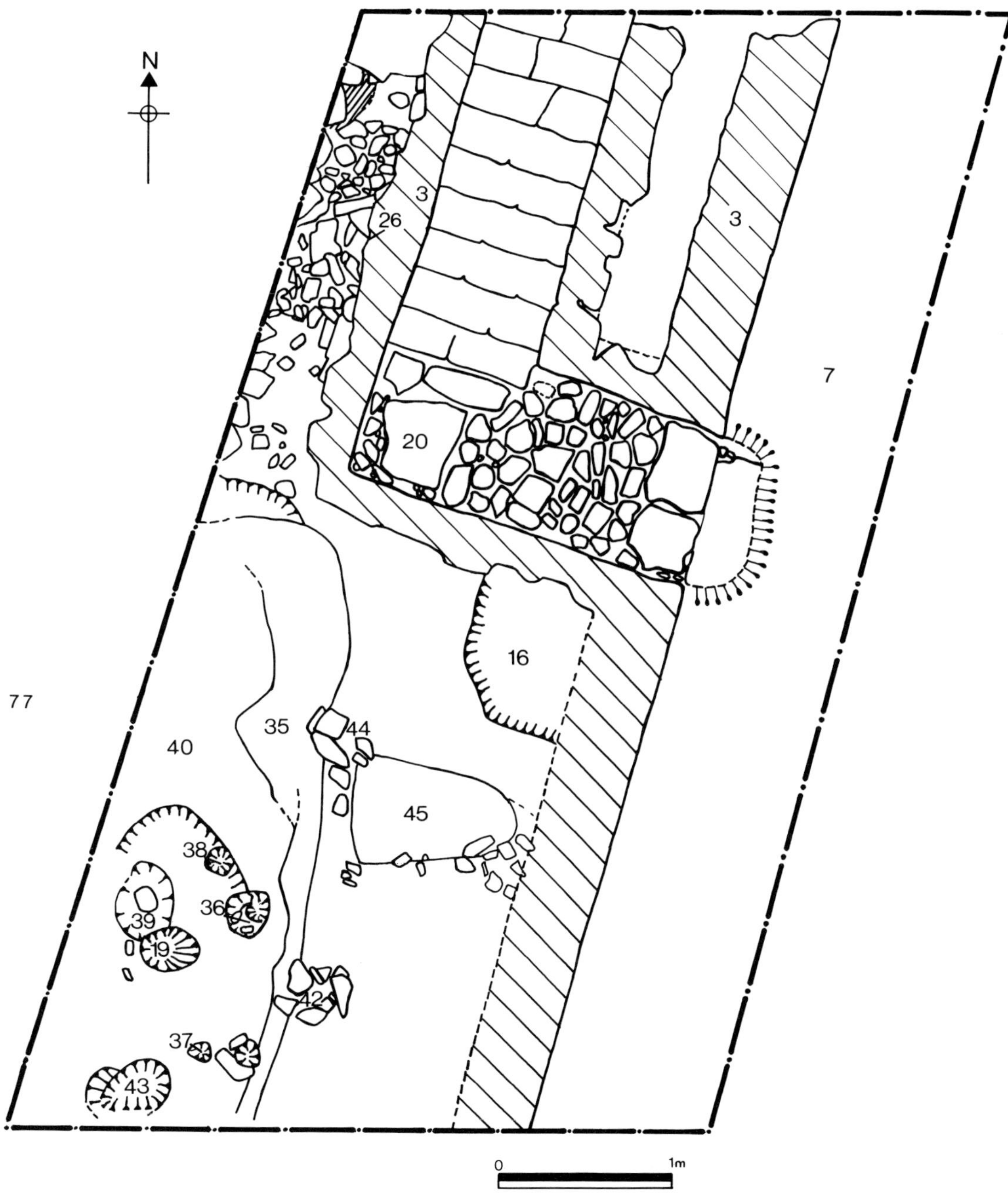

Fig 27   Castle Rushen Stores, Composite Plan Showing Earlier Features in Trench 92.102

There was a dry-stone wall blocking the entrance to the main body of the cellar (4). This was only faced on the side facing the steps and did not extend right to the cellar floor. Instead, it rested in the lowest layer of demolition fill. It appears, therefore, that this wall was built during the demolition to retain material being piled up within the main body of the cellar. The demolition fill of the steps (9) included a number of bottles and jars, some with the original paper labels surviving. One of these, an 'Apollinaris' mineral water bottle, included reference to a 'Grand Prix' at St Louis in 1904. This provides a *terminus post quem* for the date of demolition, which seems likely to have taken place early in the twentieth century. A date of between 1905 and 1910 is suggested for this event.

The cellar occupied most of the trench, leaving only small areas of undisturbed deposits for investigation. In the north-west corner of the trench, adjoining the cellar steps, was a strip some 2.5m long but only 0.4m wide (Fig 26). This was a small area to work in, making both excavation and interpretation difficult. In the south-west corner of the trench was a slightly larger area of c2.5m × 3m. This proved awkward to reconcile with the smaller area at the narrow point where they met and,

again, was difficult to interpret because of its small size.

The north-west corner of the trench
In the north-western strip the demolition deposits overlay a dark brown earthy layer (14) of late eighteenth- to early nineteenth-century date, which was different from any of the deposits in the south-western area. This deposit overlay a stony surface (26), which may have been part of a cobbled area (Fig 26). The stones were, however, rather irregular in size and layout and contained a lot of fine silty material between them, as if water had been percolating through them.

The stony surface sealed a small pit (32), which also contained silty material, suggesting that this area may have been used as some form of sump or soak-away. There was another dark brown layer (33), similar to Context 14, which in turn overlay a clay layer (41) before the natural was reached. All of these deposits (32, 33, 41) contained material dating from between 1650 and 1750. The area of these deposits available for examination was insufficient to reach many conclusions and their relationship with the cellar steps was not clear. Their presence does, however, indicate that post-medie-

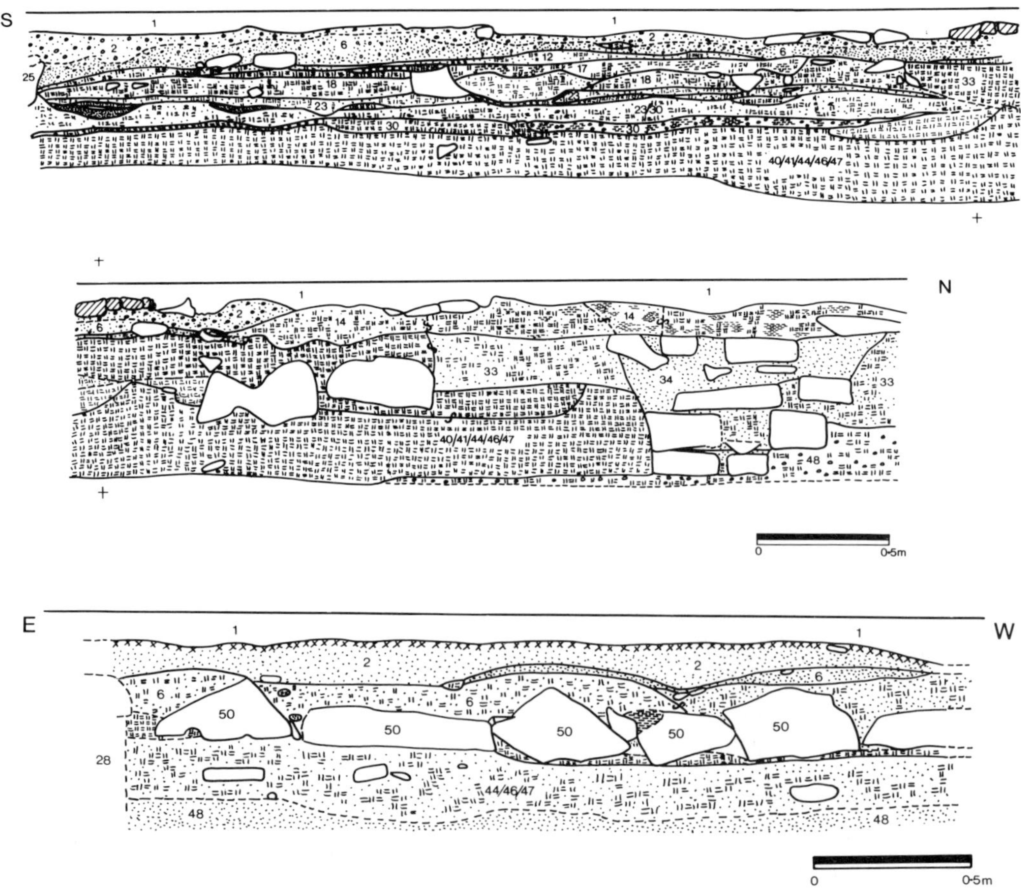

Fig 28   Castle Rushen Stores, West Section and South Section of Trench 92.102

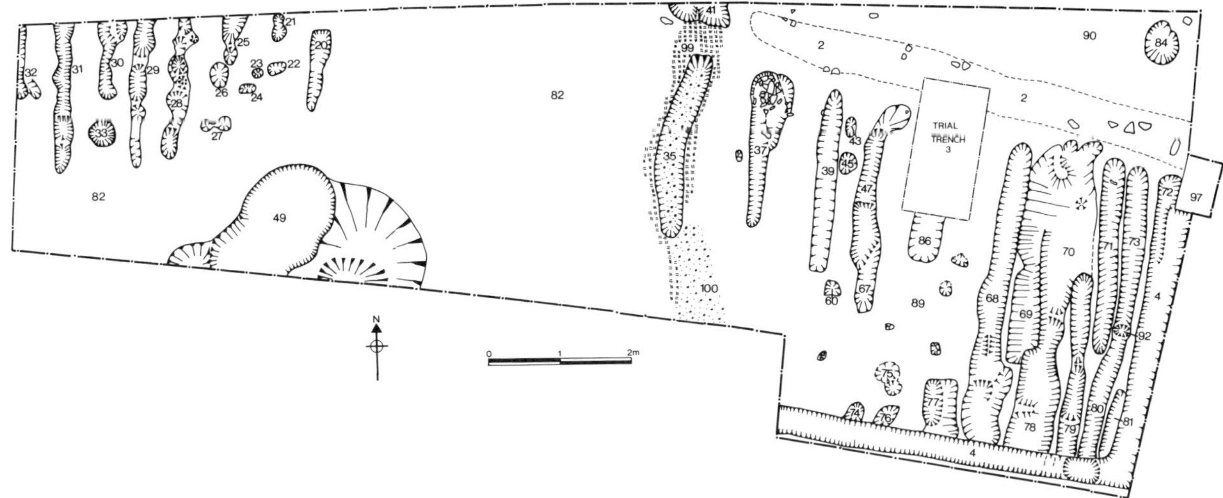

Fig 29   Castle Rushen Stores, Trench 92.103; Composite Plan Showing Eighteenth-Century and Later Garden Features and a Seventeenth-Century Pit (49)

val activity was taking place on the site and that larger areas would be well worth examining.

The south-west corner of the trench

In the larger area at the south-west corner of the site a rather different series of deposits was revealed. Essentially these consisted of a series of thin, trampled surfaces which had been cut through by the construction trenches for both the cellar and the frontage wall of the site (Fig 28). The construction trench for the cellar (28) appeared to cut that for the frontage wall (25), suggesting that the cellar was later in date (Fig 26). However, the pottery dates from the construction deposits suggest that both walls date from the late eighteenth or early nineteenth century.

The most recent trampled surfaces cut by the construction trenches were difficult to interpret, since they also appear to date from the late eighteenth or early nineteenth century. These surfaces contained various features, such as stone settings (27), but it was not clear whether they represented earlier activity on the site or trample from the building work. There was also a series of post holes (36–38 and 42), for which there was no dating evidence other than that they lay beneath a late eighteenth- to early nineteenth-century layer and cut a sixteenth-century one (Fig 27). They may date from the seventeenth or eighteenth centuries, and match the activity in the north-west of the site represented by Contexts 32, 33 and 41.

The earliest feature on the site was a truncated pit (49). This cut the natural and contained some extremely decayed fragments of bone, giving rise to the suggestion that it might be a grave or animal burial. Various visitors to the site reported that a number of graves had been found during the construction of 'Shoprite' on the opposite side of Arbory Street from the excavated area. Most of these had not been officially reported, the bones having apparently been collected up and re-buried by the JCB driver. Unfortunately, the bones from Context 49 were too decayed to enable recovery and identification.

Interpretation

Whilst it was clear that there had been a lot of activity in this area, interpretation remains a problem, particularly since it was not possible to excavate the plot or building boundaries themselves. Even though the excavation extended up to the modern street frontage wall, the footings of which were just visible in the southern side of the trench (50) (Fig 30), it was not possible to excavate to any depth because of the standing structure. The existence of earlier walls on the same lines was not established. Since the trampled surfaces could not be related to any wall lines it was not even possible to be sure whether they lay within former buildings or not. Likewise, the surviving area outside the cellar was not large enough to determine any pattern in the post holes or other features which clearly existed in this area.

Although three sherds of residual medieval pottery from Contexts 14, 23 and 44 were recovered, the earliest surviving archaeological deposits dated from the sixteenth century. These were layers which could be interpreted as earth floors within a building, although they were not particularly packed or laminar in appearance. It is perhaps more likely that they represent garden soils formed in front of buildings set further back from the street.

There was no firm evidence for seventeenth- or eighteenth-century buildings on the site, although there are various cobbled surfaces and post holes which are likely to relate to this period. By the late eighteenth century there were certainly well-packed surfaces and evidence for a wall being constructed on the present street frontage. This is likely to have formed part of the two-storey building, interconnecting with the building to the east, and with a cellar under its eastern half. This building was demolished in the early years of the twentieth century, having been used in its final years as part of Dodd's premises. Evidence for Dodd's occupation of the site is provided by a number of glass bottles marked 'T M Dodd' which were recovered from the demolition deposits. His bottles are well known on the island and he appears to have been a prominent figure in Castletown during the late nineteenth and early twentieth centuries.

T M Dodd

Trade directories in the Manx Museum Library have been searched to provide additional information about Dodd, who proved to be listed for the 25 years between 1882 and 1907. It is not known how long he remained on the site, since there are no directories between 1907 and 1940, by which time he was no longer listed. Despite this uneven record, the directories dating from 1882 to 1907 provide useful information about his activities during this period.

In Brown's directory of 1882 he is listed as a grocer, wine and spirit merchant in Malew Street. He is listed under the same headings in Brown's 1894 directory but additionally under his personal entry he is recorded as a 'grocer, ale and porter bottler, and wine and spirit merchant, 19 Malew-street; residence – Crofts'. Bent's 1902 directory gives him as a wholesale and family grocer, tea, wine, spirit and provision merchant with branches in Malew Street and Arbory Street. In Bent's 1907 directory he is merely given as a grocer in Malew Street and Arbory Street.

From these entries it is clear that he had started business in Malew Street by 1882, presumably at No 19. By 1894 he was certainly bottling ale and porter as well as being a wine and spirit merchant. At the same time he was established enough to be living in the desirable residential street known as the Crofts, rather than above the shop as might have been expected. By 1902 the directories show that he had also acquired property in Arbory Street. Presumably, he connected these with the Malew Street property to form the basic layout which has survived until the present. It may well be that the

demolition of the Arbory Street building above the cellar and the construction of the access arch and loading bay was carried out by Dodd as part of a reorganisation of the site.

Some additional references to members of the Dodd family are given by Bawden, Garrad, Qualtrough and Scatchard (1972, 252). They list an I M Dodd under Castletown Mineral Water Co in 1894, and refer to a George Dodd being secretary and John Dowis being manager of that company in 1889.

Trench 92.103

This trench was excavated within a large covered area which straddled the rear boundaries of 19 Malew Street and 20 Arbory Street. The greater part of this area had, until recently, been covered with a raised concrete floor. Since the ground in this part of Castletown falls to the north-east, there had been a drop in ground level at the eastern side of this floor. The owner of the site, Mr Callow, had recently taken up this floor as a prelude to the proposed shopping mall development so that an even gradient between the streets could be achieved. The trench was located so as to examine the largest possible area of ground that had been exposed beneath the concrete, which included the whole of Trial Trench 3 (Fig 29). The evidence from this trial trench has been amalgamated with that from the larger trench and so will not be discussed separately.

In 1868 the Ordnance Survey map shows this area to have been open ground, presumably a garden. The boundary between the Malew Street and Arbory Street properties had already gone by this date, suggesting that the properties were already in a single ownership. It is not known what deposits were lost when the floor was removed, although a scar on the side walls showed that the level had been reduced by some 300–400mm. The earth surface resulting from the floor clearance was relatively flat and had been well trampled before the excavation started. It was dark and loamy and seemed likely to represent a garden soil.

Wall and robber trenches

The most recent features, revealed when the surface (5) was cleaned, consisted of two robber trenches (2 and 4) and a pit (41) (Fig 29). The pit must have been very recent in date, since its fill included plastic packing ties. The second robber trench (4) bounded the southern and eastern sides of the excavation. It had been created by Mr Callow when he removed a low retaining wall from around the concrete floor. Part of this wall survived to the west of the excavated area, where it joined a two-storey building with a covered passage underneath. Both this building and the former wall line are shown on the OS map of 1868.

Once excavated, the wall trench (4) revealed evidence of the surfaces which had butted it to the south and east, areas now covered with concrete (101). Below the concrete to the south was a layer of ashy bedding (103) which overlay some very substantial stone flags (104). The exposed edges of these were up to 1.1m long and 120mm thick. Mr Callow said that carts used to be backed down from Arbory Street, under the covered passage, to a point under the next building to the east. This had a hoist on the first floor which was used for loading and unloading goods. To the east of the wall trench (4) the floor beneath the concrete had been made of cobbles (102) upon which a thin layer of dark soil had accumulated (115). These floors (102, 104) are likely to have been in contemporary use and later than the retaining wall since their edges were neatly laid, as though they had been butted up against it rather than cut by it. At the northern end of the robber trench (4) the remains of a step base survived (97). This had been built over the cobbles but projected into the line of the robbed wall trench. It is presumed, therefore, that this step was a later insertion cut into the wall line. Mr Callow said that these steps simply gave access to the raised concrete floor which he had removed.

On its north side the base of the step (97) butted another raised area of walling (95). Both of these features were rather roughly constructed of local stone rubble and it was not possible to determine the chronological relationship between them. The same problem arose with the robber trench (2) which ran up to the wall (95). Once again, it was not possible to see whether both had been part of the same building phase or whether one had been butted against or cut the other. The wall in the robber trench (2) must have been demolished before the raised concrete floor was laid since, according to Mr Callow, it was sealed by it. The raised stone platform in the north-east corner of the site (95) was not excavated, but appears to have been the rubble-filled remains of a small building shown on the 1868 OS map.

It would appear that in the nineteenth century the garden area was already raised above the access and cobbled yard levels, that it was retained by a wall to the south and east (4) and that, at some stage, there was another wall (2) extending westwards from the corner of the building (95). The function of this wall is not clear, particularly since it converges on the wall bounding the northern side of the site which is also shown on the map of 1868. A section was placed up against the northern wall in an attempt to date it, but it was found that the wall finished flush with the level to which Mr Callow had reduced the site. There was no widening of the footings at the base and no evidence for a construction trench. Since the wall sat on what appeared to be a continuation of Context 5, the nineteenth-century garden soil, it seems likely that it is of mid-nineteenth century date. It must also have been built with little or no footings, a feature noted in the walls examined in Trench 92.104.

Evidence of gardening activity

There were no other features apparent from a surface cleaning of the site, so a spit of the dark garden soil which extended right across the site was removed (5). This had to be removed to a depth of about 100mm before any other features became visible. It then emerged that there were two series of parallel strips at each end of the trench which were filled with a slightly darker, more humic, soil than that into which they were cut (Fig 29). Those at the western end were rather narrower and more irregular in form than those at the eastern end. These features all tended to be very shallow and faded out at their ends. Many of them contained pottery dating from the late eighteenth and early nineteenth centuries and it seems likely that they represent gardening activity of this date, possibly being the remains of trenches dug for vegetables such as potatoes or beans.

As well as the gardening activity, a number of other features emerged. There was a shallow scoop in the north-east corner of the site (84) containing soil mixed with mortar and slate fragments. This lay in an area divided from the main part of the site by a strip of well-packed light brown earth (87) (Fig 31). This mirrored the position of the robbed wall (2) and appears to have been either an earlier bank on which the wall was built, or a 'shadow' created by it where gardening activity could not introduce humic material to the subsoil. A similar strip of clay and gravel (99 and 100) divided the site in half, north to south. This proved to be the top of the former boundary bank which had divided the Arbory and Malew Street properties.

The boundary bank

The Arbory Street/Malew Street boundary proved to be quite a substantial feature consisting of a bank with flanking ditches (Fig 30). The bank had been thrown up on top of a buried soil (121). This was about 20mm deep and indicates the level of the original ground surface from which the ditches must have been cut. The buried soil contained medieval pottery and represents the only undisturbed deposit of this date from the site. Its surface was at a higher level than the sixteenth-century deposits on either side of the bank, which shows that later activity has destroyed the medieval deposits where they have not been protected by later structures. The presence of this soil supports the suggestion that there was medieval activity outside the castle, although in this area of the town almost all of the evidence appears to have been destroyed by sixteenth-century and later gardening.

The boundary bank itself (100) was 2m wide at the base and survived to a height of 600mm above the medieval ground surface. It was composed of a loose gravelly material which must have been derived from the flanking ditches (125 and 136). The western ditch (136) was about 800mm wide and cut some 500–600mm into the natural, giving a total surviving height of 1.3m from the bottom of the ditch to the top of the bank. The ditch which lay on the eastern side of the bank (125) was not so deeply cut. It had been recut as a shallow gulley (123), following a period when it appears to have become silted up (Fig 30).

The boundary clearly separated the Arbory Street and Malew Street properties from the sixteenth through to the nineteenth century. The deposits from either side of this boundary were, therefore, formed independently and are discussed separately below.

The western part of the trench

In the western (20 Arbory Street) part of the site was a dark, humic garden soil. One area of this was much darker and more clayey than elsewhere. It contained a lot of charcoal, decayed limestone and bone fragments, particularly fish. Initially this fill (48) appeared to be contained within a fairly straight-sided pit. However, its sides to the west and east proved to be poorly defined and the dark clayey material seemed to spread over a wider area. This area appears to represent a poorly defined pit or hollow (49) into which domestic refuse was being tipped, probably during the later seventeenth century (Fig 29).

Although the nineteenth-century gardening features seemed very prominent during their excavation, they were, in fact, the last surviving traces of more recent activity on the site. The dark brown soils which they cut to the west (82) and east (89) of the boundary bank proved to contain primarily seventeenth-century and earlier material, the few later finds within them almost certainly representing contamination from the trench digging.

The seventeenth-century deposits proved to be the top of uniform 'garden' soils, 500–600mm in depth, which contained very few features and had no apparent vertical stratigraphy. They were, therefore, excavated in arbitrary spits of 100–200mm in depth. These demonstrated that there was a chronological distinction between the different levels, with seventeenth-century material in the higher levels and sixteenth-century material towards the base. The soil must, therefore, have formed over a period of perhaps two centuries and was not the result of a single event. It was interesting to note that a similar sequence of soil formation was taking place at the same time on both sides of the property division, although the soils in the Arbory Street property to the west of the boundary were rather darker and more humic than those to the east. Four spits (82, 93, 94 and 110) were removed from the west of the bank before the natural was reached (Fig 30). The soil was fine

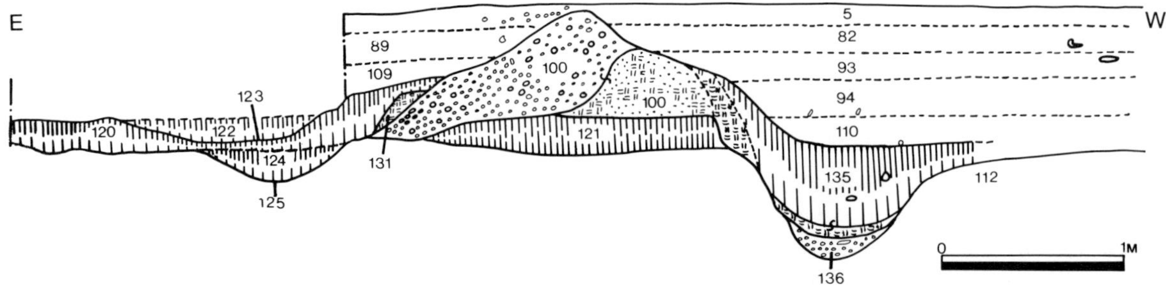

Fig 30   Castle Rushen Stores, Section through Boundary Bank and Ditches in Trench 92.103

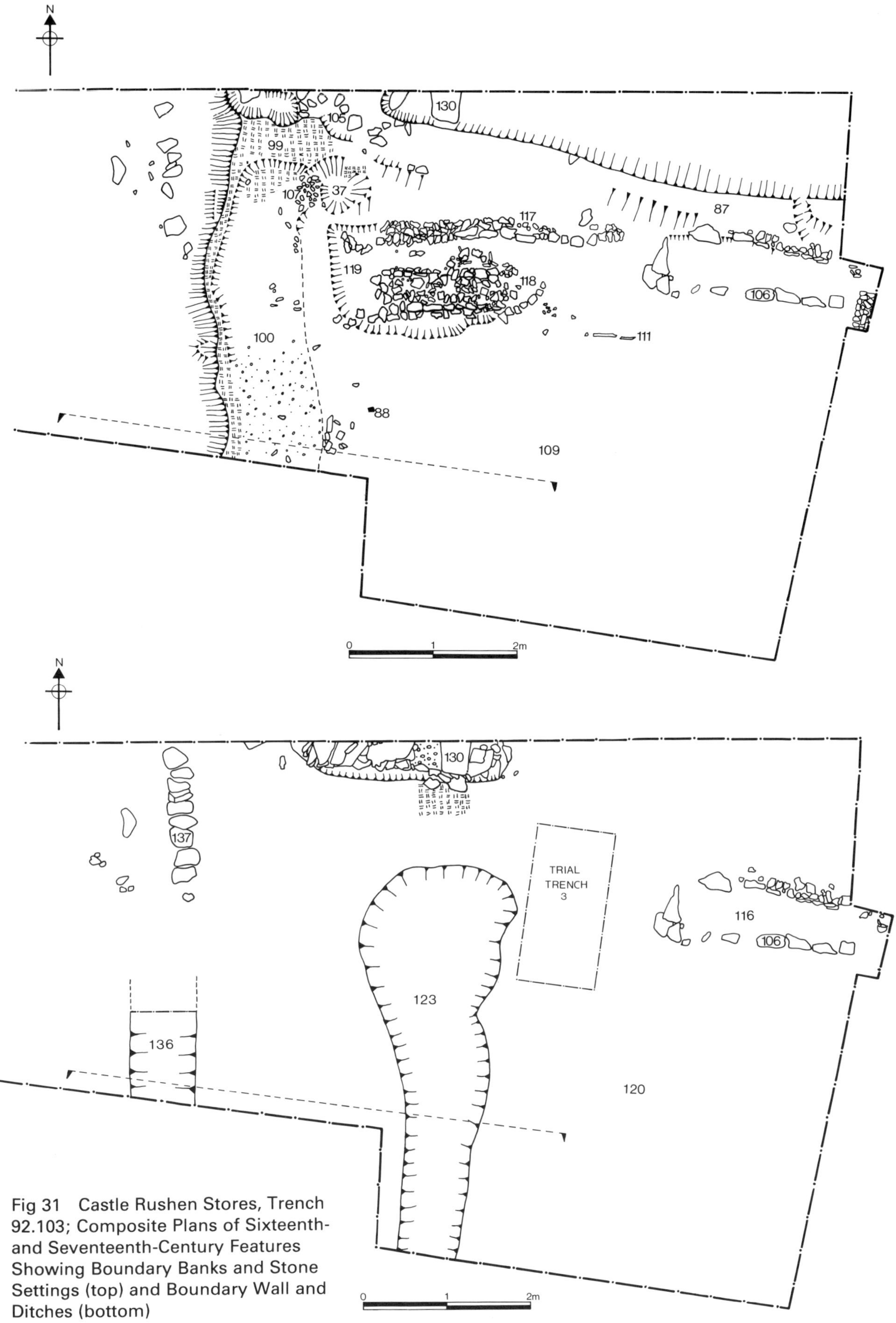

Fig 31   Castle Rushen Stores, Trench 92.103; Composite Plans of Sixteenth- and Seventeenth-Century Features Showing Boundary Banks and Stone Settings (top) and Boundary Wall and Ditches (bottom)

and crumbly, with only a very few stones in it. It became very slightly lighter in colour in the lower levels, and the density of finds seemed to decrease, but otherwise there was no distinction between these four spits.

Boundary walls and ditches

The only features located within the spits were two stone walls, Contexts 134 (not illustrated) and 137 (Fig 31). These were both contained within Context 94, a seventeenth-century deposit, and 'sitting on' Context 110, a sixteenth-century deposit. In neither case could any construction trench or contemporary ground level be discerned; the stones merely appeared to 'float' within the uniform garden soils. Both walls consisted of a single course of local stones, some of which were slightly water-rolled. Two small sections of wall (134) were exposed in the extreme north-west corner of the trench. These stones were generally 200mm across, slightly smaller than the stones of the other stone wall (137) which were generally 300mm across. This latter lay parallel to and immediately alongside the property division bank (100).

Neither of these 'walls' could have stood to any height; the small size and rather rounded shape of the stones would not have allowed it. It seems more likely that these were merely 'edging' stones, placed in a row to retain or mark the property boundaries or to revet a low bank. In this respect it may be significant that both of these 'walls' overlay earlier ditches, the wall alongside the property dividing bank (100) overlay a ditch (136), and that in the north-west corner of the site overlay another ditch (114/133), which contained sixteenth-century material. There was, however, a considerable build-up of soil (110) which had completely covered the in-filled ditches before these stones were placed on their former line.

The lowest spit (110) ended abruptly at the natural (112). This consisted of a well-bedded layer of small stones, generally less than 10mm in size, and contained within a dark orange-brown slightly clayey matrix. The top of the natural was very flat and uniform, with no apparent mixing with the soils above. It would appear that the dark 'garden' soils had been well mixed internally, but that they were quite different in character from the natural and had not disturbed the interface. The dark soils, for example, included hardly any of the small stones which made up the natural. The only features cutting the natural were the two boundary ditches mentioned above (114/133 and 136). These

were only visible where they cut the natural, since their fill was indistinguishable from the garden soils above. The ditch in the north-west corner of the site (114/133) only just fell within the trench. There was no evidence of a bank or contemporary ground surface from which it had been cut to the south, although one may have survived outside the excavated area to the north. This ditch may represent a former division of the Arbory Street plots.

The eastern part of the trench

A similar sequence of deposits to those in the western part of the trench was found to the east of the bank, that is, in the garden of the 19 Malew Street property (Fig 31). This area was defined by the gravel bank (100) to the west and to the north by a strip of lighter soil (87), which appeared to be the remains of another boundary bank. Within this area was a series of eighteenth- or nineteenth-century gardening features similar to those found in the western part of the trench (Fig 29). These appear to have been contemporary and may well have been produced at a time when both gardens had already become joined.

Below these features was a deep deposit of garden soil, very similar to that west of the bank, described above, but slightly lighter and less humic in nature. This was removed as a series of spits (89, 98, 109 and 120). As in the western area, these soils appear to have formed during the sixteenth and seventeenth centuries and finished abruptly at the natural which had not been disturbed by pits or other features, other than the boundary ditch (125) which flanked the gravel bank (100) (Fig 30).

Stone features

Contained within the garden soils were three stone features. These seem likely to be broadly contemporary since they were all sealed by a seventeenth-century soil (89), but all appear to be later than a sixteenth-century soil (109). Two of these features consisted of stone slabs which had been set on edge.

A rectangular setting of upright stones (106) had been placed tight against the possible boundary bank (87). The stones were of irregular size and shape but had been set to enclose an area about 600mm wide and at least 2m in length. The fill within this area (116) was indistinguishable from the surrounding soil to the west and south (109), although it contained pottery dating from the seventeenth century rather than the sixteenth century. To the north the lighter soil of the possible boundary bank mixed with the top of the stones, but it was not clear whether this was merely soil which had slumped over the stones or whether the bank was stratigraphically later. No construction cut for the stones could be seen but, since they could not have been free standing, it was assumed that they lined a pit which cut the surrounding soil (109). There was no evidence of a lining in the pit other than the stones, and there were some quite large gaps between these. There was no evidence of any base or floor to the feature.

About 800mm to the south-west were two further upright stones (111). These were rather thinner slabs than the upright setting (106) and they were also largely contained within the soil spit (109). There was no evidence of any construction trench for the stones, nor could they be related to any other features.

To the west of these features (106 and 111) were two sections of walling (117 and 118). These first appeared as a stony spread (108) which has been interpreted as debris from the demolition or collapse of this structure. Once this had been cleared two dry-stone walls emerged. These were of different sizes, the one to the north (117) being rather narrower and surviving higher in the ground than the one to the south (118). Both walls appeared to have been neatly constructed with well-set faces and were contained within a single shallow construction trench (119). This trench, the walling and the demolition deposits all contained seventeenth-century material.

The function of these three stone features remains obscure, although their small size and their position in what appears to be the extreme north-western corner of the Malew Street plot both suggest that they were ephemeral structures in the corner of the garden. The most likely suggestions seem to be that they were either latrines or connected with animal husbandry on the site.

The boundary bank

The possible boundary bank to the north (87) proved very hard to define. Its lighter colour soil tended to fade into the surrounding layers, as did its base. However, the alignment of this possible boundary is significant since it follows the general line of the street frontage boundary between Nos 19 and 21 Malew Street. The sharp dog-leg in the present boundary north-east of the trench may well represent a more recent re-arrangement of this area, with the bank marking the line of the former boundary. The soils north of and under the bank (90 and 126) were kept separate from those to the south, although they were otherwise very similar.

Only a small area north of the bank could be examined and only one significant feature was apparent in this area. This consisted of a patch of very substantial stones (130) (Fig 31). These stones were up to at least 600mm in size, but fairly loosely set with smaller stones and earth between. A construction trench was tentatively identified around the stones and this appeared to cut through Contexts 90 and 126, which are probably of seventeenth-century or earlier date. The stones continued right down to the level of the natural and appear to form the footings of a substantially-built structure lying to the north of the excavated area.

Trench 92.104

This trench was excavated in the back garden of 17 Malew Street and took in the area of Trial Trench 1 (Fig 32). The evidence from this trial trench has been included in the discussion below. The present building on the street frontage is of two distinct phases: the rear section appears to be of seventeenth-century construction, while the front is of nineteenth-century date. It seems that the original building was set back from the street, but that it was subsequently extended up to the present street line. A side passage gives access to the back of the plot, where there is a ruinous two-storey lean-to and a range of small outbuildings. These were not examined, but presumably consisted of an outside toilet and fuel stores. This layout of buildings was the same in 1868 when the Ordnance Survey map was surveyed. The map also shows a path running around the outside of the garden area, although no trace of this was found during the excavations.

The area in which this trench was excavated was very overgrown and partially covered with rubble from the ruinous building to the north-east. The garden has also been used for dumping rubbish so there was a large amount of modern glass, china and other debris on or very near the surface. The trench was laid out to examine the largest readily available area of ground, with extensions being placed to explore the relationship of the ruin and northern boundary wall to any surviving stratigraphy.

The surface debris was cleared and a spit of dark, rich garden soil removed (1). This was about 30cm deep and had clearly been much disturbed. The soil beneath (2) was very slightly lighter in colour but had also been much disturbed and contained material of very recent date. It was, therefore, removed

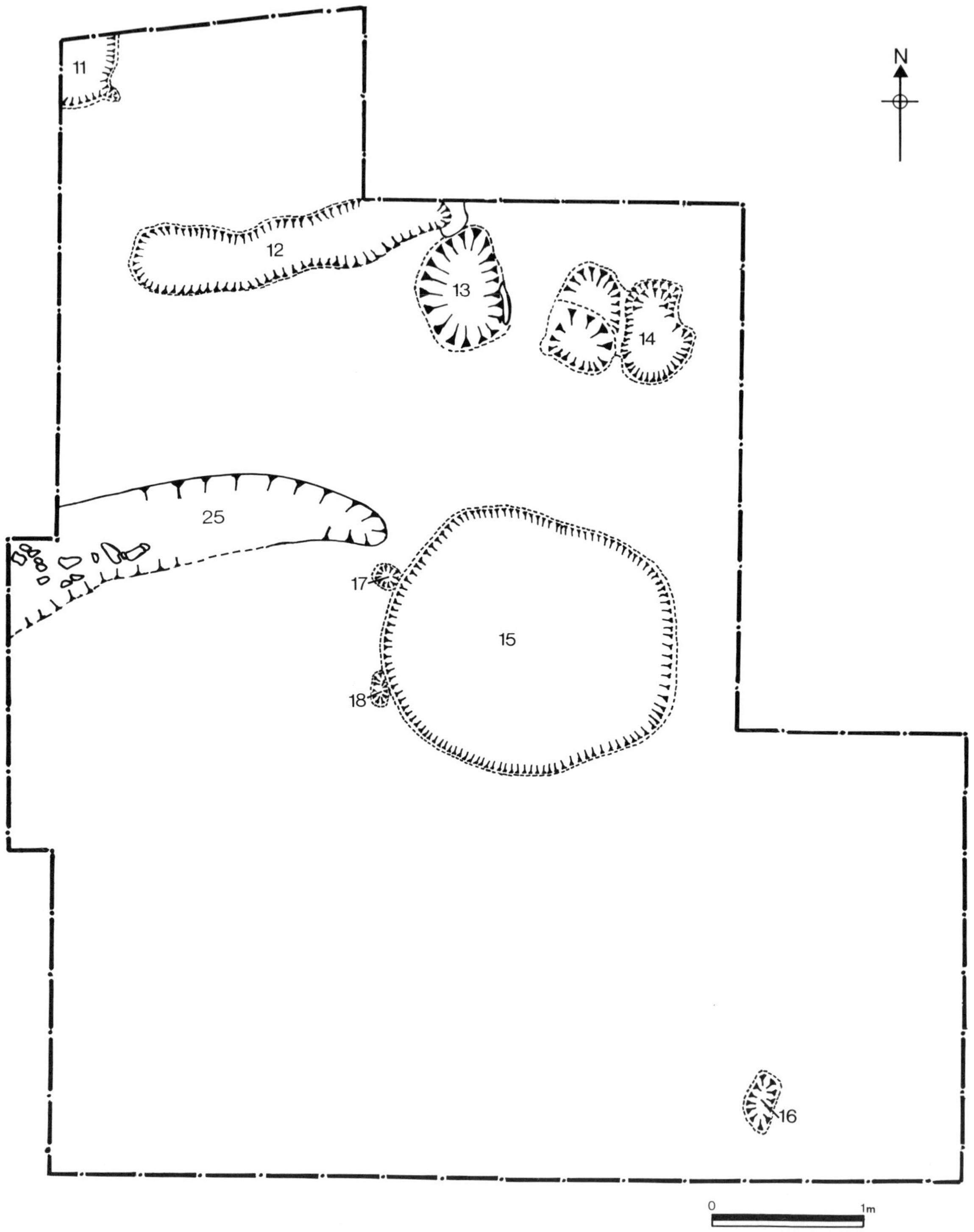

Fig 32 Castle Rushen Stores, Trench 92.104; Composite Plan Showing Nineteenth-Century and Later Features Cutting Context 19 (11–18) and a Sixteenth-Century Feature Cutting Natural (25)

as a second spit of about 150–200mm depth. There were patches of mortar and shell within this layer, especially towards the south-east corner where a small section of cobbled floor was also revealed. No attempt was made to identify or record features at this level because of the large quantities of very recent waste that were present.

Beneath Context 2 there was a slightly lighter brown soil (19), in which it was possible to see a series of pit fills (3–10) and their respective cuts

(11–18) (Fig 32). These were all of recent date and had almost certainly been cut from a much higher level. The largest of the pits (15) was nearly 2m in diameter and cut 400mm below the top of Context 19. It had fairly vertical sides and contained bands of ashy material amongst its predominantly earthy fill. It appears to have been dug and backfilled quite rapidly.

Once these late pits had been cleaned out, deep garden soils remained, very similar to those in Trench 92.103. There were no apparent features within these soils, which very gradually became lighter in colour with depth. They were removed in a series of arbitrary spits (19–23). The top spit (19) contained predominantly seventeenth-century material, although later material was also present. This almost certainly represents contamination from more modern pits which had not been recognised at a higher level. Below this lighter brown soil (19) all the spits contained sixteenth-century pottery. As with Trench 92.103, these layers suggest that there was a rapid accumulation of fine garden soil during the sixteenth and seventeenth centuries.

The lowest spit (23) finished abruptly at a fine, stony subsoil (26), identical to that found in Trenches 92.102 and 92.103. Only one feature cut this subsoil, a shallow trench (25) containing a light sandy soil very similar to the lowest spit which had been removed. This feature had also been detected in the trial trench, where it seemed to be associated with a scatter of limestone fragments, suggesting that it was the remains of a robbed-out wall. There did not appear to be any particular concentration of stone in the area excavated within the larger trench.

The excavated area extended up to two walls: the boundary wall with No 19 Malew Street and the south-west corner of the ruined building. Both of these walls were built of local limestone, as are almost all of the structures in Castletown. In both cases the walls finished without any trace of a construction trench or foundation plinth. This made it impossible to date either of the walls or tie them in to the excavated layers. Several local visitors to the site commented that Manx walls were traditionally built directly onto the ground without any foundations, which provides an explanation for the lack of any construction trench in this case.

Discussion

The excavations set out to address a number of issues relating to the history and development of Castletown: how old is the settlement; is there any evidence for a planned medieval layout; what was the building pattern on the street frontages; how were the backyard areas used; what was the material lifestyle of the inhabitants; and what is the potential for further work? Whilst the excavations may not have supplied answers to all of these questions, they have at least provided a reference point in an area of archaeology which has been little explored on the Isle of Man.

Medieval evidence

Although a little prehistoric flintwork was recovered from the excavations, it was all residual material and did not occur in sufficient quantities to suggest occupation directly on the site. There was no further evidence of activity on the site until the medieval period. Twenty-seven sherds of medieval pottery, many of them small and abraded, were recovered from the excavations. A silver halfpenny of Edward III, dating from 1335 to 1344, was also recovered. Although most of this material came from disturbed contexts, a medieval soil was found preserved beneath the boundary bank in Trench 92.103. This scatter of medieval finds, collected from a considerable area, is possibly the result of spreading 'night soil' from the town or castle over neighbouring fields. It is probable that more extensive deposits of this date have survived where they have been protected from later gardening activity by standing buildings. Despite the evidence for medieval activity, no features of this date were encountered. There was no evidence of a medieval boundary at the division between the Arbory Street and Malew Street plots, nor of any medieval boundary between the plots along either of these streets.

Boundary banks

The principal division between the Arbory Street and Malew Street properties consisted of a substantial bank with flanking ditches. There was evidence of slighter banks and ditches dividing the individual plots on both sides of this boundary. These divisions all appear to date from the early sixteenth century, since they overlay medieval deposits and soils of this date had built up against them. It appears that there had been a major reorganisation in either the land-holding or land-use at this date to explain the contemporary construction of so many new boundaries. Following their construction, the medieval soils were disturbed right down to the natural and a period of rapid soil accumulation started. Between the start of the sixteenth century, when the medieval soil was probably buried, and the end of the seventeenth century, no less than 500mm of soil built up (Fig 30 and Contexts 82, 93 and 94). This deposit exhibited no horizontal stratigraphy, suggesting that it was continually disturbed and intermixed during its accumulation. This deposit was also notably free of either small gravel derived from the underlying natural, or of larger stones from the construction or demolition of structures. This might suggest that the boundary banks were fenced or hedged, rather than having walls on them or being stone faced, and/or that the back yards were kept clear for cultivation.

Animal keeping

It used to be common practice for cows to be kept behind the houses in Castletown and some stalls still survive in backyard areas, for example, the passages which survive between the buildings shown in Figure 25. Access was provided by means of covered passages between the buildings, many of which still survive. It seems possible that the well-mixed and rich garden soils were, in fact, created as a result of keeping or mucking-out cattle in these areas. The fact that a similar sequence of soils formed in the backyard areas of all the excavated trenches suggests that, whatever the cause of this accumulation, it was as the result of a common practice in the town and not of the activity of any one individual.

Building activity

The seventeenth century seems to have been a period when a number of small stone structures were constructed in the backyard areas. These include the stone revetting walls in the western part of Trench 92.103 and the various stone structures from the eastern part of that trench. The earthy layers on the Arbory Street frontage may suggest that this area had not been built on at this date. This would tie in with the situation at 17 Malew Street, where the rear part of the surviving building appears to consist of a seventeenth-century structure, whilst the front part is a nineteenth-century addition bringing the building forward to the street frontage. It is possible that during the medieval and early post-medieval periods the settlement pattern in Castletown consisted of individual cottages set back from the street, and that from the seventeenth century onwards these were infilled and extended forward to form the frontage which exists today. This hypothesis could be tested by a combination of building survey and further excavation in the town. There was a notable absence of eighteenth-century material from any of the trenches, and then evidence of garden activity in the nineteenth century.

The finds

The finds recovered provide by far the largest sample of medieval and early post-medieval material yet recovered from an urban context on the Isle of Man. The wide range of pottery types present, both in terms of origin and of function, suggest a fairly cosmopolitan lifestyle in Castletown. This is supported by other finds, such as the imported metalwork and glass, the jettons and the coin of Philip II of Spain. As a cultural assemblage this material is comparable with groups from provincial towns elsewhere in the British Isles, and suggests that the inhabitants would have been well aware of changing fashions and tastes. Indeed, the maritime connections available to the islanders may have made 'exotic' imports such as the Saintonge chafing dishes, the Beauvais sgraffito plates or the vessel from the Iberian peninsula more widely available than at many towns on the mainland.

Pottery

P J Davey and N C Johnson

Introduction

The 1991 and 1992 excavations at Castle Rushen Stores produced a total of 4189 sherds of pottery from 120 contexts. This is the largest collection of pottery from medieval or post-medieval excavations on the Isle of Man so far recovered, exceeding that from Peel Castle by almost one thousand sherds (Davey forthcoming). It is the first collection of any size from Castletown and the only one from extensive urban excavations anywhere on the island. At the Castletown Grammar School site Cubbon retrieved 306 sherds of pottery, mostly of eighteenth-century date (Cubbon 1971). Garrad recovered a further 77 sherds, including a range of medieval and post-medieval types, from nine sites in the town in a sampling exercise in 1967 (Garrad 1969). Slightly further afield, Stenning found a small group of 23 sherds, mainly of medieval types, at the Ronaldsway smelt site (Stenning 1945) and Butler recovered small quantities of useful medieval material from Rushen Abbey (Butler 1988).

The report which follows is divided into two main sections. The first considers the evidence which is provided by the pottery for the dating and understanding of the site. The second discusses the pottery itself and its significance.

The pottery evidence and the dating of the site

TRENCH 92.102

Summary

This trench produced a total of 678 sherds of pottery from 29 contexts. The pottery evidence taken together with the provisional site matrix, suggests four major phases of activity on the site:

Phase 1, dating from the sixteenth century, comprises 34 sherds from five occupation layers in the south-west area of the site (40, 44–47).
Phase 2, possibly dating from 1650 to 1750, consists of 10 sherds from two occupation layers and one pit fill in the north-west area of the site (32, 33, 41).
Phase 3, with 466 sherds from 16 contexts, involving trampled surfaces, occupational layers and constructional debris for the cellars, appears to date from 1790 to 1820 (3, 5, 6, 10, 12, 14, 16–19, 21, 23, 28–30, 35).
Phase 4, produced 159 sherds from five contexts and dates from the very late nineteenth or early twen-

Ctxt	C19	C18	C17	C16	Med.	Total
002	8	3	4	2	–	17
003	–	6	1	1	–	8
005	1	–	–	–	–	1
006	99	88	4	4	–	195
008	66	5	–	1	–	72
009	41	1	–	–	–	42
010	10	–	–	–	–	10
011	5	3	–	–	–	8
012	13	8	–	–	–	21
013	11	9	–	–	–	20
014	37	58	20	14	1	130
016	1	3	1	–	–	5
017	5	18	5	2	–	30
018	1	4	12	4	–	21
019	–	1	–	–	–	1
021	1	1	–	–	–	2
023	–	–	1	2	1	4
028	3	5	2	14	–	24
029	–	2	–	–	–	2
030	1	1	–	1	–	3
032	–	–	1	–	–	1
033	–	2	3	3	–	8
035	1	2	1	5	–	9
040	–	–	–	13	–	13
041	–	1	–	–	–	1
044	–	–	1	3	1	5
045	–	–	–	7	–	7
046	–	–	–	7	–	7
047	–	–	–	2	–	2
u/s	2	7	–	–	–	9
Total	306	228	56	85	3	678

Table 1   Summary by context of the number of pottery sherds from Trench 92.102

tieth century. It seems to consist largely of demolition layers and fills which immediately pre-date the concrete yard surface (2, 8, 9, 11, 13).

There were nine unstratified sherds which have not been allocated to a phase.

Phase 1

This series of occupation layers produced 34 sherds in six different pottery types. Just over half consist of Manx granite-tempered wares, including glazed examples with both grey (reduced) and red (oxidised) bodies, together with two unglazed sherds. The rest are types of Cistercian-related wares probably imported from north-west England. These include both dark and clear glazed types [DRB, LRE]. The single medieval sherd recovered from Context 44 must be considered residual.

This group is difficult to date with precision as there are no continental imports. On the basis of the evidence from the Peel Town excavations, it is most likely to lie within the sixteenth century.

Phase 2

Pottery from two layers and a pit fill in the north-west area of the trench, although more difficult to date precisely, clearly represents a later phase of activity. Two sherds of granite-tempered ware [GTW] and a single piece of dark-glazed ware from Context 33 are probably of sixteenth-century date. The single sherd of Beauvais sgraffito in Context 32 is probably contemporary [BSC]. The fragments of Rainford-type yellow ware [RYW] and north Devon gravel-tempered ware [NDG] from Context 33, on the other hand, probably date from a century later. The remaining six sherds of dark-glazed wares should probably belong somewhere in the period 1600–1750. One sherd from Context 33 in particular appears to be of eighteenth-century manufacture. Overall, the evidence is consistent with a date in the later seventeenth or early eighteenth century for this phase.

Phase 3

This, the largest group of pottery from the trench, constitutes over two-thirds of all the ceramic evidence. The contexts consist of eight layers and surfaces in the south-west (6, 12, 17, 18, 19, 23, 30, 35) and one in the north-west area (14) which immediately pre-date the cellars, together with a further six which relate to the construction and use of the cellars themselves (3, 5, 10, 16, 21, 28).

Context 30 contains a blue transfer printed sherd which can be dated to 1790–1820, together with a late eighteenth-century fragment of mottled ware. This layer is separated from the sixteenth-century Phase 1 sequence by a set of post holes which did not produce any pottery (36–39, 42) and may represent Phase 2 activity in the south-west area.

The major groups of this phase which pre-date the cellar construction (12, 14, 17, 18) are indistinguishable from each other in date and include many cross joins. Neither can these layers be separated from those involved in the construction and first use of these structures (10, 16, 28). There are numerous joins between Contexts 14 and 28. Thus, a single activity is implied which includes the trampled surfaces and layers which pre-date the cellar, the cellar construction itself, including the laying of the floors, and the primary trample on the floor and steps.

The absolute dating of this phase can be estimated by taking the range of the latest datable pieces. Context 14, for example, includes four sherds of Mocha [MOC], three of pearlware [PEW], one of early shell-edged blue [SEB], 24 of late eighteenth-century or early nineteenth-century creamware [CRE] and two sherds of trailed slipware bowls of the same general date. Context 17, which includes a number of typical eighteenth-century types such as agate bodied ware [AGB], mottled ware [MOT], north Devon sgraffito [NSG], press-moulded slipware [PMS] and tin-glazed earthenware [TGE], also contains two sherds of blue transfer printed ware [BTP] and an early nineteenth-century all-over internally slipped cup rim [RSO]. The consistency of these groups is repeated in the smaller collections which belong to this phase and which should be dated to the period 1790–1820.

Context 6, a demolition deposit in the south-western area which underlay the concrete and clearance layers over the whole site, poses a problem. It has been placed within Phase 3 here on the grounds that the very large group of pottery which it produced — 195 sherds — contains types of the same period and does not include material of mid- or late nineteenth-century type. Indeed, a number of additional wares of the same period are present, including a brown stoneware oil flagon sherd [BSW] and two sherds of peasant enamel [PSE]. There are a number of joins with vessels in Contexts 14 and 17. Given the large quantity of pottery present in Phase 4, it would seem very surprising that if the demolition represented by Context 6 took place at the same time as the cellar was filled with rubble, there should be no later pottery at all in its composition.

Phase 4

This phase, which consists of the clearance layer beneath the concrete floor over the whole site (2), and a series of four fills of the cellar itself (8, 9, 11, 13), produced a total of 159 sherds. This material is characterised by the presence of red earthenware pancheons with all-over internal yellow slip, white stoneware bottles, brown stoneware ink bottles and Hartley marmalade jars. One of the white bottles has a Castletown Mineral Water Company stamp associated with Curwen Bros, a Liverpool bottle maker (9), another was made by Pearson's of Whittington Moor (8) and a third was produced by Price's of Bristol (9) (Fig 52). This combination of finds suggests a date in the early twentieth century for the backfilling of the cellar and construction of the concrete yard surface.

Phase summary

Phase 1   sixteenth century (Contexts 40, 44–47)
Phase 2   1650–1750 (Contexts 32, 33, 41)
Phase 3   1790–1820 (Contexts 3, 5, 6, 10, 12, 14, 16–19, 21, 23, 28–30, 35)
Phase 4   Late nineteenth century/early twentieth century (Contexts 2, 8, 9, 11, 13)

Phase	C19	C18	C17	C16	Med.	Total
1	–	–	1	32	1	34
2	–	3	4	3	–	10
3	173	197	47	47	2	466
4	131	21	4	3	–	159
u/s	2	7	–	–	–	9
Total	306	228	56	85	3	678

Table 2   Pottery sherd totals by phase from Trench 92.102

Phase	C19	C18	C17	C16	Med.	Total
1	–	–	3	94	3	100
2	–	30	40	30	–	100
3	37	43	10	10	–	100
4	82	13	3	2	–	100
Total	45	34	8	13		100

Table 3   Pottery sherd percentage totals by phase from Trench 92.102

TRENCH 92.103

Summary

Trench 92.103 produced a total of 1787 sherds of pottery from 62 contexts. In addition, 85 sherds were recovered from seven contexts in Trial Trench 3 (numbered between 300 and 311).

The pottery evidence, taken with the provisional site matrix, suggests four major phases of activity on the site:

Phase 1, dating from the sixteenth century, consists of bank and ditch construction which divided the area into separate plots to the east and west ends of the trench respectively. This was followed by a period of gardening activity.

Phase 2, dating from the seventeenth century, involved the construction of a number of walls on both sides of the site and further gardening.

Phase 3, dating from 1770 to 1820, consists of a gardening phase followed by the digging of a large number of linear features. Both activities appear to have disturbed earlier garden soils, as much earlier pottery was recovered throughout the phase.

Phase 4, dating from the later nineteenth and twentieth centuries, consists primarily of garden soil.

Phase 1

A gravel boundary bank (100) and associated ditches (113, 132, 135) are sealed by a soil layer (110) on the western part of the site. To the east, this phase is represented by a ditch which has been cut in two stages (124), interspersed with soil layers (109, 120, 304, 308). In addition, there is a clay strip (131) to the east of the boundary bank (100) and a soil layer preserved beneath a Phase 2 bank (126, 307). All of this material is consistently of sixteenth-century date, with a small quantity of residual medieval sherds. Beneath the gravel boundary bank (100) was a buried soil which contained two medieval sherds (121). This may represent a relic of earlier activity on the site.

Ctxt	C19	C18	C17	C16	Med.	?	Total
100	–	–	–	2	4	–	6
109	–	–	–	92	7	–	99
110	–	–	2	12	–	–	14
112	–	–	2	2	–	–	4
120	–	–	–	3	4	–	7
121	–	–	–	–	2	–	2
124	–	–	–	1	–	–	1
126	–	–	–	1	–	–	1
131	–	–	–	1	–	–	1
132	–	–	–	1	–	–	1
135	–	–	–	1	–	–	1
308	–	–	1	2	1	–	4

Table 4   Summary by context of the number of Phase 1 pottery sherds from Trial Trench 3 and Trench 92.103

Ctxt	C19	C18	C17	C16	Med.	?	Total
082	–	1	28	99	4	–	132
087	–	1	10	9	3	–	23
093	–	–	8	66	7	–	81
094	–	–	2	66	1	–	69
098	–	1	10	13	1	–	25
106	–	–	1	8	2	–	11
108	–	–	8	43	1	–	52
116	–	–	4	6	–	–	10
117	–	–	–	1	–	–	1
118	–	–	–	–	1	–	1
119	–	–	–	1	–	–	1
302	–	–	1	3	–	–	4
303	–	–	1	–	–	–	1
305	–	2	4	3	–	–	9
306	–	–	3	3	–	–	6

Table 5   Summary by context of the number of Phase 2 pottery sherds from Trial Trench 3 and Trench 92.103

Phase 2

A series of walls, two at the western end of the trench (134, 137) and two at the east (117, 118, 119, 303, 306, 311), was constructed. A rectilinear stone setting was constructed on the plot boundary at the north-east corner of the trench (87, 106, 116, 302). This construction phase was followed on the west by a sequence of garden soils (82, 93, 94) and on the east by a single garden soil (98). The walls on the east side were demolished at the end of this phase (108, 305). These contexts include considerable proportions of sixteenth-century material, implying that the digging activities produced substantial mixing in these areas.

Phase 3

On the western side of the site, sixteenth- and seventeenth-century garden soils (82) were extensively disturbed in the later eighteenth or early nineteenth century by a range of garden features (6, 8, 12, 14, 17, 18, 19, 25, 48, 99, 105, 130). In the eastern and north-eastern part of the trench, largely seventeenth-century soils (89, 90, 301) were also disturbed by a wide range of later eighteenth- and early nineteenth-century features (34, 36, 38, 44, 46, 50, 52, 54, 55, 56, 57, 61, 62, 63, 64, 65, 69, 85) and by a cobbled floor (102). Statistical analysis of the pottery groupings suggests that there was an interval of about fifty years between these two stages of activity.

Phase 4

A nineteenth-century soil extended over the whole site (5, 300). A single robbed wall (3), which post-dated the gardening, produced 18 sherds of pottery, the majority of late nineteenth-century date. An earlier robbed wall contained a wider variety of sherds. On the extreme eastern edge of the site, an area of construction activity (115, 127) also belongs to this period.

Ctxt	C19	C18	C17	C16	Med.	?	Total
006	–	1	–	–	–	–	1
008	–	1	–	–	–	–	1
012	–	–	1	–	–	–	1
014	–	–	1	–	–	–	1
015	–	2	–	–	–	–	2
017	–	3	–	–	–	–	3
018	–	1	–	–	–	–	1
019	–	1	2	–	–	–	3
025	1	–	–	–	–	–	1
034	–	1	4	1	–	–	6
036	–	6	10	–	–	–	16
038	1	5	5	–	–	–	11
044	–	–	–	2	–	–	2
046	1	–	–	–	–	–	1
048	–	–	11	7	–	–	18
050	–	1	1	–	–	–	2
052	1	8	13	1	–	–	23
053	1	6	4	–	–	–	11
054	3	7	14	1	–	–	25
055	5	20	3	1	–	–	29
056	–	2	3	–	–	–	5
057	2	8	5	–	–	–	15
059	–	–	1	–	–	–	1
061	–	–	5	–	–	–	5
062	5	8	3	3	–	–	19
063	–	1	5	–	–	–	6
064	2	17	6	–	–	–	25
065	–	–	2	–	–	–	2
069	–	–	1	–	–	–	1
085	–	–	1	–	–	–	1
089	–	6	95	33	3	–	137
090	1	9	28	6	–	–	44
099	–	–	–	2	–	–	2
105	1	1	4	1	1	–	8
130	–	–	3	1	–	–	4
301	–	8	7	3	–	–	18

Table 6   Summary by context of the number of Phase 3 pottery sherds from Trial Trench 3 and Trench 92.103

Ctxt	C19	C18	C17	C16	Med.	?	Total
001	9	9	3	5	1	–	27
003	10	5	3	–	–	–	18
005	170	325	203	60	4	–	762
115	1	–	–	–	–	–	1
127	–	–	–	2	–	–	2
300	6	18	17	2	–	–	43

Table 7   Summary by context of the number of Phase 4 pottery sherds from Trial Trench 3 and Trench 92.103

Ctxt	C19	C18	C17	C16	Med.	?	Total
u/s	1	–	–	–	–	–	1

Table 8   Summary by context of the number of pottery sherds from Trench 92.103 not allocated to any phase

C19	C18	C17	C16	Med.	?	Total
221	485	549	570	47	–	1872

Table 9   Total number of pottery sherds by century from Trench 92.103

Phase	C19	C18	C17	C16	Med.	?	Total
1	–	–	5	118	18	–	141
2	–	5	80	321	19	1	426
3	24	123	238	62	4	–	451
4	196	357	226	69	5	–	853
u/s	1	–	–	–	–	–	1
Total	221	485	549	570	46	1	1872

Table 10 Pottery sherd totals by phase from Trench 92.103

Phase	C19	C18	C17	C16	Med.	?	Total
1	–	–	3	84	13	–	100
2	–	1	19	75	5	–	100
3	5	28	53	14	–	–	100
4	23	42	27	8	–	–	100
Total	12	26	29	30	3		100

Table 11 Pottery sherd percentage totals by phase from Trench 92.103

Ctxt	DRB	GTW	LRE	NRG	RST	CPW	Med.	?	Total
020	17	7	–	1	–	1	3	2	31
021	59	25	2	3	1	–	5	3	98
022	27	22	2	2	2	–	2	–	57
023	9	9	3	–	–	–	3	–	24
024	1	–	–	–	–	–	1	–	2
107	1	1	–	–	–	–	–	–	2
109	–	1	–	–	–	–	–	–	1
Total	114	65	7	6	3	1	14	5	215
%	53	30	4	3	1		7	2	100

Table 12 Pottery sherd totals and percentages by type in Phase 1, Trench 92.104

TRENCH 92.104

Summary

This trench produced a total of 1308 sherds of pottery from 13 contexts. In addition, 322 sherds were recovered from seven contexts in Trial Trench 1 (91.129, numbered between 100 and 109). The pottery evidence, taken together with the provisional site matrix, suggests four major phases of activity from the site:

Phase 1, dating from the sixteenth century, produced 215 sherds from five contexts (20–24, 107, 109), the majority arbitrary spits in garden soil.
Phase 2, dating from the middle or end of the nineteenth century, consists of 129 sherds from a single spit in garden soil (19, 36).
Phase 3, probably dating from the late nineteenth century, produced 234 sherds from eight contexts, consisting of a variety of pits and linear features which were cut into the Phase 2 garden soil (4–7, 17, 101–03).
Phase 4, with 1047 sherds, appears to represent the late nineteenth- and twentieth-century garden soil (1, 2, 100).

Phase 1

The material from this phase includes a range of typical sixteenth-century types including coarse and fine Cistercian wares [DRB and LRE], some three sherds of the latter slip decorated [RST], granite-tempered wares [GTW], northern reduced greenware [NRG] and coarse purpleware [CPW]. Eight per cent of the assemblage is medieval, of fourteenth- or fifteenth-century date and presumed to be residual.

Phase 2

This single context (19) is by far the most mixed from the site. There are almost equal quantities of sixteenth- to nineteenth-century finds representing some 20 ware types, including, in addition, a few medieval sherds. The nineteenth-century pottery cannot be distinguished in date from the much larger groups in Phases 3 and 4, and includes a single sherd of Hartley marmalade jar which may date as late as 1900. This, together with the relatively large quantity of seventeenth- and eighteenth-century material, suggests that this level of garden soil represents the remains of perhaps two centuries of net rubbish accumulation which has been largely destroyed by intensive gardening and pit-digging in the nineteenth century and later.

Phase 3

Eight features were identified which cut Context 19 (Phase 2), but were earlier than the modern garden soil layers (Phase 4). Five of these produced a total of 113 sherds of pottery. The make-up of these finds contrasts strongly with those from Phase 2, in that in

Phase 3 the majority of the finds are of nineteenth-century or later date (62%), whereas in Phase 2 less than a quarter of the material is of this type (19%). In Phase 3 only very few finds date from the sixteenth (6%) or seventeenth centuries (13%). The dating profile of the finds is not significantly different between the various features within the phase, and it is possible that they cover the whole period 1850–1920+.

Phase 4

The two layers of modern garden soil produced a very similar range of types in comparable proportions to Phase 3. Only the quantity of sixteenth-century material is markedly reduced (2%). The pottery recovered probably covers the whole range from around 1850 to the present.

Phase summary

Phase 1   sixteenth century (Contexts 20–24, 107, 109)

Phase 2   nineteenth century (Context 19, 105)

Phase 3   mid-nineteenth century (Contexts 4–7, 17, 101–03)

Phase 4   late nineteenth and twentieth century (Contexts 1–2, 100)

Ctxt	C19	C18	C17	C16	Med.	?	Total
001	479	47	14	2	–	–	542
002	201	96	29	19	1	–	346
004	9	7	2	–	–	–	18
005	6	2	–	2	–	–	10
006	3	1	–	–	–	–	4
007	65	7	4	4	–	–	80
017	–	–	–	1	–	–	1
019	25	21	26	21	–	–	93
020	–	1	–	26	3	1	31
021	–	–	1	90	5	1	97
022	–	–	–	55	2	–	57
023	–	–	–	21	4	–	25
024	–	–	–	1	1	–	2
u/s	2	–	–	–	–	–	2
Total	790	182	76	242	16	2	1308

Table 13   Summary by context of the number of pottery sherds from Trench 92.104

Ctxt	C19	C18	C17	C16	Med.	?	Total
100	132	20	5	2	–	–	159
101	31	–	1	–	–	–	32
102	28	20	15	2	–	–	65
103	3	8	7	6	–	–	24
105	–	4	3	18	5	6	36
107	–	–	–	2	–	–	2
109	–	–	–	1	–	–	1
u/s	–	–	2	1	–	–	3
Total	194	52	33	32	5	6	322

Table 14   Summary by context of number of pottery sherds from Trial Trench 1

Phase	C19	C18	C17	C16	Med.	?	Total
1	–	1	1	196	15	2	215
2	25	25	29	39	5	6	129
3	145	45	29	15	–	–	234
4	812	163	48	23	1	–	1047
u/s	2	–	2	1	–	–	5
Total	984	234	109	274	21	8	1630

Table 15   Pottery sherd totals by phase from Trial Trench 1 and Trench 92.104

Phase	C19	C18	C17	C16	Med.	?	Total
1	–	–	–	91	7	1	100
2	19	19	23	30	4	5	100
3	62	19	13	6	–	–	100
4	78	15	5	2	–	–	100
Total	61	14	6	18	1		100

Table 16   Pottery sherd percentage totals by phase from Trial Trench 1 and Trench 92.104

TRIAL TRENCH 2

Summary

The nine sherds from two contexts from this trial trench are all of nineteenth-century date.

The pottery itself

MANX PRODUCTS

Manx granite-tempered ware (cf Garrad 1977, 1978; Parkes 1992) [GTW] (Fig 33)

This is one of the two largest groups of material from sixteenth-century contexts from all three trenches on the site. A total of 291 sherds from at least 25 vessels was found. The minimum number of vessels is almost certainly an under-estimate, as the pottery is so poorly made and variable in firing that it is difficult to be sure which sherds might or might not belong to the same vessel. A majority of the pots seem to have functioned as cooking vessels. They include quite large jars (Fig 33.5), sometimes with multiple handles (Fig 33.1), together with

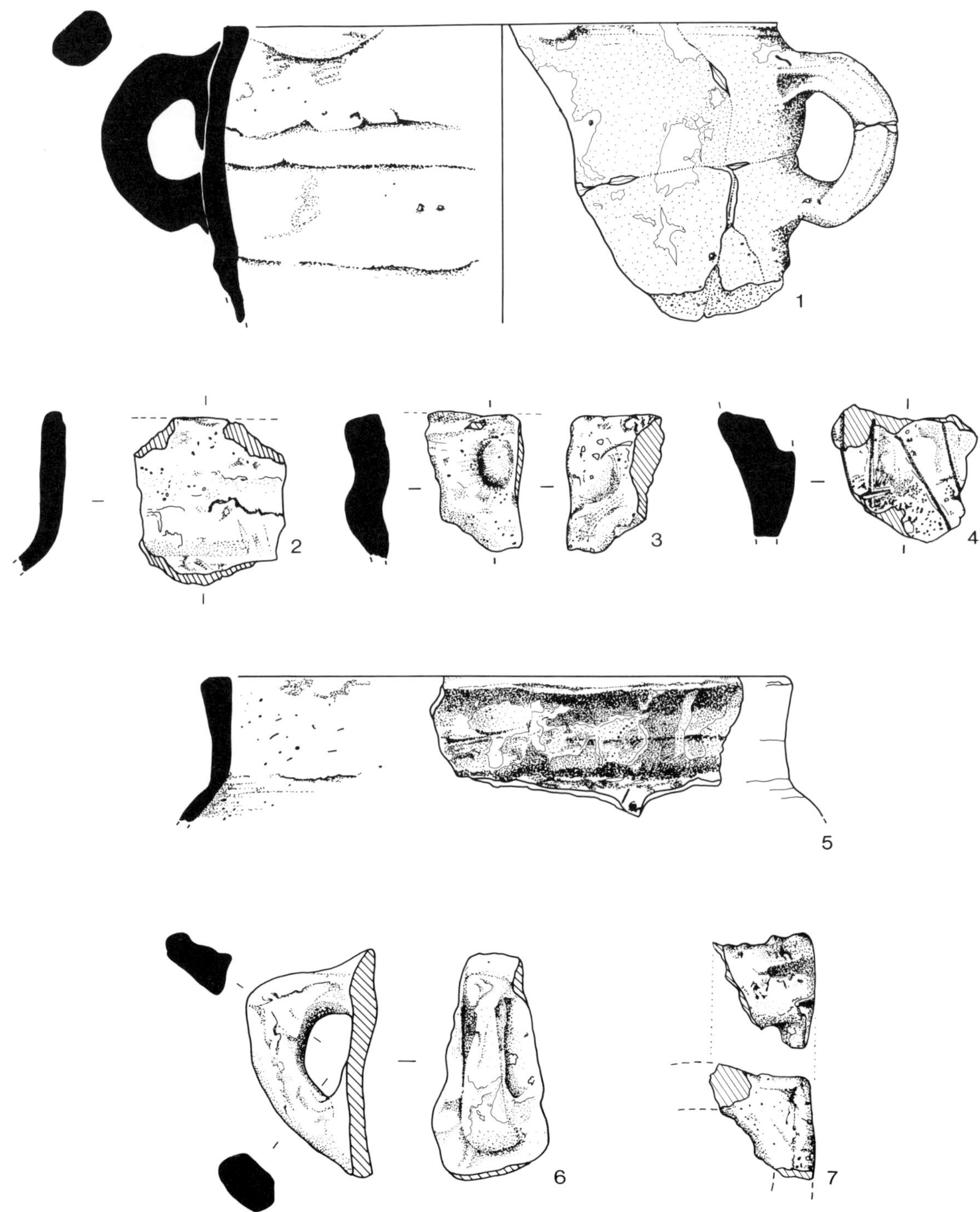

Fig 33   Castle Rushen Stores, Pottery; Nos 1–7, Fifteenth- to Sixteenth-Century Manx Granite-Tempered Ware (Scale 1:2)

skillet-shaped pieces with angular handles (Fig 33.6). Occasionally some decoration is in evidence; a rim sherd from a jar contains a thumbed indentation (Fig 33.3) and a single incised body sherd may be from a jug (Fig 33.4). A sixteenth-century date which has already been suggested for the end of this ware type seems to be confirmed at Castle Rushen Stores, where the British and continental associated pottery is so numerous and so consistent. There are no obviously earlier granite-tempered ware types present in the collection, such as were found by Bersu and Freke at Peel Castle (Wright 1980–82, 40–41, Fig 6, Nos 1–14; Davey forthcoming).

The Manx granite-free ware or 'smoothware' [MSM]

Five sherds of this material, which was common at Peel Castle in the fourteenth century and appears to have been produced by the makers of contemporary Manx granite-tempered ware, were found. Three jugs appear to be represented. It is probable that, along with the British imports, these finds are residual in the sixteenth-century garden soils of the site.

THE MEDIEVAL IMPORTS

Twenty-seven sherds of medieval wares [MED] from a minimum of 21 vessels, presumed to derive from Britain, were found on the site. Most of the pieces are very small and some are abraded. The majority appear to be from jugs, the best quality examples being in a fine gritty white ware similar to the Cockermouth type-series, held in the Department of Archaeology at the University of Liverpool. One has incised decoration around the neck

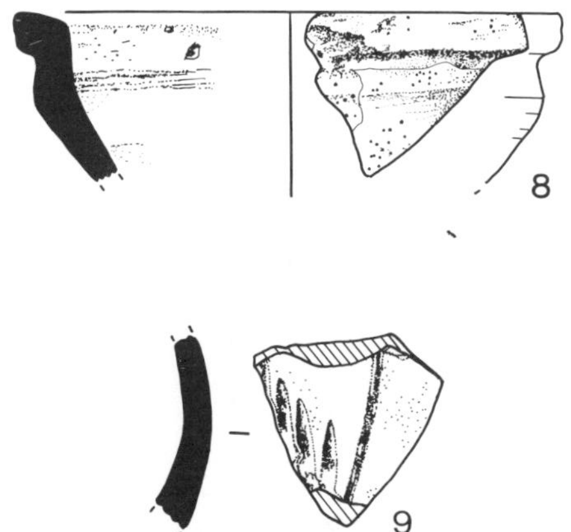

Fig 34   Castle Rushen Stores, Pottery; Nos 8 and 9, Fourteenth- to Fifteenth-Century British Earthenware (Scale 1:2)

(Fig 34.9). There are also a range of grey wares, most with a dark olive-green glaze. There are none of the Cheshire redwares or quality Bristol products which occur at both Peel Castle and Castle Rushen. These finds are difficult to date; some are of fourteenth-century types, the majority are probably up to a century later. Given the very large area excavated and the proximity of the castle, this is a small quantity of material. It suggests intermittent disposal of waste on open land rather than occupation of the area itself.

THE SIXTEENTH-CENTURY CONTINENTAL IMPORTS

France: the French earthenwares (Fig 35)

Castle Rushen Stores produced 55 sherds from a minimum of 38 vessels in wares which derive from continental Europe. The major group of 28 sherds and at least 17 vessels is from south-western France, mostly from the Saintonge. It consists of a wide range of types, including fine green cups and jugs [SAG], chafing dishes [SCD] (Fig 35.10), unglazed jugs [SUN], a late polychrome plate and jug [SPY] (Fig 35.11) and the neck of a pink Saintonge jug [SPI]. Although some of these wares were in production in the Saintonge in the fifteenth century, the whole assemblage is typical of the sixteenth century.

The second largest group consists of 15 sherds from at least 10 Martincamp flasks [MAR]. These are in all three of Hurst's types (Hurst, Neale and Van Beuningen 1986, 102–04). There are two examples of Types I and III and six of Type II. Although Type I examples may be of fifteenth-century date and the coarser of the red Type III vessels might be as late as the seventeenth century, the majority of the Matincamp finds suggest a sixteenth-century context.

Beauvais slipwares (Fig 35)

Six sherds from the same number of vessels are products of the Beauvais area of northern France (Hurst, Neale and Van Beuningen 1986, 108–16). There are four examples of Beauvais sgraffito plates [BSC] (Fig 35.12–14). Two are in 'single sgraffito', in which the design is cut through a single layer of brown slip onto the buff body beneath (Fig 35.13–14). The other two are in 'double sgraffito', in which the design uses a brown slip coat with a yellow layer on top. The fifth vessel is a green-glazed plate rim and the sixth a fragment of the base of a lead-glazed, buff earthenware plate. All of these finds are of sixteenth-century types.

Iberia: the Iberian sherd

A single base sherd in a fine red micaceous fabric is of Iberian Merida-type ware, possibly from Portugal [MER]. It is internally lead-glazed and probably formed part of a jar for the transportation of oil (Hurst, Neale and Van Beuningen 1986, 69–73).

THE SIXTEENTH-CENTURY BRITISH IMPORTS

Apart from a small group of finewares from the London area and a quantity of northern reduced greenware [NRG], which is most probably

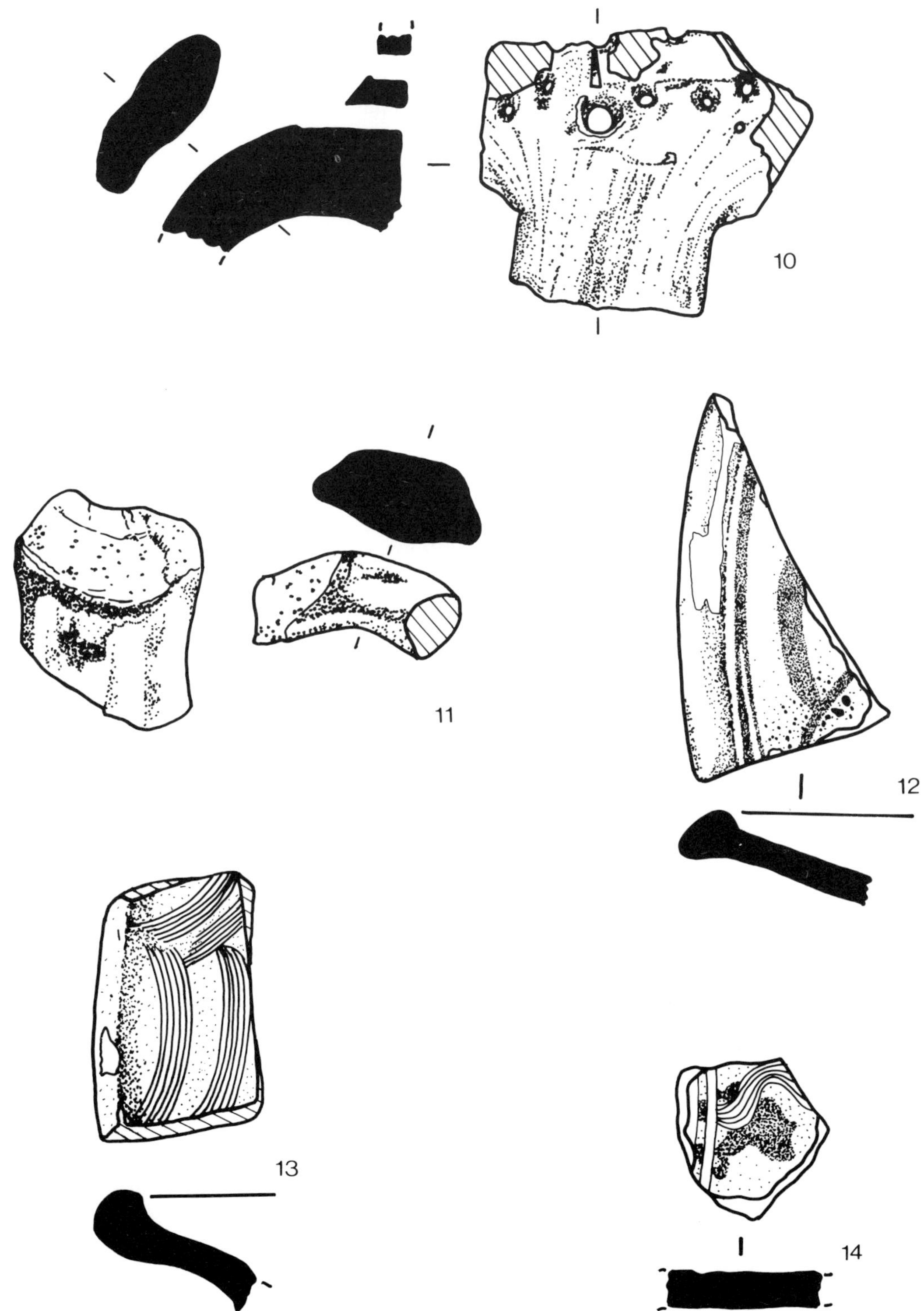

Fig 35   Castle Rushen Stores, Pottery; Nos 10 and 11, Fifteenth- to Sixteenth-Century Saintonge, Nos 12–14, Sixteenth-Century Beauvais Sgraffito (Scale 1:1)

Cumbrian or south-western Scottish in origin, the majority of the sixteenth- and seventeenth-century pottery recovered from Castle Rushen Stores appears to have been made in the south Lancashire potteries.

Surrey: Surrey white wares

Twelve sherds from at least nine vessels are in Surrey white wares (*cf* Pearce and Vince 1988) [TUD]. They range from large and small jugs to lobed cups. Although sometimes difficult to distinguish from the Saintonge products of the same period, these sherds possess a more gritty fabric and lack the mica and angular red inclusions typical of the French centre. They are most likely to date from the sixteenth century.

Cumbria: northern reduced greenware (cf White 1977) (Fig 36)

Thirty-seven sherds from at least 21 storage vessels were found. This reduced, green-glazed ware [NRG], produced in a variety of centres in northern Britain, represents an extension of the medieval tradition in an area north of the Ribble in the west and Lincolnshire in the east. Production continued in Scotland as late as the nineteenth century. These examples were probably made in Cumbria or south-western Scotland in the sixteenth century.

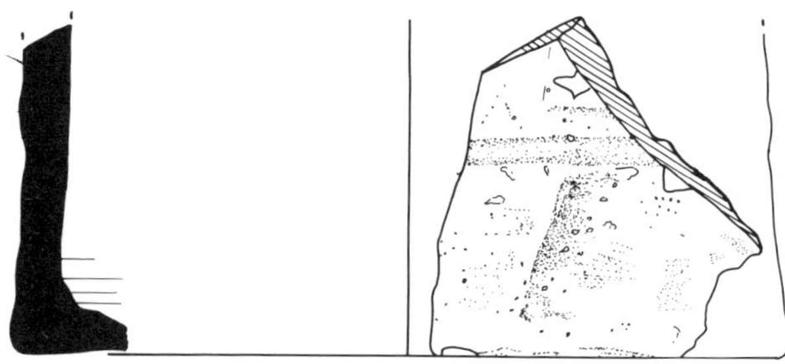

Fig 36 Castle Rushen Stores, Pottery; No 15, Sixteenth-Century Northern Reduced Greenware (Scale 1:2)

The English Midlands: Midland yellow ware (cf Woodfield 1966) [MYW] (Fig 37)

Five sherds from four vessels were found in this largely sixteenth-century ware from the English Midlands. They include a plate rim, the base of a bowl, a body sherd from a cup or posset pot, and a jar which is extensively sooted (Fig 37.16). This ware type seems to have inspired the south Lancashire potters who produced a similar, though technically inferior, product during the seventeenth century. None of the Castle Rushen Stores finds is from a sixteenth-century context.

The north-west of England: coarse earthenwares [CEW]

A small quantity of coarse gritty ware with patchy dark green glazes, often on a red slip, is present. These products, which are technically at the end of the medieval tradition, appear to have been made in the fifteenth and sixteenth century at a number of coal-measure based centres in the north-west, such as Ewloe, Clwyd (Harrison and Davey 1977), Prescot, Merseyside (Davey 1989) and, possibly, Whitehaven in Cumbria. They almost invariably represent large storage vessels and sometimes roof-furniture.

The 11 sherds from at least 10 vessels from Castle Rushen Stores include fragments of jug or pitcher-like forms and accord well with a sixteenth-century date for the main early activity on the site.

Coarse purplewares (cf Davey 1991, 126) [CPW] (Fig 37)

Thirty-nine sherds from as many as 24 vessels were found, all from large storage vessels (Fig 37.18). Although the sherds exhibit a range of wall thickness and skill in throwing, none of these finds is of sufficient quality to suggest an origin in the English Midlands. None is in the classic 'butter-pot' form and almost all are well glazed; a few have applied thumbed strip and incised line decoration. These characteristics suggest a north-western English origin for the majority of the wares. In some cases it is difficult to distinguish highly fired and partially reduced early dark wares, and it is probable that these products were made by the same potters.

Lead-glazed red earthenwares [LRE] (Fig 40)

Earthenwares with red bodies and clear glazes are relatively common on the site from the sixteenth to the nineteenth centuries. A total of 60 sherds from at least 37 vessels was recovered. The forms include jars (Fig 40.37–38), bung-hole pitchers (Fig 40.41), jugs (Fig 40.40) and more open vessels (Fig 40.39). Although a range of geographical origins is possible, most fabrics appear similar to north-west English types.

Dark-glazed wares [DRB] (Figs 42–47)

The largest group of finds from the north-west consists of both coarse and fine dark-glazed red earthenwares from sixteenth and seventeenth century contexts. These are very similar to material excavated in south Lancashire, particularly in Prescot and very probably derive from that area (Philpott 1985a, 1989). The types are similar to the Cistercian wares excavated on kiln sites in west

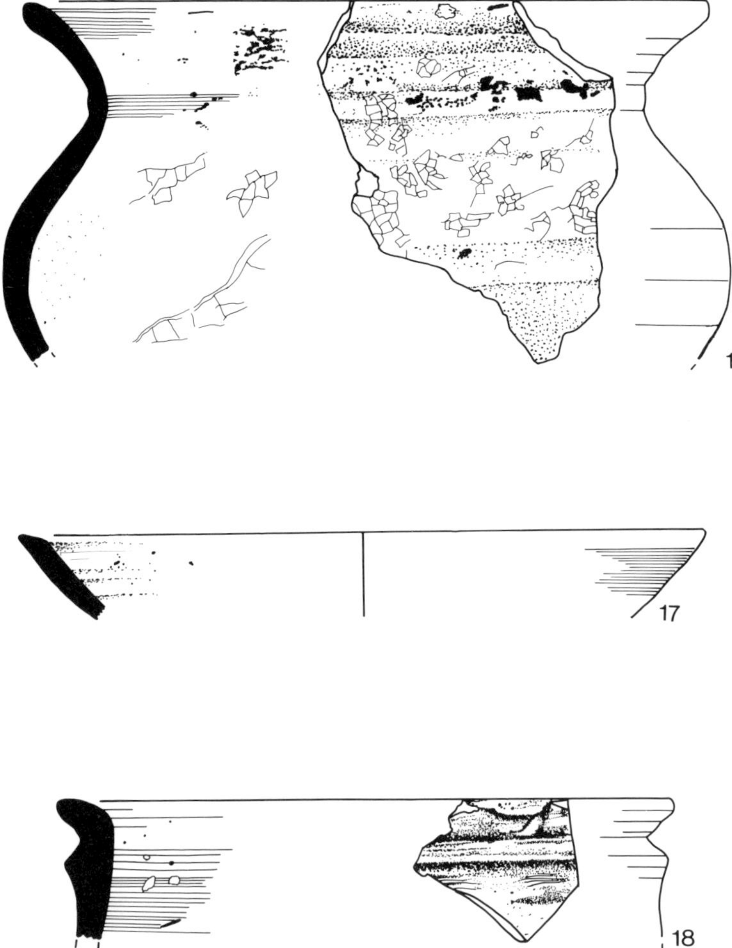

Fig 37   Castle Rushen Stores, Pottery; Nos 16–18, Sixteenth-Century Midland Yellow and Purple Ware (Scale 1:2)

Yorkshire (Brears 1967; Bartlett, Brears and Moorhouse 1971; Moorhouse and Roberts 1992, 189), but seem to constitute a north-western sub-type. From the 1500s onwards, increasing amounts of colorant were added to the glaze so that the appearance of the pottery steadily approached black. A number of centres continued to produce this ware type until the twentieth century. The divisions used here between, for example, sixteenth- and seventeenth-century examples are to a certain extent arbitrary, particularly as a technological continuum is involved. The formal distinctions established at the Wrenthorpe kiln site have been used as a guide, coupled with an assessment of the stage of development represented by the glazes involved. Castle Rushen Stores has produced the most significant group of these wares so far recovered from the Isle of Man. They include fine cups (Fig 42), a few with yellow slip decoration, and a suite of storage vessels of differing sizes (Figs 43–47). Their regular association in Castletown with other British and continental sixteenth-century wares generally confirms the estimated 'technological' date.

THE SEVENTEENTH-CENTURY BRITISH IMPORTS

There is no evidence for insular pottery production at this period. The ceramic material from Castle Rushen Stores is derived from a range of sources. First, there is a small group of north Devon wares, second, some material probably derived from the English Midlands and third, a large group from the north-west of England. With the exception of the two Westerwald stoneware sherds (Fig 51), there is no obvious continental influence.

The north-west of England: seventeenth-century Rainford-type wares (cf Davey 1991, 127–28, Fig 5)

A range of inter-locking ware types was almost certainly produced somewhere on the south Lancashire coalfield. Although the mid-seventeenth-century kiln group from Rainford provides the type site for most of these, wasters using similar production technologies have been found over a wide

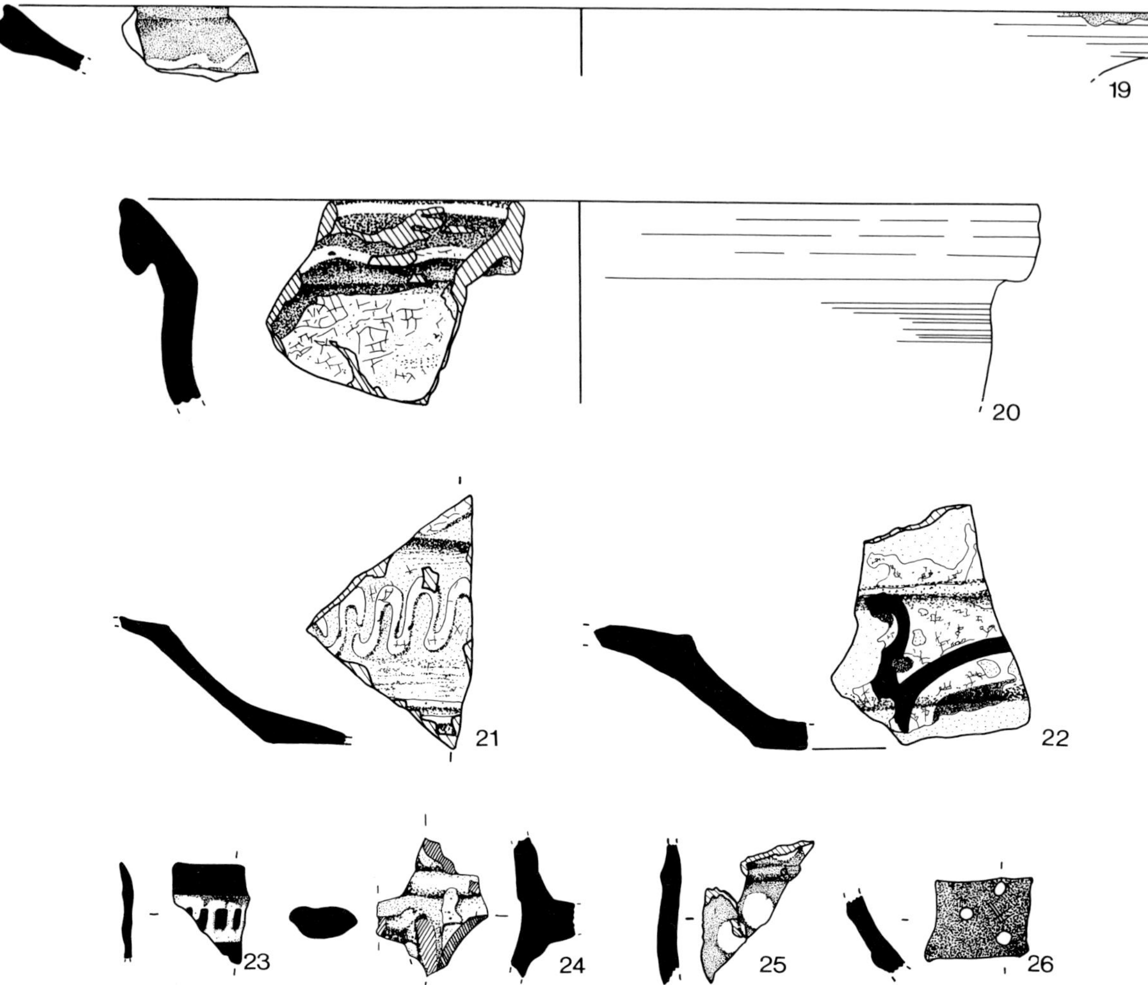

Fig 38 Castle Rushen Stores, Pottery; Nos 19–26, Sixteenth- to Eighteenth-Century Trailed Slipware (Scale 1:2)

geographical area (Davey 1991, 127). The buff-bodied, lead-glazed 'yellow ware' [RYW] seems to be a seventeenth-century attempt to reproduce Midlands Yellow. Wares with dark pink and red bodies, including those with a simple lead glaze or 'lead-glazed red earthenware' [LRE], those with a colouring impurity or additive in the body—the 'speckled wares' [RSP]—and those which have significant additive in the glaze itself, the so-called 'dark wares' [DRB], all appear to have been produced by the same industry.

The dark-glazed wares [DRB] (Figs 46 and 47)

The 'dark-glazed' wares are the most numerous and include a wide range of storage vessels as well as tablewares. Most distinctive is a tyg form with a multifaceted stem, known from the Rainford kiln site and apparently diagnostic of south Lancashire production (Fig 43.62; Davey 1991, 127, Fig 6).

Rainford-type speckled and yellow wares [RSP; RYW] (Fig 41)

Twenty-eight sherds of speckled ware from at least 14 vessels were found; all are bowls (Fig 41.42–44). The yellow ware, with only 12 sherds from five vessels, is more varied, including cups or posset pots as well as bowls.

Thrown slipwares [RST] (Fig 38)

Thirty-five sherds from at least 18 vessels were found. A wide range of types is present. These include a number of bowls with trailed decoration around the inside (Fig 38.19, 21, 22). This is a common find in Civil War deposits at Peel Castle (Davey forthcoming) and at Beeston Castle, Cheshire (Noake 1993, 197–99, Nos 88–89, 98–107). A number of more crude products may be from Buckley in Clwyd (Fig 38.20). The finds from Castletown also include a few slip-trailed hollow-wares (Fig 38.24–26). A production centre for these

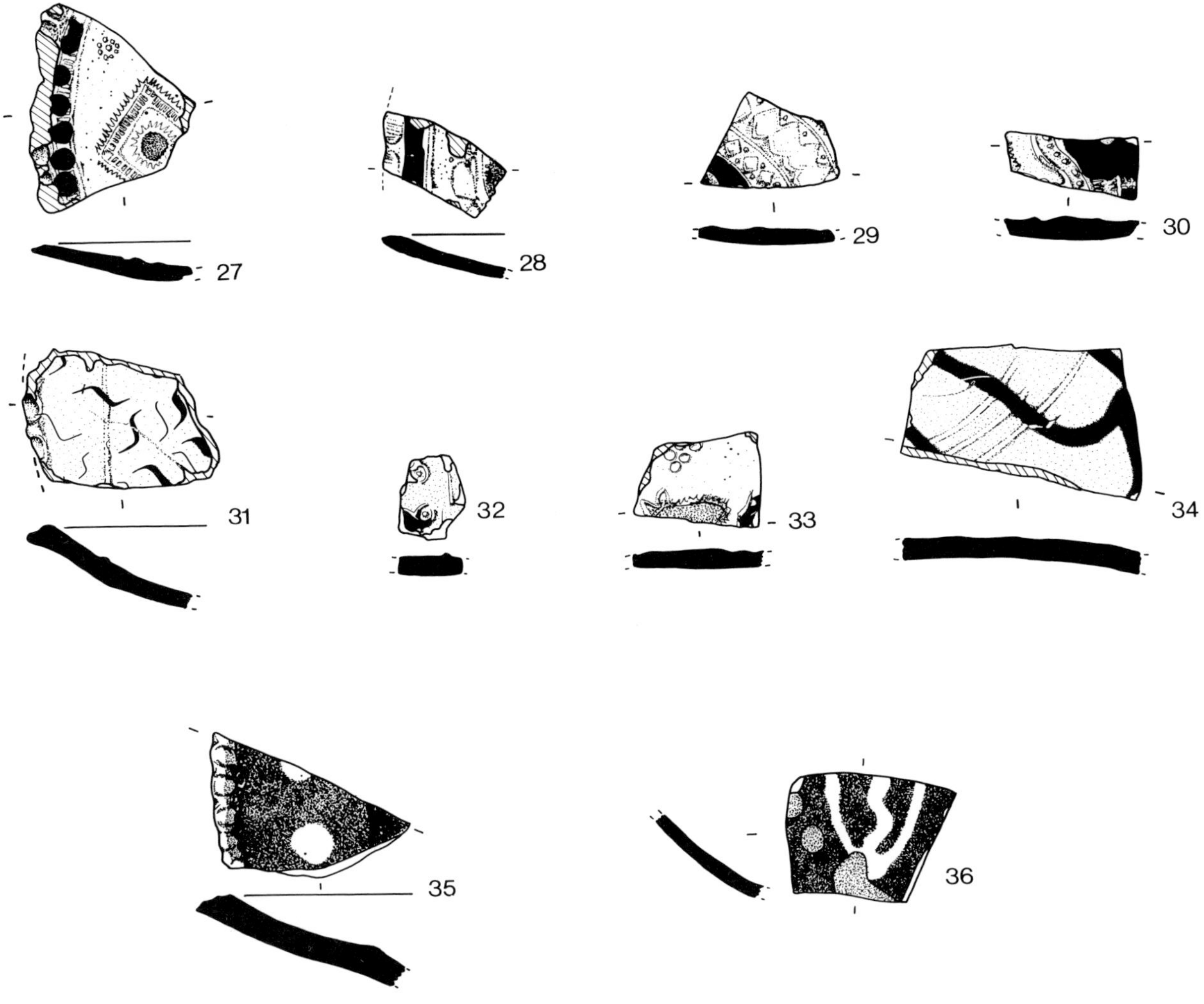

Fig 39 Castle Rushen Stores, Pottery; Nos 27–36, Seventeenth- to Eighteenth-Century Press-moulded Slipware (Scale 1:2)

wares has not so far been identified, but their distribution suggests the north-west of England.

Hollow 'reversed' slipware [HRS] (Fig 38)

Eight sherds were recovered from four vessels. These consist of fineware cups in which a buff body is coated with dark slip and then decorated with yellow trailing (Fig 38.23). This type also occurs in Civil War deposits in England (Noake 1993, 197–99, Nos 91, 108). These were probably made in the English Midlands.

Press-moulded slipwares [PMS] (Fig 39)

The site also produced a small collection of press-moulded slipwares, consisting of 35 sherds from a minimum of 18 vessels.

It includes a number of small embossed plates (Fig 39.27–30, 32–33) which may date from the late seventeenth century, as well as the more usual trailed and feathered eighteenth-century examples (Fig 39.31, 34). They were probably made in a range of centres in western and north-western England, the English Midlands and north Wales.

Press-moulded reversed slipware [PRS] (Fig 39)

Three sherds from two 'reversed' slipware plates were found (Fig 39.35–36). These probably date from the eighteenth century. The production centre for these wares is not known.

Liverpool: tin-glazed earthenware [TGE] (Fig 48)

A majority of the finds are plates (Fig 48.96–98, 100), with a few bowls (Fig 48.95, 99) and at least two *albarelli* (Fig 48.102). The *albarelli* may be London or Low Countries in origin and appear to be seventeenth-century in date. The majority of the remaining sherds have a pale 'duck-egg blue' glaze, which is typical of the eighteenth-century Liverpool potteries.

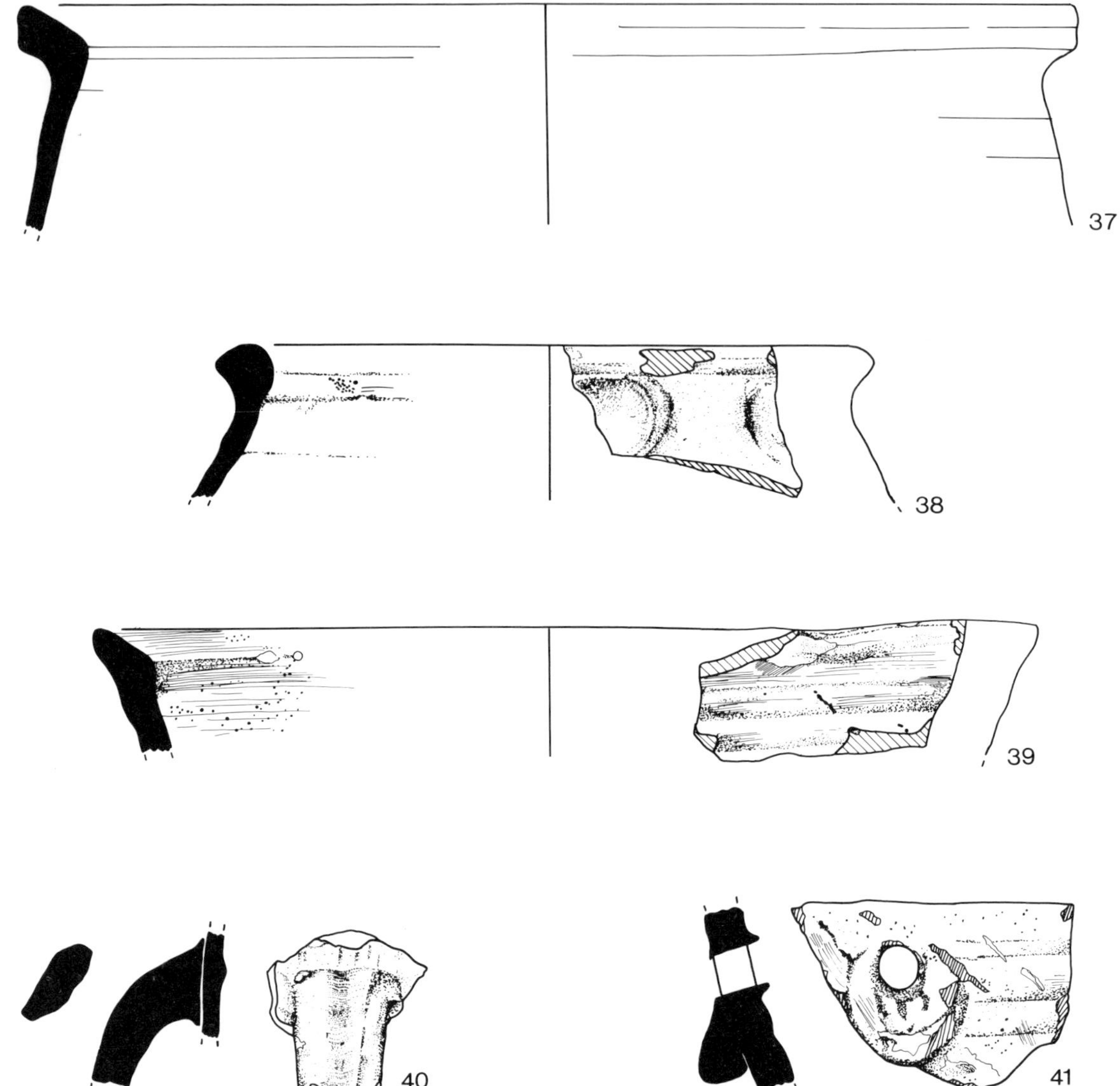

Fig 40   Castle Rushen Stores, Pottery; Nos 37–41, Sixteenth- to Seventeenth-Century Lead-glazed Red-bodied Earthenware (Scale 1:2)

North Devon: the north Devon wares
(cf *Watkins 1960; Evans 1979; Grant 1983)*
(Figs 49 and 50)

Four main types of north Devon products are represented: gravel-tempered ware [NDG], smoothware [NSM], slipware [NSL] and sgraffito [NSG]. The largest group consists of 39 sherds from a minimum of 13 vessels in gravel-tempered ware. This consists of straight-sided bowl fragments (Fig 49.103–05) and plates (Fig 49.108–09), together with a small cup (Fig 49.106). Seven sherds of smoothware were found, all of which appear to be from internally glazed jars (Fig 49.110). In addition there are fragments of two sgraffito plates (Fig 50.111–12) and the body sherd of a slipware jug. Although the majority were probably made during the seventeenth century, almost all are from eight-

eenth- and nineteenth-century contexts. In general, the Castle Rushen Stores finds repeat the range of north Devon products which were found at Peel Castle in the Civil War deposits. The two sgraffito sherds are the first recovered from the Isle of Man.

STONEWARES

German stonewares (Fig 51)

Five sherds from at least four German stoneware drinking mugs were also found. One of these is probably from Cologne [CSW], two from Raeren [RSW] and the fourth, in two sherds, from Wester-wald [WES] (Fig 51.113–14; Hurst, Neale and Van Beuningen 1986, 176–225). With the exception of the latter, these are of sixteenth-century date.

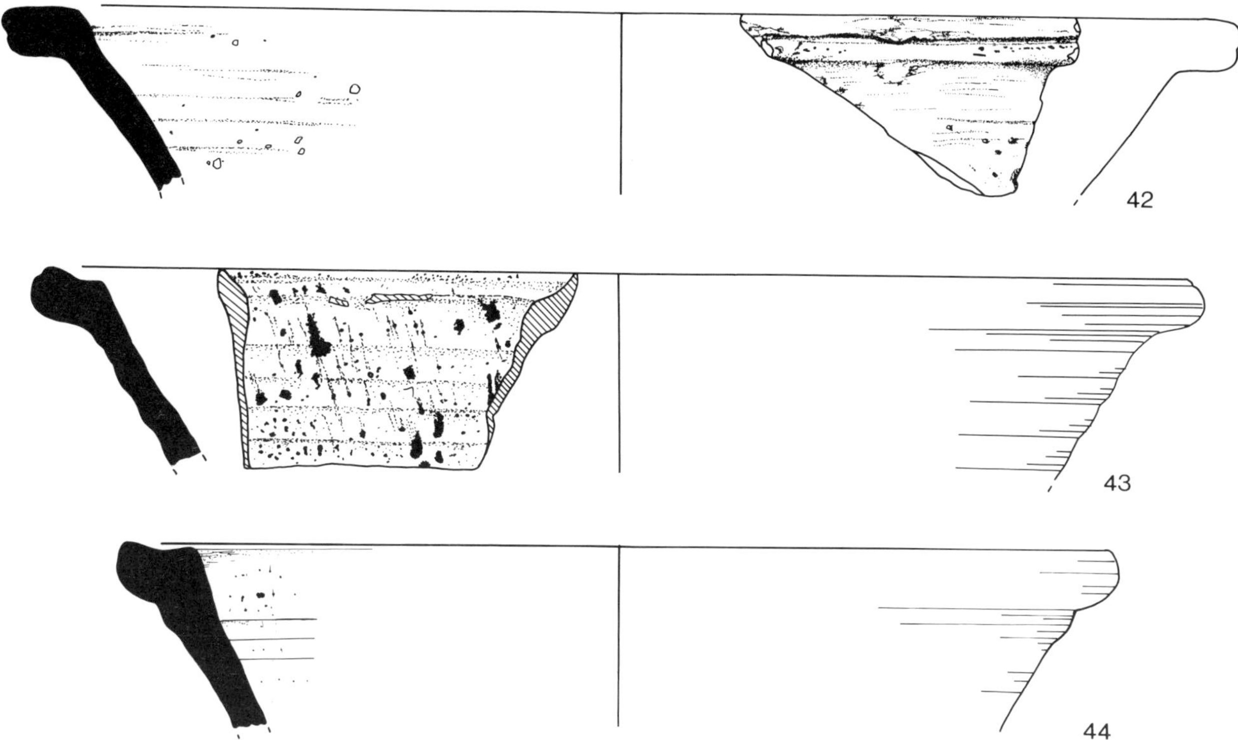

Fig 41   Castle Rushen Stores, Pottery; Nos 42–44, Seventeenth-Century Rainford-type Speckled Ware (Scale 1:2)

Summary

The excavations at Castle Rushen Stores have prouced the largest groups of sixteenth- and seventeenth-century pottery from the Isle of Man. They have established that the inhabitants of Castletown in the sixteenth century used a wide range of ceramic vessels for a variety of purposes. The changes in table manners which characterise the end of the medieval period seem to have arrived on the island at much the same time as in neighbouring areas of England. The move to the use of fine drinking vessels and tablewares, mostly made in the north-west of England but including significant quantities from northern and south-western France, seems to have occurred at some time before 1500. For dairy and kitchen purposes, locally made granite-tempered ware was still in widespread use.

In the seventeenth century, local wares disappear and the pottery assemblage is almost indistinguishable from that recovered in any town in the north-west of England. The rather high quantities of north Devon products are really the only exception to this. It must be assumed that by the middle of the seventeenth century, the Stanleys had brought the island very substantially into their south Lancashire economic orbit.

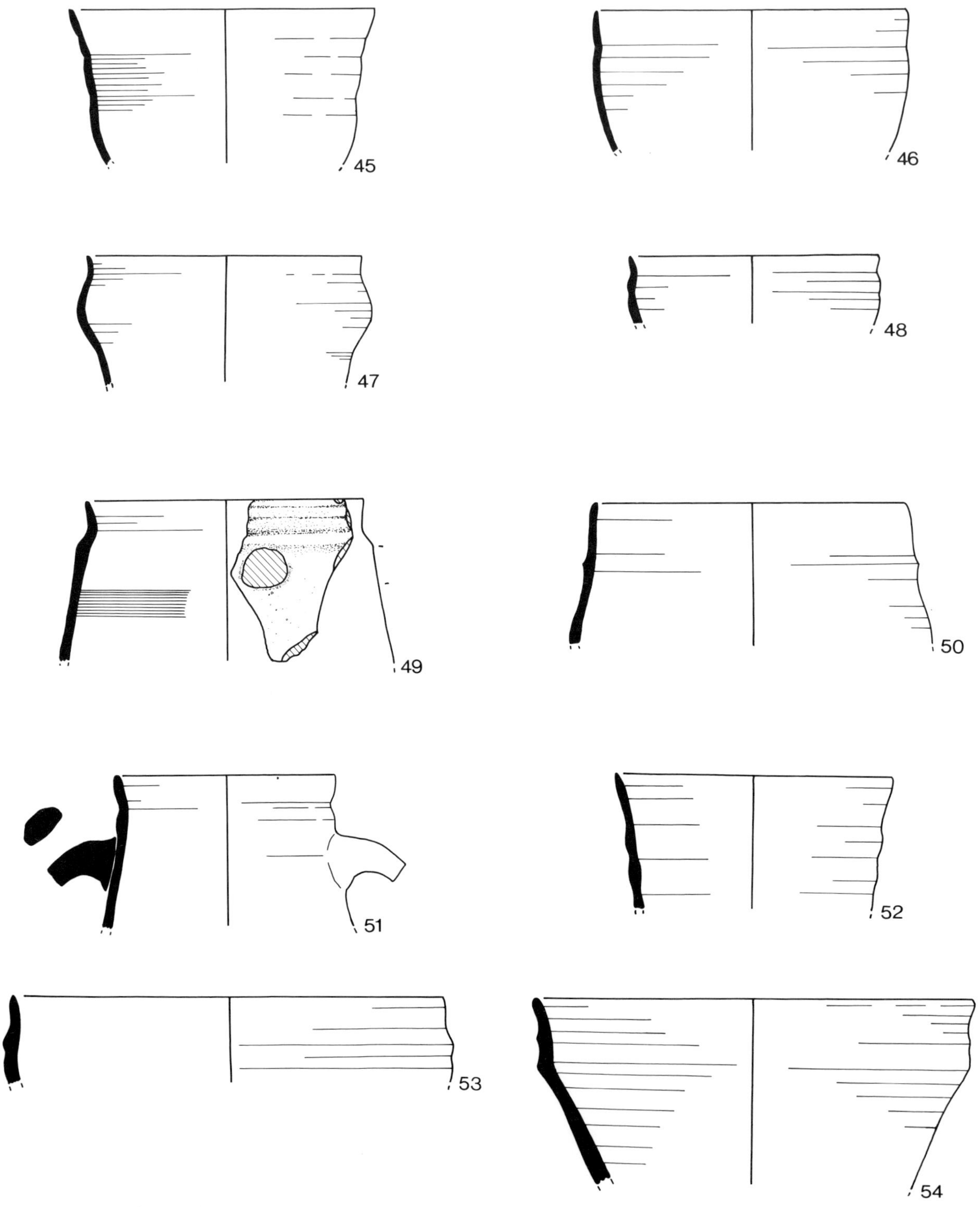

Fig 42   Castle Rushen Stores, Pottery; Nos 45–54, Sixteenth- to Seventeenth-Century Dark-glazed Red-bodied Fine Earthenware (Scale 1:2)

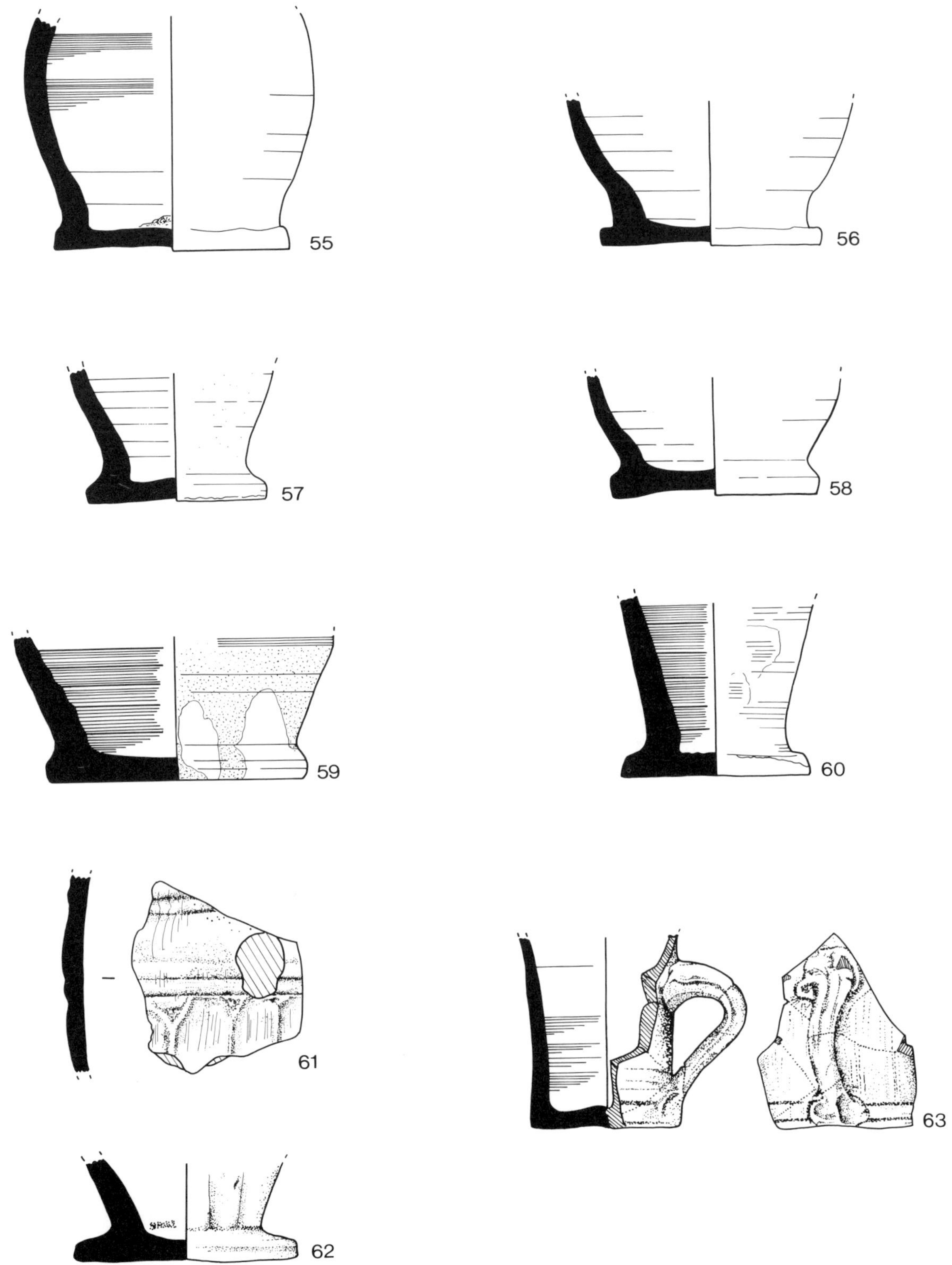

Fig 43   Castle Rushen Stores, Pottery; Nos 55–63, Sixteenth- to Seventeenth-Century Dark-glazed Red-bodied Earthenware (Scale 1:2)

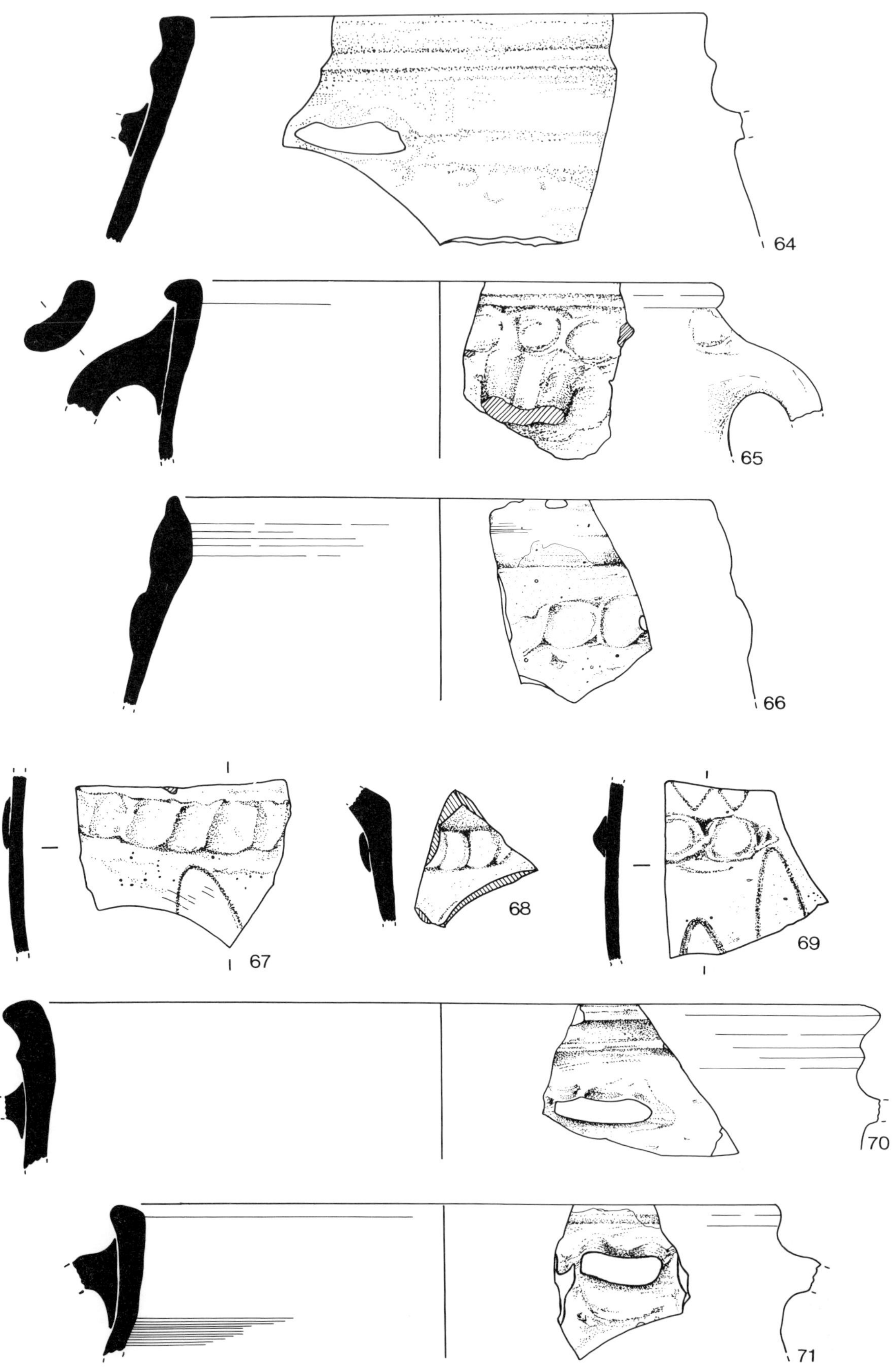

Fig 44 Castle Rushen Stores, Pottery; Nos 64–71, Sixteenth- to Seventeenth-Century Dark-glazed Red-bodied Earthenware (Scale 1:2)

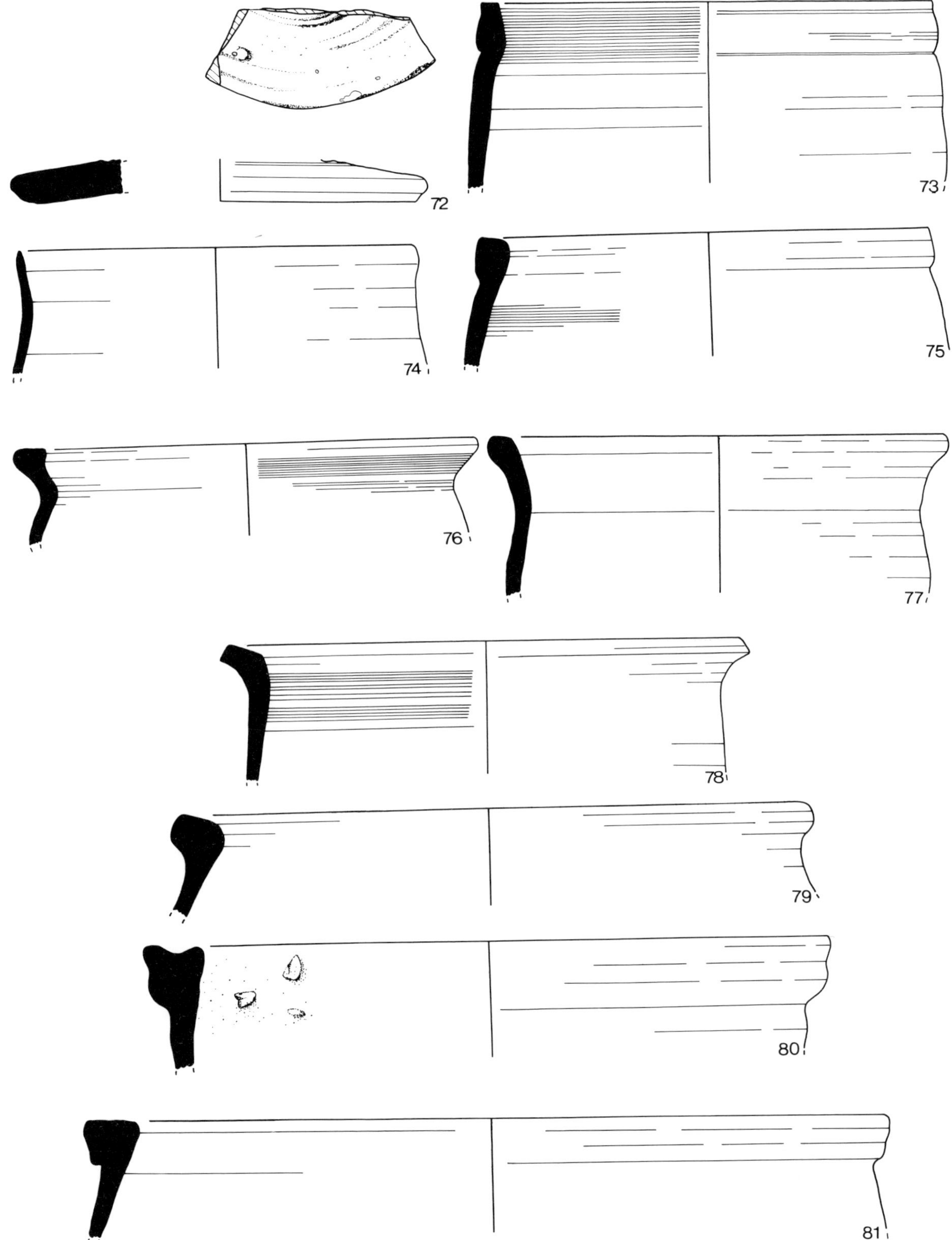

Fig 45   Castle Rushen Stores, Pottery; Nos 72–81, Sixteenth- to Seventeenth-Century Dark-glazed Red-bodied Earthenware (Scale 1:2)

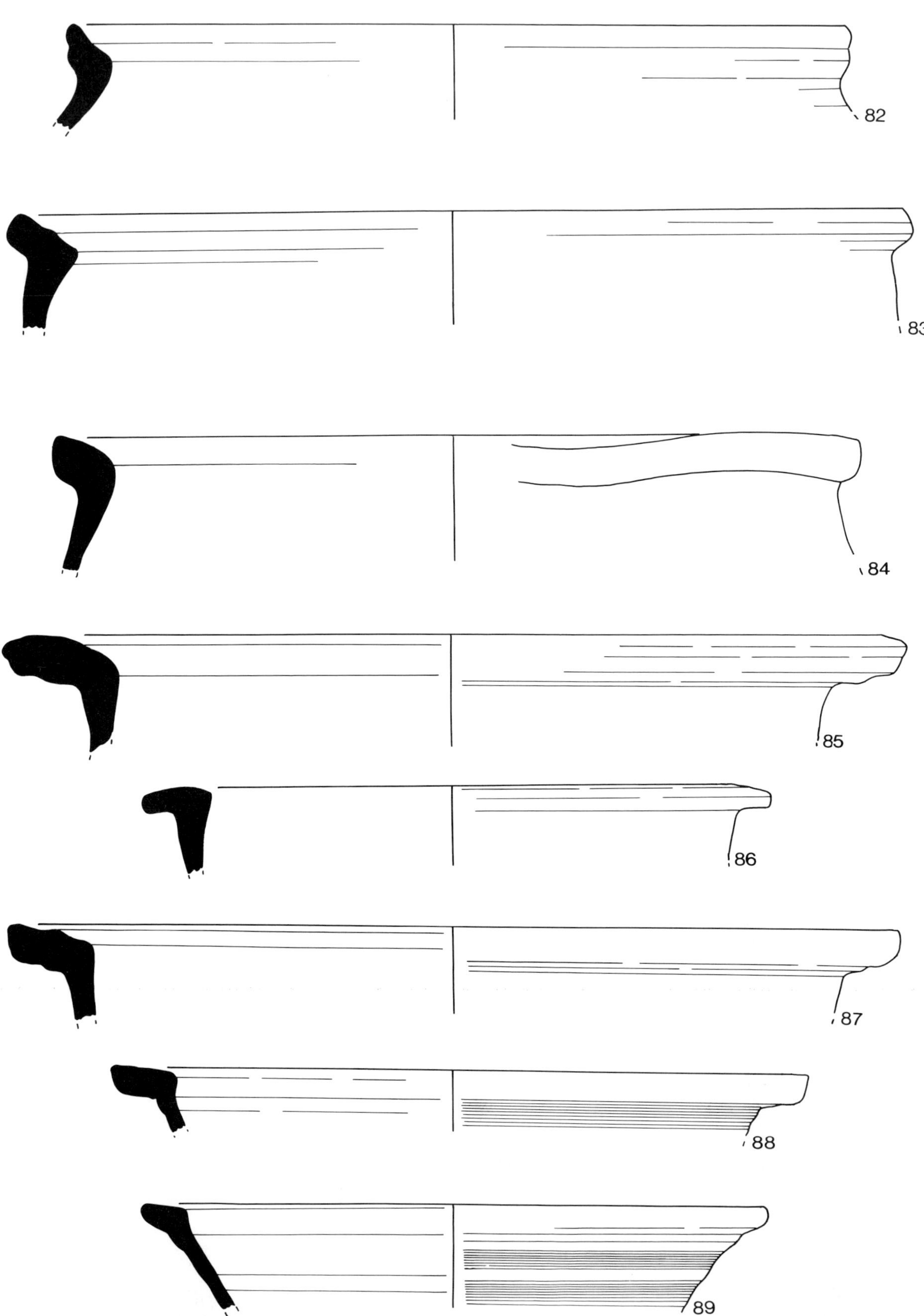

Fig 46   Castle Rushen Stores, Pottery; Nos 82–89, Sixteenth- to Seventeenth-Century Dark-glazed Red-bodied Earthenware (Scale 1:2)

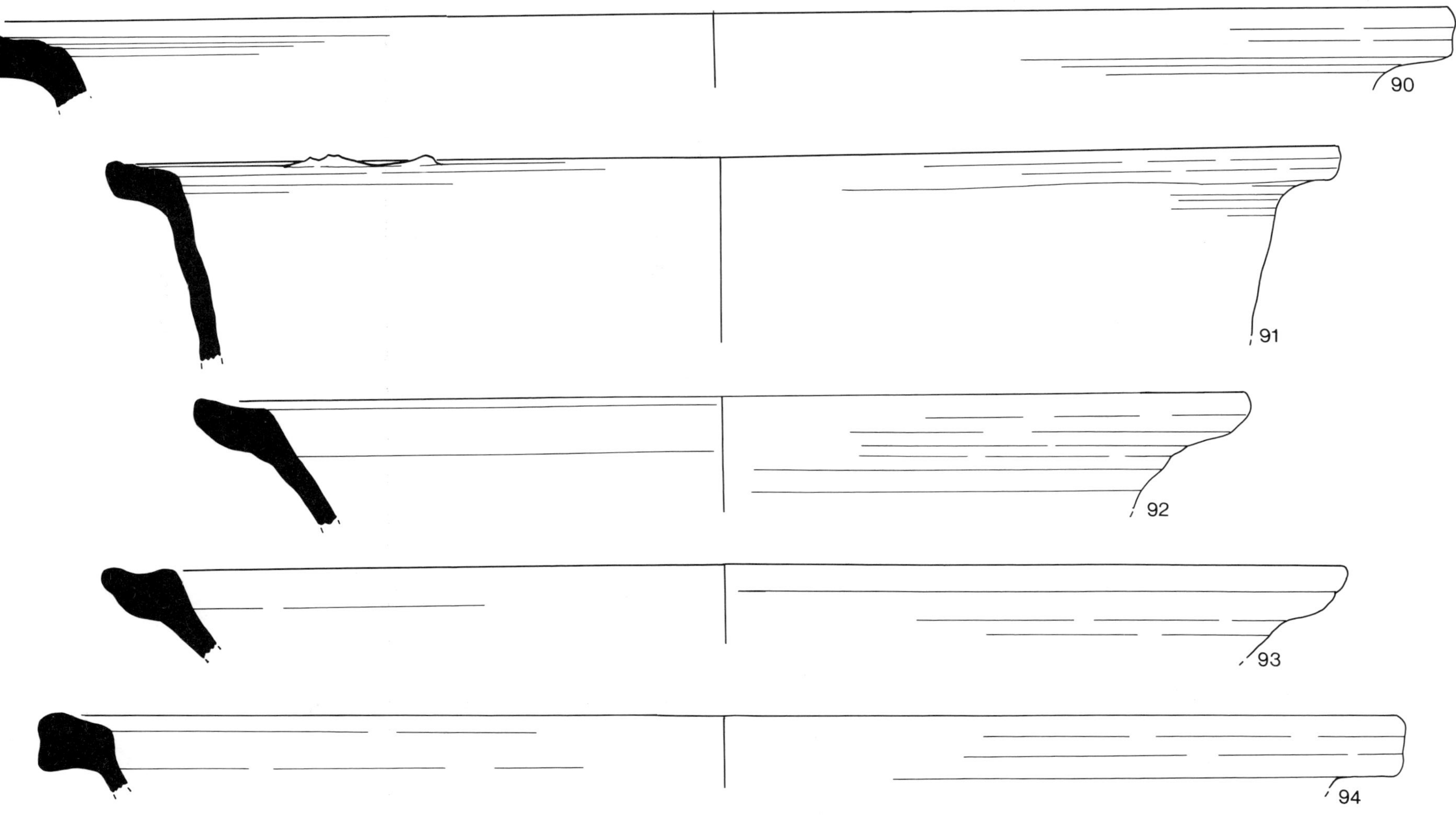

Fig 47 Castle Rushen Stores, Pottery; Nos 90–94, Sixteenth- to Seventeenth-Century Dark-glazed Red-bodied Earthenware (Scale 1:2)

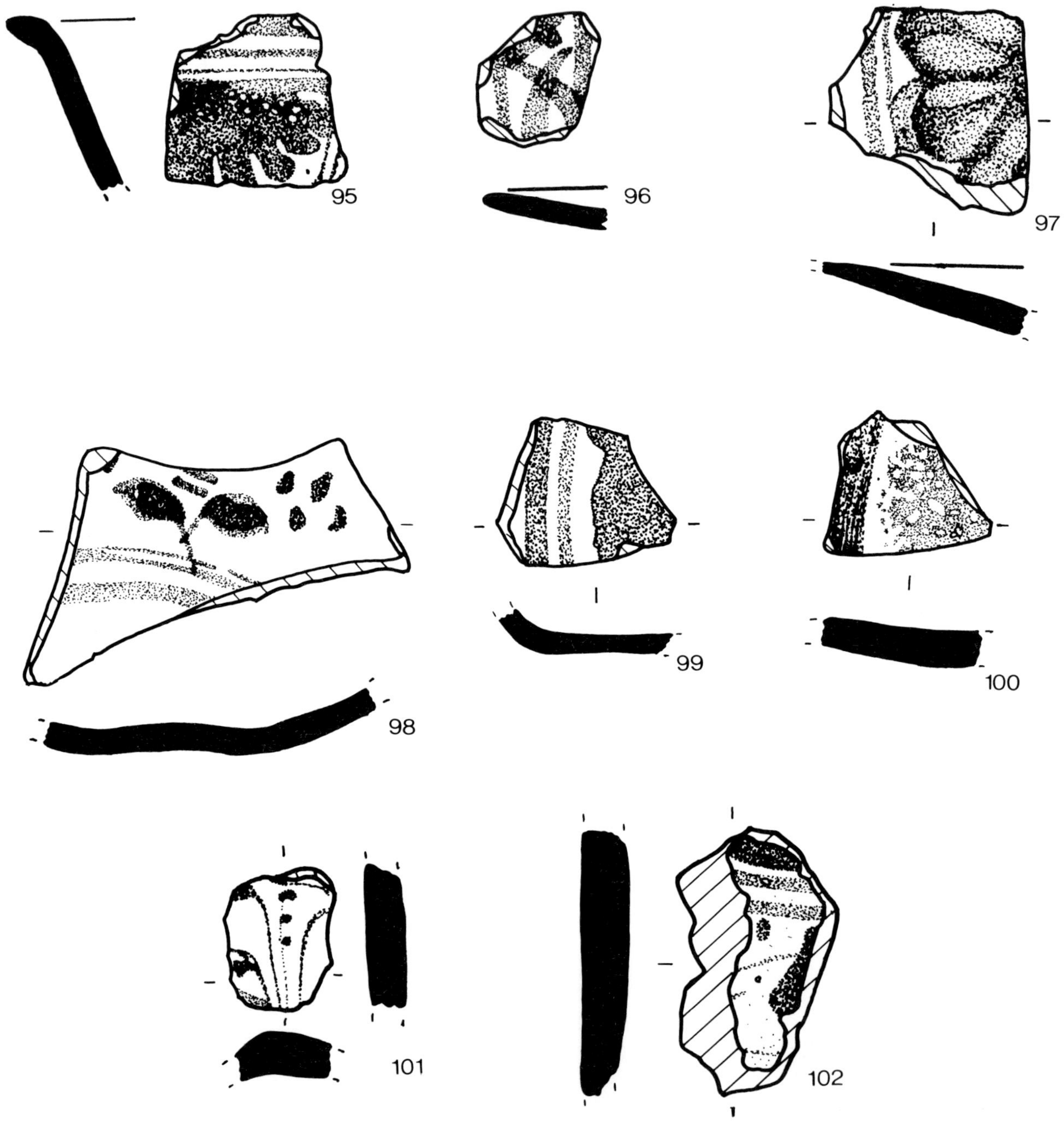

Fig 48   Castle Rushen Stores, Pottery; Nos 95–102, Eighteenth-Century Tin-glazed Earthenware (Scale 1:1)

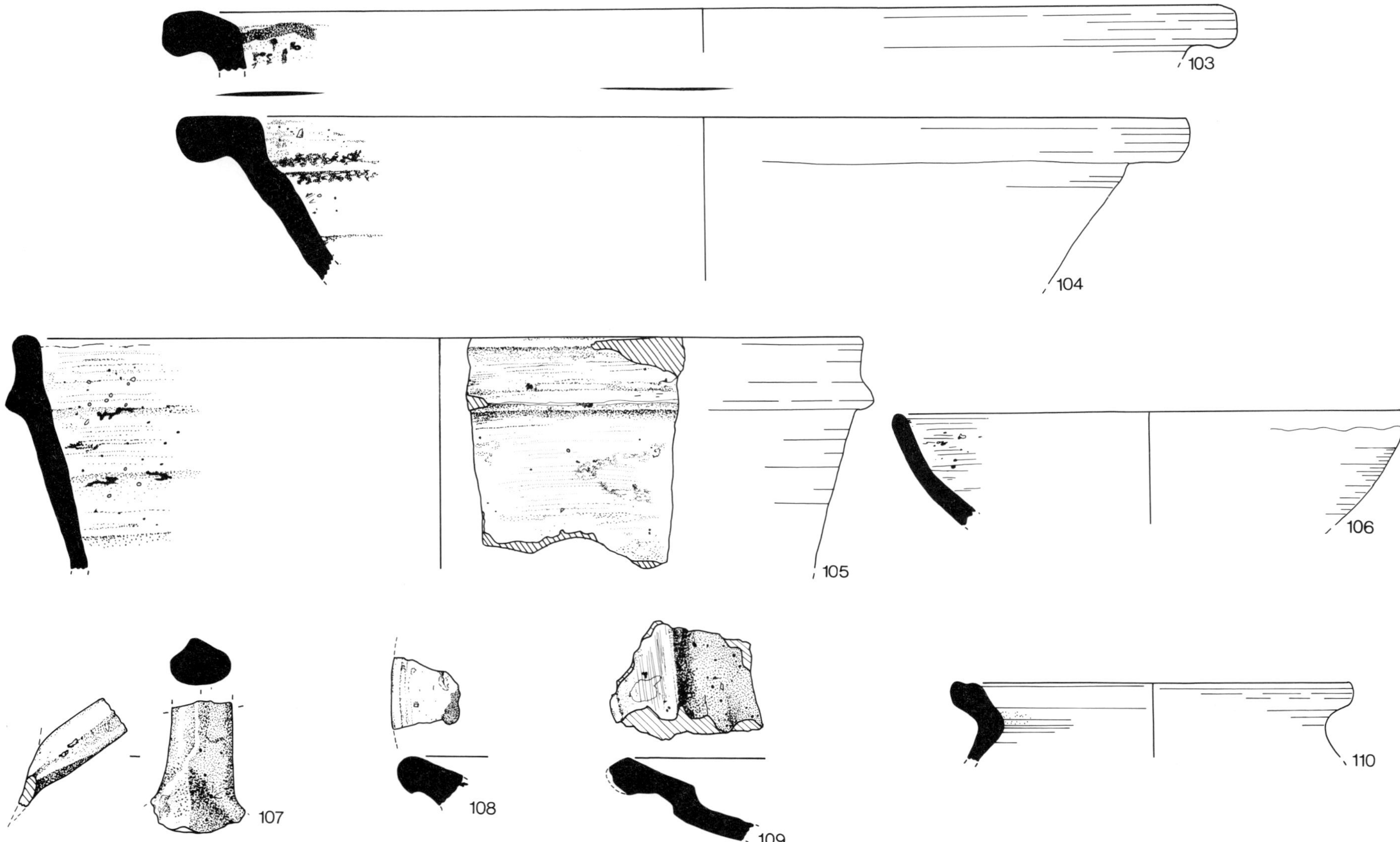

Fig 49   Castle Rushen Stores, Pottery; Nos 103–109, Seventeenth-Century North Devon Gravel-Tempered Ware, No 110, Seventeenth-Century North Devon Smoothware (Scale 1:2)

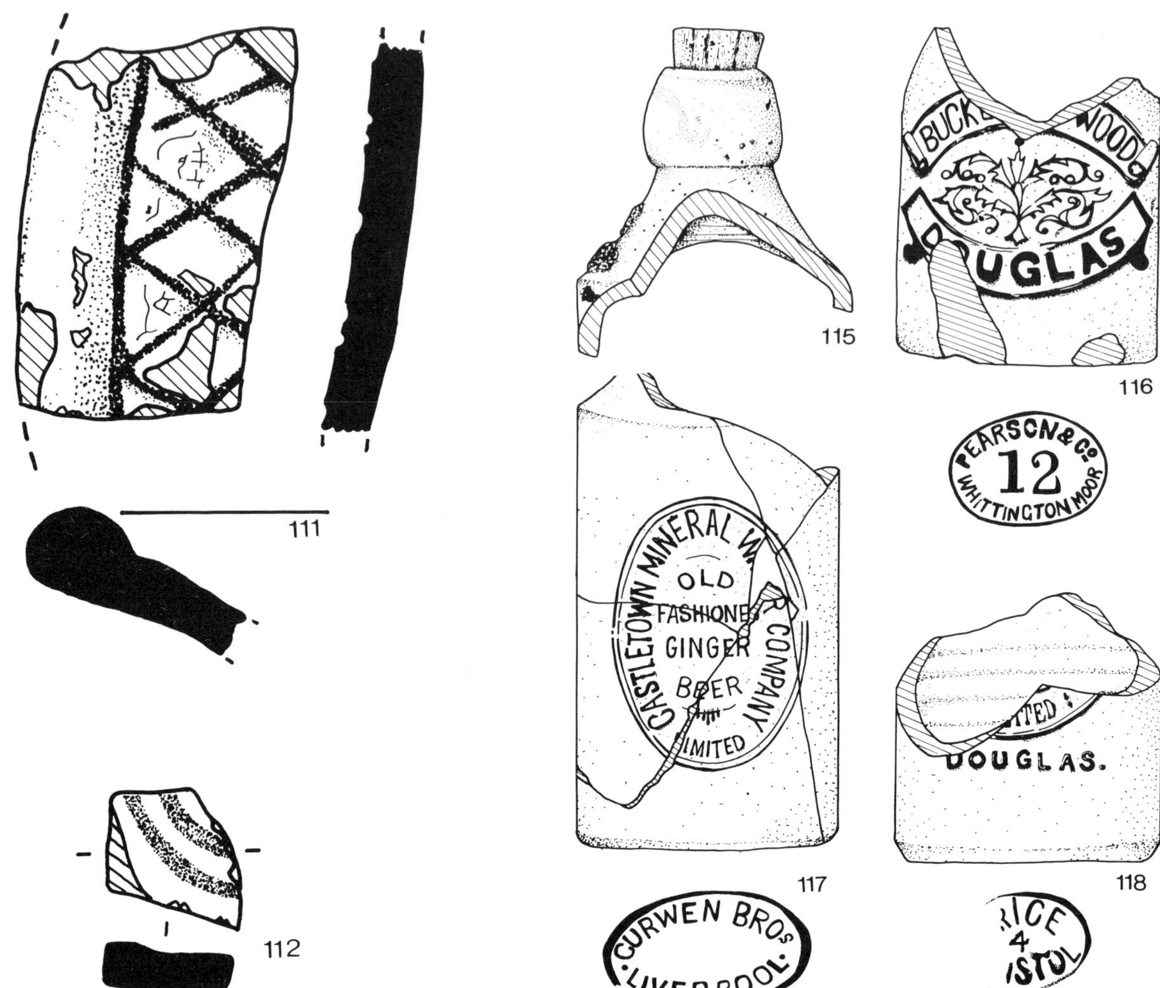

Fig 50   Castle Rushen Stores, Pottery; Nos 111 and
112, Seventeenth-Century North Devon Sgraffito
(Scale 1:1)

Fig 52   Castle Rushen Stores, Pottery; Nos 115–118,
White Stoneware Bottles (Scale 1:2) and Stamps
(Scale 1:1)

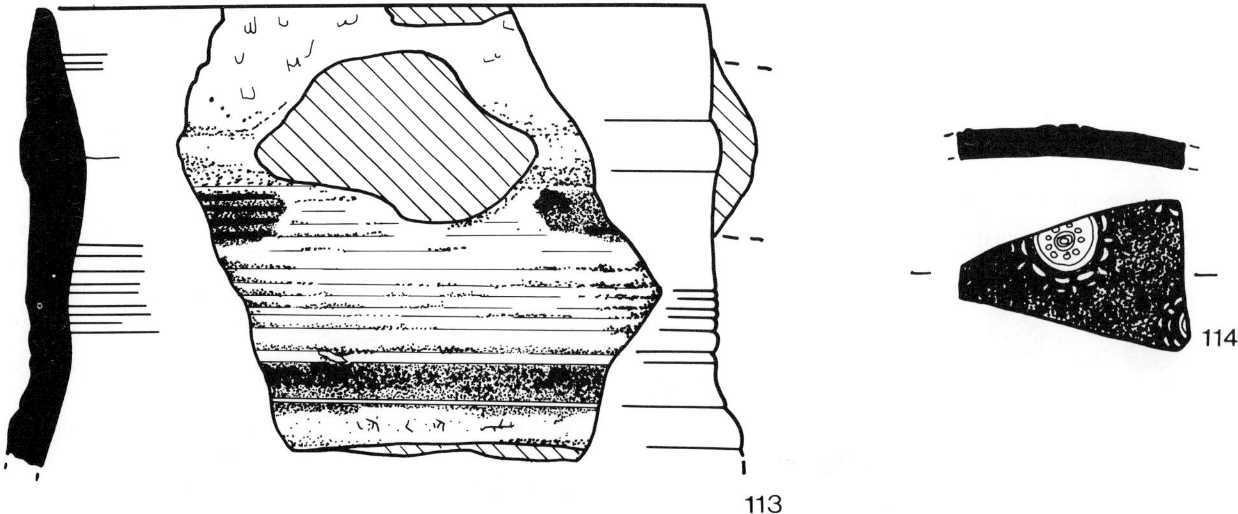

Fig 51   Castle Rushen Stores, Pottery; Nos 113 and 114, Seventeenth-Century Westerwald Stoneware
(Scale 1:1)

Floor Tiles (Fig 53)

D A Higgins

Nine fragments of floor tiles, three plain and six decorated, were recovered from the excavations. All of the pieces are rather small and battered and all were derived from garden soils of seventeenth-century or later date. Most of the pieces show clear evidence of wear and so must represent a floor or floors which were broken up and the pieces scattered, probably during the seventeenth century.

Although all of the fragments recovered came from 92.103 they did not seem to be evenly distributed across the trench. One piece of plain tile was found in Context 93, a garden soil to the west of the boundary bank (100), that is, in the garden of the Arbory Street property. Another piece of plain tile was found in a garden soil (90) to the north of a possible boundary bank (87). The date and nature of this boundary are not as well defined as the boundary bank (100), but this deposit would certainly have been in the garden of a Malew Street rather than an Arbory Street property.

All of the remaining pieces came from the garden soils to the south of the possible bank (87) and east of the main boundary bank (100). This area would have been the bottom of a property fronting onto Malew Street and it may have been a different property to that containing Context 90. Some 35–40 square metres of this plot were excavated, about half of the total trench area, and yet it produced seven out of the nine fragments of floor tile, including all of the decorated pieces. A similar area of the adjoining Malew Street property to the south was examined in Trench 92.104, but this did not produce any fragments of floor tile at all. It seems clear that the floor tiles are particularly associated with the Malew Street property at the eastern end of Trench 92.103.

Fabric

All of the tiles are made of a very similar fabric, the slight differences in two of them probably being no more than the result of firing conditions or subsequent burning. They are made of a rather soft, sandy fabric which has oxidised to a light orange colour throughout. The body contains occasional grits and stones up to *c*10mm in size, and occasional voids where small pieces of vegetable matter have burnt out. One of the plain tiles (89) has a rather redder fabric with a grey reduced base. One of the decorated tiles (Fig 53.2) has a rather mottled body of orange with patches of grey, particularly towards the base. It may have been burnt after it was broken.

Glaze

All of the fragments have the remains of glaze on the upper surface and, in the case of two of the plain tiles, of glaze splashes on the underside as well. Where the glaze has fused properly it is transparent with a slight greenish tint, but it appears slightly orange due to the body beneath. In several cases, however, the glaze does not appear to have fused properly, leaving a rather dull opaque surface of olive-green or whitish colour. Two of the plain tiles have a particularly greenish glaze which may have been achieved by adding some copper to the basic lead glaze.

Production

All of the tiles have a simple flat back without any trace of keying. The sides are knife cut, with a slight bevel to facilitate tight joints at the surface. Four of the decorated tiles had measurable thicknesses: 31, 31, 36 and 37mm. The three plain tiles have thicknesses of 36, 37 and 42mm. In general terms thicker tiles tend to be later in date and particularly thick examples, such as the third of the plain ones, are typical of sixteenth-century products.

Decoration (Fig 53.1–6)

At least three and probably four different patterns are represented by the six decorated pieces recovered. In each of these the pattern is line-impressed or relief-moulded and without the use of slip inlay.

1   Edge fragment of tile, 31mm thick, decorated with part of a boldly executed oak leaf pattern (5). This design is well known from Rushen Abbey, where numerous examples have been found (Jewitt 1885, Kermode and Herdman 1914, Butler 1988). A reconstruction of the full tile has been published by Butler (1988, Fig 13.9) who dates it to the fifteenth century. Brotherton-Ratcliffe (forthcoming) has recorded examples of this pattern from the Dominican friary in Chester.

2   Central fragment of a tile, 31mm thick, decorated with two parallel lines flanked on either side by further decoration. Faint traces where the glaze has flaked away suggest a lobed central pattern. There may also have been some form of decorative motif between the two

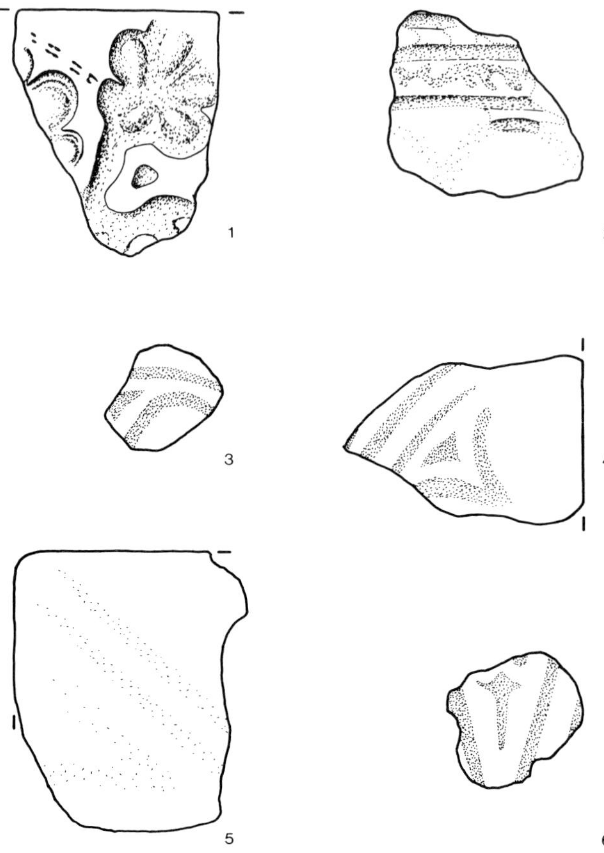

Fig 53 Castle Rushen Stores, Floor Tiles (Scale 1:2)

6 Small fragment of incomplete thickness which appears to be from a similar but different design to Fig 53.3–5 above. The converging lines appear to be from a lobed pattern, but in this case enclosing a decorative motif which the previous ones lacked. Also, the angle of these lines suggests a design with 12 segments rather than 8. No parallel from the island can be found for such a design (98).

Discussion

The absence of inlaid tiles, the use of line-impressed or relief decoration and the presence of some quite thick plain tiles, all suggest that this is a relatively late group, probably dating from the fifteenth or early sixteenth centuries. By far the largest collection of tiles from the island comes from Rushen Abbey at Ballasalla, some 3km to the north-north-east of Castletown. At least two of the decorative types can be paralleled there. Tiles were also found in 1905 on the floor of a former chapel in the north tower of Castle Rushen. These were of the same types as those found at the abbey and were presumed to have come from there (Kermode and Herdman 1914, 117). Although possible, this need not have been the case, since Castle Rushen was the administrative centre of the island and was owned by the Lords of Man. As such, it may well have been furnished with tiles in its own right. There are also some secular buildings, such as Bagnio House in Arbory Street ('The Lord's Bath House' in the Manorial Roll of 1511), which might conceivably have had tiled floors.

There are clearly a number of known or possible sources from which these tiles could have come. It is not known what sort of building occupied the Malew Street plot during the fifteenth to seventeenth centuries. It is just possible that it was an important secular building with its own tiled floors, but it seems more likely that the tiles were brought to this property, for whatever reason, from elsewhere.

The tiles themselves can be paralleled with examples from Ireland, Wales and England and show that the Isle of Man was keeping abreast of developments in the material and design of flooring during the fifteenth and sixteenth centuries.

Clay and Briar Tobacco Pipes

D A Higgins

The 1991 and 1992 excavations produced a total of 309 pieces of clay tobacco pipe consisting of 41 bowl, 255 stem and 13 mouthpiece fragments. Two

parallel lines (55). The curve of these lines suggests that this formed part of a 16-tile composition. Only one other fragment from a 16-tile composition appears to be known from the island (Butler 1988, Fig 13.6), but insufficient of this example survives to be able to tell whether it is the same.

3–5 Three examples, probably from tiles of the same design (89, 89, 36). The first two examples are 37mm and 36mm thick respectively; the third is in a very poor state of preservation and the thickness cannot be determined. The complete pattern has been reconstructed by Jewitt (1885, Fig 4) and would have consisted, when laid, of double lined lozenges surrounding double lined circles, within which were octofoils. The spandrels were filled with a sexfoil flower and foliage. Butler (1988, 92) dates this design to the fifteenth century and quotes parallels from Rievaulx, Chester and Valle Crucis; Campbell (1986, Fig 8) illustrates a similar design from Drogheda in Ireland. Brotherton-Ratcliffe (forthcoming) notes that the design on these tiles was originally in very high relief but that, in a worn condition, they look like line-impressed tiles.

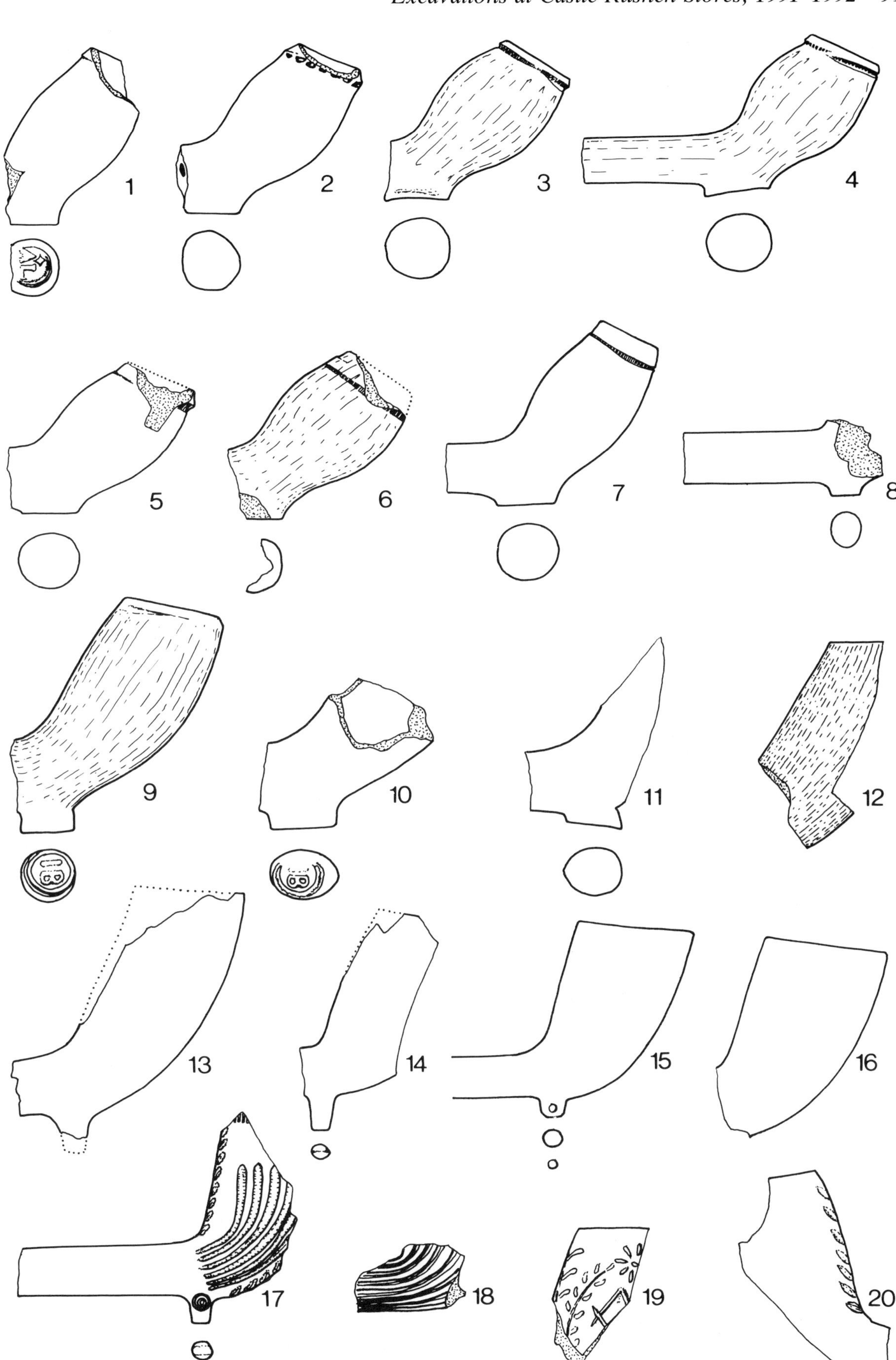

Fig 54   Castle Rushen Stores, Clay Tobacco Pipes; Nos 1–20 (Scale 1:1)

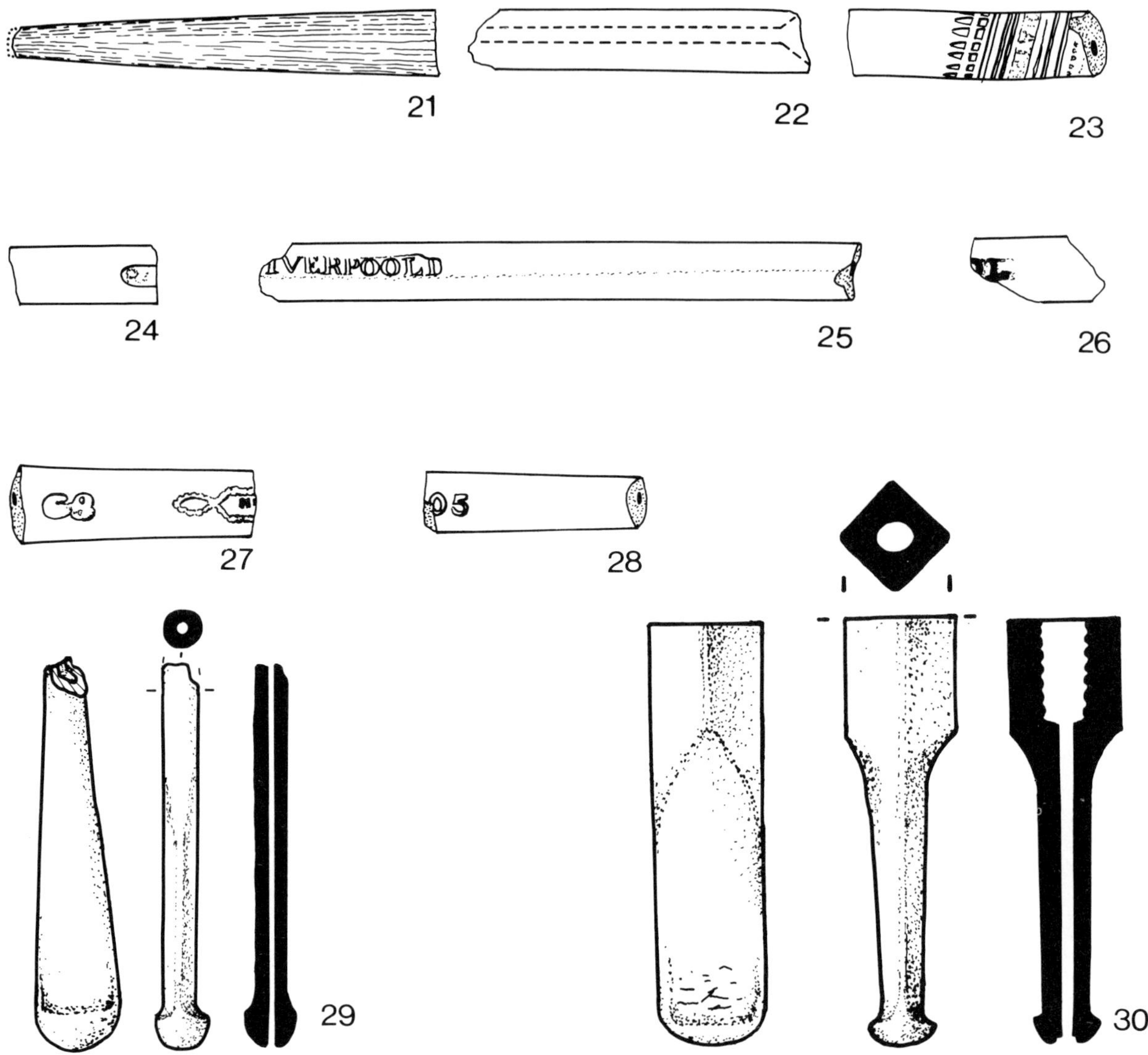

Fig 55   Castle Rushen Stores, Clay Tobacco Pipes; Nos 21–28, and Briar Pipe Mouthpieces, Nos 29–30 (Scale 1:1)

mouthpieces from briar pipes were also recovered. These pipes constitute one of only three significant assemblages so far recovered from the Isle of Man. The other two are both from excavations at castle sites: the 1982–87 excavations at Peel Castle, which produced 704 fragments, and the 1989 excavations at Castle Rushen, where 159 were found. The Castle Rushen Stores group is the only substantial assemblage so far recovered from a purely domestic site on the Isle of Man.

The clay pipes were recovered from a total of 51 contexts. Only five of these contexts contained ten or more pieces of pipe, and all of these were disturbed garden soils containing material of mixed date. Although lacking any individually significant groups, the assemblage as a whole is sufficiently large to provide a valuable indication as to the changing styles of pipe which were used in Castletown.

The clay pipes

The earliest pipe recovered appears to be a stem fragment from Context 92.103/82 (Fig 55.21). This has an unusually pronounced taper towards the mouthpiece and has been finely burnished all over. Both of these features tend to be associated with very early pipes and it is likely that this fragment dates from the late sixteenth or early sevententh century. Pipes of this date are rare anywhere in the British Isles, and this fragment represents the earliest known evidence for smoking on the Isle of Man.

Apart from the single early stem it is not until the 1620s or 1630s that the next evidence for smoking occurs on the site. From this date the habit appears to have been much more common and pipe fragments occur regularly amongst the domestic waste. There are ten bowls dating from the period 1625 to

1660 (for example, Fig 54.1–7). All of these are heeled forms and all are made of a fabric which has fired to a light buff colour on the surface. The fabrics of these pipes are generally moderately gritty although in some cases, such as the AL pipe (Fig 54.1), it is very fine with no inclusions visible to the naked eye. The bowl forms are generally rather crude and of average finish. Only one of the pipes is marked and this can be attributed to the Chester maker Alexander Lanckton (Fig 54.1; see below for fuller discussion). The pipes are generally well-milled and half of them have a burnished surface. The forms, fabrics and finish of these pipes can all be paralleled in the north-west of England, and it seems likely that this is where they originated.

The period between 1650 and 1680 is less well represented, although there is a heel fragment from Context 92.104/4 which probably dates from this period, as does a bowl fragment from Context 92.103/5. As with the earlier examples, these pipes are made of 'local' north-western type fabrics. The bowl fragment also has part of a Rainford style stamp facing the smoker. This particular form of mark almost invariably occurs on spurred pipes, thus indicating their presence during the seventeenth century, even though no spurs were actually recovered from the site. There is also an unusually small heel fragment which dates from between 1630 and 1680 (Fig 54.8).

The link with the north-west appears to have been maintained during the late seventeenth and early eighteenth centuries. During this period more pronounced and often flared heels (Fig 54.9–11) were in use alongside spurred forms (Fig 54.13). These pipes were still being made of 'local' fabrics. Burnishing also occurs, although milling is not generally found on these forms. Two of these pipes are marked (Fig 54.9–10) and both are likely to have been made in Rainford, south Lancashire. There is also a marked stem (Fig 55.23) which was probably produced in Rainford or Liverpool.

No fragments attributable to the mid-eighteenth century were recovered. Material of this date is often scarce, probably as a result of both the reduction in smoking due to the popularity of snuff, and because of the introduction of thin-walled bowls which were easily crushed.

A number of fragments dating from the late eighteenth century onwards were recovered (Fig 54.14–20). By this date fine white 'imported' clays from the west country were being used to make the pipes. The late eighteenth- and early nineteenth-century pieces appear to have come principally from the north-west, for example, the decoration on Figure 54.19 is typical of that area and some of the marks, such as Figure 55.25, have clearly come from Liverpool. The later nineteenth-century pipes, however, appear to have come from more diverse sources and there are certainly some Scottish pieces present, for example Figure 55.27. Quite a number of later nineteenth-century Scottish pipes are known from the island.

Marked and decorated pipes

Twelve marked pipes (seven stamped and five moulded) and four decorated pipes were recovered from the excavations. All but one of these are illustrated and are discussed in the catalogue entries below. The only piece not illustrated is a bowl fragment from 92.103/5, which dates from about 1650 to 1680. This has just the very edge of a Rainford style crescent-shaped border facing the smoker on the bowl and would probably have been produced in Rainford or Liverpool. The stamped marks are shown in Figures 54.1, 9, 10 and Figures 55.23–25, the moulded marks in Figures 54.15, 17 and Figures 55.26–28 and the decorated pipes in Figures 54.17–20.

Glazed mouthpieces

Six stem or mouthpiece fragments with glaze were recovered. One of these consisted of a 'nipple' type mouthpiece from Context 92.103/5 which survives to a length of 12mm and is entirely covered with a yellowish-brown glaze. It probably dates from between 1850 and 1910. The other five pieces all have a thin olive-green glaze. Two pieces, from Contexts 91.129/300 and 92.103/5, are mouthpieces surviving to lengths of 37mm and 32mm respectively. Both pieces have simple cut ends, typical of long-stemmed pipes, and are entirely covered with glaze for their surviving lengths. The other three fragments are all from near the mouthpiece and have varying amounts of glaze. They come from Contexts 92.102/10, 92.102/12 and 92.103/5. All of these pieces date from the nineteenth century.

'Reused' pipe

Sometimes pipe fragments, generally stems, are recovered which have been carved after firing. The form of this carving varies considerably and the reason for it is not always apparent. Suggestions include reusing a broken pipe, making whistles or hair curlers or simply doodling. One stem which may fall into this last category was recovered from Context 92.102/14. The stem fragment survives to a maximum length of 47mm, has a stem bore of 6/64″ and probably dates from the late seventeenth or early eighteenth century. At the thicker end something sharp has been inserted into the bore and twisted to form a conical depression — the bore and cone are shown dotted in Figure 55.22.

The briar pipe mouthpieces

Two briar pipe mouthpieces were recovered from Context 92.104/7, a large ash pit which dates from the earlier part of the twentieth century. These reflect the continuing habit of smoking at a time when clay pipes had fallen out of common use. Both are made of a hard man-made material, almost certainly 'bakelite', and are illustrated in Figures 55.29–30.

Discussion

The single late sixteenth- or early seventeenth-century stem fragment constitutes the earliest evidence for smoking from the Isle of Man. It shows that new trends were being taken up at an early date and argues against any suggestion that the island was in any way a cultural backwater. It was not until the second quarter of the seventeenth century, however, that pipes start to form a regular part of the excavated assemblage. This is in keeping with the date at which pipes regularly occur in English assemblages and suggests that, as in England, this was the date that smoking became widely disseminated through Manx society.

For the rest of the seventeenth century and throughout the eighteenth century, the forms, marks and decoration of the excavated pipes can be paralleled in numerous assemblages from the north-west. Whilst this does not preclude Manx makers having copied these styles, or there being imports from other areas of the Irish Sea basin, it seems most likely that the bulk of these examples were actually imported from that part of England.

It is even possible to suggest the principle source of these pipes. During the seventeenth century Chester pipes generally had a finer fabric than those from south Lancashire. Between about 1690 and 1790 Chester also produced a distinctive series of pipes with decorated stems. Apart from the single AL pipe these finer fabrics and decorated stems are not represented amongst the excavated finds, and so it is unlikely that Chester was a supply source for pipes. On the other hand, the coarser fabrics and distinctive marks found in groups from south Lancashire and Liverpool are well represented amongst the excavated material. It seems likely that the majority of the pipes used in Castletown were produced in the workshops of either Rainford or

Liverpool and that they were shipped out to the island from the docks at Liverpool.

This suggestion is borne out by the finds from Castle Rushen and Peel Castle, where there were also very few Chester pipes but a large number of south Lancashire products. These sites, however, did seem to include a greater diversity of material, for example, some CR pipes which do not appear to be of a north-western form and some examples of Dutch pipes. These more exotic imports may hint at the wider maritime contacts enjoyed by the island. At present it is impossible to say whether these are real differences reflecting the higher social status of the castle sites, or merely a product of the small body of evidence which is available for study.

After about 1850 the supply of pipes seems to have changed, with Scottish pipes from Glasgow finding a significant place in the Manx market. Although there is only one Scottish pipe from the excavations there are numerous other examples from the island, including examples made by the firms of Coghill, McDougall and White. These were, no doubt, circulating amongst other pipes from the north-west and pipes which were being produced on the island at this date, but more study material is needed before it will be possible to assess the relative importance of these different nineteenth-century supply sources.

The illustrated pipes (Figs 54 and 55)

1 Heeled bowl from between 1625 and 1650 with the stamped mark AL. Glossy surface but not apparently burnished; stem bore 7/64″ (92.103/5). None of the surviving rim is milled, a feature typical of Alexander Lanckton of Chester, to whom this pipe can be attributed. Lanckton is recorded in 1657 and probably left Chester about 1664 (Rutter and Davey 1980, 246).

2 Fully milled heeled bowl; 1625–50. This has a stem bore of 6/64″ and very coarse, deeply impressed milling all around the rim (92.102/18).

3 Fully milled heeled bowl; 1625–55. This has a good burnish on the bowl and an unusually small stem bore of 5/64″ (92.102/23).

4 Fully milled heeled bowl; 1625–50. It has a poorly burnished surface and a stem bore of 6/64″ (92.102/18). There are distinctive mould flaws on both sides of the heel, which suggest

that this pipe was made in the same mould as an unstratified heel fragment recovered from Trial Trench 1 (91.129).

5   Heeled bowl; 1630–60. Probably half milled originally, stem bore 7/64″ (92.103/5).

6   Heeled bowl; 1640–60. Probably fully milled originally and with a stem bore of 8/64″ (92.104/2). Average burnish.

7   Fully milled heeled bowl; 1640–60. North-western type, stem bore 7/64″ (92.103/89).

8   Fragment of a pipe with an unusually small heel; 1630–80. Origin uncertain but made of quite a fine 'local' fabric. Stem bore 7/64″ (92.104/2).

9   Heeled bowl with a good burnish but not milled; 1680–1720. The heel is stamped IB; probably a Rainford product, where there were numerous makers with these initials. Stem bore 7/64″ (92.103/5).

10   Heeled pipe; 1690–1720, stamped IB. Probably a Rainford product. Not milled, stem bore 6/64 (92.103/89).

11   One of two very similar fragments from this context with flared heels; a typical north-western form, 1690–1720. Both have fine fabrics, possibly imported, and stem bores of 5/64″ (92.103/5).

12   Two fitting bowl fragments of north-western form; 1690–1720. These have a finely bur-nished surface which has given an extremely glossy, glass-like finish (92.103/5).

13   Part of a north-western type spurred bowl; 1690–1730. Stem bore 7/64″ (92.103/5).

14   Fragmentary spurred bowl; 1790–1840. Stem bore 5/64″ (92.103/5).

15   Plain bowl with a relief moulded dot on either side of the heel; 1800–40. Stem bore 4/64″ (92.104/2).

16   Plain bowl found lying on the surface of the excavation; probably late nineteenth- or early twentieth-century. Stem bore 5/64″ (92.103/5).

17   Bowl with relief moulded decoration consisting of moulded milling above flutes and with leaf decorated seams. There is also a symbol mark,

consisting of a double ring motif on each side of the spur. This mark and the decorative scheme are both typical of north-western products of 1800–40. Stem bore 5/64″ (92.104/2).

18   Fragment of a spurless fluted bowl of 1840–1910. The design consists of seven thick flutes flanked by thin lines on each side of the bowl. Stem bore 4/64″ (92.104/2).

19   Bowl fragment with relief moulded plant decoration surrounding a square and com-passes. These decorative elements are typical of pipes produced in the north-west; 1800–40 (92.102/14).

20   Bowl fragment with large, crudely executed leaf decoration on the seam, 1800–40. Stem bore 5/64″ (92.103/5).

21   Very unusual stem fragment with a pro-nounced taper to the mouthpiece. The whole stem is finely burnished. Stem bore 7/64″ (92.103/82). Probably late sixteenth- or early seventeenth-century.

22   Stem fragment of late seventeenth- or early eighteenth-century date with a stem bore of 6/64″ (92.102/14). A conical hollow has been made in the thicker end of the stem by twisting a sharp implement in the bore. This was clearly done after the pipe had been broken. There is no obvious function for this hollow, which may well be the result of someone doodling with a piece of broken pipe. The bore and hollow are shown dotted.

23   Stem fragment with a Rainford style roller-stamped mark of 1710–40. The maker's name should occupy the central band of the mark, but is almost illegible in this example. It poss-ibly reads 'John Atharton' or 'Tho Atharton'. The Atherton family were working in both Rainford and Liverpool. Stem bore 6/64″ (92.104/1).

24   Burnt stem fragment with part of a name stamp. This is almost illegible but may start 'R T'. The mould seams are not visible on this example, but this style of mark was usually placed on the top of the stem. This type of mark was most commonly used by the Liver-pool makers, 1790–1840. Stem bore 5/64″ (92.103/5).

25   Stem fragment of 1790–1840 illustrated from above to show the end of a Liverpool maker's

mark alongside the mould seam. The die is distinctive in that it has an additional vertical line, possibly a 1, at the end of the mark. There is a 'W. Morgan', Liverpool mark with the number 7 at the end in the Manx Museum. The Castle Rushen Stores example had a hard, highly fired fabric. Stem bore 5/64″ (92.103/89).

26   Small stem fragment with incuse moulded lettering; 1850–1910. Only that on the right hand side survives, possibly an 'O' followed by an 'L'. This may be the end of 'Liverpool'. Stem bore 5/64″ (92.104/7).

27   Stem fragment with an incuse moulded number, possibly 68 or 69, and the incuse moulded lettering Mc/ /GOW in a relief moulded border. Made by McDougalls of Glasgow, who were working from 1846–1967. Stem bore 5/64″ (92.104/1).

28   Stem fragment with part of a relief moulded number on the left hand side. The other side is blank. Stem bore 4/64″ (92.104/1).

29   Briar pipe mouthpiece. Brown bakelite, damaged at the bowl end, surviving to a length of 53mm (92.104/7).

30   Briar pipe mouthpiece. Black bakelite, 57mm in length. The end nearest the bowl is square and has a threaded hole for the pipe bowl and stem to be attached. The mouthpiece has numerous teeth marks visible where it has been clenched or chewed (92.104/7).

Hair Curler

D A Higgins

Although wigs are known to have been worn since at least the late sixteenth century, it was the period between 1660 and 1800 when they were at the height of fashion (Le Cheminant 1985). Hair curlers, or wig curlers, were used to fashion the curls and during this period would have been everyday objects.

One hair curler was recovered from Context 92.102/14, a deposit which pre-dated the nineteenth-century cellar on the Arbory Street frontage. The curler is likely to date from the later seventeenth or eighteenth century, when wigs were in vogue. The curler is a short example (Fig 56), having a length of only 42mm, and is made of a light brown clay with gritty inclusions. It has a slightly

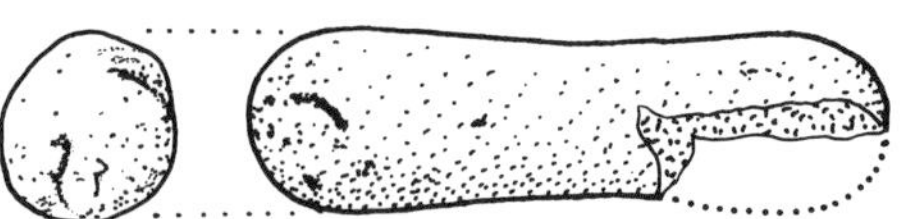

Fig 56   Castle Rushen Stores, Hair Curler (Scale 1:1)

uneven form, suggesting that it was hand rolled, and has been poorly fired, leaving the fabric soft and friable.

This curler is unusual both because of its short length and because of its fabric. Usually curlers were between 50mm and 100mm in length (Le Cheminant 1985, 345) and made of well-fired white pipeclay. An example from Liverpool has been thin-sectioned, showing it to have been made of 'an extremely inclusion free pure clay' (Davidson and Davey 1982, 336). Sometimes curlers were stamped with the maker's initials on their ends. A few of these examples are known to have been made by tobacco pipe makers, but the majority of the marked examples bear the initials of a small number of individuals who appear to have been specialist hair curler manufacturers.

There were plenty of pipe makers in the northwest who could have made curlers for the local and Manx markets and a wide range of curlers were produced by the specialist hair curler manufacturers, examples of which, in a buff/brown clay, have been excavated at South Castle Street in Liverpool (Philpott 1985b). None of these, however, is as short or made of such a friable brown fabric as the Castletown example. It is possible that the Castletown curler was made on Man in response to local demand. Whatever its origin, the presence of this curler demonstrates both that wigs were being used in Castletown and that contemporary fashions were being followed on the island.

Clay Marbles

D A Higgins

Two clay marbles were recovered from the excavations. Both are made of a fine white pipeclay which has been well fired. They were recovered from recent contexts and are likely to be of nineteenth- or early twentieth-century date. The marbles are described below.

1   Half a marble, 18mm diameter. This marble has some sparse gritty inclusions, probably quartz, in the fabric. It had a regular spherical form but with a number of striations and small scratch marks on the surface. These run in a number of orientations and appear to have been made when the clay was in a leather hard state. They

may result from the marble having been lathe turned (92.102/2).

2 Complete marble, 15–16mm in diameter. This marble has a smooth surface with a 'fold' mark in the clay at one point. It has a slightly uneven form and has almost certainly been hand rolled. Without a broken section it is impossible to determine the nature of any inclusions in the clay (92.104/1).

Brick

N C Johnson

Introduction

The excavations provided a total of 108 fragments of brick clay from 36 contexts, distributed widely over the site. Most, but not all, of the phases identified by the analysis of the pottery are represented.

Method

In the majority of cases all brick fragments excavated were retained, recorded and subsequently stored in context groups. Where very large quantities of relatively modern brick fragments were encountered, however, a representative sample was taken. Where this was the case, it is noted below.

The nature of the material precluded the legible marking of individual fragments; identification of pieces in the archive is based on the bags and labels with which they are stored.

Trench 92.102

The Trench 92.102 finds assemblage includes 23 fragments of brick, some of substantial proportions, from 12 contexts. This total number of fragments does not represent the whole quantity of brick produced by the trench, since two contexts (7 and 9) were sampled only. These contexts consisted of building rubble and formed the back-fill of the cellar in this trench. As such, they contained a mass of brick material, the majority of which was modern; the brick retained was characteristic of the whole.

The single fragment from a Phase 2 context (as identified in the pottery report) was recovered from Context 41, a layer behind the wall adjoining the cellar steps. It has one very smooth face and is

Context	Phase 1	Phase 2	Phase 3	Phase 4
004	–	–	–	2
006	–	–	1	–
007	–	–	–	1
008	–	–	–	1
009	–	–	–	2
014	–	–	5	–
016	–	–	1	–
017	–	–	3	–
028	–	–	1	–
030	–	–	3	–
033	–	–	2	–
041	–	1	–	–
Totals	–	1	16	6	23

Table 17   Brick fragments from Trench 92.102 by context and phase

remarkably hard-fired, although not in a fully controlled kiln, being part-reduced, part-oxidised. The fabric is relatively fine, with some sand present. It is not entirely credible to place this fragment in the late seventeenth century/early eighteenth century and, therefore, it has to be regarded as the result of contamination from the construction trench (28).

The material from Phase 3 is mainly small, most pieces being no larger than 64 cubic cm. It is quite homogeneous, with a relatively fine fabric, small 1.5 cubic mm voids, and fired to an even hue. Some fragments are sooted.

One larger fragment from Context 14 possibly represents four sides of a corner, with a thickness of 49mm. It appears sooted or heavily weathered, and retains some lime mortar. The iron content of this piece is higher than others from this group, but not as high as some of those from Trench 92.103.

There are two other relatively large fragments in the Phase 3 group, from Contexts 14 and 28. One of these (28) appears highly fired, and has discrete small patches of reduced material within it, representing the addition of grog. The fabric is fine, with only a few small inclusions.

The Phase 4 material is modern. Context 4 produced a half brick with frog originating from Glenfaba Brickworks, a company incorporated in 1927 (Bawden *et al* 1972, 135). This example measures 78mm × 109mm. The fragment recovered from Context 8 retains the arc of a cylindrical hole through it, characteristic of modern cored bricks. The two representative examples retained from Context 9 are both sooted, but are of differing types. One is possibly a Ballacoarey brick and measures 75mm × 113mm × 230mm; it retains mortar on all faces and has no frog. The other, a half brick, measures 72mm × 110mm, and is of unknown origin, with a higher iron content than Ballacoarey bricks and no frog. The half brick example reserved from Context 7 is also probably a Ballacoarey brick, has no frog and measures 75mm × 102mm.

The brickworks at Ballacoarey was in operation from at least the latter half of the eighteenth century until the first quarter of the twentieth century, with a break caused by the First World War; sales of stockpiled bricks continued beyond 1925 (Bawden *et al*, 1972, 134).

The half brick found in the dry-stone wall (4) is a fire brick and, therefore, imported. It measures 68mm × 108mm.

Trench 92.103

A total of 74 fragments of brick was recovered from this trench, from 17 contexts.

Two of these fragments derive from contexts given a sixteenth-century date by the pottery analysis (110, 120). They are both too small, however, to admit of firm conclusions concerning the use of brick at this location at this time. Indeed, one fragment is more likely to be burnt daub rather than brick, possibly residue from a burnt-down clay daub structure.

The material recovered from those contexts allocated to Phases 2 and 3 in the pottery report can be characterised by its homogeneity. Most of the fragments possess an even colour throughout the fabric, with an almost complete absence of inclusions, and small (1 cubic mm) voids. They do not appear to be particularly highly fired. Two fragments (from 82 and 89) possess both faces: these are 53mm and 48mm across respectively. The fragment from Context 89 is sooted. The few inclusions present in this group appear to be of granite, less than 0.9 cubic mm in size, and, in considerably smaller proportion, small sub-rounded stones of less than 8.0 cubic mm.

Two fragments from contexts in these phases (52, 90) appear to have a higher iron content. The fabric is sandier, and has a higher proportion of inclusions. One fragment from Context 52 carries grass impressions from the drying stage of manufacture.

No distinctions were possible between material apparently belonging to Phase 2 contexts and that from Phase 3 contexts.

A clear division exists within the material from Phase 4 contexts. There is a small group of fragments of highly fired brick, and a much larger group which strongly resembles the majority of the material described above. The highly fired group consists of six fragments in total, an equal number from each of Contexts 3 and 5. Those from Context 3 retain traces of cement and lime-wash; one has both faces intact, and measures 74mm across. One fragment from Context 5, from the larger group, retains grass impressions on an intact face.

The majority of the fragments recovered are small in size, being no larger than 90 cubic mm.

Trench 92.104

Eleven fragments of brick were recovered from this trench, from seven contexts. A number of modern bricks and brick fragments, present on the surface of the area proposed for excavation, were removed during site clearance: no examples were reserved.

Three fragments of brick derived from Phase 1 contexts: two from Context 20, and one from Context 21. The latter has a coarse fabric, with

Context	Phase 1	Phase 2	Phase 3	Phase 4	
001	–	–	–	1	
003	–	–	–	3	
005	–	–	–	28	
036	–	–	2	–	
050	–	–	1	–	
052	–	–	3	–	
055	–	–	1	–	
082	–	10	–	–	
089	–	–	10	–	
090	–	–	7	–	
093	–	1	–	–	
094	–	2	–	–	
098	–	1	–	–	
105	–	–	1	–	
108	–	1	–	–	
110	1	–	–	–	
120	1	–	–	–	
Totals	2	15	25	32	74

Table 18 Brick fragments from Trench 92.103 by context and phase.

Context	Phase 1	Phase 2	Phase 3	Phase 4	
002	–	–	–	4	
004	–	–	2	–	
007	–	–	2	–	
020	2	–	–	–	
021	1	–	–	–	
Totals	3	–	4	4	11

Table 19 Brick fragments from Trench 92.104 by context and phase

some granitic inclusions and an even colour throughout. One fragment from Context 20 resembles the majority of the material from Trench 92.103; it cannot, however, be regarded as representative. It is possible that it retains an intact face.

Phase 2 was not represented.

The Phase 3 contexts held four fragments: two in Context 4 and two in Context 7. Three of these are very small, being no larger than 80 cubic mm. They are all different from each other. One fragment is similar to the majority of the Trench 92.103 material, whilst the remaining piece, a fire brick, has an untypical fabric. Two faces mutually perpendicular remain intact, one with a modern cement render adhering. This brick also retains traces of a lime mortar.

Four brick fragments were recovered from Context 2, and belong to Phase 4. Three of these are all different from each other and do not appear to resemble other material from the site. They are, however, very small (less than 80 cubic mm) and do not allow secure analysis. The remaining fragment is a typical fire brick, manufactured from coal-measures clay. It has three intact faces, and measures 38mm across.

Discussion and overview

The evidence provided by the brick assemblage from this site is limited by the considerable homogeneity of the material across the boundaries provided by the pottery phasing, and by the minimal representation of other types. The majority of the brick recovered in Trench 92.103 derives from the seventeenth- and eighteenth-century garden soils, present on both sides of the boundary bank; the fact that the majority of the fragments from the final phase of activity identified for this trench are indistinguishable from this earlier group is not surprising, since it almost certainly represents reworked material. The conflation of Phase 2 and 3 material in this trench possibly represents a degree of contamination by historical digging activity, but may also imply longevity of either the brick-built structures themselves, or the manufacturing source.

The presence of this brick does, in the first instance, invite inquiry concerning the need for and use of it; the extant buildings are almost exclusively constructed from stone or modern brick, and there is no particular reason, at the moment, to suppose that they were preceded by seventeenth- or eighteenth-century brick structures, given the perceived higher status value of such construction.

The Trench 92.102 group was mostly recovered from Phase 3 contexts, when the ground surface was exposed and in use, prior to the major construction work represented by the cellar and subsequent buildings. The more confined and slightly later date of this Phase 3 compared with that of Trench 92.103 perhaps explains the partial, not entire similarity between the brick material from the two trenches. The almost certainly imported and, therefore, decontextualised building rubble used to backfill the cellar, and to provide hardcore for the concrete yard surface (1), has limited value archaeologically.

It can be concluded, on the basis of the Trench 92.103 group, and some of the Trench 92.102 material, and with the rider that only small quantities have been recovered from both trenches, that one particular source of brick was available for some time. The homogeneity of the material across phase boundaries dating from the mid-seventeenth century could be related to an entry in a Castle Rushen inventory *c*1694: a large stockpile of bricks 'computed to ninety thousand' is recorded at Bagnio House (*The Journal of the Manx Museum*, Volume II, No. 26, March 1931, 13). Derby House in Castle Rushen itself was constructed in the 1690s; it is thought that the bricks were manufactured at Red Gap (NGR SC 258 678) (Cowin pers comm). It is also apparent that brick construction became more prevalent at a point subsequent to the building of the cellar in Trench 92.102, so that it became available as rubble, even if only as a small proportion compared with masonry. By this time different brick types were available.

Building Materials
D A Higgins

A variety of building materials was encountered during the excavations. The following samples were retained.

Asbestos

One fragment from Trench 92.103/5.

Marble

A cut stone tile was found in the early twentieth-century demolition deposit in 92.102/8. This is a roughly square tile, approximately 77mm by 79mm by 25mm thick. It is made of a soft, powdery white stone with a crystalline structure, which is marble.

Mortar and plaster

Almost all of these samples came from topsoil or modern demolition deposits. Samples from earlier deposits tend to be small and their identification as mortar is often uncertain, some of them almost certainly being pieces of decaying stone. The only significant pieces came from the early twentieth-century demolition deposits in Contexts 92.102/8 and 9. These included pieces retaining whitewash or a red ochre colour, reflecting the colours used in the building.

Salt-glazed brick or pavier

Two small pieces were recovered from Context 92.104/1.

Salt-glazed drain pipe

Four pieces were recovered from the early twentieth-century demolition deposits in Trench 92.102. There were three pieces in Context 8 and one piece in Context 9.

Slates

Samples of Manx slates with possible peg holes, suggesting that they had been used for roofing, were retained from Contexts 5, 36, 82 and 118 in Trench 92.103. Contexts 82 and 118 both date from the seventeenth century and show that local slate was in use as a roofing material at this time. Context 36 of the same trench also produced a fragment of what appears to be an imported slate, possibly from Wales. This context dates from the late eighteenth or nineteenth century.

Glass

N C Johnson
with a note on Fine Glass by
R Hurst Vose

Introduction

The 1991 and 1992 excavations recovered 2521 fragments of glass from 46 contexts.

Method

The excavated material was retained and recorded by context. After washing, all fragments were marked with the Manx Museum accession code, and bagged separately according to context. The flat (window) glass was divided from the vessel glass.

All the material was catalogued longhand, noting colour, dimensions, weight and distinguishing marks, and relief moulded designs sketched. This catalogue has been deposited in the site archive.

Fragments of the finer and apparently earlier glass were sent for examination by R Hurst Vose, whose report appears separately. The consequences of her findings have been incorporated into the overview with which this concludes.

In the report which follows, descriptions of individual fragments from the various trenches have been grouped under headings of glass types.

Statistical analysis

Trench 92.102
This trench produced a total of 423 sherds of glass, weighing in total 5.594kg, from 18 contexts. The weight of flat (window) glass fragments amounted to 7.5% of the total glass recovered.

Trench 92.103
This trench incorporated Trial Trench 3 (91.129/300 to 311). Two contexts from the trial produced glass, a total of ten sherds amounting to 0.134kg. In 1992, 317 sherds were recovered, weighing 2.379kg, from 26 contexts. Flat (window) glass fragments made up 3.9% of the total weight of glass material.

Trench 92.104
Trial Trench 1 (91.129/100 to 110) formed part of the boundary of the 1992 excavation. It was not re-excavated. In 1991, a total of 151 sherds was recovered, weighing 0.807kg; 16% of these were flat (window) glass. Four contexts from the 11 produced glass. In 1992, nine contexts from a total of 26 produced 1620 sherds (weighing 15.032kg). Flat (window) glass pieces amounted to 27.8% of weight of glass recovered.

A summary of the weights and numbers appears in Tables 20 and 21.

Fine vessel glass

No more than single figure quantities of sherds in this category were recovered from any one trench. Surviving sherds were very small in size—usually less than 0.009kg—and were generally present as individual pieces not related to each other. These factors combined to hinder identification. Very pale yellow-green and colourless glass was found, varying in thickness from 0.8mm to 1.8mm. Trench 92.102 produced four pieces of a colourless drinking glass rim with a metal thickness of 1.2mm (14). Four further sherds were found, all colourless and 1mm thick (6). Three fragments of drinking glass rims were recovered from Contexts 92.103/3, 5 and 57, all colourless, with another from Trial Trench 3, colourless, with white patination (300). Two rim sherds were excavated from Contexts 92.104/1 and 5. A further 11 fine vessel sherds were recovered (1, 2, 5 and 6), with two of these apparently from the same vessel (2). Two colourless rim sherds were recovered from Context 91.129/100, along with another six sherds of a colourless white patinated metal 1mm thick (101).

Green bottle glass

This category includes examples covering a colour range from olive-green to blue-green. A number of complete and semi-complete examples of this type were recovered, including one with labelling largely intact: the 'Apollinaris' bottle, found in Context 92.102/9. A *terminus post quem* is provided by the label, which records that the manufacturer was awarded a prize for this mineral water in 1904.

The total weight of green glass recovered from the various trenches is as follows: Trial Trench 1: 0.296kg; Trial Trench 3: 0.054kg; Trench 92.102: 3.092kg; Trench 92.103: 1.719kg; Trench 92.104: 3.117kg. It was not possible, however, to separate most of the material into quantities or numbers for either mineral bottles (of the Apollinaris type) or wine bottles. Comment, therefore, is reserved for those pieces positively identified. Some dimensional information concerning the glass in this category was recovered, allowing some grouping.

The 'Apollinaris' mineral bottle, although not complete, provided dimensions as follows: neck, 25mm diameter; shoulder, 58.5mm; and base, 57mm. On the basis of these, it is possible to say that there were four other sherds from Contexts 92.102/8 and 9 which derive from a similar bottle, one from Context 92.103/1 and five from Contexts 92.104/1 and 2.

A second type of bottle can be identified from an intact example recovered from Trench 92.102. This bottle exhibits a well-rounded shoulder, is of larger volume than the 'Apollinaris' bottle, and is more olive-green in colour. Its principal dimensions are: neck, 28.5mm diameter; shoulder, 68mm; base, 65.5mm. A total of four bottles of this type were found in Contexts 92.102/2 and 9.

Apart from these divisions, only generalised categorisation is possible. Both Contexts 92.102/14 and 92.104/2 produced an example of a neck sherd with a diameter of 31mm. Two contexts in Trench 92.103, relatively closely related to each other, produced base sherds of similar dimensions: Context 5 contained a sherd 72mm in diameter, while Context 58 held one 74mm in diameter. Metal colours and thicknesses, however, bore little relation to each other.

In 1992, Trench 92.104 produced a base sherd from Context 1 with a diameter of 90mm, while Context 100, in 1991, held a sherd of the same diameter. Metal thickness in this case is comparable. A further base from Context 92.104/1 measured 100mm in diameter.

Two bases from Trench 92.102 exhibited a pontil mark, one from Context 6, the other from Context 38. The latter was found in two joining pieces, and measured 62mm in diameter.

Markings on the sherds recovered in this category were limited.

Mineral bottles (mainly Codd's Patent type)

A total of 280 sherds was recovered belonging to this group. Two principal types of bottle could be identified. One had dimensions of 25–27mm neck diameter, 57–62mm shoulder diameter, and a base 51–65mm in diameter. These were sealed by a marble held by gas pressure against a rubber or cork ring. The second type was larger, and sealed either by the same arrangement, or by a bung of some description. (Insufficient sherds were found to ascertain the full dimensions of this bottle.) The moulded maker's mark of 'Cannington Shaw, St Helens' was present on a number of the smaller bottles, in a variety of forms of wording. In all, 65 sherds were recovered from Trench 92.102 (1.479kg); 34 from Trench 92.103 (0.147kg); one from Trial Trench 3 (0.055kg); 150 from Trench 92.104 (3.287kg); and 30 from Trial Trench 1 (0.362kg).

Three traders were positively identified. A fairly complete bottle marked 'Silverburn Glen Aerated Water' (trade directory entry for 1889) was found in Context 92.104/7. Pieces of bottles from Robert Williamson, Laxey Glen (trade directory entries for 1882, 1889, 1894), were found in Trench 92.104 and in the trial trench which preceded it (eight firmly identified sherds, plus two likely to derive from these bottles: Contexts 2, 7 and 91.129/100). T M Dodd (trade directory entry 1894) is known to have had a bottling plant on the site: three firmly identified pieces of this trader's bottles were found in

Contexts 92.102/8 and 11, with one further fragment in this trench (8), one in Context 92.103/3, and seven in Contexts 92.104/1 and 2 probably of this provenance.

The very pale green colour of this group of sherds showed, in a very few cases, some slight variation towards the blue or yellow ends of the green spectrum. Varying degrees of patination and wear were observed. A proportion of the material recovered from Trench 92.102 exhibited the same clouding of the metal as the flat glass (see below). Metal thicknesses varied within an extreme range of 1.8–10mm; most pieces lay within the range of 4–7mm. Fifteen marbles were found: nine from Trench 92.102; one from Trench 92.103; the remainder from Trench 92.104, including one from the trial trench.

A notable feature of these bottles is the unique batch number allocated by Cannington Shaw, the manufacturer, to particular sequences of trader's bottles. Dodd's bottles are numbered 4010 and 4012, Williamson's 1128, Silverburn Glen's (proprietor John Davies) 1528. One bottle number cannot be identified, the only numbers surviving being 7 and 9.

Brown glass

A small quantity of material—0.340kg—in this category was recovered over the two years. Trench 92.102 was the most productive (0.180kg). A sherd from an elliptical jar 44mm × 28mm was recovered from Context 92.104/1. Otherwise there did not appear to be any exceptions to a rule of bottle type sherds, for which dimensional information was insubstantial.

Medicine bottles

Sherds of this type were characterised by having one or all of the following: ribbed bodies; gradations; lettering indicating gradations in 'tablespoons'; blue metal colour.

Sherds from this category were present only in Trench 92.104. Context 1 produced five sherds, three of which appeared associated. In addition, one sherd was recovered from Context 2 and a collection of nine sherds from Context 6, all of which were from the same vessel.

Miscellaneous bottles and jars

A considerable variety of material was recovered in this category, most of it, predictably, from Trench 92.104. There were three exceptions: a phial sherd with a base diameter of 25mm, of colourless metal 1.2mm thick from 92.102/8; a base/body sherd from the same context of very pale green metal 1.5mm thick with a base diameter of 33.5mm, and the remains of a printed label, possibly indicating that the contents would have been a perfume of some description; and an example of a whole 'Lea and Perrins' Worcestershire sauce bottle from Context 92.103/102, in very pale green patinated metal about 2.5mm thick, measuring 23mm diameter at the neck, 50mm diameter at the shoulder, and 52mm diameter at the base.

Context 92.104/1 produced a rich variety of glass containers, a number of which were intact. Perfume, nail varnish, glue and sauce bottles were identified, along with a piece of tube, a pipette, a stopper to fit a jar with a 40mm internal neck diameter, another stopper (with an associated neck sherd) marked 'GARTON'S', and a sherd from a glass bowl.

Another stopper was found in the same trench (2). This was to fit a neck of 12mm maximum internal diameter, and was marked 'GARTON'S'. This context also produced three sherds from sauce bottles, two of them from square bases with dimensions respectively of 45mm and 46mm.

In Context 5, one of the small pits, there were two associated sherds from a storage jar, and one sherd from a sauce bottle. Another pit (6) contained ten fragments making up almost all of a bottle of the type used to store domestic cleaning liquids, with a neck diameter of 21mm, shoulder dimensions of 38mm × 85mm, and base dimensions 30mm × 58mm. A large proportion of the body of another glass vessel was also found in this pit: 17 fragments in total, with a neck diameter of 31mm and a shoulder diameter of 60mm.

The large almost circular pit (7) produced three fragments of a heavy glass bowl (two rim sherds and one base sherd); two phial sherds; and two complete storage jars, one measuring 75mm at the neck, the other 74mm, and both 72mm in diameter at the base. Finally, this same context contained two pieces of a heavy, press-moulded drinking glass.

Flat (window) glass

The trial trenches produced a small quantity of glass in this category. Twenty-four sherds were recovered from Trial Trench 1 (from Contexts 100, 101 and 102); three more came from Trial Trench 3 (from Contexts 300 and 301). One example was pale blue; the remainder were colourless or very pale green, sometimes tinged yellow. Metal thickness was in the range 1–2.5mm, with one piece 3mm thick (a piece of 'obscured' glass) and the pale blue sherd 3.5mm thick. One sherd (from Context 101) was cut with a 90 degree angle.

Trench 92.102

In Trench 92.102, the 149 sherds of flat (window) glass recovered were, for the most part, almost colourless, with the slightest hint of very pale green. Twenty-one pieces were heavily patinated. Metal thickness varied from 0.8mm to 2.8mm, with most pieces lying in the range 1–2mm. A characteristic of the glass recovered from this trench was opacity: chemical action by the mortar in the demolition layers which provided most of the material is thought to have been responsible for this.

Twenty-eight of the sherds had an identifiable cut edge, normally diamond; one piece, however, from Context 8, had been nibbled. Five sherds exhibited a thickened, rounded edge (14, 17, 28).

Trench 92.103

Trench 92.103 produced only 65 sherds of flat glass, probably for reasons explained elsewhere. A wide colour variation was evident here compared with the other trenches, from an almost colourless very pale green, through pale green to green, with examples of pale blue and completely colourless glass. Metal thickness lay in the range 1–3mm, with most pieces 1–1.8mm. Four sherds were less than 1mm thick, and a single sherd was 4mm thick. Nineteen of the 65 sherds appeared to have a cut edge: one piece, from Context 5, had a thickened, rounded edge.

Trench 92.104

Trench 92.104 was the most productive, with a total of 1083 sherds in this category. More than half of the recovered material had at least one cut straight edge, and a sixth of this quantity had parallel cut edges. More than two-fifths of the straight edge sherds had a 90 degree cut angle.

Thickness of the majority of the sherds from this trench lay in the range 1–2.5mm. Almost all of the glass was a nearly colourless very pale green (with variations towards a more blue or a more yellow green), or colourless. One dark green sherd was recovered, three pale green, one pale blue, and one with a slight rose tint. Some sherds (19) had residual putty marks. Seven sherds appeared to have a curved cut edge. Two fragments of mirror, 1.5mm thick, were recovered from Context 7.

By far the most productive contexts in Trench 92.104 were 6 (1.238kg) and 5 (0.915kg). A quantity of glass (0.369kg) from Context 1 had been partly welded together by heat.

Trench	Flat/ Window	Vessel/ Bottle	Annual Totals	Combined Total
92.102	149	274	423	423
91.129 (3)	3	7	10	
92.103	65	252	317	327
91.129 (1)	24	127	151	
92.104	1083	537	1620	1771
Totals	1324	1197	2521	2521

Table 20   Quantities of glass recovered from 1991 and 1992 excavations

Trench	Flat/ Window	Vessel/ Bottle	Annual Totals	Combined Total
92.102	0.419	5.175	5.594	5.594
91.129(3)	0.003	0.131	0.134	
92.103	0.095	2.284	2.379	2.513
91.129 (1)	0.064	0.743	0.807	
92.104	4.332	10.700	15.032	15.839
Totals	4.913	19.033	23.946	23.946

Table 21   Weight (in kg) of glass recovered from 1991 and 1992 excavations

Overview

Little or no glass was recovered from contexts representing the earliest period of known activity on the site. This period has been identified as dating from the sixteenth century, when it can be assumed that the use of glass, certainly in this area of Castletown, was restricted in the extreme.

Evidence from the glass for the site as a whole for the seventeenth century and much of the eighteenth century is insubstantial. It may be significant that most of the fragments recovered from Trench 92.103, from contexts dated to this period, derive from the western end of the trench. The exceptions (108 and 118) are described in R Hurst Vose's report.

The late eighteenth-century and the early nine-teenth-century phases mark a considerable upturn in activity on the Arbory Street properties. Whether this is trade or domestic in origin is obscure; the evidence from Trench 92.102 includes a drinking glass rim and mineral bottle fragments, whilst that from Trench 92.103 includes mainly mineral bottle sherds. There is no comparable evidence from Trench 92.104.

The next increase in activity takes place in the late nineteenth century: evidence for this is provided by all three trenches. There remains a distinction, however, in Trenches 92.102 and 92.103 the material recovered is mostly bottle glass, certainly indicating trade activity at the location of Trench 92.102, and in the vicinity at least of Trench 92.103. In Trench 92.104 glass fragments and substantially whole vessels were recovered from discrete rubbish pits. The markedly higher proportion of flat (window) glass in this trench is characterised by the number of relatively small pieces with parallel cut edges. The quantity of this type of glass (3.51kg) would appear to indicate the deliberate refenestration of formerly leaded windows in the locality, and confirms the open and waste nature of this ground, whilst the area investigated by the other two trenches was in use for industrial or horticultural purposes. Considerable variation in the thickness of the glass (1.2–3.0mm) indicates a non-mechanised method of manufacture, without the precise method being evident. By comparison, the later phase in this trench includes scattered modern window glass in much smaller quantity.

The vessels from Trench 92.104, also buried in pits in the late nineteenth/early twentieth century, are mixed in origin, and are more likely to represent domestic rubbish than trade activity. It is notable that the Codd's mineral bottles from this phase are mainly from other sources than T M Dodd, the proprietor of the Arbory Street grocery business, partly located on ground covered by Trench 92.102. The Phase 4 period of Trench 92.104 does produce Dodd's bottles, and continues to be domestic in character.

Early Post-Medieval Fine Glass

R Hurst Vose

This report concerns 13 sherds of glass, from eight contexts, from the Castle Rushen Stores excavation in 1992.

Trench 92.102

1   Small fragment from a bottle base with kick in thick greenish-brown clear glass of good quality, with shiny fire finish. Base diameter where bottle base touches surface is *c*70mm (12). Late eighteenth- to nineteenth-century.

2   Body fragment from a straight-sided cylindrical thin-walled vessel/container; the metal, or glass fabric, clear greenish-brown, full of bubbles, the surface pitted with weathered spots. Diameter 100mm. The quality is crude but it has a polished fire finish, suggesting the higher temperatures of a coal-fired furnace, dating no earlier than *c*1615 (13). Probably seventeenth-century.

Fig 57   Castle Rushen Stores, Glass (Scale 1:1)

3–4   Two joining fragments forming a vessel base, probably from a beaker, in clear colourless glass; the metal of good quality with some seeds; the surface with opaque iridescent weathering. The base has a shallow kick, at the centre of which is a small pontil mark. A thick glass trail has been applied to its outer edge and flattened whilst still hot to give added stability as well as decoration. Very little of the vessel walls remains, but a plain outcurved slightly bulbous form is indicated. Walls 1.5mm thick, base diameter 600–650mm (Fig 57). The technique of applying a band of trailed glass to the edge of a glass base is an old one, and was certainly in use in medieval times. In the later sixteenth and early seventeenth centuries, English forest glasshouses were producing more or less cylindrical beaker glasses in green tinted glass. Bases of such beakers were slightly kicked with a trail of glass laid around the basal angle and pressed in the horizontal plane so that the glass would stand flat. This form copied its betters in clear colourless or crystal glass, and is often associated with beakers with chequered spiral trail decoration both in green and crystal glass (Charleston 1984, 89). It is obvious from the metal that this glass was an import, and may be *façon de Venise* from the Continent, perhaps the Netherlands (Tait 1967, 98). Fine colourless glass products appeared on English sites from the thirteenth century, however, probably imported from Italy (Charleston 1984, 18–19), and it is possible this base may be associated with these earlier finds. The metal itself appears heavy for *cristallo*. It is an example of luxury ware of the time, since clear colourless glass products were then limited to the rich and powerful, appearing on sites such as palaces and the houses of rich merchants (38).

Trench 92.103

5–6   Two joining fragments from a small bottle or phial base in clear pale green glass with shallow kick. The metal is quite good with smooth fire finish, but there is a film of surface weathering on both sides. Walls 1mm thick, base diameter 40mm. Probably late sixteenth- or seventeenth-century (5).

7   A small distorted glass thread in clear colourless glass. Perhaps glasshouse waste or subjected to intense heat elsewhere (5).

8   A small fragment of vessel/bottle glass in clear pale green tinted metal of poor quality with much seed and bubbles, but with shiny fire finish and no weathering. Walls 1mm thick. A raised line on the outer surface suggests a mould seam (5). After 1615.

9   Fragment of furnace waste or glass melted in a fire, pitted by surface contact whilst still hot. Probably once clear green glass which has devitrified to opaque pale green (94).

10   A small clear yellowish tinted vessel glass fragment of good quality, with a little seed and surface hair lines. The fragment is possibly from a straight-sided cylindrical vessel such as a beaker, but it is too small to be conclusive. It is decorated on the outer surface with either moulded decoration, or more likely chequered spiral trail decoration, although again the fragment is too small to be absolutely certain. A distinct chequer pattern in relief was produced by applying a spiral trail of hot glass to the original gather of glass, then inflating the glass in a vertically ribbed mould. Examples of chequered spiral decoration have been found on English forest glasshouse sites at Rosedale, Woodchester, Newent, Bickerstaffe and Haughton Green in green tinted glass. The quality and colour of this fragment, however, suggest that it is an import. Examples of such imports have been found in England, notably in London, and also in the Lower Rhineland and the southern Netherlands, all probably originating from the Antwerp area during the late sixteenth and early seventeenth centuries (Tait, 1967, 98, 112). Vessel wall 2mm thick (108).

11   One small vessel fragment in clear colourless glass with very slight iridescent surface weathering. Metal of quite good quality with seeds. The fragment came from a straight-sided cylindrical vessel with vertical ribbed moulded decoration. Vessel wall 1–2mm thick. Sixteenth- to seventeenth-century (108).

12   One small fragment, 1mm thick, in good quality slightly brownish clear colourless glass, with some seeds and slight surface weathering. Probably *cristallo*, Venetian or *façon de Venise*. The sherd suggests a straight-sided cylindrical form. It has been decorated with white enamelling or *lattimo* applied to the outer surface, being perhaps blobbed decoration or the end of two trails. Trailed *lattimo* decoration was used by Venetian glassmakers, the technique being spread by these craftsmen to many parts of Europe during the sixteenth and seventeenth centuries. Trailed *lattimo* decoration appears on German and Dutch glass in the sixteenth century and was used on English glass attributed to the Italian glassmaker Verzelini, who worked in London in the last quarter of the sixteenth century (118).

Trench 92.104

13   A fragment of green tinted bottle glass 2–3.5mm thick, with bubbles, slight iridescent surface weathering and good fire finish. The glass was mould blown and from a multi-sided container (see Hume 1961, Fig 1). Probably second half of the eighteenth century (21).

Ironwork (Figs 58 and 59)
S D White

The excavations produced a total of 742 iron objects, of which 373 were identified as nails and 296 were unidentified pieces of iron or iron sheet. The remaining objects included an iron buckle, pieces of wire and pipe, horseshoes, scissor blades and washers.

From each trench a number of the unidentifiable objects were selected for X-ray, but in most cases the very heavy corrosion proved to be too dense and further identification was impossible. However, a chain (Fig 58.2) from Context 92.102/10, the cellar steps, produced a very clear X-ray showing details of a swivel between the main links and the end rings. It is suggested that this chain may be part of a heavy-horse harness, a hame chain, or a chain which was used to fasten a drag to the horse

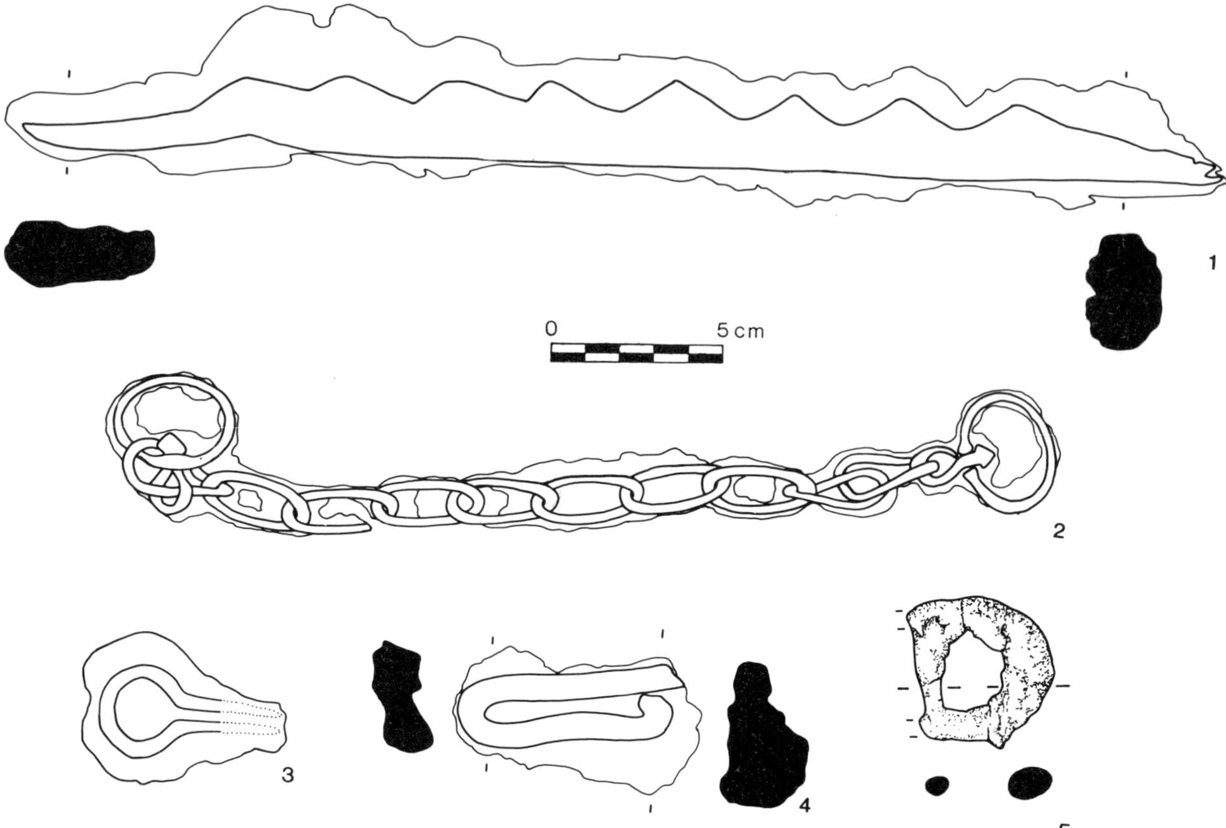

Fig 58   Castle Rushen Stores, Iron Objects; Nos 1–4, drawn from X-rays (Scale as shown); No 5, Buckle (Scale 1:1)

harness. An object from Context 92.102/7, the demolition fill of the cellar, appears on X-ray to be a ratchet (Fig 58.1). This item may be from a piece of machinery, or possibly part of a ratchet spit support from a side iron (Moorhouse 1971, 56, Pl IIIb). From Context 92.102/18, a layer dating from the late eighteenth/early nineteenth century, came an object that proved, after X-raying, to be a Jew's harp (Fig 58.3). The only other X-ray that produced a reasonable image was that of an object from a recent ash pit, Context 92.104/7 (Fig 58.4), which appears to be a folded iron bar.

Four items, which were originally thought to be of non-ferrous metal, were examined by G Egan. They included a buckle from Context 92.103/89 (Fig 58.5). This is incomplete and corroded and may, originally, have had an oval double-loop frame. It measures 28–19mm (if originally symmetrical) and comes from a late eighteenth- to nineteenth-century deposit. Other finds identified by G Egan were some wire fragments with a diameter of approximately 1mm, from Context 92.104/20, a seventeenth-century deposit; a screw which was 25mm in length from Context 91.129/82; and an unidentified fragment from Context 92.103/82, dating to 1650 or earlier.

The 373 nails recovered from the site have been tabulated (Tables 22–26) in an attempt to show the distribution of types throughout the site. The nails have been divided into six main types (A–F) which are illustrated in Fig 59 and defined as follows:

Type A—square flat head
Type B—oval flat head
Type C—clench nail
Type D—horseshoe nail
Type E—rounded head
Type F—triangular head

Tacks (T) and screws (S) have also been included in the tables as have objects which are possible nails (?) and those which are parts of nails (N), either the head or the shaft itself. No nails were recovered from Trial Trench 2.

Nails are widely distributed in most of the sixteenth-century and later contexts from the site. The Type C nails only occur in Context 22 in Trench 92.104, a sixteenth-century layer. The Type D nails, which are horseshoe nails, appear in Trenches 92.102 and 92.104, but only in those contexts of eighteenth-century or earlier date. Trench 92.103 is different in that there are five examples of Type D nails in contexts of late eighteenth- to early nineteenth-century date.

A full list of all the ironwork, including a sketch, forms part of the archive material for the site.

Ctxt	Date	A	B	C	D	E	F	T	S	N	?
100	17th–19th C	1	–	–	–	1	–	–	–	–	2
103	15th–19th C	–	–	–	1	–	–	–	–	–	–
105	15th–16th C	2	2	–	1	1	–	–	–	–	–
Total: (11)		3	2	–	2	2	–	–	–	–	2

Table 22   Nails from Trial Trench 1 (91.129)

Ctxt	Date	A	B	C	D	E	F	T	S	N	?
300	17th–20th C	–	–	–	–	–	1	–	–	–	–
301	17th C	–	–	–	1	–	–	–	–	–	–
303	?17th C	1	–	–	–	–	–	–	–	–	–
305	?17th C	–	–	–	–	–	–	–	–	–	1
306	?17th C	–	1	–	–	–	–	–	–	–	–
308	?17th C	–	2	–	–	–	–	–	–	–	1
Total: (8)		1	3	–	1	–	1	–	–	–	2

Table 23   Nails from Trial Trench 3 (91.129)

Ctxt	Date	A	B	C	D	E	F	T	S	N	?
002	19th–20th C	–	1	–	–	–	–	–	–	–	–
006	17th–18th C	–	–	–	–	1	–	–	–	–	1
007	17th–20th C	–	–	–	–	–	–	–	–	–	1
008	17th–20th C	1	2	–	1	–	–	–	–	–	–
011	17th–20th C	1	1	–	–	–	–	–	–	–	1
012	17th–19th C	–	1	–	–	–	–	–	–	–	–
014	17th–19th C	–	1	–	–	–	–	–	–	–	3
016	?18th C	–	1	–	–	–	–	–	–	–	–
017	17th C	–	1	–	–	–	1	–	–	–	–
018	17th–18th C	–	1	–	1	–	–	–	–	4	–
019	17th C	1	–	–	–	–	–	–	–	1	–
023	17th C	–	–	–	–	1	–	–	–	3	1
024	17th–18th C	–	–	–	–	–	–	–	–	2	–
028	17th–18th C	–	–	–	–	–	–	–	–	1	–
030	?18th C	–	1	–	–	1	–	–	–	2	–
033	17th C	–	–	–	–	1	–	–	–	–	1
035	?	1	–	–	–	–	–	–	–	–	–
036	?	–	–	–	–	–	–	–	–	–	1
040	?16th C	–	–	–	–	–	–	–	–	1	–
Total: (43)		4	10	–	2	3	1	–	–	14	9

Table 24   Nails from Trench 92.102

Ctxt	Date	A	B	C	D	E	F	T	S	N	?
001	17th–19th C	–	1	–	–	1	2	3	1	4	–
005	17th–20th C	7	7	–	–	1	2	–	2	22	–
036	18th–19th C	–	–	–	1	–	–	–	–	–	–
038	18th–19th C	–	–	–	1	–	–	–	–	–	–
040	18th–19th C	4	–	–	–	–	–	–	1	4	–
046	18th–19th C	–	–	–	1	–	–	–	–	–	–
048	18th–19th C	–	–	–	–	–	–	–	–	1	–
052	18th–19th C	–	–	–	–	–	2	–	–	–	–
053	18th–19th C	–	–	–	–	–	–	–	–	1	–
054	18th–19th C	–	–	–	–	–	–	–	–	4	–
055	18th–19th C	–	–	–	2	–	–	–	–	–	–
056	18th–19th C	–	–	–	1	–	–	–	–	–	–
064	18th–19th C	–	–	–	–	–	–	–	–	3	–
065	18th–19th C	–	–	–	1	–	–	–	–	–	–
082	17th C	8	5	–	1	6	–	–	–	30	–
087	17th C	–	–	–	–	–	–	–	–	8	–
089	17th C	–	–	–	1	–	–	–	–	13	–
090	17th–18th C	–	–	–	–	–	–	–	–	4	–
093	Pre 1600	1	–	–	–	4	–	1	–	19	–
094	16th C	–	–	–	–	1	–	2	–	11	–
095	18th–19th C	–	–	–	–	–	–	–	–	1	–
098	?17th C	–	–	–	1	–	–	–	–	3	–
100	17th/18th C	–	–	–	–	–	–	–	1	4	–
106	18th/19th C	–	–	–	–	–	–	–	–	1	–
108	?17th C	1	–	–	–	–	–	–	–	1	–
109	?17th C	2	–	–	–	2	–	–	–	5	–
110	16th–17th C	–	1	–	–	–	–	–	–	5	–
120	16th–17th C	–	–	–	–	–	–	–	–	3	–
135	?16th C	–	1	–	–	1	–	–	–	1	–
Total: (203)		23	15	–	10	16	6	6	5	148	–

Table 25   Nails, tacks and screws from Trench 92.103

Ctxt	Date	A	B	C	D	E	F	T	S	N	?
001	17th–19th C	–	2	–	–	–	–	–	–	2	1
002	17th–19th C	–	1	–	–	1	–	–	–	3	1
004	1660–1690	–	–	–	–	–	–	–	–	1	–
005	?	–	–	–	–	–	1	–	–	2	1
006	?	–	–	–	–	–	–	–	–	1	–
007	18th–19th C	–	–	–	–	–	–	–	–	7	3
019	? 17th C	–	1	–	2	1	–	–	–	10	–
020	? 17th C	–	7	–	2	1	–	–	–	5	–
021	? 16th C	–	2	–	–	1	–	–	–	10	–
022	? 16th C	–	1	3	–	5	–	–	–	9	–
023	15th–16th C	–	–	–	–	–	–	–	–	3	1
Total: (91)		–	14	3	4	9	1	–	–	53	7

Table 26   Nails from Trench 92.104

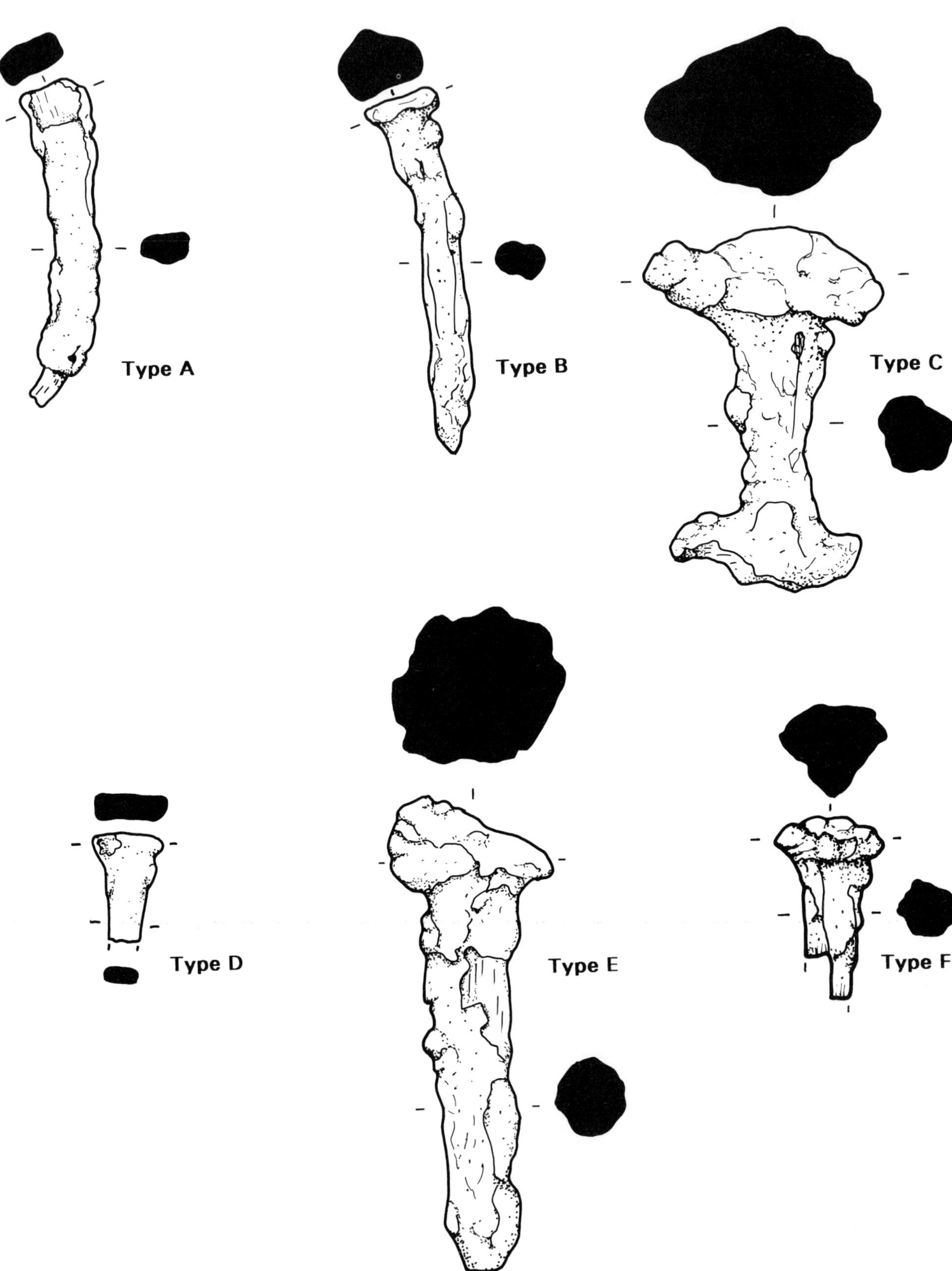

Fig 59   Castle Rushen Stores, Nail Type Series (Scale 1:1)

Non-Ferrous Metal (Figs 60 and 61)

G Egan

The range of copper-alloy and non-ferrous white-metal finds recovered from the site is wide, and this is largely because of the use of a metal detector in skilled hands. None of the items is definitely earlier than the fifteenth century; there is a small amount of sixteenth-century material, increasing numbers of finds from seventeenth-century layers, but very few from the eighteenth century. All these finds are individually catalogued below. The very large number of nineteenth- to twentieth-century items, which at this stage add very little to the archaeological perspective, are dealt with more summarily, with only a small selection included below, apart from a few categories where there is a continuity of similar items (pins and lace chapes), or where unusual finds from the later deposits may reflect those from the earlier ones, for example, bullet cartridges and lead shot, all of which are described. Many of the latest finds are too fragmentary to identify from this period of great proliferation and expanding diversity in material culture, and few categories have received any systematic study from archaeologists.

No significant variation from urban and rural assemblages across England stands out amongst the finds, and none of the items is necessarily of Manx manufacture. A couple of specific parallels for early metalwork items from London and beyond underline the case for mainland or even continental manufacture (Figs 60.2 and 11).

The number of pieces of shot, with apparent counterparts in the later cartridges, together with buttons from commercial airline uniforms, point to the strategic significance of the island, and its developing transport links.

Amongst the items probably of eighteenth-century or earlier date, the dress accessories comprise a decorated strap end from the close of this medieval tradition (Fig 60.1); a sixteenth-century decorated hooked tag (Fig 60.2) with parallels in London and the Netherlands; 26 pins of standard form from the sixteenth to the twentieth centuries; 11 simple lace chapes from the sixteenth to eighteenth centuries; buttons—generally of plainer forms, two of copper and eight of lead—from the seventeenth century onwards (including the later ones from BEA uniforms and one from a fireman's uniform); and a sixteenth-century wire loop (Fig 60.8), which may be a fastener or part of the reinforcing from a purse. The earlier of the rumbler bells (Fig 60.9) is probably of seventeenth-century date, and could be a dress item, though a pet or draught animal seems more likely to have worn it.

Tools include a needle from a seventeenth-century deposit (Fig 60.10), a decorative knife-end cap (Fig 60.11), characteristic of a sixteenth-century fashion well known on the mainland, and part of a handle. These finds, however, provide little evidence for specific activities. There is a cast copper-alloy fragment, probably from a vessel of some kind (Fig 61.14), and a range of roves, wire, sheet offcuts, lead runnels and a hammered lead bar, from the sixteenth century onwards, though again there is no clear focus for defining the activities they represent. Of the seven shot balls, five date from the seventeenth century. A small fragment of decorated lead from an unidentified item (Fig 61.18), possibly of sixteenth-century date, may be from a cheap mass-produced trinket like a brooch.

The assemblage provides useful indications of the local material culture from the sixteenth century onwards. Decorative items such as the hooked tag from Context 92.104/20 (Fig 60.2) and the knife-end cap from Context 92.103/93 (Fig 60.11) underline from their parallels the wide availability of some of the more distinctive finds.

CATALOGUE

Copper alloy

Strap end (Fig 60.1)

Front sheet from composite strap end, ?terminal broken off, 56 × 17mm; sub-circular aperture at attached end; engraved with grid of five pairs of rectangles, each alternate one having engraved zigzags to give a checker-like pattern; two iron rivets. The presence of iron rivets on a copper-alloy accessory may well indicate re-use. Possibly sixteenth-century (92.104/22).

Hooked tag (Fig 60.2)

Trapezoidal attachment loop, circular decorative panel with edge beading and openwork cross having triple-branched arms; asymmetrically angled hook; 37mm × 17mm; from a sixteenth- or early seventeenth-century context (92.104/20).

A number of decorative hooks of this general kind are known, including three from London and two from the Netherlands of precisely the same design as this example (Museum of London acc nos 80.406/99 and 101 and 86.141/2; Hopstaken 1987, 46). The second of those from London has been published as dating to the early seventeenth century (Murdoch *et al*, 1991, 109 and 111, No 214) though the two continental finds are from a site that was apparently overwhelmed by flooding in 1530. Other excavated examples, of different designs, are from

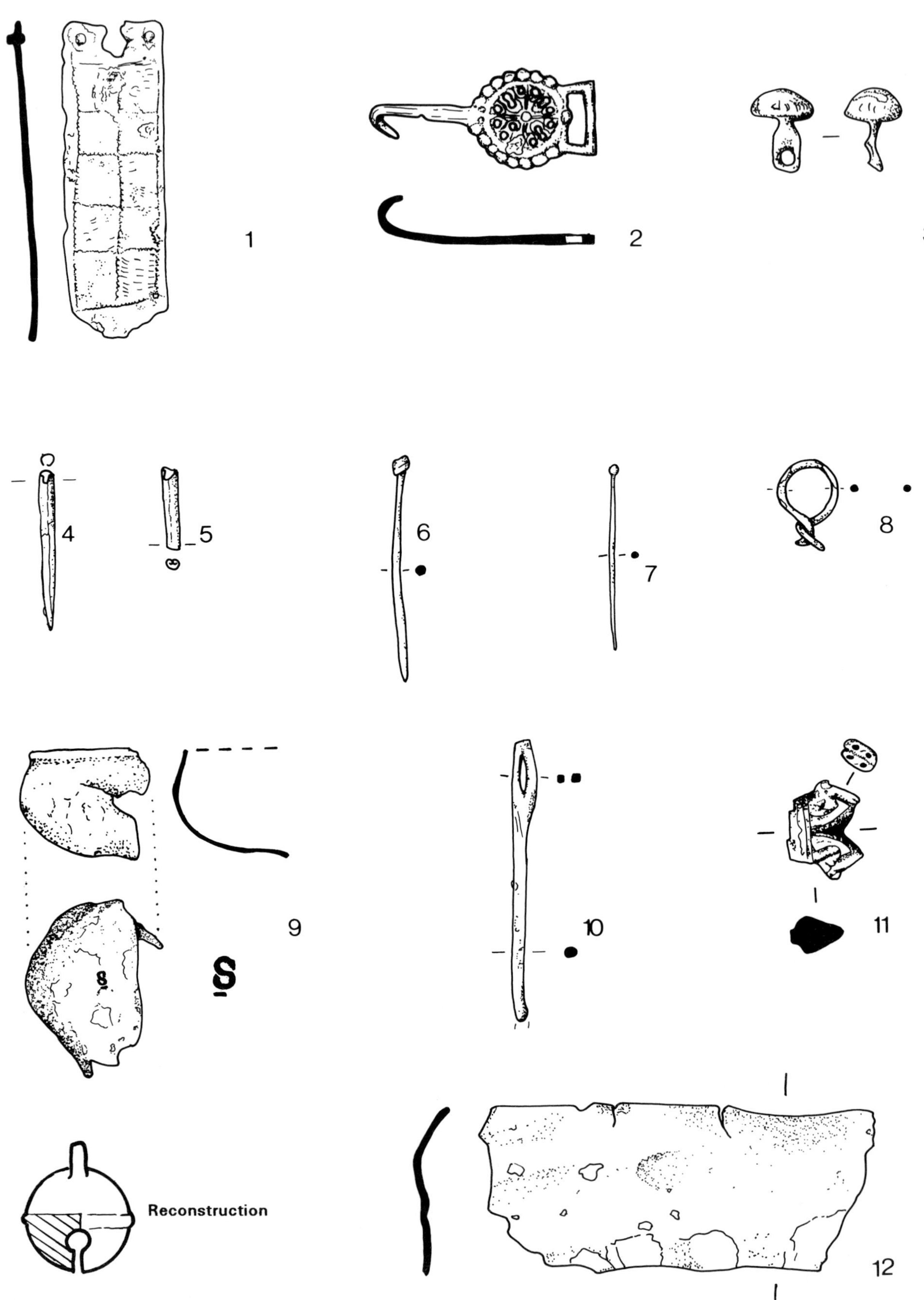

Fig 60   Castle Rushen Stores, Non-Ferrous Metal; Nos 1–12 (Scale 1:1)

contexts of diverse date, for example, Sandal Castle, W. Yorks—1485–1645 (Goodall 1983, 232–23 Fig 1, No 30); Hull—early to mid-sixteenth century (Armstrong 1977, 66–67, Fig 28, No 112); Coventry—*c*1545–*c*1557/8 (Woodfield 1981, 96 and 98, Fig 6, No 105); Chelmsford—*c*1700–1730 (Goodall 1985, 42–43, Fig 27 No 25); and Winchester—early to mid-nineteenth century (Hinton 1990, 549–52, Fig 149, No 1428). Three decorative chains found in Amsterdam, lengths between 240mm and 330mm, and with similar hooks at each end, are from deposits dated to the sixteenth to early seventeenth centuries, and are interpreted as cloak fasteners (Baart *et al* 1977, 154–55, Nos 162–64). Whilst this identification is plausible, there seems to be no specific evidence for it; the dating appears most probable, the hooks from later deposits presumably being residual.

Buckle
D-shaped frame, 28mm × 23mm; bar slightly set back; pin. Nineteenth- or twentieth-century (92.104/6).

Buttons (cf Fig 60.3)
Thirteen buttons were recovered, as follows:

1 Cast, plano-convex; diameter 13mm; loop for attachment. Early twentieth-century or later (92.102/6).

2 Corroded and incomplete convex head; diameter 17mm; bevel near edge. Late eighteenth- or early nineteenth-century (92.102/12).

3–5 Three buttons similar to preceding item; diameter 12mm. Late eighteenth- or early nineteenth-century (92.102/14).

6 Cast; plano-convex; diameter 9mm; faint, radiating grooves near perimeter; tapered tab with drilled hole for attachment at back. Seventeenth-century (92.103/82; Fig 60.3).

7 Corroded; cast disc head; diameter 21mm; ?integral loop. Eighteenth-century or later (92.103/127).

8–9 Two plano-convex buttons with plastic backs; diameter 25mm; crown over BEA; obliquely hatched border; FORMICA LONDON on backs; looped wire shanks. From British European Airways uniform; recent (92.104/1).

10–12 Three plain buttons, forms as preceding items, but with heads in two parts; diameter 23mm; recent (92.104/1).

13 Plain, flat-headed, two-part metal button; diameter 13mm; two holes for attachment; recent (92.104/1).

Stud
Corroded; convex bone inset diameter 14mm at one end, brilliant-cut glass gem at the other. Nineteenth-to twentieth-century (92.104/7).

Popper
Male part, diameter 17mm, six holes for attachment; recent (92.104/1).

?Eyelet
Fragment of possible C-section eyelet; diameter *c*7mm; recent (92.103/3).

Mounts
1 Elongated octagon, 35mm × 20mm, with arched section lengthwise; in centre radiating beading, and gems all defined by a line of beading, with gems each surrounded by beading and dividing transverse lines of beading (the gems are all brilliant-cut glass, several are missing); looped strip (distorted) for attachment at back. Possibly an ornament for the hair; recent (92.104/2).

2 Stamped sheet plain ring with rosettes and decorative rococo arcs around, maximum diameter 31mm. Nineteenth- to twentieth-century (92.104/5).

Lace chapes (cf Figs 60.4 and 5)
Sheeting bent into tubes for the ends of laces of textile or leather. These were used on jerkins and other clothing, but apparently not on shoes. Only two have rivets.
Fold types: I ◯ , II ◑◑ .

1 Length 12mm+; end corroded, shaft diameter 2mm; ?sixteenth-century (92.102/40).

2 Length 17mm+; end corroded, shaft diameter 2.5mm; with robust oval rod of uncertain material (?not a lace); ?sixteenth-century (92.102/40).

3 Length 18mm+; diameter at end 2mm; Fold type I; nineteenth-century or later (92.130/5).

4 Length 20mm+; diameter at end 3mm; Fold type I; nineteenth-century or later (92.103/5).

5   Length 24mm+; diameter at end 2mm; with rivet; Fold type I; nineteenth-century or later (92.103/5).

6   Length 20mm; diameter at end 2.5mm; diameter at tip 1.5mm; tip ?rounded; Fold type I; seventeenth-century or earlier (92.103/93).

7   Length 22mm+; shaft 3mm × 1.5mm; Fold type I; seventeenth-century or earlier (92.103/93).

8   Length 31mm; diameter at end 2mm; diameter at tip 1.5mm; tip ?rounded; Fold type I; seventeenth-century or earlier (92.103/93).

9   Length 14mm+; shaft diameter 3mm; Fold type II; seventeenth-century (92.103/98; Fig 60.4).

10   Length 28mm; diameter at end 3mm; diameter at tip 1mm; tip rounded; with rivet; Fold type I; seventeenth-century (92.103/98; Fig 60.5).

11   Length 24mm; diameter at end 2.5mm; diameter at tip 2mm; tip ?broken off; Fold type II; sixteenth- to seventeenth-century (92.103/108).

Pins (cf Fig 60.6 and 7)

Twenty-six pins were recovered and are as follows. They have wound-wire heads unless stated otherwise. Lengths are only given for complete examples.

1   Length 31mm, wire diameter c0.75mm (92.129 Area 3, U/S).

2   Length 34mm, diameter 1mm. Seventeenth-century context (92.129/303).

3   Length 35.5mm, diameter 1mm. Seventeenth-century context (92.129/305).

4   Diameter c0.75mm. Early twentieth-century or later (92.102/6).

5   Length 32mm. Early twentieth-century or later (92.102/8).

6   Incomplete and corroded, diameter of wire c1mm (92.102/11)

7   Diameter c0.75mm. Late eighteenth- to early nineteenth-century context (92.102/27).

8   Diameter c1.25mm. Late eighteenth- to early nineteenth-century context (92.102/30).

9   Length 48mm. Nineteenth-century or later (92.103/5).

10–11   (At least two) diameter c0.75mm. Nineteenth-century or later (92.103/5).

12   Length 32mm. Late eighteenth-century or later (92.103/54; Fig 60.7).

13–17   Five pins diameter c0.75mm. Late eighteenth-century or later (92.103/55).

18   Diameter c1.25mm. Late eighteenth-century or later (92.103/55).

19   Diameter c0.75mm. Seventeenth century (92.103/89).

20   Diameter c0.75mm. Seventeenth-century or earlier (92.103/93).

21   Diameter c0.75mm. Seventeenth-century (92.103/94).

22   Length 29mm. Seventeenth-century (92.103/108).

23   Length 31mm. Seventeenth-century (92.103/108).

24   Diameter c0.5mm. Seventeenth-century (92.103/108).

25   Length 39mm, diameter c1.25mm. Probably sixteenth-century (92.103/109; Fig 60.6).

26   Length 39mm. Probably sixteenth-century (92.103/109).

Twisted wire loop (Fig 60.8)

These common items seem to have been sewn onto textile and leather accessories, and some found in human burials in Norwich have been interpreted as fasteners (Margeson 1993, 20). A pouch found in Southampton has the surface covered with these loops to act as a cheap reinforcement, perhaps against cut purses (cf Egan forthcoming a). It is not yet clear whether either of these functions, or both, represent the regular usage of these simple objects, or if they served other purposes as well.

Diameter of loop 10mm. Probably sixteenth-century (92.103/109).

Rumbler bell (Fig 60.9)
Possibly from human dress, but it is more likely to be from a pet's collar or a horse harness, as a later one from Context 91.129/100 almost certainly is.

1 Rim fragment of cast bell, diameter *c*80mm. Nineteenth- to twentieth-century (91.129/100).

2 Distorted fragment of lower sheet hemisphere, diameter *c*28mm; an incuse S may be a maker's mark. Seventeenth-century (92.103/82; Fig 60.9).

Needle (Fig 60.10)
Incomplete (point missing), length 49mm+, punched eye. Late seventeenth-century (92.103/93).

Point of pin or needle
Surviving length 43mm. Late seventeenth-century (92.103/93).

Cutlery (cf Fig 60.11)
1 Spoon bowl fragment. Early twentieth century or later (92.102/8).

2 Knife-end cap in form of two stylised, out-splayed, horse's hooves; 17mm × 12mm; nails are represented by shallow holes to the sides of a central groove; circumferential groove near point of attachment; part of iron tang survives (92.103/93; Fig 60.11).

   Several parallels are known on complete knives found in London and attributed to the sixteenth century (see Somers Cocks and Blair 1979, 4 and 6, No 9); a simple hoof motif also appears on pewter spoons thought to be of slightly later date and perhaps of French origin (Hilton Price 1908, 33, Fig 17). Late seventeenth-century or earlier.

3 Four-pronged fork, length 167mm; expanded handle with round top. Early twentieth-century or later (92.104/7).

Keyhole escutcheon
Rectangular plate, 49mm × 18mm, with bevelled, rectangular hole cover on pivot. Nineteenth- to twentieth-century (92.104/4).

Handles
1 Robust, oval drop handle, 61mm × 37mm; thickened outer edge; bevelled, octagonal-section attachment loop with traces of rust; possibly from a metal vessel. Nineteenth- to twentieth-century (92.104/8).

2 Oval drop handle. Early twentieth-century or later (92.102/8).

?Picture hanger
Sheet object, 20mm × 13mm; keyhole-like aperture towards rounded end, two smaller holes in centres of each of a pair of lobes at other end. ?The larger hole was to accommodate a nail head for attachment and two tack holes were for fixture. Early twentieth-century or later (92.102/11).

Tacks
Two tacks, lengths 13mm and 17mm; square-section shanks and sub-round heads. Nineteenth- to twentieth-century (92.104/6).

Roves
1 Rove-like object, diameter 14mm, with thickened inner and outer edges, the latter with beading; rod-like extensions on each side, one with rabbeted end, the other corroded; recovered from recent garden soil (92.129/100).

2 Irregularly rounded, maximum diameter 21mm. Sixteenth-century context (92.129/105).

Wire
1 Multiple, offset coils, diameter *c*15mm; possibly a spring. Early twentieth-century or later (92.102/13).

2 Pair of wires with a third coiled around the central part, and a fourth partly spiralled around one pair of ends. Early twentieth-century or later (92.102/13).

3 Fragments. Early twentieth-century or later (92.102/13).

4–5 Two pieces, nineteenth- or twentieth-century (92.104/4).

6 One piece, nineteenth- or twentieth-century (92.104/6).

Sheeting (cf Fig 60.12)
Nine pieces of copper-alloy sheeting were recovered, as follows:

1 Two fragments. Nineteenth- to twentieth-century (92.102/13).

2 Fragment. From a seventeenth-century context (92.102/41).

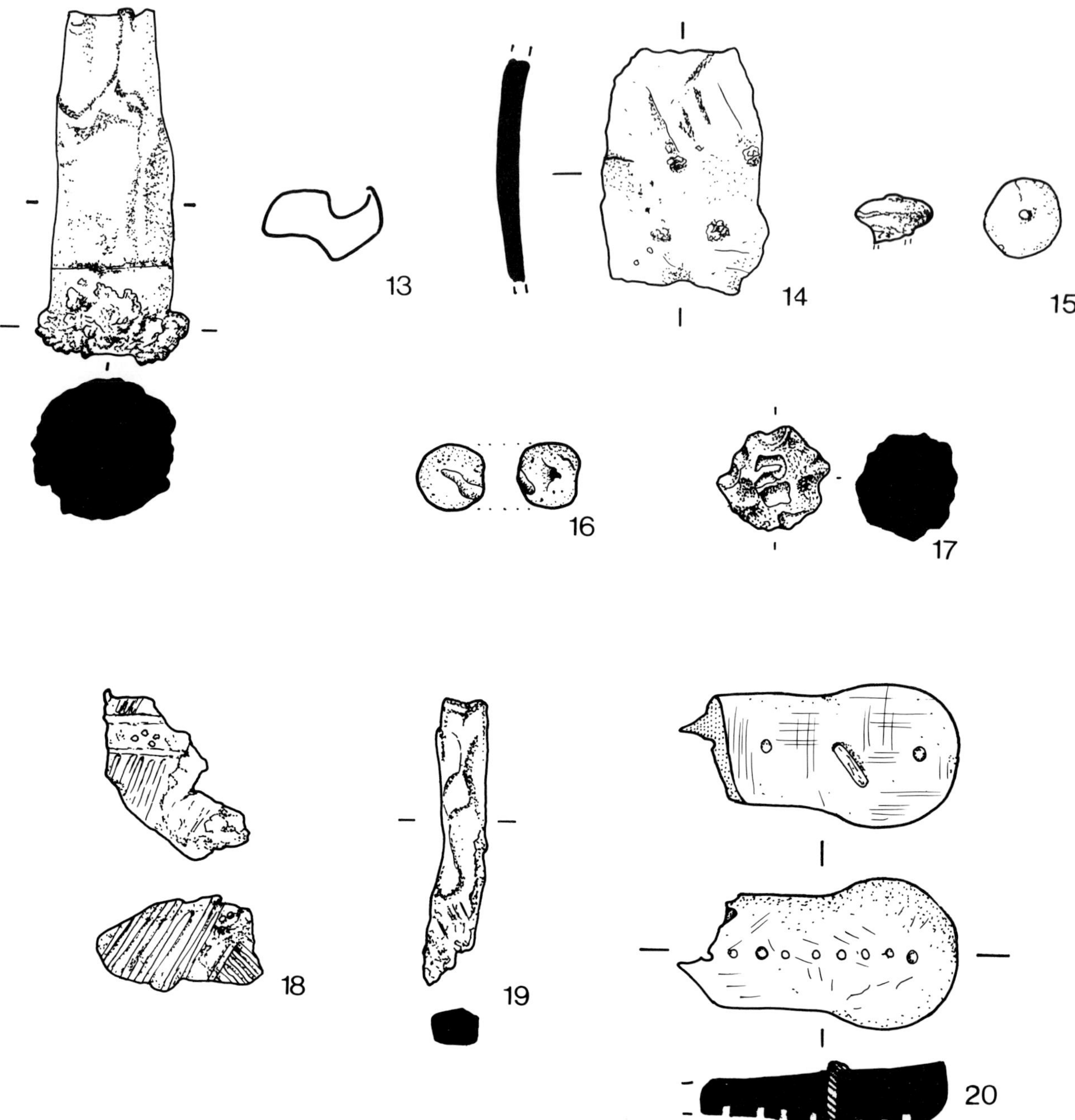

Fig 61   Castle Rushen Stores, Non-Ferrous Metal: Nos 13–20 (Scale 1:1)

3 Fragment. From a probable sixteenth-century context (92.102/49).

4 Roughly lozenge-shaped; 15mm × 14mm; off-central hole. Late eighteenth-century or later (92.103/63).

5 Rectangular piece, 16mm × 8mm. Seventeenth-century or earlier (92.103/93).

6 Two sheet strips, the larger 35mm × 10mm, with one rounded, pierced end, broken off at the other, and a smaller fragment. Seventeenth-century (92.103/94).

7 Fragment. From a sixteenth-century context (92.104/22).

8 Fragmentary strip, 68mm × 27mm; the longer sides are nearly parallel; broken off at both ends. From a sixteenth-century context (92.104/22; Fig 60.12).

9 Smaller fragment as preceding item. From a sixteenth-century context (92.104/22).

Cartridge cases (cf *Fig 61.13*)

1 Corroded and distorted cylinder, length 50mm; separate end cap, diameter 20mm. Early

twentieth-century or later (92.102/11; Fig 61.13).

2   Corroded end cap, diameter 18mm. Early twentieth-century or later (92.104/7).

Miscellaneous (cf *Fig 61.14*)

1   Fragmentary ring of tubular sheeting, diameter *c*35mm. Recent (91.129/100).

2   Irregular rod, length 20mm; thickened at one end, pointed at the other. From a context containing sixteenth-century and later material (92.129/103).

3   Electrical wire with cover of wound textile tape; recent (92.103/5).

4   Electrical component strip. Early twentieth-century or later (92.104/4).

5   Cast, curved fragment; broken off on all sides, 36mm × 45mm; roughly finished; hint of taper at one end; possibly from a vessel. From a seventeenth-century context (92.104/20; Fig 61.14).

6–11   Seven unidentified scraps from Trench 92.102 as follows: six from late eighteenth- or early nineteenth-century contexts (6, 12, 14, 17, 24, 28) and one from a sixteenth-century context (44).

Lead and other non-ferrous white metals

Buttons (cf *Fig 61.15*)

1   Corroded, possibly a button; convex; diameter 12mm; ?ligatured, cursive initials in beaded border. Nineteenth- or twentieth-century (92.102/8).

2   Crude, biconvex; diameter 13mm; central, raised boss; trace of ?iron shank. Late eighteenth-century or later (92.103/1; Fig 61.15).

3   Corroded; diameter 18mm; convex centre, with illegible maker's name around; traces of black coating. Nineteenth- to twentieth-century (92.104/7).

Vessel

Distorted fragment (possibly the base); thickened rim; cast, circumferential lines internally. Recent (92.104/2).

?Lid

Corroded; vertical-sided, diameter 50mm. Nineteenth- or twentieth-century (92.104/5).

Shot (cf *Fig 61.16 and 17*)

1   Corroded, diameter 14mm. From a probable sixteenth-century context (92.102/40).

2   Diameter 11mm. Seventeenth-century or earlier (92.103/93).

3   Diameter 16mm; ?impact mark. Seventeenth-century or earlier (92.103/82).

4   Diameter 10mm; ?impact marks. Probably seventeenth-century (92.103/89; Fig 61.16).

5   Very irregular surface, diameter approx. 15mm; presumably a piece of shot, with indentations. Probably seventeenth-century (92.103/89; Fig 61.17).

6   Diameter 17mm; gnawed by a rodent. Probably seventeenth-century (92.103/89).

7   Diameter 16mm. Late eighteenth-century or later context (92.103/62).

Rove

Slightly dished, diameter 19mm, ?separate sheet on one face; recent context (91.129/102).

?Rivet

Convex head, diameter 27mm, with slight groove diametrically, shaft corroded; recent context (91.129/102).

?Machine part

Slightly convex disc, diameter 26mm, with shallow groove diametrically; iron geared disc diameter *c*35mm attached to back; recent context (91.129/102).

Pencil sharpener

Corroded sharpener of conical form, surviving length 30mm; initials (?H)B in oval ?indicating maker; decorative handle at end; rusted iron blade. Nineteenth- to twentieth-century (92.104/7).

Thimble

Machine-made, domed thimble; height 23mm, diameter at base 17mm; black lettering ?COMEM-FORME; floral motif around end. Early twentieth-century or later (92.102/9).

Candle holder

Incomplete and corroded pewter candle holder cup base, with flanged foot and basal rivet; surviving height 28mm. Nineteenth- to twentieth-century (92.104/4).

Tubes

1 Corroded, slightly curved piece of sheet tube, length 46mm, diameter *c*3mm. Recent (91.129/ 100).

2 Bent tube, partly corroded; diameter 10mm, length *c*150mm; collar near broken-off end. Early twentieth-century or later (92.102/8).

Miscellaneous (cf Fig 61.18 and 19)

1 Corroded, non-ferrous white-metal disc; diameter 14mm; tab at one end (too thick for a cloth seal) (92.102 U/S).

2 Incomplete and distorted fragment; length 55mm; flange at right angle along edge; two round stubs. Early twentieth-century or later (92.102/9).

3 Arched tie or staple, now distorted; holes for attachment at the rounded ends; raised strengthening ridge to each side of mid-point; present length *c*80mm, width 13mm. Recent (92.103/1).

4 Sub-round, flat object; 42mm × 40mm, thickness 7mm; cut off on one side; expanded, convex-headed ?rivet at centre, holding rusted iron fragment, with solder. Recent (92.104/1).

5 Flattish, D-section bar; length 262mm, width 14mm, with four holes for attachment. Nineteenth- to twentieth-century (92.104/6).

6 Flat, sub-triangular object, 22mm × 20mm, with raised border; loop on one side, trace of a possible second on another. Nineteenth- to twentieth-century (92.104/10).

7 Fragments of thin, ?round-edged object cast with parallel hatching in three areas, one divided from the others by a band having four pellets and raised edges. Parallels for this kind of crude decoration are found particularly amongst cheap dress accessories and toys of late medieval to seventeenth-century date, though no specific identification can be suggested. From a sixteenth-century context (92.104/21; Fig 61.18).

8 Irregular, partly hammered bar; 42mm × *c*6mm × 5mm. Seventeenth-century or earlier (92.103/ 93; Fig 61.19).

Sheeting

1 44mm × 44mm; folded in half. Recent (92.102/ 1).

2 Folded, irregularly cut fragment; 63mm × 24mm. Nineteenth-century or later (92.103/5).

3 Strip folded into tube, length 54mm. Nineteenth-century or later (92.103/5).

Miscellaneous scraps

1 One piece. Nineteenth-century or later (92.103/ 5).

2 One piece. Nineteenth-century or later (92.103/ 5).

3 One piece. Probably seventeenth-century (92.104/20).

4 One piece. Probably sixteenth-century (92.104/ 21).

5 One piece. Probably sixteenth-century (92.104/ 22).

6 One piece. Possibly fifteenth- to sixteenth-century (92.104/23).

Runnels

1 One piece. Recent (91.129/100).

2 Probable runnel. Probably sixteenth-century (91.129/105).

3 One piece. Recent (92.102/1).

4 One piece. Recent (92.103/1).

5 Three pieces. Seventeenth-century (92.103/ 82).

6 One piece. Probably seventeenth-century (92.103/89).

7 One piece. Seventeenth-century (92.103/90).

8 Five pieces. Probably sixteenth-century (92.103/110).

9   Irregular, flattish casting, 49mm × 26mm, from within a right-angled container, raised ridge along straight sides. Recent (92.104/2).

10   One piece. Possibly seventeenth-century (92.104/19).

11   Two pieces. Probably seventeenth-century (92.104/20).

12   Two pieces. Probably sixteenth-century (92.104/21).

13   One piece. Probably sixteenth-century (92.104/22).

14   Group of recent items of metal—several electrical components, etc. (92.104/1).

Composite objects

Bone handles (cf *Fig 61.20*)

1   Incomplete tool handle, scale, >47mm × 10mm; tapers near one end and towards the other; two holes for rivets — one of copper alloy survives, along with part of the iron tang and a trace of the other scale. From a small tool, such as a knife or boot hook, etc. Early twentieth-century or later (92.102/11).

2   Fragmentary, knopped end of cutlery handle scale, >40mm × 23mm; copper-alloy rivets (one survives, staining from others) and series of decorative holes on same alignment, some with copper-alloy insets; probably late eighteenth/early nineteenth-century (92.102/23; Fig 61.20).

Plastic buttons

1   Plano-convex; diameter 22mm; NFS in raised border; plain back; shank is round plate with central hole; National Fire Service uniform button. Recent (92.104/1).

2   Probably a button; fragment of convex ?head; diameter 21mm; central stem on back; abraded. Recent (92.104/1).

Coins
M M Archibald

Fifteen coins were recovered from the excavation at Castle Rushen Stores, as follows:

1   United Kingdom. Victoria, penny 1862. This coin is corroded but is relatively unworn. It is likely to have been deposited, at the latest, by *c*1900 (92.102/7).

2   Isle of Man. Victoria, farthing 1839. This coin is corroded but is relatively unworn. It is likely to have been deposited, at the latest, by *c*1900 (92.102/8).

3   England. Elizabeth I, sixpence, date illegible. This coin is very corroded but unclipped. It appears to have been in better condition than such coins found in Civil War contexts, so was probably deposited by *c*1600, but a later survival cannot be ruled out (92.102/16).

4   Spain. Philip II (1556–98), *cuartillo*, Cuenca mint, after 1566 (92.103/5). (Fontecha y Sanchez, 1968 No: PII, 47)

5   Germany. Nuremberg jetton, late sixteenth- to early seventeenth-century. Maker's name illegible. *Reichsapfel* 3 crowns and 3 *lis* around rose type. Diameter: 21mm (92.103/82).

6   Germany. Nuremberg jetton fragment, sixteenth-century. *Reichsapfel* 3 crowns and 3 *lis* around rose type. Diameter: estimated at about 24mm. This jetton is very corroded and only about one-third of it is present. The four letters visible of the obverse inscription are part of the place-name Nuremberg, and the name of the issuer is absent (92.103/89).

7   United Kingdom. Edward VII, halfpenny 1903. This coin is hardly worn. It is likely to have been deposited by *c*1920 (92.104/1).

8   United Kingdom. Victoria, halfpenny 1862. This coin is corroded but is relatively unworn. It is likely to have been deposited, at the latest, by *c*1900 (92.104/1).

9   United Kingdom. George VI, halfpenny 1937. This coin is very corroded, but appears to have been relatively unworn. It is likely to have been deposited, at the latest, by *c*1950 (92.104/1).

10   United Kingdom. George VI, halfpenny 1942. As above (92.104/1).

11   United Kingdom. George VI, halfpenny 1938. As above (92.104/1).

12   Isle of Man. Douglas Bank, halfpenny token 1811. Obverse with view of Peel Castle (Davies

1969, No 10). This token is somewhat worn, and has been deliberately defaced with intersecting scores on the obverse (92.104/7).

13   Isle of Man. James Stanley, Earl of Derby 1702–36, halfpenny token, cast type 1709 (Seaby 1984, 7402). This token is likely to have been deposited, at the latest, by 1786 when regal issues for the Isle of Man began (92.104/19).

14   England. Elizabeth I, sixpence, initial mark bell 1582–3; London, date illegible (North 1980, II, No 1997 or No 2015). This coin is chipped and corroded (92.104/21).

15   England. Edward III, halfpenny (fragments). Second Coinage, London 1335–44 (North 1980, II, No 1102). This coin is slightly worn. Such coins had a long life in currency, and although it is more likely to have been deposited in the mid-fourteenth century, a date as late as the early fifteenth century cannot be ruled out (92.104/23).

Flint (Fig 62)

S B McCartan

The assemblage comprises 28 pieces, 11 of which are natural. With the exception of one natural piece of schist (?), the rest are flint. Flint occurs around the Castletown area as gravel and pebbles on the nearby beaches, where schist is probably also found. Thirteen of the 17 worked pieces are partially or wholly patinated. This alteration can occur as a result of mineral action within the soil and/or exposure to the natural elements.

Very few pieces preserve evidence of primary flaking technology. It would not appear that hard hammer percussion was employed, but there is a suggestion that medium and soft hammers, together with platform preparation, were used in the production of some pieces. None of the artifacts exhibit signs of secondary technology or retouching, but the majority have edge damage which may or may not have occurred during use.

There is no evidence for *in situ* material. The assemblage may represent prehistoric material disturbed by later activity, such as the construction of the plot boundary between Arbory Street and Malew Street, property boundaries, gardens and buildings. It is also possible that some of the worked and natural flint was originally in soil brought into the area to build up the sixteenth- to nineteenth-century gardens. Similarly, it may also have been contained in gravel or other building materials used in the construction of banks, walls and buildings.

Most of the flint was recovered from Trench 92.103, which probably reflects the much larger area excavated, but it was also where the greatest evidence for boundary construction and gardens was recovered.

Given the meagre evidence for both primary and secondary technologies, and the absence of prehistoric features, it is not possible to ascribe the flint stone assemblage to a particular prehistoric period or periods. Pieces such as that from Context 92.103/48 (Fig 62.2) and from Context 92.103/110 (Fig 62.4), however, would not look out of place in an early Mesolithic assemblage. The nearby sites of Cass ny Hawin, Pooilvaaish, Strandhall and Port St Mary attest to early Mesolithic settlement along the eastern coastal areas of the island.

The Castle Rushen Stores flint industry may represent prehistoric activity in the area. The proximity of the site to the Silver Burn and the coast would have made it an attractive area for either permanent settlement, or as a temporary encampment to exploit seasonal riverine and coastal resources. It is not unusual for quantities of worked and natural flint to be found during urban excavations, as repeated use of a site will obviously result in the destruction of earlier evidence, as already seen with the archaeological excavations within the walls of Castle Rushen and Peel Castle. However, the possibility that the flint may have come from soil or building materials brought into the area from elsewhere must also be considered.

CATALOGUE

Notes to catalogue

1   All pieces are flint unless otherwise stated.
2   During analysis all pieces were held with the dorsal face uppermost and the proximal end towards the observer.
3   Patination refers to the discolouration of the flint. Due to problems with current terminology, no distinction has been made between patination and cortication.
4   Edge damage refers to the removal of small flakes from the piece. Without the use of a high powered microscope it is not clear whether the damage is due to use or to post-depositional processes.
5   Dimensions are given in millimetres in the order: length: width: thickness.

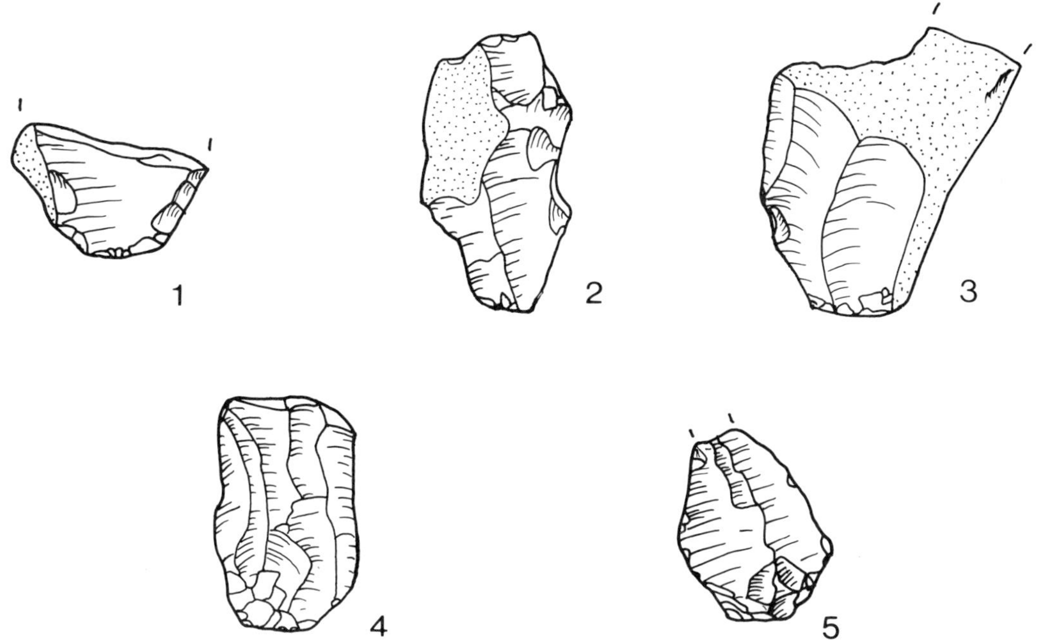

Fig 62   Castle Rushen Stores, Flint (Scale 1:1)

Trench 92.102

1   Secondary flake; grey; abraded; proximal surviving; edge damage; 14:25:04 (6; Fig 62.1).

2   Natural (16).

3   Natural (23)

4   Natural (schist?) (23)

5   Natural (30)

Trench 92.103 and Trial Trench 3

1   Secondary flake; toffee brown/orange; patinated; abraded; segment surviving; edge damage; 15:18:07 (91.129/300).

2   Natural (5).

3   Natural (5).

4   Natural (5).

5   Secondary flake; grey; partially patinated; proximal surviving; edge damage; 24:29:16 (34).

6   Secondary blade: grey and red; partially patinated; small fragment missing at distal; extensive edge damage; 37:18:04 (48; Fig 62.2).

7   Primary flake; cream/toffee brown; patinated; abraded; edge damage; 24:20:08 (87).

8   Primary flake; grey; one lateral surviving; edge damage; 19:13:09 (89).

9   Natural (89).

10   Natural (89).

11   Inner flake; toffee brown; hinge fracture; 13:10:02 (90).

12   Secondary flake; yellow/grey; partially patinated; proximal surviving; edge damage; 17:32:08 (108).

13   Inner flake; yellow/grey; partially patinated; hinge fracture; edge damage; 28:19:05 (108).

14   Secondary flake; toffee brown; partially patinated; small fragment missing from distal; edge damage; 39:30:10 (91.129/308=92.103/109; Fig 62.3)

15   Secondary blade; grey/white; patinated; modern edge damage; 33:18:06 (110).

16   Secondary flake; toffee/orange; patinated; abraded; edge damage; 30:18:05 (110; Fig 62.4).

17   Inner flake; grey/white; patinated; proximal surviving; edge damage; 14:11:05 (135).

Trench 92.104 and Trial Trench 1

1   Secondary flake; grey; abraded; extensive edge damage; 55:41:27 (91.129/103).

2   Secondary flake; grey; partially patinated; distal surviving; edge damage; 32:27:09 (22).

3   Natural (23).

4   Natural (23).

5   Secondary flake; grey/white; patinated; abraded; small fragment missing from distal; edge damage; 25:17:04 (23; Fig 62.5).

6   Secondary flake; toffee brown; partially patinated; distal surviving; edge damage; 32:43:17 (23).

Coal, Coke, Cinder and Burnt Stone

N C Johnson

The excavations at Castle Rushen Stores recovered fragments of coal, coke, cinder and burnt stone material in the following quantities:

Coal:	186
Coke:	49
Cinder:	6
Burnt stone:	31

This material derived from a total of 52 contexts, distributed over the whole site. It also covered the full range of phased use as identified by the pottery report, with the single exception of Phase 2 in Trench 92.104.

Method

Standard excavation practice was followed; the material was collected in discrete context groups and noted in the site records, and subsequently was bagged and stored in these context groups. Due to the nature of the material, individual pieces were not marked with the accession number; the bag and label provide the sole sourcing record. The tables below indicate the total quantity of fragments recovered from each context, together with an indication of the maximum volume of the largest piece in cubic centimetres.

Context	Coal		Coke		Cinder		Burnt Stone	
	No	Vol	No	Vol	No	Vol	No	Vol
002	–	–	–	–	1	<4	–	–
006	3	<2	–	–	–	–	1	<1
012	1	<4	–	–	–	–	–	–
014	3	<1	–	–	–	–	–	–
018	1	<1	–	–	–	–	–	–
019	–	–	–	–	1	<1	–	–
023	–	–	1	<8	–	–	–	–
024	–	–	2	<8	–	–	–	–
030	6	<27	–	–	–	–	–	–
036	5	<8	–	–	–	–	–	–
038	3	<175	–	–	–	–	–	–
040	1	<4	–	–	1	<1	–	–
041	–	–	2	<3	–	–	–	–
046	3	<1	–	–	–	–	1	<1

Table 27   Coal, coke, cinder and burnt stone from Trench 92.102

Trench 92.102

Fragments of coal and cinder are present in this trench from an early period in its development: Contexts 40 and 46 both produced a small, but significant number, indicating a use of coal in the neighbourhood of the site in the sixteenth century.

The distribution of fragments of coal, with some coke, across other later contexts is fairly widespread, with a bias towards occupation surfaces.

Trench 92.103

Sixteen coal fragments were recovered from a sixteenth-century context (109) in this trench. The

Context	Coal		Coke		Cinder		Burnt Stone	
	No	Vol	No	Vol	No	Vol	No	Vol
001	1	<2	–	–	–	–	–	–
005	10	<9	4	<8	–	–	8	<25
'012	1	<1	–	–	–	–	–	–
014	3	<1	–	–	–	–	–	–
015	2	<6	–	–	–	–	–	–
016	2	<8	–	–	–	–	2	<8
019	–	–	–	–	–	–	1	<6
036	8	<8	–	–	–	–	1	<1
038	1	<1	–	–	–	–	–	–
040	–	–	2	<1	–	–	–	–
046	2	<4	–	–	–	–	–	–
048	12	<15	7	<1	–	–	–	–
052	1	<2	–	–	–	–	1	<1
053	–	–	2	<1	–	–	–	–
054	2	<5	–	–	–	–	–	–
056	–	–	1	<1	–	–	–	–
057	4	<8	–	–	–	–	–	–
064	1	<3	–	–	–	–	4	<100
082	18	<8	2	<8	–	–	–	–
087	4	<8	–	–	–	–	–	–
089	13	<15	12	<8	2	<1	2	<1
090	3	<3	–	–	–	–	–	–
093	1	<4	–	–	–	–	–	–
094	2	<6	–	–	–	–	–	–
098	2	<1	–	–	–	–	–	–
106	3	<1	–	–	–	–	–	–
108	20	<9	2	<8	–	–	–	–
109	16	<8	5	<8	–	–	–	–
116	1	<4	–	–	–	–	–	–
118	3	<1	–	–	–	–	–	–

Table 28   Coal, coke, cinder and burnt stone from Trench 92.103

relatively high number of these compared with other contexts make it unlikely that they represent contamination, although their location solely within one context indicates that this evidence should not be overloaded with significance.

Distribution, both vertically and horizontally, of coal fragments in the Phase 2, seventeenth-century layers, is much more widespread. Fragments were recovered from both ends of the trench, either side of the boundary bank. The total number increases towards the upper levels of this phase; the quantity recovered from Context 89 may indicate some contamination.

A similarly wide range of distribution is shown by the material recovered from Phase 3 contexts, whilst Phase 4 is represented by a quantity of fragments from Context 5, which is small relative to its large geographical area. Only two cinder fragments were recovered from this trench, both of them from Context 89.

Trench 92.104

The chronology of the coal finds from this trench is comparable with the others. A single fragment was recovered from Context 23, a sixteenth-century soil immediately overlying the natural, and a number of others from the group of layers just above it which have been allocated to Phase 1.

No material was retrieved from Context 19 (Phase 2), but further finds were made in the soils and pit fills belonging to the late nineteenth and twentieth centuries. A large ash pit (7) was notable for containing a number of pieces of burnt stone, perhaps indicating the quality of the coal imported.

Context	Coal		Coke		Cinder		Burnt Stone	
	No	Vol	No	Vol	No	Vol	No	Vol
001	1	<1	1	<1	–	–	–	–
002	6	<12	–	–	1	<1	–	–
005	2	<9	–	–	–	–	–	–
007	7	<60	5	<45	–	–	8	<15
020	3	<10	–	–	–	–	–	–
021	1	<2	–	–	–	–	–	–
022	2	<2	–	–	–	–	–	–
023	1	<6	–	–	–	–	–	–
u/s	1	<4	1	<64	–	–	2	<3

Table 29   Coal, coke, cinder and burnt stone from Trench 92.104

Discussion

The most significant point to emerge from the excavated material, from all three trenches, is the date at which coal appears to have been in use in the Castletown area. Each trench produced coal fragments from sixteenth-century contexts, suggesting that coal was in common use. The availability of wood on the island has long been questioned; this ubiquity of coal fragments would suggest that the absence of timber and the favourable maritime location led to a relatively early use of coal. It may also have implications for the nature of industrial processes in the locality.

Certainly, it would appear from the following extract from the Exchequer Book of the Isle of Man (1696, 66–67) that there was a pollution problem in the island by the seventeenth century, although the exact source and type of fuel is not evident:

For as much as by the general want of Chimneys throughout this Isle and more especially in Markett, and other townes, the smoke coming out of the doores is a very great Inconvenience both to the Inhabitants and passers by. For remedy whereof, and the better to prevent fire for the time to come, You are to give notice to all householders within your Sheading who already have not Chimneys to their respective dwelling houses that on or before the tenth day of December next upon paine of ten shillings fine for the first offence To be forthwith levied they make not only a sufficient Chimney but also a convenient range for the more effectuall carrying up the said Smoke, and if any person doe neglect therin (after due notice given), he or they soe offending shall for every week the same is unfinished after the said tenth of December forfeit the sume of two shillings and six pence to be levied as aforesaid and for the better performance hereof you are to make presentments of every default att the next Chancery Court, as you will answer the court att your uttmost will. Given under my hand att Cstle Rushen this twenty third Day of October Anno Domini 1696.

Nicholas Sankey.

To the Coroners of the Severall Sheadings within this Isle. 27th October. Copies of the above said order are this day sent to the severall Coroners.

(Manx Museum Microfilm RB 449a)

Vitreous and Burnt Debris

E A Slater

Overall, the three areas yielded different forms of material: Trench 92.102—corroded iron and lead; Trench 92.103 and Trial Trench 3—iron concretions and corroded iron; Trench 92.104—heated material or material produced by heating: cinder, baked clay/daub, heated lithics.

Four main types of material are represented.

1 **Cinder** Defined as very light-weight, extremely friable, porous material, often light in colour and in small pieces. Typical of residue from domestic or non-industrial fires.

2 **Heated lithic** Lithic with reddening or porosity showing the effects of low level heating. No true vitrifaction, ie a vitreous or glassy phase that might result from prolonged heating in contact with a flux like wood ash.

3 **Iron concretions** Either the corroded remains of iron objects or iron pans formed via the deposition of iron compounds from an iron-rich environment.

4 **Natural stones** (lithic samples)

All samples were weighed, examined with the naked eye and under an optical microscope at ×20 and ×80. They were all tested with a magnet for the presence of metallic iron, metallic nickel or magnetic compounds of iron (magnetite, Fe_3O_4, being the main possibility in this context). Pieces were removed for X-ray diffraction analysis from all samples except cinder and pieces of corroded iron. The aim was not to identify the compounds present, which can be difficult and complex for this type of material, but to check for the presence of certain forms of iron silicates (fayalites), iron oxides, etc. that may indicate iron slags.

Trench 92.102

1   1 piece; natural lithic 19g (6).

2   16 pieces; corroded iron, clay concretion, lithics 106g (14).

3   2 pieces; corroded iron, ?head of a nail 23g (14)

4   1 piece; lead carbonate concretion. Possibly some copper corrosion, ie small flecks of green mineral phase, but the presence of copper compounds was not detected with X-ray diffraction; 14g (46).

Trench 92.103 and Trial Trench 3

1   1 piece; lithic 1.9g (91.129/306).

2   6 pieces; 1 stone, 5 iron concretion 20g and 403g (5).

3   1 piece; heated lithic 22g (5).

4   1 piece; iron concretion 29g (14).

5   1 piece; iron concretion 197g (89).

6   1 piece; lithic 3g (103).

7   1 piece; lithic 3g (103).

8   3 pieces; lithic 102g (109).

9   1 piece; lithic with iron corrosion on the surface 64g (116).

10   1 piece; lithic 51g (116).

11   1 piece; lithic 71g (126).

12   3 pieces; iron concretion 717g (135).

Trench 92.104

1   1 piece; heated lithic. Surface colouration suggests non-intensive heating (2).

2   4 pieces; 1 lithic, 3 cinder 41g (2).

3   8 pieces; cinder 181g (5).

4   2 pieces; heated lithic 37g (5).

5   4 pieces; cinder 14g (7).

6   1 piece; baked clay vitrified on one surface 79g (21).

7   1 piece; ?lithic. No slag phases 91g (23).

Slate Pencil (Fig 63)
S D White

A small stone rod was recovered from Context 92.102/12, which probably dates from the late eighteenth- or early nineteenth-century. The rod is 42mm long and approximately 5mm in diameter, and appears to be made of slate. It has been deliberately shaped along its long axis to produce seven facets.

Fig 63   Castle Rushen Stores, Slate Pencil (Scale 1:1)

Worked Bone and Shell (Fig 64)
S D White

The excavations produced eight pieces of worked bone and the remains of four mother-of-pearl buttons. The bone items included four buttons, three of which were plain bone discs with a single hole pierced in the centre, the remains of two handles and two unidentified objects, both of which had been cut along their long axes to form a number of facets. The objects recovered are catalogued below.

Buttons
1   Bone button, diameter 17mm with concentric rings visible on one side, pierced at the centre with a single hole. From nineteenth-century garden soil (92.103/5; Fig 64.1).

2   Bone button, diameter 19mm, maximum thickness 3.5mm; a slight depression in the centre of the button is pierced with four holes. From nineteenth-century garden soil (92.103/5; Fig 64.2).

3   Bone button, diameter 14mm, pierced at the centre with a single hole. Late eighteenth to nineteenth century (92.102/57; Fig 64.3).

4   Bone button with a diameter of 11mm; pierced at the centre. From modern garden soil (92.104/2; Fig 64.4).

5–8   Remains of four mother-of-pearl buttons; 26mm diameter; pierced at the centre with four holes. The backs of the buttons are quite rough, but the fronts have two scored circles. One button is slightly damaged but otherwise complete (Fig 64.5); one button has been broken in half; the five remaining fragments appear to belong to one, and possibly two, other buttons of the same design. From an early twentieth-century deposit (92.104/7).

Handles
1   Part of a bone handle 46mm × 17mm tapering to 15mm × 6.5mm, end of handle curved and slightly worn. From nineteenth-century garden soil (92.103/5; Fig 64.6).

2   Part of a bone handle, 93mm × 14mm × 5mm; one end is round, the other tapers to form a 'neck' which is 5mm wide. From the modern garden soil (92.104/1; Fig 64.7).

Miscellaneous
1   Part of an unidentified bone object 49mm × 7mm tapering to 5mm × 5mm; roughly shaped, leaving a series of facets. From a seventeenth-century deposit (92.103/108; Fig 64.8).

2   Part of an unidentified bone object 14mm × 5mm × 4.5mm. Probably seventeenth century (92.103/89; Fig 64.9).

Leather
D A Higgins

A number of leather objects were recovered but these are all likely to be of modern date. Eight

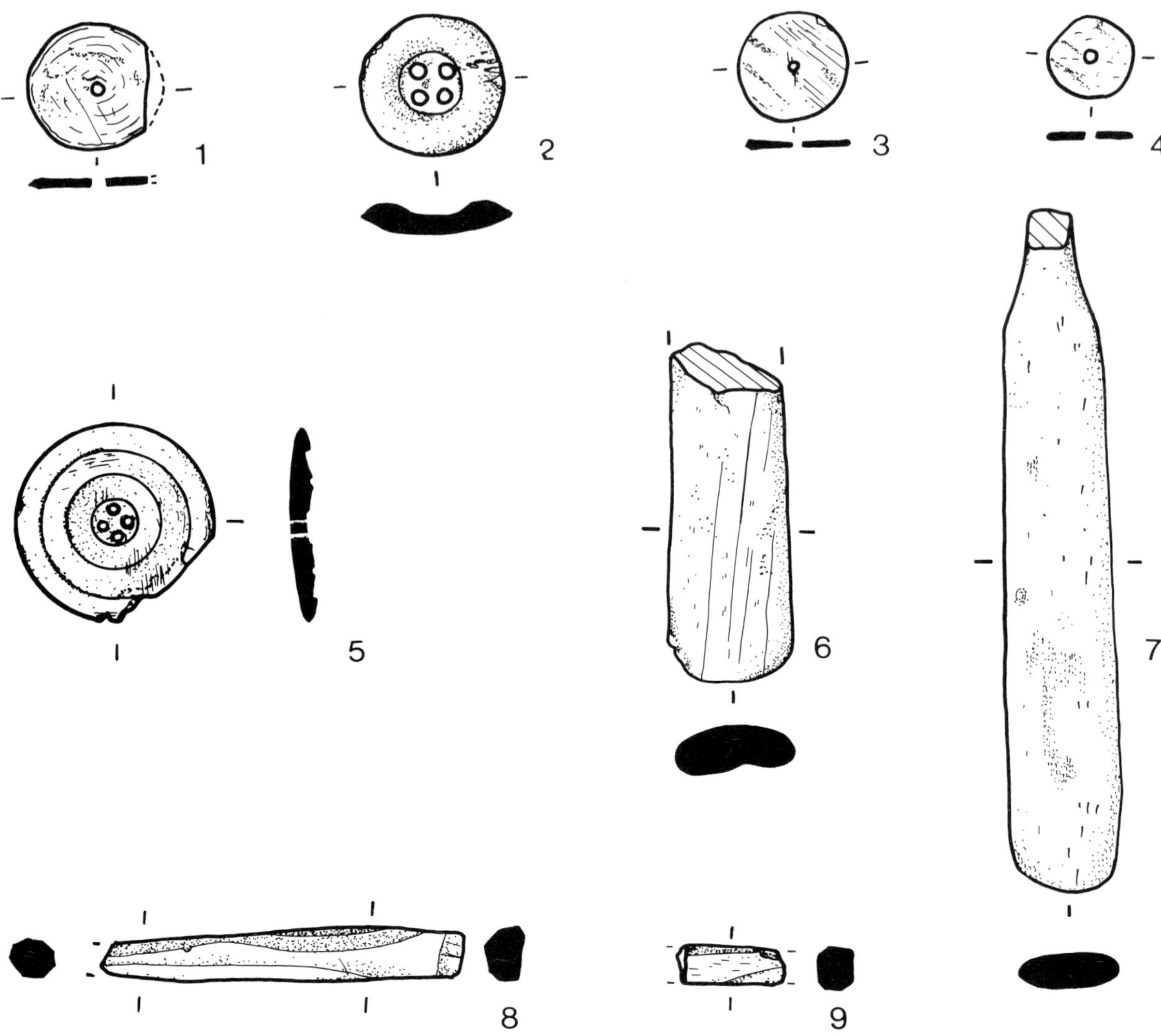

Fig 64   Castle Rushen Stores, Worked Bone and Shell (Scale 1:1)

pieces were recovered from the early twentieth-century demolition deposits in Trench 92.102. These had been preserved by being sealed under the concrete yard surface. Another four pieces were found in the uppermost layers and pits of Trench 92.104. This trench was in an overgrown garden which had been used extensively for dumping rubbish during the course of this century. The fragments recovered were:

1   Front half of a boot sole, with hobnails. Some very small portions of the upper survive (92.102/6).

2   Fragmentary remains of a shoe. Part of the heel survives with iron hobnails (92.102/8).

3   Several small fragments of leather, unidentified (92.102/8).

4   Three small fragments of leather which appear to be offcuts (92.102/10).

5   A sheet of leather without any apparent stitching holes. This would have been roughly rectangular with dimensions of 120mm × 100mm, although one of the shorter sides has an 'S' shaped cut across it (92.102/11).

6   Sole of a small shoe, probably a woman's, made of several layers of leather (92.102/14).

7   Heel of a small shoe with traces of iron nails (92.104/1).

8   Small fragment of leather, unidentified (92.104/6).

9   Virtually complete shoe sole made up of layers of leather held together with copper alloy pins (92.104/7).

10   Heel of a shoe, made up of four layers of leather held together with copper alloy pins. There are also some iron studs (92.104/7).

Fibre

S D White

A single piece of fibre was recovered from Context 92.102/46. This material was examined microscopically by Dr P R Tomlinson, who identified it as animal hair. As the surface scales of the hairs were missing, it was not possible to attribute it to any one species.

Wood

D A Higgins

A number of wood fragments were recovered. A few of these were from the upper layers of Trench 92.103. This was a covered area which had recently had its concrete floor removed. It seems likely that the majority of these fragments represent modern debris arising from this floor clearance. The remainder of the fragments were preserved in the early twentieth-century demolition deposits in Trench 92.102.

LIST OF WOOD FRAGMENTS BY CONTEXT

1   Two small plain fragments and two worked fragments. One of these is part of a moulded glazing bar from a window. It survives to a length of 160mm and is *c*25mm × 15mm in section. It is painted white and retains putty insets from the glass. The other piece survives to a maximum length of 110mm, is painted a yellow-ochre colour and was part of a larger object or structure. It has a large, looping projection at one end and a groove carved all down one edge (92.102/8).

2   Two pieces: one sawn, possibly part of a plank, the other a painted wooden bar. This bar survives to a maximum length of 200mm. In section it is 20mm in one dimension but tapers from 27mm to 24mm in the other. It has been painted a dull yellow-ochre colour (92.102/9).

3   Three slivers of wood, up to 65mm maximum length (92.102/10).

4   Fragment, less than 25mm maximum length (92.102/17).

5   Fragments, less than 30mm maximum length (92.102/21).

6   Fragment of wood, approximately 85mm × 25mm × 10mm (92.102/23).

7   One small fragment (92.102/40).

8   Several small fragments (92.103/3).

9   Ten assorted fragments, including a small wooden peg. This is cylindrical, 32mm in length and tapering from 7.5mm to 6mm in diameter (92.103/5).

10   Wooden post, surviving to a length of 340mm. The main section is 63mm × 40mm and has three iron nails embedded in it. It tapers to a blunted point which is 44mm × 25mm. The post was set in the soil beneath the concrete floor and may well have been driven in before this area was roofed and floored (92.103/89).

Bottle Corks

D A Higgins

The early twentieth-century demolition deposits in Trench 92.102 produced a total of 77 bottle corks. The majority of these were wine bottle types which ranged in size from 31mm long with a diameter of 20mm, to 40mm long with a diameter of 23mm. Some of the corks retained traces of marks on them, but these were all too degraded to be legible. All of the corks appear to have been damaged where they have been pulled from a bottle with a corkscrew. In addition to the wine bottle corks there were a number of other stoppers or bungs present.

The totals recovered from each context were:

1   One cork, wine bottle type (2).

2   15 corks: 13 wine bottle type and two bungs, one 33mm deep and tapering in diameter from 28mm to 24mm, the other 9mm deep and tapering from 30mm to 26mm (8).

3   53 corks: 52 wine bottle types and one bung. This was 30mm deep and tapered from 30mm to 26mm (9).

4   Eight corks, all wine bottle types (11).

ENVIRONMENTAL EVIDENCE FROM CASTLE RUSHEN AND CASTLE RUSHEN STORES

Animal bone

M McCarthy

Introduction

In recent years the town centre of Castletown has received considerable archaeological investigation. Excavations undertaken by D J Freke in Castle Rushen in 1989 uncovered the remains of several structures and features, most of which were associated with late medieval activity at the castle. Further excavations outside the castle by J M Lewis and D A Higgins during the summers of 1991 and 1992, in the area known as Castle Rushen Stores, revealed some structural evidence and successive layers of garden soils. Ceramic finds indicated that most of the garden features had built up during the post-medieval period.

The faunal remains recovered during these excavations represent a reasonable sample of the meat requirements of both the occupants of the castle and the residents of nearby houses. As there are no other reports on assemblages of animal bones excavated in the Isle of Man, this material from Castletown is of particular significance in providing the first opportunity to examine the diet of the island's medieval and post-medieval residents. The analysis has also presented the opportunity to determine how and to what extent differences in status between the occupants of the castle and the householders at Castle Rushen Stores are reflected in the faunal refuse.

Recovery

The animal bones that form the basis of this report were all recovered by hand during normal trench excavation. In the absence of sieving, it is most likely that the bones of small birds, small mammals and fish are under-represented. It seems a safe assumption that fish must have been exploited to a greater extent than the sample of bones recovered would suggest. Examination of residues from sieved soil samples from Peel Castle indicated that fish were significant food items. It can be concluded, therefore, that their low representation at both Castle Rushen and Castle Rushen Stores is linked to the on-site recovery methods.

Methods

The identification of the animal bones was mostly carried out in the Manx Museum and the Centre for Manx Studies. The material, which was examined by area and phase, was first sorted into identifiable and non-identifiable groups. The non-identifiable group included those bones which, although they could not be positively identified to species level, could be categorised into a size class. For example, when a bone could not be assigned with certainty to pig or sheep, the category 'medium mammal' (MM in tables) was used. In the same way, bones that could not definitely be recorded as cattle were classed as 'large mammal' (LM in tables) fragments.

The identifiable sample was sorted into elements and species using the rather limited comparative material housed in the Manx Museum and with reference to Schmid's (1972) *Atlas for the Identification of Animal Bones*. Problematic bones were taken to Ireland for identification with the more extensive skeletal collections in the Department of Archaeology, University College Cork. These were returned to the Isle of Man after identification.

Sheep were distinguished from goat on the basis of diagnostic morphological features outlined by Boessneck (1969) and Prummel and Frisch (1986). In addition, the position of the nutrient foramen was recorded on all suitable sheep femora, as this may be an indication of breed (Noddle 1978). The native breed of sheep, the Manx Loaghtan, apparently lacks a foramen in the proximal midshaft area of the bone (Bazin 1984). The ovicaprid bones are all referred to as 'sheep' in the text as many of them bore anatomical features distinguishing them to that species.

Ageing evidence was derived from the eruption and wear patterns of teeth, using the methods of Grant (1975) and Silver (1971), and from the less accurate method of the fusion of the epiphyses to the shafts of long bones, with reference again to Silver's work. The relative abundance of the species present was expressed in terms of the percentages of bones that were identified and, in the case of the three main domesticates, by estimating the minimum number of individuals present. All measurements were taken with hand-operated digital callipers, following the methods outlined by von den Driesch (1976). The figures are presented in tabular form to an accuracy of 0.1mm.

Medieval 14th Century	Horse	Cow	S/G*	Pig	Deer	Dog	Cat	Rat	Rabbit	LM*	MM*
Curtain Wall 178	–	4	3	2	–	–	–	–	1	9	–
Moat Fills 65, 121, 134, 190	–	31	13	5	–	–	–	–	–	23	15
Pit Contexts 149, 154, 160, 172, 186, 197	2	302	77	37	4	53	4	7	–	137	46
Late Medieval **15th–17th Century**											
Drains 56, 63, 77, 114, 140, 143, 145, 155, 156, 167, 173, 184	1	535	226	47	5	59	10	86	3	275	119
Pit Contexts 170, 171, 198	–	31	15/1	3	–	1	–	–	–	24	6
Ash Layers 50, 72	5	147	70	17	3	28	6	2	1	119	45
Cobbles 80, 89, 129, 132	–	76	16	2	–	4	–	–	–	34	13

S/G* Sheep/Goat   LM* Large mammal   MM* Medium mammal

Table 30   Castle Rushen; number of animal bones by period and context grouping

	Horse	Cattle	S/G*	Pig	Dog	Cat	LM*	MM*	Totals
Cranial	–	6	–	2	–	–	–	3	11
Maxilla	–	1	1	3	–	–	–	–	5
Mandible	–	2	–	6	3	–	–	–	11
Teeth	1	6	4	10	1	–	–	–	22
Atlas	–	3	1	–	1	–	–	–	5
Axis	–	3	–	–	–	–	–	–	3
Vertebrae	–	61	5	2	9	2	6	–	85
Humerus	–	22	8	5	5	–	2	–	42
Radius	–	18	6	–	3	1	4	–	32
Ulna	–	11	–	3	5	–	–	–	19
Scapula	–	19	10	–	7	–	8	3	47
Femur	–	32	12	1	2	1	9	–	57
Tibia	–	18	14	1	4	–	5	1	43
Pelvis	–	25	3	1	2	–	8	–	39
Astragalus	–	9	–	–	–	–	–	–	9
Calcaneum	–	10	1	–	–	–	–	–	11
Carps/Tars*	–	14	–	–	–	–	–	–	14
Metatarsus	1	8	7	–	7	–	–	–	23
Metacarpus	–	7	4	1	3	–	–	–	15
Phalanx	–	20	1	–	–	–	–	–	21
Ribs	–	–	–	–	–	–	61	30	91
LBF*	–	–	–	–	–	–	34	9	43
Other	–	7	–	2	1	–	–	–	10
Totals	2	302	77	37	53	4	137	46	**658**

S/G* Sheep/Goat   LBF* Long bone fragment   LM* Large mammal   MM* Medium mammal   Carps/Tars* Carpals/Tarsals

Table 31   Castle Rushen; domestic mammals, Period 1, pit contexts

Condition of the material

The condition of the material varied considerably between the two sites and also between different contexts within individual sites. Overall, the bones from Castle Rushen were better preserved than those excavated at Castle Rushen Stores. Within Castle Rushen material itself, the samples from the medieval deposits were the best preserved, showing very little evidence of gnawing (2%) and weathering (6%). This suggests that the bones did not lie on the surface of the ground for any great length of time, but were deposited into the pits and middens relatively soon. A much larger percentage of the bones from Period 2 had been gnawed and exposed to weathering, indicating perhaps that the castle area was not kept as clear of food waste during the post-medieval period.

Burning was quite common, particularly in the Castle Rushen Stores material. This may point to different cooking methods or to a different approach to rubbish disposal, with the occupants of the houses at Castle Rushen Stores burning a certain amount of their animal debris. Most of the animal bones from Castle Rushen Stores were recovered from garden soils which also contained a range of other domestic debris. The highly fragmented and weathered condition of the sample indicates that the deposits accumulated slowly, with bones being exposed to trampling and gnawing or exposure over a long period of time. Canid gnawing was recorded on almost 20% of the bones, indicating that dogs also played a significant role in the degeneration of the faunal sample.

Castle Rushen

The vast majority of the bones (72%) found at Castle Rushen are late to post-medieval in date, but a small number of bones were also recovered from fourteenth-century contexts. The bone material was found for the most part in pits, drains and moat fills. The context numbers and their grouping within the different periods recognised by the excavators are given in Table 30.

Period 1: fourteenth century

Faunal material dating to the fourteenth-century occupation of the castle consists of 775 bone fragments. These have been derived from numerous features across the site which have been grouped together under the following context headings: moat fills; pit contexts; and a deposit from the area of the curtain wall. The highest concentration of animal bones occurred in individual pit samples. This patterning may be attributed to refuse disposal practices, with bone material being deliberately discarded into pits, whilst other contexts remained relatively bone free. The material is described below by context grouping.

The moat fills
Eighty-eight fragments of bone derived from various fills of the castle moat, of which 50 (57%) could be positively identified. Cattle are the most common species, comprising 31 (62%) of the identifiable sample. Sheep are represented by 13 bones (26%) and pig by just five (10%) fragments. There was evidence for a single lamb under six months. The other 38 bones could not be identified as a particular species but were classed as the remains of large and medium-sized mammals.

Evidence that cattle were used for traction was attested by the recovery of a phalanx which had severe eburnation (polishing) on the proximal joint surface as well as moderate exostosis around the proximal shaft area. The moat fills provided evidence of a possible additional food resource in the vertebra of an immature cetacean, probably a porpoise. This single occurrence does not necessarily imply the deliberate hunting of marine mammals for food. The fact that the bone belongs to an immature individual may indicate that it represents a young animal which, having strayed from the family group, eventually ended up being washed ashore near Castletown. The absence of any trace of human modification on the vertebra is noteworthy, as is the presence of canid marks, suggesting that the bone might easily have been brought into the castle area by a dog.

The pit contexts
Six hundred and sixty-nine fragments of bone were examined from six pits. Favourable preservation conditions meant that the bulk of the material was identifiable, with only 180 (27%) bones being grouped into size categories. Table 31 shows the mammal species and skeletal element representation for the pit material as a whole. A list of the identified species is also given for each pit in Table 32. As the contents of the individual pits did not vary significantly in terms of species composition, the results are combined together in the following description.

Over 535 (80%) of the bones were stained dark brown with no traces of gnawing or erosion, suggesting that the bones were quickly incorporated into the pits and covered with soil. In contrast with the other two context groupings in this period, the pit samples produced quite a diversity of animals,

	Pit 149	Pit 154	Pit 160	Pit 172	Pit 186	Pit 197
Cattle	30	85	57	87	10	33
Sheep/Goat	3	15	13	26	–	20
Pig	4	10	9	7	2	5
Horse	–	1	–	–	–	1
Dog	2	6	4	37	4	–
Cat	–	1	–	3	–	–
Deer	–	2	2	–	–	–
Hare	–	–	–	–	–	–
Rat	1	4	–	1	–	1
LM*	3	41	23	40	11	19
MM*	1	10	6	21	–	8
Totals	44	175	114	222	27	87

LM* Large mammal   MM* Medium mammal

Table 32   Castle Rushen; Period 1, animal bones from pit contexts

although again the large domestic mammals form the greater part of the assemblage.

Cattle bones are by far the most numerous amongst the finds, accounting for 303 (62%) of the total identifiable sample. Although all parts of the body are represented, the bovine sample is dominated by the remains of upper meatier bones, implying that the pits functioned more as disposal areas for waste from the table than for primary butchery debris. A cattle metatarsus showed slight degeneration of the proximal articular surface, with pitting and polishing caused by some form of joint disease such as osteoarthritis.

Sheep are second in importance, with 78 (16%) of the identifiable bones coming from this species. The species is slightly better represented in terms of the number of individuals represented (21%). Lamb seems to have been favoured, with at least two individuals occurring in a single pit. An analysis of the elements present provided similar results to cattle in that the bones seem to consist mainly of food waste from the kitchen and table, with the products of primary butchering waste forming a low proportion of the assemblage.

The remains of pig are very poorly represented, accounting for just 39 (8%) of the identifiable sample. The bones of the head are the most common element, which is probably not unusual as a pig's head was considered a delicacy in the medieval period and often appeared as a centrepiece on a table prepared for a banquet or feast. The presence of three piglet bones indicates that the flesh of suckling pigs was also chosen, again perhaps for a special event.

The pit grouping produced the second largest assemblage of dog bones from Castle Rushen, with the deep pit against the curtain wall (89.159/172) alone accounting for 37 of the 53 bones recovered.

The remaining dog bones were scattered evenly and in small amounts amongst the other four pits. There are at least three individuals represented of varying sizes: 302mm, 323mm and 405mm at the shoulder. Three thoracic vertebrae showed slight lipping (osteophytosis) around the area of the centrum, which is indicative of a degenerative joint disease.

Other species were only nominally represented in the pits. Two vertebrae, a radius and a femur from an immature cat, and a tooth plus a metatarsus from a horse made up the remainder of the domestic assemblage. The horse metatarsus was incomplete and did not allow for a wither's height to be established for the animal. Tooth wear evidence indicated that it came from an individual aged somewhere between six and ten years.

There was very little evidence for wild species of animals. Single rat bones recovered from four of the six pits listed in Table 32 represent individuals probably regularly frequenting refuse areas in search of fodder. Finally, fragments of two metatarsi, a carpal and a humerus from a species of deer, probably red deer, *Cervus elaphus*, on the basis of size, produced the sole evidence for the exploitation of wild game. Three of the deer bones came from the deep pit against the curtain wall (89.159/154), in which a small quantity of piglet bones was also found. Together, these bones may represent waste from a single meal.

The curtain wall

Only 19 fragments of bone were recovered from a deposit associated with the curtain wall (89.159/ 178) and ten (52%) of these were identified as cattle (four), sheep (three), pig (two) and rabbit, *Oryctolagus cuniculus* (one). The remaining nine bones were classified as long bone fragments of large mammals.

The rabbit bone, the central portion of a pelvis, showed some superficial knife marks probably related to skinning. It is not known when rabbits were first introduced into the main island of Man (Garrad 1972) but it is documented that in the sixteenth century they were deliberately brought onto the Calf by the Lords of Man to increase the number of nest sites for their shearwaters (McCarroll, Garrad and Dackombe 1990, 76). Rabbits are first found in Britain and Ireland in the thirteenth century, when they were introduced by the Normans to meet the food requirements of a new wealthier class. Whilst it is tempting to record this specimen from a fourteenth-century context at Castle Rushen as providing evidence for the presence of rabbits on the island at a date earlier than is generally accepted, it would be unwise given that the deposit from which the bone was recovered

	Horse	Cattle	S/G*	Pig	Deer	Dog	Cat	LM*	MM*	Totals
Horn Core	–	1	–	–	–	–	–	–	–	1
Antler	–	–	–	–	1	–	–	–	–	1
Cranial	–	5	15	–	–	2	–	9	–	31
Maxilla	–	–	–	1	–	3	–	–	–	4
Mandible	–	4	3	1	–	3	1	–	–	12
Teeth	1	9	10	5	–	6	–	–	–	31
Atlas	–	4	2	–	–	1	1	–	–	8
Axis	–	5	–	–	–	–	–	–	–	5
Vertebrae	–	107	35	15	1	16	–	19	6	199
Humerus	–	22	20	4	1	4	6	24	3	84
Radius	–	27	26	1	–	2	–	5	2	63
Ulna	–	11	4	2	–	3	–	–	–	20
Scapula	–	17	13	3	–	2	–	9	3	47
Femur	–	51	18	2	1	–	2	13	3	90
Tibia	–	39	38	1	1	5	–	12	–	96
Pelvis	–	28	15	2	1	–	–	15	–	61
Astragalus	–	25	6	1	–	2	–	–	–	34
Calcaneum	–	24	1	3	–	2	–	–	–	30
Carps/Tars*	–	38	3	–	–	–	–	–	–	41
Metatarsus	–	19	9	–	–	2	–	–	–	30
Metacarpus	–	24	7	4	–	5	–	8	–	48
Phalanx	–	67	1	1	–	–	–	–	–	69
Ribs	–	–	–	–	–	–	–	117	67	184
LBF*	–	–	–	–	–	–	–	44	35	79
Other	–	8	–	1	–	1	–	–	–	10
Totals	1	535	226	47	6	59	10	275	119	**1278**

S/G* Sheep/Goat   LBF* Long bone fragment   LM* Large mammal   MM* Medium mammal   Carps/Tars* Carpals/Tarsals

Table 33   Castle Rushen; Period 2, drain contexts

	Horse	Cattle	S/G*	Pig	Dog	Cat	LM*	MM*	Totals
Horn Core	–	3	–	–	–	–	–	–	–3
Cranial	–	1	–	–	14	–	–	4	19
Maxilla	–	–	–	5	–	–	–	–	5
Mandible	–	–	–	–	1	–	–	–	1
Teeth	5	6	1	3	2	–	–	–	17
Atlas	–	1	1	1	–	–	–	–	3
Vertebrae	–	8	10	–	2	1	8	6	35
Humerus	–	4	4	–	1	–	5	–	14
Radius	–	3	9	–	1	–	2	–	15
Ulna	–	3	2	–	–	–	–	–	5
Scapula	–	12	1	1	1	–	10	2	27
Femur	–	7	9	1	1	1	9	–	28
Tibia	–	18	9	–	1	–	8	2	38
Pelvis	–	6	3	1	–	–	4	–	14
Astragalus	–	6	1	–	–	–	–	–	7
Calcaneum	–	5	4	1	1	–	–	–	11
Carps/Tars*	–	13	5	–	–	–	–	–	18
Metatarsus	–	11	1	–	2	–	7	–	21
Metacarpus	–	16	1	–	–	–	4	–	21
Phalanx	–	23	6	4	1	1	–	–	35
Ribs	–	–	–	–	–	–	45	21	66
LBF*	–	–	–	–	–	–	17	10	27
Other	–	1	3	–	–	3	–	–	7
Totals	5	147	70	17	28	6	119	45	**437**

S/G* Sheep/Goat   LBF* Long bone fragment   LM* Large mammal   MM* Medium mammal   Carps/Tars* Carpals/Tarsals

Table 34   Castle Rushen; domestic mammals, Period 2, ash layers

appeared to have been subjected to later contamination (Johnson, pers comm).

Summary—Period 1

The major part of the faunal assemblage from fourteenth-century deposits at Castle Rushen consists of the remains of domestic cattle and sheep, with lesser quantities of pig bones. Cattle provided the major food source, beef seemingly accounting for over 60% of all the meat eaten in the castle. Mutton was also a significant food item and young lamb seems to have been especially prized. It would appear that pork was seldom eaten, although there is evidence that pigs' heads and suckling pig were regarded as delicacies. The recovery of the remains of at least three young pigs plus two deer bones from a single pit (89.158/154) suggests that these may have been eaten together at a single banquet to mark a special celebration or feast day.

There was very little evidence for industrial deposits. Only three cattle horn cores were recovered, all of which were chopped at the base. There was no evidence at all for goat horn cores, elements which were highly valued during the medieval period for object manufacture. This may indicate that horn cores, together with their sheaths, were carefully removed from the skull at the primary stage of butchering and then taken to a horner's workshop either elsewhere in the castle area or in some quarter of the medieval town. Overall, the fourteenth-century samples were small, the only two species of note being an immature cetacean and a rabbit, and the latter was probably intrusive.

Period 2: fifteenth to seventeenth century

Period 2 produced the bulk of the animal bones from the excavations at Castle Rushen. As with Period 1, the material was sorted into four major context groupings and is described below under these headings.

The drains

The complex network of drains uncovered outside the keep proved to be the most productive in terms of bone recovery, with almost 66% of the entire assemblage coming from 13 drain contexts. The condition of the material is quite poor in comparison with that from the earlier medieval deposits. Over 15% of the specimens were flaky and brittle, a condition which no doubt contributed to the fragmentary nature of the sample. Some of the breakage may also be due to trampling, since the bones were recovered from outside the keep in an area probably used by many pedestrians.

Gnawing was also more evident in the material from the drain contexts. Altogether, the condition of the material indicates that bones were left scattered around the yard surface of Castle Rushen before they finally became incorporated into the drain deposits. Altogether, 13 drain contexts yielded 1248 bones. A list of all bone-producing contexts and the species and elements represented is given in Tables 30 and 33 respectively.

The predominant species is cattle, which accounted for 535 (61%) of the total identifiable sample and is represented by at least 19 juvenile and adult individuals. There was no evidence that calves had been killed for their veal. After cattle, sheep are the next most commonly occurring animal, contributing 226 (26%) bones to the identifiable material with at least 10 individuals being present. It would seem that lamb was equally favoured in Period 2, with 20 bones being recovered representing at least three individuals. Pig is again rather uncommon, comprising 47 (5%) bones, with only one adult individual being represented. The presence of three young pig bones indicates that suckling pig was popular, whilst the recovery of two neo-natal bones suggests that farrowing may have taken place within the castle walls.

In terms of body parts the major food animals are best represented by meat-bearing elements such as upper limb bones, scapulae and pelves, although non-meaty foot elements like phalanges and metapodia are more numerous in this period than in the earlier fourteenth-century deposits.

The remains of dog outnumber those of pig, the 59 (7%) bones identified representing at least two individuals, one about the size of a small sheepdog, the other somewhat larger; perhaps labrador size. Cats appear for the first time in reasonable quantities, with no fewer than four individuals occurring in the drains.

The drain contexts yielded the largest sample of deer bones from the castle. Six bones were identified, five of which came from the fore and upper portions of the body and represent the remains of meat joints of high value. The remaining element consisted of a sawn portion of antler, which may indicate boneworking activity in the vicinity of the area excavated.

The proportion of other wild animals is quite high for the site. Three rabbit bones, two showing evidence for skinning, were recovered from Contexts 89.159/77 and 114. The recovery of 86 rat bones from 15 individuals may explain why the cat population increased in Period 2. Examination of the cranial material indicated that all of the bones originated from the black rat, *Rattus rattus*, the species to be expected in pre-eighteenth-century deposits.

Element	Measurement	N	Range	Mean
Humerus	Bd	9	63.6– 71.5	67.4
	BT	9	60.3– 65.9	63.3
Radius	Bp	28	64.6– 76.9	68.8
	BFp	28	58.9– 69.5	63.5
	Dp	27	38.1– 32.3	36.2
	Bd	17	55.9– 67.7	60.3
	BFd	17	52.3– 61.7	60.3
	Db	17	32.2– 43.3	37.6
Tibia	Bd	77	42.7– 59.2	53.1
	Dd	77	34.1– 46.5	39.5
Metatarsus	Bp	64	35.2– 50.5	41.4
	Dp	58	35.6– 42.4	39.1
	Bd	54	44.0– 57.2	47.7
	Dd	58	23.7– 31.4	26.5
	GL	5	199.1–240.2	213.4
Metacarpus	Bp	46	44.8– 55.7	48.9
	Dp	41	27.2– 34.2	29.6
	Bd	57	47.2– 59.7	51.3
	Dd	62	22.8– 31.6	26.9
	GL	5	163.2–182.1	171.2
Astragalus	GLl	86	48.8– 62.9	57.3
	GLm	86	46.7– 59.6	52.5
Calcaneum	GL	20	107.1–131.9	115.8
Phalanx I	Bp	92	22.4– 32.4	25.9
	GL	92	45.9– 58.7	51.6
Phalanx II	Bp	68	21.7– 29.6	25.3
	GL	68	30.8– 39.1	33.6
Scapula	GLP	36	50.3– 67.1	59.2
	GLG	36	44.3– 56.8	50.2
	BG	35	35.7– 46.4	40.3
	SLC	27	42.8– 55.9	47.4

Table 35   Castle Rushen; summary of cattle measurements

Measurement Abbreviations
Bd   Distal breadth
BFd   Breadth of the Facies articularis distalis
Dd   Distal depth
BT   Breadth of trochlea
Bp   Proximal breadth
BFp   Breadth of the Facies articularis proximalis
GL   Greatest length
GLl   Greatest lateral length
GLm   Greatest medial length
GLP   Greatest length of the Processus articularis
GLG   Greatest length of the glenoid cavity
BG   Breadth of the glenoid cavity
SLC   Smallest length of the Collum scapulae

Element	Measurement	N	Range	Mean
Humerus	Bd	48	24.8– 30.1	27.6
	BT	48	23.3– 28.5	26.1
Radius	Bp	23	26.9– 31.2	25.9
	BFp	23	23.3– 28.5	–
	Dp	23	13.1– 15.1	–
	Bd	9	24.6– 26.7	25.7
	BFd	9	20.3– 25.3	22.6
	Dd	9	14.2– 18.1	16.1
	GL	4	127.0–149.0	–
Tibia	Bd	47	21.9– 27.3	23.9
	Dd	47	16.2– 20.4	17.1
	Bp	5	34.3– 38.7	35.9
	Dp	5	33.5– 38.3	35.7
Metatarsus	Bp	6	17.8– 19.3	18.4
	Dp	6	17.6– 19.9	18.3
	Dd	5	13.5– 14.6	13.7
	GL	1	112.0	–
Metacarpus	Bp	8	19.6– 22.7	21.3
	Dp	8	14.2– 16.2	15.2
Calcaneum	GL	5	48.8– 51.4	50.4
Astragalus	GLl	30	23.6– 33.8	26.5
	GLm	30	22.5– 31.3	25.2
Phalanx I	Bp	20	10.5– 14.3	11.7
	GL	20	29.5– 35.5	31.5
Phalanx II	Bp	8	8.7– 10.8	9.8
	GL	8	18.4– 20.3	19.3
Scapula	GLP	13	28.1– 33.7	30.3
	GLG	13	21.7– 26.6	23.8
	BG	13	16.4– 20.2	18.5
	SLC	12	17.1– 21.1	18.7

Table 36   Castle Rushen; summary of sheep measurements

Element	Measurement	N	Range
Radius	Bp	2	25.7–28.5
	Dp	2	16.4–19.3
Astragalus	GLl	1	35.9
	GLm	1	32.9
Scapula	GLP	1	30.9
	GLG	1	25.5
	SLC	1	21.4
Phalanx I	Bp	3	16.3–18.9
	GL	3	33.7–38.6

Table 37   Castle Rushen; summary of pig measurements

Pit contexts

Eighty-one bones were recovered from three pit contexts, of which 51 (63%) were identified and 30 (37%) were classified as large and medium mammal remains. The assemblage was characteristic of domestic rubbish, consisting largely of food waste. The material was in a good state of preservation, which indicates that not only was the material lying in a primary position but that it was deposited there fairly soon after use. With the exception of a single dog pelvis from Context 89.159/171, the remainder of the bones from this pit grouping consist of cattle, sheep and pig (Table 31). Cattle again dominate the sample, contributing 31 (61%) of the 51 bones identified. There are 15 sheep bones. Pig is just nominally represented. The three fragments identified as pig are all porous and may have belonged to a single immature individual. The only clear evidence for goat was a horn core from Context 89.159/171, which had been chopped horizontally at the base, presumably with the intention of using the core for artifact manufacture. Other evidence for bone working was attested by the recovery of the distal portion of a cattle metatarsus, which was sawn horizontally roughly two-thirds of the way down the length of the shaft. This specimen represents an off-cut from boneworking; the remainder of the shaft was probably fashioned into some sort of artifact.

The ash layers

The ash layers (89.159/50 and 72) together produced 437 bones. The animal bones were generally less well preserved than in the pits, but the survival of bone was still significantly better than in the drain and cobble features.

A significant number of bones, 30 (7%), especially the unidentified material, was burnt, mostly to a white colour. The totally calcined nature of these bones implies that bones left lying around the floor surface were swept into the fire and remained there for some time before being dumped along with the ashes into designated refuse areas outside the castle.

These deposits are similar to the drain contexts in providing a wide range of mammal species (Table 34). Cattle and sheep are, predictably, the most dominant species, with cattle outnumbering sheep by a little over 2:1 in terms both of the total number of fragments recovered and the minimum number of individuals represented. Almost all parts of the cattle skeleton are represented, with particularly high values for tibiae and lower limb bones, and a notable absence of mandibular and maxillary fragments.

With the exception of a single tooth there are no cranial remains of sheep, whilst all other parts of the skeleton are present. This suggests that the heads of cattle and sheep were not considered good eating and must therefore have been discarded at the earliest stage of butchering. Pig is again characterised by a dearth of remains. Only 17 (3%) bones were identified of this species, probably representing just one individual which was under two years of age at death. Five fragments of horse were identified and the species is thus slightly better represented than in other deposits. The remains consist entirely of teeth and belong to a mature individual of between six and ten years.

Other domestic animals include cat and dog. Numbering 28 (6%), dog bones are more common than the remains of pig although the numbers are probably unrepresentatively high, given that almost half of the remains represent fragmentary cranial material conceivably belonging to the one individual. Metrical evidence did indicate, however, that three individuals are present. Two humeri belong to dogs 390mm and 470mm at the shoulder, whilst a tibia comes from an animal a little larger than a terrier.

The complement of wild animals consists of deer, rat and rabbit. There are three deer bones, two of which bear marks associated with disjointing. The other bone, a phalanx, comes from a juvenile individual. Rat is present as two tibia fragments, and there is a single occurrence of rabbit.

Cobble features

The cobble features produced just 145 bones of which 98 (67%) were positively identified. The bones were scattered in small numbers in four contexts and only domestic species are present. Cattle bones, 76 (78%), are the most abundant, followed by lesser quantities of sheep, 15 (16%). As in the other context groupings, pigs were found in small numbers and all belong to an immature individual. The only other animal to be represented is dog.

Summary

The major part of the Castle Rushen faunal assemblage consists of the bones of domestic cattle, sheep and pigs. Cattle and sheep were clearly the most important economically, whilst remains of pig were extremely scarce in all deposits. Although cattle are always the most dominant species, sheep are slightly better represented in Period 2 than in the earlier fourteenth-century layers. There are also more horse bones from the later deposits, although most of these are loose teeth.

92.102	Horse	Cow	S/G*	Pig	Deer	Dog	Rabbit	LM*	MM*
Phase 1	–	5	5	1	–	–	1	32	21
Phase 2	–	2	1	1	–	–	–	2	1
Phase 3	–	21	21	1	–	–	2	32	52
Phase 4	–	3	5	–	–	1	1	5	5
92.103									
Phase 1	1	141	77	17	–	3	–	167	177
Phase 2	3	43	361	84	3	34	–	542	577
Phase 3	–	36	38	9	–	13	–	37	60
92.104									
Phase 1	1	110	54	–	–	–	–	73	46
Phase 3	–	49	13	3	–	–	–	12	11
Phase 4	–	62	77	15	–	–	–	49	25

LM* Large mammal   MM* Medium Mammal

Table 38   Castle Rushen Stores; number of animal bones by trench and phase

	Cattle	S/G*	Pig	Rabbit	LM*	MM*	Totals
Cranial	1	–	–	–	–	1	2
Teeth	2	2	2	–	–	–	6
Atlas	1	–	–	–	–	–	1
Vertebrae	–	1	–	–	–	–	1
Radius	1	–	–	–	–	–	1
Tibia	–	–	–	1	–	–	1
Metatarsus	–	1	–	–	–	–	1
Metacarpus	1	1	–	–	–	–	2
Phalanx	1	1	–	–	–	–	2
Ribs	–	–	–	–	14	6	20
LBF*	–	–	–	–	20	15	35
Totals	7	6	2	1	34	22	**72**

S/G* Sheep/Goat   LM* Large mammal   MM* Medium mammal   LBF* Long bone fragment

Table 39   Castle Rushen Stores; mammalian bone in Trench 92.102; Phases 1 and 2 (numbers of fragments)

Cats and dogs were kept as pets and probably also to control what would seem to have been a vermin problem in the post-medieval period, given the recovery of no fewer that 15 rats from the drains contexts alone. The presence of the butchered remains of deer and rabbit indicates that whilst wild animals were hunted, their flesh principally served to add variety to a diet that consisted mainly of beef and mutton. Perhaps the most notable feature in the Castle Rushen assemblage is the occurrence of a rabbit bone in a fourteenth-century context. Too much significance cannot be attached to this find, however, given that the deposit appeared to have been subjected to some degree of recent disturbance.

Castle Rushen Stores

In 1991 three trial trenches (1–3) were opened in order to assess the archaeological potential of the site. The excavation area was considerably extended in the following year, with the opening of three larger trenches (92.102, 92.103 and 92.104) which resulted in Trenches 1 and 3 from the previous season being subsumed into Trenches 92.104 and 92.103 respectively. Trench 2 remained as an isolated excavation trench, but as no faunal material was recovered from here it is not considered further in this report.

The entire Castle Rushen Stores assemblage consists of 3615 bones distributed throughout four phases of activity, dating variously from the sixteenth to the eighteenth centuries. The majority of the bones, over 2530 (70%), came from back-garden deposits which had built up gradually from the post-medieval period to modern times. The garden soils contained examples of post-medieval and modern pottery and metalwork, together with numerous animal bones discarded from nearby properties. The surface appeared to have been extensively trampled, which resulted in the survival of very few complete bones and high values for loose teeth. The faunal material is described below by the three main trenches opened in 1992 and by the different phases of activity recognised by the excavators in each trench. The list of species recovered from each trench and from the phase divisions within these trenches is given in Table 38.

Trench 92.102

Trench 92.102 produced the smallest sample of animal bones, which was distributed across four phases of site activity.

Phases 1 and 2, which date from the late sixteenth to the seventeenth or eighteenth century, produced just 73 bones (Table 39). These came from general occupation layers and a pit located in the area of the trench which had not been destroyed during the construction of a nineteenth-century cellar. The excavators were unsure whether these contexts were located inside or outside previous buildings.

The samples were generally poorly preserved, with high values for loose teeth and eroded and gnawed bones, 15 (21%). As a result, the percentage of identifiable material from Phases 1 and 2 is very small, 16 (22%), most of the material being classified as the remains of large and medium-sized mammals. The three major domesticates are all represented, cattle (seven specimens) and sheep (six specimens) being present in almost equal numbers. Pig is present as two eroded molars, and there is just one rabbit bone.

There were 149 bones in the Phase 3 and 4 contexts, which date from the late eighteenth to the nineteenth century on the basis of the pottery. Some of the bone material came from trampled surfaces and occupation layers, but the bulk of the remains were associated with the demolition layers and subsequent fills of the cellar. Once again, the incidence of erosion and gnawing is high, 35 (24%), which no doubt affected the survival potential of young animal, as well as fish and bird, remains.

Sheep are present in slightly higher numbers than cattle in terms of fragment numbers (Table 40), and they are equally represented by the minimum number of individuals present. Pig is extremely scarce, with just a fragment of a humerus to attest to its presence. Rabbit is represented by three bones, two of which came from immature individuals, implying perhaps that rabbits were kept for breeding in the back-gardens of houses. The small size of the samples from Trench 92.102 precluded a detailed analysis of the material. At all times cattle and sheep are present in almost equal numbers,

	Cattle	S/G*	Pig	Dog	Rabbit	LM*	MM*	Totals
Cranial	1	5	–	–	–	5	–	11
Maxilla	2	–	–	–	–	–	–	2
Mandible	2	–	–	–	–	–	–	2
Teeth	3	2	–	–	–	–	–	5
Atlas	1	–	–	–	–	–	–	1
Vertebrae	3	5	–	–	–	–	–	8
Scapula	–	1	–	–	–	–	–	1
Humerus	1	2	1	–	1	–	–	5
Radius	1	1	–	–	–	–	–	2
Pelvis	1	–	–	–	–	–	–	1
Femur	1	1	–	–	2	–	–	4
Tibia	1	4	–	–	–	–	–	5
Metatarsus	5	1	–	1	–	–	–	7
Metacarpus	2	1	–	–	–	–	–	3
Phalanx	–	3	–	–	–	–	–	3
Ribs	–	–	–	–	–	12	23	35
LBF*	–	–	–	–	–	20	34	54
Totals	24	26	1	1	3	37	57	**149**

S/G* Sheep/Goat LM* Large mammal MM* Medium mammal LBF* Long bone fragment

Table 40 Castle Rushen Stores; mammalian bone in Trench 92.102; Phases 3 and 4 (numbers of fragments)

	Horse	Cattle	S/G*	Pig	Dog	LM*	MM*	Totals
Cranial	–	3	6	1	–	17	34	61
Maxilla	–	–	–	1	–	–	–	1
Mandible	–	6	4	1	–	–	–	11
Teeth	1	42	38	2	–	–	–	83
Atlas	–	–	–	–	–	–	–	–
Axis	–	1	–	2	–	–	–	3
Vertebrae	–	15	–	–	–	–	–	15
Scapula	–	2	2	–	–	3	29	36
Humerus	–	8	2	3	–	20	21	54
Radius	–	5	2	–	–	18	–	25
Ulna	–	1	1	–	2	–	–	4
Pelvis	–	6	–	4	–	–	–	10
Femur	–	3	2	1	–	16	–	22
Tibia	–	2	–	18	–	26	–	–
Astragalus	–	3	1	–	–	–	–	4
Calcaneum	–	1	2	–	–	–	–	3
Metatarsus	–	9	4	–	1	–	–	14
Metacarpus	–	4	5	–	–	–	–	9
Phalanx	–	22	2	–	–	–	–	24
Ribs	–	–	–	–	–	16	24	40
LBF*	–	–	–	–	–	59	69	128
Other	–	8	2	–	–	–	–	10
Totals	1	141	77	17	3	167	177	**583**

S/G* Sheep/Goat   LM* Large mammal   MM* Medium mammal   LBF* Long bone fragment

Table 41   Castle Rushen Stores; mammalian bone in Trench 92.103; Phase 1 (numbers of fragments)

	Horse	Cattle	S/G*	Pig	Deer	Dog	LM*	MM*	Totals
Horn Core	–	–	1	–	–	–	–	–	1
Cranial	–	18	17	4	–	–	130	101	270
Maxilla	–	5	1	–	–	–	–	–	6
Mandible	–	22	12	7	–	3	–	–	44
Teeth	1	77	99	26	–	4	–	–	207
Atlas	–	3	5	–	–	1	–	–	9
Axis	–	3	3	–	–	–	–	–	6
Vertebrae	–	54	20	–	–	10	–	–	84
Scapula	–	9	8	5	–	1	36	64	123
Humerus	–	24	27	9	–	2	20	49	131
Radius	–	12	41	4	1	3	16	41	118
Ulna	–	8	3	6	–	1	–	–	18
Pelvis	–	16	11	4	–	1	–	10	42
Femur	–	9	11	1	–	–	35	20	76
Tibia	–	7	23	5	–	1	13	21	70
Astragalus	–	11	3	2	–	–	–	–	16
Calcaneum	–	2	8	3	–	3	–	–	16
Metatarsus	1	30	30	–	–	4	7	–	72
Metacarpus	–	34	26	2	–	–	5	–	67
Phalanx	1	75	11	6	2	–	–	–	95
Ribs	–	–	–	–	–	–	100	58	158
LBF*	–	–	–	–	–	–	180	213	393
Other	–	17	1	–	–	–	–	–	18
Totals	3	436	361	84	3	34	542	577	**2040**

S/G* Sheep/Goat   LM* Large mammal   MM* Medium mammal   LBF* Long bone fragment

Table 42   Castle Rushen Stores; mammalian bone in Trench 92.103; Phase 2 (numbers of fragments)

whilst pig bones, as in the Castle Rushen assemblage, are conspicuously low in number.

Trench 92.103

Trench 92.103 yielded the largest sample of animal bones from the site, with a total of 2805 fragments being recovered from the three earliest phases of site activity. The results are discussed below by individual phase.

Phase 1

The pottery evidence indicated that this phase dates from the sixteenth century. On the western side of the trench faunal material was recovered from a gravel boundary bank and from fills in its associated ditches. A ditch on the eastern side of the trench also produced quantities of animal bones. Other bone-rich contexts included a number of garden soils, a clay strip to the east of the boundary bank and a soil layer preserved beneath a Phase 2 bank. As there were no significant differences in terms of species and element composition between the different contexts, and as the samples are all relatively small, the material is discussed together below.

Altogether, 583 bones were associated with the earliest phase of activity in this trench. The material is characterised by high levels of erosion, which may explain the abundance of loose teeth (Table 41). The predominant species is cow, which accounts for

141 (59%) of the total identifiable mammal bone and represents at least eight individuals. All parts of the skeleton were found, with bones from the head and lower regions of the limbs being the most common. There are 77 sheep bones from at least five individuals, two of which were under six months of age at slaughter. Bones from the head, including loose teeth, are common whilst the complete absence of vertebrae is of note. Pigs again rank a poor third, contributing just 17 bones. Eleven of these belonged to young piglets. Other domestic animals identifiable in the assemblage are horse and dog. Horse is present with an example of one upper molar, whilst the three dog bones are from widespread locations and represent a mature animal.

Phase 2

With the exception of a small sample of bones from the rectilinear stone setting at the north-eastern side of the trench, the bone material from Phase 2 came entirely from successive layers of garden soil, all of which dated from the seventeenth century on ceramic evidence. In all, 2040 bones were recovered of which 921 (45%) were identified to species level. The overall occurrence of each species is shown in Table 42. It can be seen that the various categories of unidentified material formed a comparatively high proportion of the faunal sample.

Cattle are the most common mammals present, with a total of 436 (47%) of the identifiable mammal

	Cattle	S/G*	Pig	Dog	LM*	MM*	Totals
Horn Core	–	1	–	–	–	–	1
Cranial	1	1	–	–	–	5	7
Mandible	1	1	4	–	–	–	6
Teeth	13	17	–	1	–	–	31
Atlas	–	1	–	1	–	–	2
Axis	–	1	–	–	–	–	1
Vertebrae	5	6	3	7	–	1	22
Scapula	1	–	–	1	–	–	2
Humerus	–	1	1	–	–	–	2
Radius	1	1	1	–	–	–	3
Ulna	1	–	–	1	–	–	2
Pelvis	1	1	–	1	–	–	3
Femur	1	–	–	–	–	–	1
Tibia	2	1	–	–	–	–	3
Astragalus	3	–	–	–	–	–	3
Metatarsus	1	3	–	–	–	–	4
Phalanx	3	2	–	–	–	–	5
Ribs	–	–	–	–	3	19	22
LBF*	–	–	–	–	34	35	69
Other	2	1	–	1	–	–	4
Totals	36	38	9	13	37	60	**193**

S/G* Sheep/Goat   LM* Large mammal   MM* Medium mammal   LBF* Long bone fragment

Table 43   Castle Rushen Stores; mammalian bone in Trench 92.103; Phase 3 (numbers of fragments)

bones being from this species. Most bones of the skeleton are present, although again the most common parts of the body are the head and lower portions of the limbs. In total 361 (39%) of the identifiable mammal bones come from sheep. These are from all parts of the body, with loose teeth (99 specimens) predominating. Pig bones were found throughout the deposits in small numbers, making up 9% of the identifiable material. Twenty-six of the 84 fragments identified are loose teeth; most of the remaining bones belong to the upper regions of the body. Ten bones originated from piglets.

Dog bones were found in relatively large quantities, contributing 34 fragments from at least two individuals. Of seven lumbar vertebrae recovered, two were chopped right through in a transverse direction, whilst two more displayed superficial knife marks on the dorsal surface. Judging by the butchery marks these bones would appear to represent food remains meant for humans, as it is unlikely that such care would have been taken if the carcass was intended to be fed to dogs. Whilst it seems rather unlikely that the post-medieval or early modern residents of Castletown had to resort to dog flesh as a food source, it is possible that a particularly impoverished household would have had no other option.

Phase 3

The animal bones in Phase 3 were all recovered from a range of eighteenth- and nineteenth-century garden features. Preservation was poor and a large percentage of eroded fragments plus loose teeth were recovered. In all, 193 fragments of bone were associated with this phase, of which 129 (67%) were identifiable to species level (Table 43). Of these, 38 fragments are from sheep, 36 from cattle, 9 from pig and 11 from dog. Seventeen of the sheep bones are loose teeth, representing 45% of the total material from this species. Loose teeth are also the most common element amongst the cattle sample, contributing 13 (36%) fragments. Altogether the number of bones from this phase is too small to be very significant, but it is noted that sheep bones are slightly more numerous than cattle.

Trench 92.104

Work in Trench 92.104 revealed eight features containing faunal remains. Some 600 bones were recovered from these, from three different phases of activity. The material is rather poorly preserved, displaying severe erosion and weathering. In addition, the recovery of a concentration of fresh bones from Context 1 showing very neat, professional butchery techniques of recent origin, indicated that the area had been subjected to a certain degree of modern disturbance.

	Horse	Cattle	S/G*	LM*	MM*	Totals
Cranial	–	3	1	21	11	36
Mandible	–	2	3	–	–	5
Teeth	–	25	19	–	–	44
Atlas	–	2	–	–	–	2
Axis	–	1	–	–	–	1
Vertebrae	–	9	–	–	–	9
Scapula	–	4	2	6	2	14
Humerus	–	8	5	8	–	21
Radius	–	8	6	4	–	18
Ulna	–	2	–	–	–	2
Pelvis	–	2	1	–	–	3
Femur	–	4	8	1	–	13
Tibia	–	3	4	–	–	7
Astragalus	–	1	–	–	–	1
Calcaneum	–	4	–	–	–	4
Metatarsus	–	8	2	–	–	10
Metacarpus	–	1	3	–	–	4
Phalanx	1	16	–	–	–	17
Ribs	–	–	–	7	3	10
LBF*	–	–	–	26	30	56
Other	–	7	–	–	–	7
Totals	1	110	54	73	46	**284**

S/G* Sheep/Goat LM* Large mammal MM* Medium mammal LBF* Long bone fragment

Table 44   Castle Rushen Stores; mammalian bone in Trench 92.104; Phase 1 (numbers of fragments)

Phase 1

This phase produced 284 bones, all originating from sixteenth-century garden features. Cattle fragments, as in the earlier phases in Trenches 92.102 and 92.103, comfortably outnumber those of sheep, contributing 110 (67%) bones to the total identifiable sample (Table 44). Sheep account for 33% of the material, whilst the remains of pig are completely absent. Bones of the head and those from the upper regions of the body are present in larger numbers than most other parts of the skeleton. No other mammalian bones were associated with Phase 1.

Phases 3 and 4

Bone material from these phases is described together in view of the small sample sizes and the relative contemporaneity of the deposits. Altogether 316 bones were dated to the nineteenth- and twentieth-century use of the site. Only the three major stock animals are present in any numbers with cattle, again, providing most of the bones, 161 (51%). Sheep are better represented in these contexts than in the earlier sixteenth-century deposits and their remains actually outnumber those of cattle in Phase 4. Pigs, whilst present in Phases 3 and 4, are again characterised by their small numbers, making up only 8% of the total identifiable bone.

Not included in this total is the complete skeleton of a pig which was found in Trench 1 (104) during

	Cattle	S/G*	Pig	LM*	MM*	Totals
Cranial	1	–	–	3	–	4
Teeth	3	3	2	–	–	8
Axis	1	–	–	–	–	1
Vertebrae	7	5	–	–	–	12
Scapula	1	1	–	1	–	3
Humerus	7	–	–	–	–	7
Radius	–	1	–	–	–	1
Pelvis	11	–	–	–	–	11
Femur	16	1	–	3	–	20
Phalanx	2	2	1	–	–	5
Ribs	–	–	–	1	8	9
LBF*	–	–	–	4	3	7
Totals	49	13	3	12	11	**88**

S/G* Sheep/Goat LM* Large mammal MM* Medium mammal LBF* Long bone fragment

Table 45   Castle Rushen Stores; mammalian bone in Trench 92.104; Phase 3 (numbers of fragments)

	Cattle	S/G*	Pig	LM*	MM*	Totals
Cranial	–	–	–	5	2	7
Mandible	–	1	–	–	–	1
Teeth	6	8	2	–	–	16
Atlas	1	1	–	–	–	2
Axis	1	–	–	–	–	1
Vertebrae	17	5	–	–	–	22
Scapula	4	2	–	2	3	11
Humerus	4	11	1	–	–	16
Radius	1	8	3	–	–	12
Ulna	1	–	2	–	–	3
Pelvis	6	4	2	–	–	12
Femur	9	17	–	3	–	29
Tibia	1	13	1	2	–	17
Astragalus	–	1	–	–	–	1
Calcaneum	–	2	–	–	–	2
Metatarsus	–	–	1	–	–	1
Metacarpus	2	2	1	–	–	5
Phalanx	7	1	2	–	–	10
Ribs	–	–	–	24	10	34
LBF*	–	–	–	13	10	23
Other	2	1	–	–	–	3
Totals	62	77	15	49	25	**228**

S/G* Sheep/Goat LM* Large mammal MM* Medium mammal LBF* Long bone fragment

Table 46   Castle Rushen Stores; mammalian bone in Trench 92.104; Phase 4 (numbers of fragments)

the 1991 season of excavations. The skeleton belonged to an individual a little under a year at death. As there were no marks of any description on the bones, it is likely that the animal died from an illness and was buried in the back garden of one of the houses. The only other mammalian species present in this period is horse. The bone, a third phalanx, came from an individual over two years of age.

The sizes of the bone samples from Trench 3 are really too small to draw valid conclusions about economy and animal husbandry. It would seem, however, that the two most important domestic species were cattle and sheep, that pigs provided an additional but minor supplement to the diet and that wild species of animals were rarely exploited.

Summary

The deposits at Castle Rushen Stores were not ideally suited for the preservation of animal bone, and any conclusions drawn about the economy must take this into consideration. Also, the methods of recovery employed on the site meant that the bones of larger animals stood a better chance of being collected than those of small mammals and fish. Assuming that the figures do reflect the real situation, cattle and sheep were clearly the most important suppliers of meat in all three phases, with sheep numbers increasing in the nineteenth to twentieth centuries, perhaps as a response to an increased demand for wool. The presence of pigs in such small numbers suggests that they served as an occasional supplement to the diet, possibly being kept as domestic scavengers in the back gardens of houses.

As at Castle Rushen, wild animals do not appear to have been exploited to any great extent, with deer just occurring as three post-cranial fragments in Trench 92.103 and rabbit recorded from Trench 92.102 only. The Castle Rushen Stores assemblage is probably most remarkable for the recovery of four butchered dog vertebrae from a late context, reflecting perhaps the extreme poverty of certain residents of the town during the eighteenth or nineteenth century.

Discussion

The size of the animals

The dimensions of all suitable post-medieval bones are given in Tables 35–37 for Castle Rushen and in Tables 47 and 48 for Castle Rushen Stores. The measurable sample from the medieval deposits at Castle Rushen was small and has not been represented in tabular form. Size comparisons relied on British (Coy 1981) and Irish (McCarthy 1988) material, as the results of the metrical analysis from Peel Castle have yet to be made available. Overall, the size analysis suggested that the cattle bones recovered are typical of those found on most British and Irish post-medieval urban sites, despite the seventeenth-century description of Manx cattle as being 'little, low and poor' (Moore 1900). The most common measurements were on the metapodia and tibiae and there was quite a considerable range in size (Tables 35 and 47). The larger bones could be interpreted as males, perhaps bulls, or as an improved breed of cattle introduced into the island from either Britain or Ireland.

Sheep produced a number of useful measurements, all falling well within the range obtained for other contemporary Irish and British sites. The sheep were probably of a variety of breeds, cranial evidence indicating the presence of both polled and horned individuals. There were no four horned varieties of sheep, although the absence of the nutrient foramen in the proximal portion of the femur indicated that over 30% of the sheep may have been Loaghtans. Seventeenth-century documents inform us that, whilst Manx sheep were as fat and as palatable as their English counterparts, they were smaller in stature (Moore, 1900). It is likely that by the eighteenth and nineteenth century there was considerable interbreeding between the native Manx sheep and the new improved breeds introduced from Britain.

Pig measurements were extremely scarce, given the small samples recovered for this species and the fact that most of the bones belonged to immature and juvenile individuals. The few measurements obtained differ in no way from any other post-medieval material examined by the writer.

None of the horse bones were suitable for accurate size reconstruction, but direct comparison with modern reference material indicated that the remains belonged to relatively large ponies, of perhaps Connemara-pony size.

The ageing of the animals

The most accurate and reliable method of ageing is that based on mandibles but these were not abundant at either site. There were just 15 complete mandibles from Castle Rushen and eight from Castle Rushen Stores. Only one context produced as many as three and that was from Trench 92.103 at Castle Rushen Stores.

The seven cattle jaws from Period 2 at Castle

Element	Measurement	N	Range	Mean
Radius	Bd	2	57.3–63.7	–
	Dd	2	37.7–43.1	–
Tibia	Bd	1	55.1	–
	Dd	1	49.2	–
Metatarsus	Bd	11	44.7–65.4	50.6
	Dd	11	23.9–32.1	25.1
	Bp	8	40.6–48.8	43.5
	Dp	8	37.2–49.2	41.5
	GL	1	201.0	–
Metacarpus	Bd	2	49.2–52.1	–
	Dd	2	25.3–26.9	–
	Bp	5	46.2–51.2	48.2
	Dp	5	26.7–31.6	29.1
Astragalus	GLl	3	58.0–59.5	–
	GLm	3	52.9–55.1	–
Phalanx I	Bp	19	22.7–31.7	26.8
	GL	19	46.1–58.1	48.7
Phalanx II	Bp	13	22.6–29.1	26.2
	GL	11	32.1–38.5	35.5
Scapula	GLP	1	81.1	–
	GLG	1	64.9	–
	BG	1	57.1	–

Table 47   Castle Rushen Stores; summary of cattle measurements

Element	Measurement	N	Range	Mean
Humerus	Bd	15	25.6– 39.7	28.8
	BT	15	23.5– 35.3	27.1
Radius	Bd	8	25.2– 31.4	27.9
	BFd	7	22.1– 28.9	24.8
	Dd	6	15.9– 20.8	17.9
	Bp	11	26.2– 39.8	31.2
	BFp	10	24.8– 33.9	26.8
	Dp	11	12.9– 20.1	15.6
	GL	2	138.2–154.5	–
Tibia	Bd	6	22.2– 29.8	24.3
	Dd	6	17.5– 23.7	19.1
	Bp	1	25.2	–
	Dp	1	28.4	–
Metatarsus	Bp	8	16.7– 20.2	17.5
	Dp	8	15.9– 19.8	18.3
	Bd	2	22.3– 22.9	–
	Dd	2	14.8– 15.5	–
Metacarpus	Bp	9	17.2– 22.1	20.1
	Dp	9	12.8– 16.1	14.7
	Bd	3	23.5– 24.7	–
	Dd	3	14.1– 15.2	–
	GL	1	112.5	–
Astragalus	GLl	5	26.5– 35.5	29.1
	GLm	5	25.2– 33.6	27.6
Calcaneum	GL	1	48.8	–
Phalanx I	Bp	14	10.3– 12.2	10.6
	GL	14	30.9– 37.2	32.7

Table 48   Castle Rushen Stores; summary of sheep measurements

Rushen were all from adults. Five of these had wear patterns which suggested that the animals were over five years of age at death. Epiphyseal fusion data showed that whilst a few animals were slaughtered when young, most were adults, suggesting that cattle were perhaps equally valued as sources of milk and hides. The available ageing data for the medieval period at Castle Rushen seemed to indicate that all cattle were kept to an old age, since no bones from young animals were found.

For sheep, the five mandibles from Castle Rushen were all from old individuals, where the third molar was in an advanced stage of wear. The evidence of slaughter age from epiphyseal fusion suggested the presence of both young and old animals, with an abundance of sheep over 2.5–3.5 years old at death (52%). The few individuals older than this probably represent breeding stock.

Tooth wear and long bone fusion evidence for the pigs eaten at Castle Rushen indicated that all were in their first or second year at death. Almost 8% of the pigs were under six months old, revealing that suckling pig was a popular dish.

The sample of ageable bones from Castle Rushen Stores was small but the results show a similar pattern to that observed at Castle Rushen. For the sixteenth- and seventeenth-century material the low ratio of immature to adult cattle and sheep indicates that the local economy was geared towards dairying and wool production. There was some evidence that the animals being supplied to the castle during the late medieval period were slightly younger than those found in contemporary deposits at Castle Rushen Stores, but the samples are too small to be convincing.

A slightly higher ratio of immature to adult animals in the eighteenth and nineteenth centuries is probably linked to the expansion of Castletown as an urban settlement, resulting in an increased demand for meat. Most of the cattle and sheep from this period were apparently killed at between two and three years of age and very few were over five years at slaughter. The remains of piglets and lambs were not as numerous as at Castle Rushen, whilst the recovery of some foetal or neo-natal fragments from Trench 92.103 may point to breeding of pigs nearby.

Methods of butchery

The general pattern of butchering was broadly similar throughout the different periods of occupation at both sites, and was little different for the two most important mammal species involved. Most marks took the form of cuts and chops on the upper limb bones and were associated with the division of the carcass into manageable portions. The types of fracture observed on these bones are consistent with their having been broken by means of a blow across the shaft by a heavy chopping implement.

The majority of the vertebrae had been chopped axially, which indicates that cattle and sheep carcasses were halved, a method of butchery requiring suspension of the carcass. Lateral chop marks on both sides of a number of vertebrae from fourteenth-century deposits at Castle Rushen demonstrate that some animals were butchered on the ground, as was common practice during the early Christian and early medieval periods (McCarthy 1988).

Extensive knife cuts on the surfaces of the four major limb bones and the vertebrae suggest that a certain amount of filleting was also practised, whilst nicks and scratches on the metapodia and phalanges of cattle provide evidence for skinning. Other long bones exhibit signs of butchery consistent with preparation for marrow extraction. There were a number of sheared atlases and occipital condyles, where heads were severed from bodies and knife marks on mandibles suggest separation of the lower jaw from the skull and also the removal of the tongue. Some sheep and pig skulls were cleaved along the midline by dorsal blows, presumably for access to the brain.

The post-medieval bones, especially those from Castle Rushen Stores, included many instances of sawing in layers associated with seventeenth- or eighteenth-century and modern pottery. These marks are typical of modern butchery techniques and one particular concentration of sawn bones from Trench 92.104 at Castle Rushen Stores is probably very recent in origin.

Summary of species present

The major part of the faunal assemblages from Castle Rushen and Castle Rushen Stores consists of the bones of domestic cattle, sheep and pig, most of which appear to be the product of food refuse. Leaving aside such biasing factors as selective recovery and poor conditions of preservation in many deposits, the methods used to calculate the relative importance of the animals present indicated that the two major species were cattle and sheep, these providing over 80% and 90% of the identifiable material from Castle Rushen and Castle Rushen Stores respectively.

Cattle and sheep
Cattle would at all times have provided most of the meat eaten, although sheep occasionally provided

more fragments and individuals in the eighteenth- and nineteenth-century levels at Castle Rushen Stores. At Castle Rushen also, sheep increase in significance from 17% in the fourteenth century to 23% in the fifteenth to seventeenth centuries. The rise in importance of sheep in the later periods may indicate that an increased European demand for wool encouraged Manx farmers to enlarge their flocks. Goats were clearly unimportant as a source of meat, being present only as horn cores and in extremely small numbers.

Pig

Pig was the least frequently occurring of the three main domestic species, and both sites had a significantly lower percentage of pig bones in comparison with contemporary urban sites in Britain and Ireland. Although specific ratios are not given, the faunal assemblages excavated at Peel Castle are also characterised by small numbers of pig bones (Roberts pers comm). Whilst it could be argued that the quantity of pig bones from Castletown is an effect of survival, this seems unlikely given that pigs were no more numerous in those deposits where preservation was considered excellent, for example the pit groupings.

Noddle (1975) has attributed the relative scarcity of pig bones at British medieval sites to a depletion in woodland in which pigs were turned out to fatten on mast during the autumn. The deforestation of the Isle of Man apparently commenced very early on, with historical sources documenting that forest clearance was at such an advanced stage by the eleventh century that Magnus Barefoot ordered the men of Galloway to provide timber for the purpose of building wooden forts on the island (Freke 1990, 117). The extremely low proportion of pig bones from both these excavations compared with remains of domestic ruminants indicates that there was insufficient woodland in the surroundings of Castletown to maintain a large pig population, and this accords well with the presumed early depletion of forests in the Isle of Man.

Horse

The proportion of horse bones was low, but this may not necessarily represent the actual numbers of horses kept, since the faunal samples from both sites consisted almost entirely of domestic refuse and the eating of horseflesh had presumably been banned by the Church at a much earlier stage in the island's history. A large number of dog bones in both assemblages indicates that these animals were kept as pets and for guarding properties.

Deer

Red deer was present in the form of butchered post-cranial remains and, in a single instance, as a sawn antler tine. Deer bones were more abundant in the castle deposits but the small quantity overall indicated that venison was at best only a supplement to the diet. Although red deer has been recorded on the island since the early Holocene, it disappeared sometime during the eighteenth century following an attempt at herd management in the seventeenth century by the Earl of Derby (Garrad 1972b, 192). Various attempts to introduce the fallow deer, *Dama dama*, a species which was brought to Ireland and Britain in the thirteenth century by the Normans, have proved unsuccessful (Garrad *ibid*).

Wild game

The only other species of wild game represented was the rabbit, whose remains, with the exception of a single pelvis bone, were all recovered from late medieval and post-medieval contexts. One species of wild mammal which might have been expected but is not represented is the hare, a species recorded as early as the fifteenth century (Garrad 1990, 76). Overall, the very low percentage of wild animals recovered adds support to the theory that the area around Castletown was not very heavily wooded during the medieval and post-medieval periods.

Animal processing and management

The assemblages for the three main domesticates include bone remains from all stages of animal processing, from initial slaughter to the eventual consumption of the meat. This indicates that animals were brought into Castletown from the surrounding countryside on the hoof and were slaughtered in the vicinity of the excavated areas. A higher percentage of the upper regions of the body from Castle Rushen seems to imply that a certain amount of the meat was coming into the castle kitchens in the form of prepared joints or halved carcasses, much as one sees in butchers' stalls today. A disproportionate number of cranial and lower parts to meatier bones in the town assemblage suggests that some of the preparation of carcasses intended for the castle may well have been carried out in the area of Castle Rushen Stores.

Indicators of a difference in status between the occupants of the castle and the residents of nearby houses are evidenced in the ageing data. For the late medieval period in particular, there is some evidence that the cattle and sheep bones from the castle assemblage represent slightly younger animals than those eaten at Castle Rushen Stores. The remains of piglets and lambs are also more numerous in the castle samples. This would imply that the occupants of Castle Rushen were sufficiently affluent to afford the tender flesh of young animals on a more regular basis than the townspeople. Ageing data from the sixteenth- and seventeenth-century levels at Castle Rushen Stores showed that more animals were kept well into maturity, presumably to fulfil other economic roles such as the provision of milk, hides and wool before being slaughtered. Much of this is rather speculative, however, and clearly larger assemblages of better preserved bones are needed before more definitive statements on past animal management in the island can be made.

One of the major drawbacks of the analysis of the animal bones excavated at Castle Rushen and Castle Rushen Stores is that it has not been possible to compare the results with other Manx material, as these bone assemblages are the only relatively large faunal samples to be examined from the Isle of Man. In addition, the bulk of the animal bones for this report came from post-medieval and early modern levels which, although of inherent interest in themselves, precluded a detailed examination of changes in diet and husbandry techniques from the earlier to the later period. The excavations at Peel Castle yielded larger samples of bones, with a broader date range than either of the two Castletown sites, and the results of a detailed analysis of this material are eagerly awaited. Finally, examination of faunal assemblages from other Manx sites is also essential before a more complete picture of the economy and past animal husbandry practices on the island will be obtained.

Bird bone

C T Fisher

Introduction

A total of 920 fragments of bird bone was recovered from the Castle Rushen and Castle Rushen Stores excavations, from a total of at least 34 species. Minimum numbers for each species from each of the sites are presented in Table 49. The discussion which follows attempts to present the collected data in terms of the size and age range of the most common species. There is also an analysis of the presence and absence of particular species at differing phases of the sites. Evidence for butchery, burning or tooth marks is also presented by site and by species.

Discussion

As would be expected, most of the bones retrieved from these excavations were from the two most commonly domesticated birds, chicken (56%) and goose (21%).

Chickens

Of the chicken bones, the most frequent size is medium, about equivalent to a Rhode Island Red. Most of the birds were probably females kept primarily for egg-laying, although four tarsometatarsi (all medium sized or slightly bigger) in the Castle Rushen excavation were found to have spurs and were therefore from cockerels. At least 14% of the bones from the two excavations were juveniles or immatures. Juvenile bones probably represent chicks that did not survive, but immatures point to the fact that many birds must have been eaten before they were fully adult.

Geese

Goose bones are most likely to have come from domesticated birds; wild greylags are uncommon visitors to the island. As evidence for this, many of the goose bones are larger than those of the wild ('standard') bird's skeleton. Of those bones which *are* standard size, many also show indications of domestication, such as increased porosity (presumably due to factors including diet and lack of exercise). Nearly a tenth of all the goose bones come from birds which appear to be unusually short but sturdy-limbed.

The excavations at Peel Castle (Fisher, C T forthcoming) also yielded bones belonging to this dwarf variety, which is possibly the same as the 'little form of greylag, no more than pinkfoot size' kept by Norsemen in dark-age Shetland (Fisher, J M Mc 1966).

It is also notable that in the Castle Rushen excavation a quarter of all goose bones come from the distal wing, and are thus possibly connected with pinioning, or with the production of small hand brushes, quill pens or thread bobbins (Harrison and O'Connor, *in litt* and pers comm). A large proportion of these bones (36%) are from the dwarf form. No such preponderance of wing bones (or bones from dwarf birds) occurs amongst the goose bones from Castle Rushen Stores, however.

Ducks

There were also considerable numbers of mallard bones from both excavations (3%). Most match in size the standard wild bird (although like the goose remains these may well represent small domestic varieties) but a quarter are the size of the large domestic Aylesbury variety. Mallard and teal do breed on the island, but the other duck identified from this excavation, wigeon, occurs only as a

Species	Fragment Numbers				
	Castle Rushen	**Min No**	**Castle Rushen Stores**	**Min No**	**Total**
Chicken *Gallus gallus*	405	186	113	80	518
Greylag Goose *Anser anser*	163	77	34	25	197
Mallard *Anas platyrhynchos*	18	14	13	7	31
Manx Shearwater *Puffinus puffinus*	7	5	18	15	25
Raven *Corvus corax*	13	11	9	6	22
Herring/L. Black-Backed Gull *Larus argentatus/fuscus*	11	10	3	2	14
Puffin *Fratercula arctica*	11	9	3	3	14
Rock Dove/Feral Pigeon *Columba livia*	10	6	1	1	11
Chough *Pyrrhocorax pyrrhocorax*	9	3	2	2	11
Teal *Anas crecca*	9	6	0	0	9
Shag *Phalacrocorax aristotelis*	5	1	2	2	7
Black-Headed Gull *Larus ridibundus*	0	0	6	5	6
Woodcock *Scolopax rusticola*	6	4	0	0	6
Carrion or Hooded Crow/Rook *Corvus corone/frugilegus*	6	3	0	0	6
Curlew *Numenius arquata*	5	5	0	0	5
Jackdaw/Magpie *Corvus monedula/Pica pica*	2	2	2	2	4

Table 49   Bird species present in the excavations in order of frequency (continued overleaf)

winter visitor. Interestingly, bones from two of probably six individual teal found in the excavations were from the distal wing, as was the single wigeon bone. Possibly these birds were caught alive and then pinioned until needed for food, or to act as ornamental birds.

Manx shearwaters

The numbers of Manx shearwater bones from both excavations are most significant. This cliff-nesting bird was of very great economic importance to the island, and was so named by the ornithologist Francis Willughby in 1676 with reference to the breeding population on the Calf of Man. These birds fly very close to the wavetops (hence the name 'shearwater'), and breed in burrows left by other animals such as rabbits. The Manx shearwater bred in considerable numbers on the Isle of Man until the end of the eighteenth century, when it began to decline, and now probably nests on the Calf only in very small numbers (Airne 1964, Cullen and Slinn 1983).

The shearwaters were harvested in huge quantities by the islanders. They were most palatable when pickled or salted. According to Pennant (1776), 'they are salted and barrelled, and when they are boiled are eaten with potatoes'. The birds leave their young alone in the burrow during the day, so it was easy for the islanders to climb the cliffs in August and drag the fat chicks out with iron hooks (Airne 1964). This is presumably why well over half the bones from the Castle Rushen excavations are from immatures. Of the eight bone fragments recovered from the excavations at Peel Castle (Fisher, C T forthcoming), seven were from immatures.

The main profit from Manx shearwaters, however, came from feathers and oil. In 1600 an official feather gatherer, Katherine Moore, collected

Species	Fragment Numbers				
	Castle Rushen	Min No	Castle Rushen Stores	Min No	Total
Grey Heron					
Ardea cinerea	1	1	2	2	3
Blackbird					
Turdus merula	3	3	0	0	3
Cormorant					
Phalacrocorax carbo	3	2	0	0	3
Coot					
Fulica atra	3	2	0	0	3
Golden Plover					
Pluvialis apricaria	3	2	0	0	3
Starling					
Sturnus vulgaris	3	1	0	0	3
Great Auk					
Pinguinus impennis	1	1	1	1	2
Kestrel					
Falco tinnunculus	0	0	2	2	2
Common Guillemot					
Uria aalge	0	0	2	2	2
Turnstone					
Arenaria interpres	2	1	0	0	2
Wigeon					
Anas penelope	1	1	0	0	1
Mute Swan					
Cygnus olor	1	1	0	0	1
Buzzard					
Buteo buteo	0	0	1	1	1
Moorhen					
Gallinula chloropus	1	1	0	0	1
Partridge					
Perdix perdix	1	1	0	0	1
Turkey					
Meleagris gallopavo	1	1	0	0	1
Whimbrel					
Numenius phaeopus	1	1	0	0	1
?Redwing					
Turdus ?iliacus	0	0	1	1	1
Total of at least 34 species	705	361	215	159	920

Table 49 (Cont'd)   Bird species present in the excavations in order of frequency

twenty stone weight (127 kg) of feathers; in 1660 the harvest yielded ten thousand birds (Airne 1964).

The decline of the colony in the early nineteenth century was probably not simply due to over-exploitation by man, but because of predation by rats which colonised the island after a Russian ship was wrecked on the Calf in 1786 (Airne 1964). These were most likely to have been brown rats (*Rattus norvegicus*); according to Parslow (1967), it was through the accidental introduction of this species that several island colonies of shearwaters were reduced or made extinct. The main British breeding populations are now on islands such as Skokholm and Skomer in Wales and Rhum, Scotland (Cramp and Simmons 1977).

Puffins and guillemots

Birds of the auk family (which includes guillemots and puffins) were also harvested for food, oil and feathers on the Isle of Man. Puffins (or 'sea parrots', a name bestowed on account of the peculiarly sturdy and colourful bill) still breed on the Calf of Man and in other Manx localities including the Chasms, about four miles west of Castle Rushen. They were particularly noted by Townley (1791):

Size of bone	Castle Rushen	Castle Rushen Stores
bantam	93 (34)	23 (8)
medium/bantam	5	6
medium	237 (23)	55 (4)
medium/gamecock	70 (4)	29 (1)
Total (518 (74))	405 (61)	113 (13)

Table 50   Number of chicken bones excavated (immatures in brackets)

Size of bone	Castle Rushen	Castle Rushen Stores
large	35 (3)	19 (1)
dwarf but sturdy	15	2 (1)
standard	113 (12)	13
Total (197 (17))	163 (15)	34 (2)

Table 51   Number of goose bones excavated (immatures in brackets)

Context	Fragments	Min No
072	1 (1)	1 (1)
074	1 (1)	1 (1)
103	5 (4)	3 (2)
Total	7 (6)	5 (4)

Table 52   Castle Rushen; number of adult and immature Manx shearwater bones (immatures in brackets)

Date	Fragments	Min No
19th/20th Century	2 (1)	2 (1)
18th/19th Century	7 (5)	6 (5)
17th Century	6 (2)	4 (1)
16th Century	*3 (2)	3 (2)
Total	18 (10)	15 (9)

*one adult femur with knife marks across shaft

Table 53   Castle Rushen Stores; number of adult and immature Manx shearwater bones (immatures in brackets)

We got a second refreshment from our stores, to which was added, by the very civil old lady, a dish of cold parrots, with an assurance from her that they were excellent food, and that they afforded a broth, or soop, that was uncommonly good and nourishing. I tasted one of the birds, and found it savoury, not ungrateful to the palate, and was therefore induced to purchase the new-taken ones. . . .

According to Simon (1944), 'when pickled and preserved with spices, they are admired by those who love high eating'. He also remarks that puffins once provided the staple food of the Faeroe Islanders, who dried and exported the flesh.

In modern times common guillemots are still extremely abundant cliff-nesters on the Isle of Man. In Townley's day they were very numerous on the Calf and high cliffs of the adjacent main island. Madoc (1934) describes how they come to the island regularly every spring, the colonies sounding like 'a hen-run, . . . sometimes like a pack of hounds . . . some bring off a squeak like that of a stuck pig'. Both fragments of common guillemot recovered in this excavation were from Castle Rushen Stores, one sixteenth century, the other from the seventeenth century.

Great auks

Although guillemots and other members of the auk family are not usually eaten fresh, they are said to be palatable when salted. The eggs were very commonly collected and the birds were also good sources of oil. There was one auk that was undoubtedly of huge commercial importance—the now-extinct great auk (or 'garefowl'). Once numerous on both sides of the Atlantic, this unfortunate bird was done to death by overharvesting—like the oddly similar dodo, huge numbers of great auks and their eggs were taken, particularly by sailors as a convenient source of meat on long voyages. The birds were also sometimes harvested for their feathers, which were detached from the skin by parboiling the dead birds. On treeless islands like Funk, off Newfoundland, the fuel was provided by burning the fat bodies of the birds, thus consuming even more carcasses (Grieve 1885). The last authenticated sighting of great auks was a pair captured on the Icelandic island of Eldey in 1844; their single egg was thrown away.

Two fragments of great auk bone were found in the excavations, one at Castle Rushen (a humerus crossed by two fine knife cuts) and one (which is very fragmentary, and must be treated as a tentative identification) at Castle Rushen Stores. There is only one other known record of bones of this species recorded from the Isle of Man—in a cave deposit dated about 90 AD from Perwick Bay, about three miles west of Castle Rushen (Garrad 1972a). The Isle of Man is, however, the setting for the earliest picture known to depict the great auk, a colour wash of a single bird by Daniel King painted about 1652 (Williamson 1939). The picture, unmistakably of a great auk despite the vastly exaggerated bill, is captioned 'These kind of birds are about the Isle of Man'. The bird is in full breeding plumage, and is depicted on a flat rock close to the water's edge. Both factors suggest that great auks bred on the Isle of Man; the flightless, strong-swimming birds rarely came ashore except to breed, and tended to lay their eggs on rocks easily accessible to the water. One other report of great auk on Man has been published (Gawne 1944). John Gawne, of Fistard, read Ken Williamson's paper on the King painting, and was reminded of a conversation he had 50 years previously.

> This must be the bird Bill Corlett, a Port St. Mary fisherman, told me about in the summer of 1895. It was a flightless bird, which used to come at a certain time to the Flat Rocks south of the Point, and Bill Corlett pronounced the name as 'Big Uig'. He had been told about it when a boy (perhaps about 1840–50) by old men, the same as he told me. . . . I think the time of year those old fisherman would be likely to see the birds would be between April and the end of July, as that was the time they would be passing the Point and the Flat Rocks on their way to the fishing grounds. . . .

Great auks are known to have bred on St Kilda, in the Orkneys and at Colonsay and Oronsay in the Hebrides – as well as on the south-east Irish coast—but by the mid-seventeenth century the breeding colonies had been virtually destroyed on all but the remote St Kilda.

Shags and cormorants

Shags and cormorants were probably also exploited for oil and, usually as juveniles (which, according to Simon (1944), are said to taste like roast hare), for food—both are common breeding birds, especially on the Calf of Man and Maughold Head. The Peel Castle excavations produced a considerable proportion of immature bones from these two species, supporting the belief that there was summer harvesting of young birds for food. There were no immatures bones at all amongst the ten identified (from probably only two individuals of each species) from the Castle Rushen excavations, but there is some evidence that adult birds were also eaten. According to Fenton (1976) the inhabitants of the Scottish Northern Isles would bury cormorants for 24 hours to tenderise them, and to remove some of the fishy taste. Another possible reason for the presence of cormorants at Castle Rushen is to catch fish—they were domesticated by the Japanese and Chinese and taught to retrieve fish for their masters; a ring round the neck prevented them from swallowing their catch. Apparently, these birds were also trained in seventeenth-century Britain—according to Pennant (1776) Charles I had a 'Master of Cormorants'—but there is no evidence of the shag being used in the same way.

Gulls

Bones which might represent either herring or lesser black-backed gull are most probably attributable to the former species, a cliff-nester, which according to Ralfe (1905) 'is perhaps the dominant bird of Man'. The lesser black-backed gull is less common, both as a breeding and wintering species. The other gull species represented (from the Castle Rushen Stores excavation) is the black-headed. This small gull is common on the island in winter, but most birds leave in spring to breed in adjacent parts of the British Isles. Two of the six black-headed gull bones, however, are tentative identifications. The gull carpometacarpus and humerus in the seventeenth-century context 92.103/82 are very similar to black-headed gull bones, but may just possibly be from kittiwake, a gull that also nests on the Isle of Man.

Gulls are known to have once been popular as food in the British Isles, being netted and then fattened during the winter months in the poultry yard—which also helped to dissipate the strong fishy taste. Indeed, 'During the seventeenth century young Black-headed Gulls, termed Puets, were netted and held in high esteem as a delicacy after being fed on bullock's liver or with corn or curds from the dairy, which may have imparted a more pleasant flavour' (Simon 1944). Out of 14 bones attributed to herring/lesser black-backed gull, 10 are from the distal wing; for black-headed gull the number is four out of six (one carpometacarpus is possibly from a kittiwake). This strongly hints at some level of pinioning, which would support the idea of temporary captivity.

Pigeons

The pigeon bones may have come from feral birds, perhaps associated with the castle as scavengers. However, historical evidence concerning the wild rock dove, from which the feral pigeon is descended, seems to point towards many of these bones being remains of rock doves collected from the south-western cliffs. Townley (1791) described, during an excursion from Port Erin to the Calf in the late seventeen hundreds, how he saw 'great numbers of wild pigeons, that lodge and breed in the holes of the tremendous rocks which surround and guard that westerly peninsula of Mona; but they were so very wild as not to allow us to come within gun-shot of them'. He reported that they were good eating.

Crows

Several members of the crow family (*Corvidae*) were found in the excavation and may have been associated with man as scavengers or possibly as pets. Corvids are known to have been eaten, but usually only as juveniles ('crow pie'); there are only three immature bones (two from raven, one from chough) amongst 43 corvid bones identified. The species identified are jackdaw or magpie, rook or crow (only found in the Castle Rushen excavation), raven and chough. Of the four small crow bones, three are definitely jackdaw, the fourth indeterminate between jackdaw and magpie. Both are common on the island; the jackdaw is known to have been an inhabitant of Castle Rushen itself. Rook and crow post-cranial bones are even more difficult to distinguish. Both species are now common on the Isle of Man (where most crows, and nearly all breeding crows, are of the hooded form), but in Townley's day the rook was a very scarce bird (Townley 1791).

A note in Airne (1949) suggests that Norse influence—epitomised by Odin's relationship with this large, intelligent bird—led to the commonplace habit of keeping ravens as pets. This theory is reinforced by the fact that, of the 22 bones recovered from both parts of the excavation, over half are from the wing and may be bones discarded after pinioning. An ulna from Castle Rushen has a single puncture mark which may have been made by the pinioning knife.

Chough are mostly associated with the sea cliffs and do not have such a close connection with man as the other corvids, but nevertheless make good pets. Ralfe (1905) describes how a 'young bird taken from a nest on the Calf was brought up by the late Mr Keene, of Castle Rushen, and proved a tame, amusing, and high spirited pet, until it met the common fate of such favourites, by drowning itself in a water barrel'. The Isle of Man is now one of the remaining breeding strongholds of the chough, along with Islay and Colonsay and the west coasts of Ireland and Wales.

Birds of prey

Birds of prey too were regarded as status symbols as captive birds. The three bones found (all from Castle Rushen Stores, from the seventeenth century) are from the leg and so there is no evidence of pinioning, or indeed of the removal of feathers for fletching. The kestrel bones, from a female, could have originated from a falconer's bird, or from a wild bird killed to protect livestock. Buzzards, however, are very infrequent visitors to the island (although this might not have been the case in the seventeenth century) and the single bone is more likely to have been from a captive bird.

Miscellaneous

Many of the other bird bones probably represent species caught for food, many of them readily available on the shores or in the moorland interior of the island. It is notable that—of the few woodland species—most also frequent other habitats, such as marsh and heath, which occur more commonly on the island.

Members of the closely related families *Phasianidae*, *Rallidae*, *Charadriidae* and *Scolopacidae* (the pheasants, rails, plovers and waders), make good eating; these include partridge, coot, moorhen (which 'when skinned and then fried in hot fat makes an excellent salmi or braise' (Simon 1944)), golden plover, curlew, whimbrel, woodcock and turnstone, which were all identified from the excavations. Golden plover and curlew bones were also found to be frequent in the Peel Castle excavation.

To the dinner table list must be added mute swan (which was identified by a single heavily scraped and gnawed lower leg bone) and grey heron. Herons, which are resident breeding birds on the Isle of Man, were also eaten, although the bones are filled with a strong-tasting fluid which had to be extracted before the bird could be cooked. This

	Chicken	Min No	Goose	Min No
Late 19th & 20th Century	18	13	8	5
relative frequency	69%	72%	31%	27%
18th & 19th Century	27	20	4	4
relative frequency	87%	83%	13%	17%
17th Century	46	33	15	13
relative frequency	75%	72%	25%	28%
16th Century	22	14	7	3
relative frequency	75%	82%	24%	18%
Total	113	80	34	25
relative frequency	77%	76%	23%	24%

Table 54   Castle Rushen Stores; comparative numbers of chicken and goose bones over time

Date/Species	Fragments	Min No
Late 19th and 20th Centuries:		
Gallus gallus	18(4)	13
Anser anser	8	5
Puffinus puffinus	2(1)	2(1)
Anas platyrhynchos	5	4
Corvus corax	1	1
Fratercula arctica	2	2
Total:	**36**	**27**
18th and Early 19th Centuries:		
Gallus gallus	27(2)	20
Anser anser	4	4
Puffinus puffinus	7(5)	6(5)
Larus ridibundus	1	1
Fratercula arctica	1	1
Phalacrocorax aristotelis	1	1
Pyrrhocorax pyrrhocorax	1	1
Turdus ?iliacus	1(1)	1(1)
Total:	**43**	**35**
17th Century:		
Gallus gallus	46(5)	33
Anser anser	15(2)	13
Puffinus puffinus	6(2)	4(1)
Anas platyrhynchos	8	3
Corvus corax	6	4
Larus ridibundus	?4	?3
Larus fuscus/argentatus	3	1
Phalacrocorax aristotelis	1	1
Ardea cinerea	2	1
Falco tinnunculus	2	1
Uria aalge	1	1
Pyrrhocorax pyrrhocorax	1	1
Buteo buteo	1	1
Pinguinus impennis	1	1
Columba livia	1	1
Columba monedula/Pica pica	2	2
Total:	**100**	**71**
16th Century:		
Gallus gallus	22(2)	14
Anser anser	7	3
Puffinus puffinus	3(2)	3(2)
Corvus corax	2	1
Uria aalge	1	1
Total:	**35**	**22**

Table 55 Castle Rushen Stores; comparative numbers of bones per species in different periods (immatures in brackets)

Ctxt	Species/Bone	Mark Type
	Chicken	
005	humerus	knife/scrape marks
033	ulna	scrape mark
033	tarsometatarsus	heavily chewed
037	femur	tooth mark
057	tibiotarsus	gnawed
068	humerus	knife mark
068	ulna	scrape marks
068	femur	knife marks
068	tibiotarsus	knife marks
072	tibiotarsus	bite mark
072	tibiotarsus	burned
074	radius	knife marks
077	humerus	bite mark
077	humerus	cut across epiphysis
103	femur	bite mark
115	tarsometatarsus	gnawed
	Goose	
004	carpometacarpus	knife marks
007	ulna	cooked/burnt
008	carpometacarpus	small knife cuts
008	tibiotarsus	large tooth impression
020	humerus	tooth mark
033	radius	gnawed
077	humerus	cut across base
077	radius	puncture mark
103	humerus	knife cuts
134	ulna	burned
134	radius	burned
143	tarsometatarsus	cut marks across epiphysis
	Mute Swan	
036	tarsometatarsus	heavily scraped and gnawed
	Great Auk	
068	humerus	two fine knife marks across bone
	Raven	
149	ulna	single puncture may be bite mark, or result of pinioning?

Table 56   Castle Rushen; butchery, burning or tooth marks

fishy fluid, however, 'was excellent for applying to all sorts of cuts and cracks' (Simon 1944, after May Byron's Home Cookery Book 1932).

Bird frequencies over time

It was noted in the Peel Castle excavations (Fisher, C T forthcoming) that there are some differences between the numbers of certain species of bird recovered from each of three periods: post-medieval, medieval and pre-medieval. Unfortunately, the contexts from Castle Rushen itself have not yet been closely dated, but four historical periods can be established for Castle Rushen Stores (Table 55). By far the most productive period, both for different species and for numbers of bone fragments, is the seventeenth century. At Peel Castle, the most significant change over time seemed to be that goose became superseded by chicken as a domestic bird. No such evidence is afforded by the statistics from Castle Rushen Stores, albeit from a much smaller sample (Table 54).

Date/Context	Species/Bone	Mark Type
18th/19th Century	**Chicken**	
92.102/23	right humerus	tooth mark
92.103/54	left coracoid	knife marks
	right femur	burnt
92.103/64	left ulna	ends chewed/cut off
17th Century		
92.102/41	right tibiotarsus	tooth crush mark
92.103/116	right tibiotarsus	puncture/tooth mark
16th Century		
92.103/109	left ulna	knife mark
92.103/110	right ulna	scrape marks
92.104/21	left femur	dual tooth puncture marks
92.104/23	left humerus	dual tooth puncture marks
17th Century	**Goose**	
92.103/48	left tibiotarsus	much scored with knife
16th Century		
92.103/110	left femur	knife and scrape marks
16th Century	**Manx Shearwater**	
92.103/109	left femur (adult)	knife marks across bone

Table 57   Castle Rushen Stores; butchery, burning or tooth marks

Butchery, burning or tooth marks

Many of the bird bones, particularly those of chicken and goose, bear knife and bite marks. Many of the bite marks must be from animals such as cats and dogs rather than humans, and so may have occurred after disposal of the bones—as would the marks of rodent teeth. Of particular interest is the evidence of knife marks on great auk and Manx shearwater bones, helping to confirm the once-great economic importance of these birds to the inhabitants of the Isle of Man.

Molluscs

P J Davey

Introduction

The molluscan evidence from both Castle Rushen and Castle Rushen Stores consists largely of the shells of limpets, oysters, edible periwinkles and flat periwinkles. The few other species recorded are in insignificant numbers.

The tabulated results present a summary of the molluscan remains recovered from the excavations (Tables 58 and 59 below). They have been laid out by site and by phase. Full listings of the finds, together with measurements of individual fragments is retained in the site archive. Taxonomy follows Bruce *et al* (1963); English names follow Barrett and Younge (1980). During the excavation the shells were collected by hand, during trowelling, and were then washed, bagged and stored by context.

This report considers the contextual evidence for each of the species present and then attempts an assessment of the whole assemblage. The species are discussed in order of frequency.

Summary of species present

Common limpet (Patella vulgata)

Limpets occur throughout the sequence at both Castle Rushen and Castle Rushen Stores. They are the dominant component of the assemblage and form some 54% of the total number of individuals collected from the two sites. They are in the majority, particularly in the later phases at Castle Rushen and in Trench A at Castle Rushen Stores where they represent two-thirds of the collection (Tables 58 and 59). The majority of the specimens are undamaged.

Common or edible periwinkle (Littorina littorea)

The edible periwinkle is an important component of the molluscan assemblage from both sites, forming 20% of the total collection. It is the dominant mollusc from Trench B at Castle Rushen Stores, where it occurs in seventeenth- to nineteenth-

Species	Phase								
	1	**2A**	**2B**	**3**	**4A**	**4B**	**4C**	**Total**	**%**
Patella vulgata (common limpet)	1	2	3	7	9	109	162	293	60
Littorina littorea (edible periwinkle)	–	1	5	9	9	35	35	94	19
Ostrea edulis (flat oyster)									
lower valve	12	3	1	2	5	13	46	82	17
upper valve	(11)	(2)	(1)	(3)	(10)	(13)	(51)	(91)	–
Littorina littoralis (flat periwinkle)	1	1			2	3	3	10	2
Pecten maximus (great scallop)	–	1	–	–	–	2	2	5	1
Buccinum undatum (common whelk)	–	–	–	–	1	–	–	1	1
Cardium edule (edible cockle)	–	–	–	–	–	–	1	1	1
Helix aspera (garden snail)	–	–	3	–	2	1	1	7	1
Total no of individuals:	14	8	12	18	28	163	250	493	100

*In the case of *Ostrea edulis* the number of individuals is based on the number of lower valves present; the number of upper valves is shown in brackets

Table 58   Castle Rushen 89.159; molluscs by phase

Species	Trench/Phase											
	A				**B**			**C**				
	1	**2**	**3**	**4**	**2**	**3**	**4**	**2**	**3**	**4**	**Total**	**%**
Patella vulgata (common limpet)	2	1	36	4	1	5	16	1	1	7	74	39
Littorina littorea (edible periwinkle)	1	–	9	1	6	9	8	–	7	3	44	23
Ostrea edulis (flat oyster)												
lower valve	–	–	1	–	–	2	2	1	1	28	35	19
upper valve	–	–	(1)	–	–	(1)	(1)	(1)	–	(27)	(31)	–
Littorina littoralis (flat periwinkle)	–	–	8	–	1	6	3	–	1	–	19	10
Pecten maximus (great scallop)	–	–	4	–	–	–	–	–	–	–	4	2
Cardium edule (edible cockle)	–	–	–	1	–	–	–	–	–	–	1	1
Helix aspera (garden snail)	–	–	–	–	–	11	–	–	–	–	11	6
Total no of individuals:	3	1	58	6	8	22	40	2	10	38	188	100

*In the case of *Ostrea edulis* the number of individuals is based on the number of lower valves present; the number of upper valves is shown in brackets

Table 59   Castle Rushen Stores; molluscs by phase within Trenches 92.102–104

century phases. At Castle Rushen it occurs from the medieval period onwards, but in small quantities.

Flat or native oyster (Ostrea edulis)

Oysters were found in some numbers at both sites. With the exception of the 12 individuals from the medieval moat at Castle Rushen, they appear to become important only in the later nineteenth century. At Castle Rushen oysters form 8% of Phase 4B and 18% of Phase 4C. At Castle Rushen Stores they appear in significant numbers only in Trench C in Phase 4 (nineteenth century), where they form 74% of the assemblage. Opening marks were not in evidence (Llewellyn-Jones and Pain 1980, 147).

Flat periwinkle (Littorina littoralis)

Flat periwinkles occur in small numbers on both sites at most periods, amounting to 4% of the total collection.

Great scallop or clam (Pecten maximus)

Fragments of at least eight individuals were found, four from each site. There are too few examples to show any clear period bias, although one specimen was recovered from late medieval deposits at Castle Rushen.

Common cockle (Cardium edule)

Single cockle shells were found in nineteenth-century deposits at both Castle Rushen and Castle Rushen Stores.

Common whelk or buckie (Buccinum undatum)

A single individual was recovered from a nineteenth-century context at Castle Rushen.

Garden snail (Helix aspera)

This, the only species of terrestrial mollusc recovered from the excavations, formed less than 3% of the whole assemblage. Almost all of the finds were from nineteenth-century contexts. At Castle Rushen Stores all of the garden snail finds came from the topsoil of Trench C. At Castle Rushen, the three pre-nineteenth-century individuals from Phase 2B, which is dated by the pottery to the fifteenth century, may well be intrusive, as the relevant contexts contained many voids into which snails might have penetrated at a later date.

Discussion

Considering the situation of the Isle of Man, the length of its coastline and the richness of its marine resources, molluscan remains from archaeological excavations have rarely been reported. Probably the most important find was made by Swinnerton in 1888 at Port St Mary, where a megalithic tomb had been constructed over an earlier mesolithic midden. The contents of the 'refuse heap' are described as 'shells which lay in great quantity among the (human) bones, . . . principally of the common limpet, periwinkle, and others common still on the neighbouring shore' (Boyd-Dawkins 1890, 138). At Balladoole, Kermode (1924) described 'great accumulations of discarded shells in the many hollows on the summit plateau' and Cornwall (1974) refers to 'discarded shells in habitation debris at all levels. . ... The shells, obviously food waste, are those of the periwinkle (*Littorina littorea*), and of the limpet (*Patella vulgata*), together with broken pieces of crab shell, *Cancer pagurus*. All are still abundant on the adjacent foreshore.' The Castletown finds, which date from the medieval and post-medieval periods, confirm the continued dominance of these two species in Manx shellfish diet until the nineteenth century.

Limpets and periwinkles

The importance of limpets, called 'flitters' in Manx English dialect, is remembered in a children's variant of 'Oranges and Lemons' current in the 1870s (Swinnerton 1912):

> Pancakes and flitters is the way of cantailers,
> I owe you three farthings . . . etc.

This is thought to refer to the custom of picking limpets on Shrove Tuesday and putting them in a tin can to serve on that day, Ash Wednesday or Good Friday breakfast (Swinnerton 1912, 41; Radcliffe 1991, Information Card 12). Despite their importance in a Manx context, limpets are not the overwhelming element in the excavated assemblage that can be seen in prehistoric sites in the Western Isles of Scotland, such as Ardnave, Islay (Evans 1983, 353, Table 3) or in North Wales, such as the Ty Mawr hut-circles, Holyhead (Evans and Evans 1987, 58, Table 8).

Periwinkles were sufficiently important to have given their name to a fair which was held annually on 6th February at Pooylvaaish, until about 1840 (Moore 1900, 107).

The importance of these two species is probably derived from their abundance throughout the island, representing a renewable resource which is difficult to over-fish. Limpets have a relatively high protein value of around 13%, though large numbers would have to be eaten to sustain life (Townsend 1967). The paucity or absence of other species such as cockles, mussels, queenies and scallops from the Manx excavated assemblages is probably due to the much more restricted areas in which these species can prosper in Manx waters, and the degree of management which is needed to sustain viable communities. Bruce, Colman and Jones (1963, 216) record the cockle from only a handful of locations. Mussels are locally very abundant at Queen's Pier, Ramsey, but 'not common in the south of the island' (*ibid*, 211). Although queenies and scallops are common 'all round the coast' (*ibid*, 212–13), they have only recently become popular as food (Radcliffe 1991, Information Card 12).

Oysters

Oysters are described as 'present in small numbers all round the island' (Bruce, Colman and Jones 1963, 212). Their presence in medieval deposits at Castle Rushen suggests that they have been fished since at least that period. For a later period this is confirmed by Cubbon who records finding 'many oysters' in an early eighteenth-century deposit beneath the Castletown Grammar School site (Cubbon 1971, 11). There have clearly been problems in sustaining renewable populations over the years as in Ramsey Bay, for example, a short-lived eighteenth-century oyster fishery was reactivated in the later nineteenth century only to be over-fished within a few years. The Sea Fisheries Act of 1894 belatedly attempted to protect the native stocks from over-fishing by imposing a closed season from 1st May to 31st August (Radcliffe 1989, 171).

Other stocks of oyster were fished from time to time. For example, one of the interviewees in the Manx Folk Life Survey in 1949 is recorded as saying 'there was once oyster fishing from the Niarbyl but it was not a great success' (Manx Museum Library Records C/33–B).

The finds from the Castletown excavations seem to confirm the latter part of the nineteenth century as an important one for the consumption of oysters.

Molluscan contribution to diet

In all of this discussion an assumption has been made that the molluscan remains recovered represent human food. The limpets, for example, do not bear any sign of having been used as bait. On the other hand, there is no suggestion that shellfish were the sole source of protein. Even at Port St Mary 'small mammal bones' were also recovered. In Castletown, very considerable quantities of animal and bird bones should also be taken into account when the contribution of shellfish to diet is considered.

Flat periwinkles

One species which may have arrived in the town accidentally is the flat periwinkle. This is described as being 'common everywhere on algae, chiefly fucoids' (the wracks). A number of the specimens collected from the excavations are very small; one has an overall length of not quite 2mm. Although edible, it seems likely that some or all of the examples of this species arrived on the sites attached to seaweed, which was being applied to the gardens or fields as a fertiliser. On the other hand, in the Norse and pre-Norse levels at Buckquoy, Orkney, flat limpets occured in considerable quantities with other shellfish and were considered to represent human food debris (Evans and Spencer 1976–77).

Summary

The molluscan evidence from the Castletown excavations confirms the importance of the common limpet and edible periwinkle in Manx gastronomic history from the thirteenth to the nineteenth centuries. Oysters were of some significance throughout this period, but did not become important until the later nineteenth century. No other species were in evidence in any quantity. Commonly eaten shellfish such as cockles, mussels and scallops were either rare or absent. The total numbers of shells recovered is small considering the large areas excavated, particularly at Castle Rushen Stores. Apparent trends in the data must be considered tentative until much larger groups from all periods can be studied.

Plant Remains
D A Higgins

One small plant fragment was preserved by the corrosion products of an Elizabethan silver coin in 92.102/16. This was kindly identified by Dr P R Tomlinson as a piece of *Calluna vulgaris* (heather). Whilst heather is widely distributed on the island, it would not be expected to grow in an urban setting and this fragment may have been brought to Castletown to be used as fuel, fodder or animal bedding.

Charcoal fragments were present in many of the layers. Although these were not systematically collected, individual pieces from the following layers were saved: Trench 92.102/19; Trench 92.103/48, 82, 94, 108, 110, 117; and Trench 92.104/23.

EPILOGUE

P J DAVEY

'The urban archaeologist, therefore, should not be concerned with the town as an isolated artifact. One of his most readily identifiable priorities is the need to investigate more fully the relationship between the town and its wider context' (Schofield, Palliser and Harding 1981, v).

The excavations reported on in this volume have begun to address some of the archaeological questions discussed in the Introduction.

Chronology

A number of both relative and absolute chronological issues have been clarified. The standing masonry of the castle keep and curtain wall were preceded by other structures, including a stone building and a wide ditch or moat. The fills of the moat included medieval pottery dating probably to the later thirteenth or early fourteenth century. Further research will be needed to elucidate the form of this earlier phase of the castle's history. No evidence was recovered for earlier medieval or prehistoric structures, such as have been found at Peel Castle.

Sequence and Change

The Castle Rushen Stores excavations have provided clear evidence of sixteenth-century and later occupation of the area, although they did not locate any earlier settlement evidence in that part of the town. The few sherds of medieval pottery and an early coin may best be interpreted as the result of 'night soil' dispersion from neighbouring houses or the castle. The considerable clay banks which form the division between the Malew Street and Arbory Street properties, and the lesser structures between individual properties, all give the appearance of a planned extension of the town away from the waterfront, towards the end of the fifteenth century or at the beginning of the sixteenth. The structure of the area remained more or less unchanged until 1992, when the excavations took place. The Collins chart of 1693 supports this idea in that it implies that the major focus of settlement is the river and sea frontage, with the castle as a focus in the centre (Fig 2). Until this sixteenth-century suburb was created, the area consisted of fields or gardens. This new evidence also suggests an expansion of population and greater prosperity at this period.

Industrial Activity and Consumption of Goods

Although the recent excavations provide little evidence for industrial activities on the sites, apart from the nineteenth-century bottle works, they produced very considerable quantities of domestic waste, which gives a clear indication of the quality and sources of goods and materials consumed in the town, particularly from around 1500 up to 1900. The evidence of material culture is much more comprehensive that any previously discovered on Man.

Building materials recovered from Castle Rushen and Castle Rushen Stores indicate that brick and Manx Series roofing slates were in use by the sixteenth century and window glass by the seventeenth. Coal was in general use by the sixteenth century.

Imported Goods

The ceramic evidence is uneven, particularly at Castle Rushen. Where it is possible to make direct comparisons, no difference in the quality of the ceramics in use in the town and the castle can be discerned. A high proportion of the medieval fragments from both sites are from sources in Britain, with a small but significant group from the Saintonge in south-west France. In the sixteenth century a wide range of finewares from Beauvais and Martincamp in northern France, the Saintonge and north-west England is in evidence. These occur even in the small groups from Bank Street, which boasts fine Cistercian ware cups and a sherd from a Martincamp flask, as well as the normal range of coarse wares. The picture of a cosmopolitan trading centre is further advanced by the presence of fine glass drinking vessels from Venice, together with German stoneware tankards and dress accessories from London and further afield.

The seventeenth-century finds assemblages

appear to contain far less exotic material, with much of the pottery, glass and clay pipes probably being produced in the north-west of England. Compared with towns in Cheshire or Lancashire, there is an unusually large proportion of north Devon material in evidence. This is almost certainly a reflection of its central position in the northern Irish Sea and the activities of the Bideford and Barnstable shipmasters in bringing ceramic material northwards as ballast, in order to return to the south-west with much higher value products from Ireland and northern England (Grant 1983).

Environmental Evidence

The environmental evidence produced by the excavations consists almost entirely of animal, bird bones and shellfish. The animal bone assemblages consist largely of cattle and sheep from the sixteenth century and later, with a smaller quantity of pig bones. Domestic animals, not apparently consumed as food, are represented by numbers of both horse and dog bones. This evidence is difficult to interpret as there are no other comparable assemblages published from the island. A longer chronological range is also needed in order to show how the management of these animals developed over time. A wide range of bird bones was represented, with at least 34 species evident. Whilst the majority consisted of chicken and greylag goose, a number of other species, such as mallard, shearwater, pigeon, puffin, chough and herring gull, all seem to have been eaten by the inhabitants of both town and castle. Limpets and periwinkles formed a small element in Castletown's diet throughout the period represented by the excavations.

Economic Relationship with Other Towns and Settlements in Man

The question of the economic relationship between Castletown and the other towns in the Isle of Man, and the nature of the internal Manx market, is a much more difficult one. This is largely because, apart from the one metre quadrats in Peel, there is no evidence with which to make a comparison. At Peel, unlike Castletown, medieval domestic structures were encountered in the town, together with small artifact assemblages. The sixteenth-century material found in the silted-up harbour included many of the pottery types found at Castle Rushen Stores, such as late Saintonge green-glazed wares, a fragment of Martincamp flask and numbers of fine Cistercian ware drinking vessels (Davey 1992b, 65–66). In summary then, the available evidence suggests that Peel and Castletown shared a similar level of material culture at this period.

The relationship between the towns and rural settlements is very difficult to assess. A number of stray finds, such as the pink Saintonge fragment from Sulby and the Normandy gritty ware find from Braddan Vicarage (Davey forthcoming), do suggest that the island may probably need to be considered as a single market and that many of the goods which arrived in the towns found their way to rural sites quite readily. Recent field walking in the area of Cregneash Village has provided a few sherds of imported medieval pottery analagous to that found in Castletown. A serious programme of excavations at rural sites, in particular at the quarterland farms, will be needed in order to place these finds from Peel and Castletown into a Manx context.

APPENDICES

Appendix 1—Castletown Cottages

J Roscow

Notes on the 'Cottages of Castletown' documents

The original list of the cottages in Castletown can be found in a document in the Derby Papers, held in the museum library, in which they are listed as a 'Survey of the Rents in the Isle of Man' and dated 1506. The document carries the reference 1715–2 and appears to have been unrecognised as the Manorial Roll of the south of the Isle of Man, because it was written in a different order to the other extant Manorial Rolls. The document starts with a list of the cottages of Castletown and goes on to list the rest of the treens of Kirk Malew. The standard order for listing is Rushen, Arbory, Malew, Santon and so on, commencing with the treens of the parish and then proceeding to list the cottages and intacks.

A search through some of the museum's microfilms revealed that there were entries recorded in the 'Lord's Composition Book' for 1506. An examination of microfilm GL 839 revealed a few pages similar to the 1506 Derby Survey, but in a different hand and in poor physical condition. Fortunately, the record of the 'cottages of Castletown' has survived in a readable condition, providing a secondary check on this Roll in the Isle of Man. Unfortunately only the south is covered by the 1715–2 document, and even less by the 'Composition Book'. Both state that the land was let for seven years, this being the first year. The comprehensiveness of this statement, inserted after every holding, indicates that this was a new survey and it was presumably to set the land-holding on a new and detailed basis. This suggestion is borne out by the fact that the survey is entered at the beginning of the 'Lord's Composition Book', which normally only records changes and additions of ownership. Some earlier records from the north are known. Crellin (1969) attributes these to around 1495. They have no details of the actual holding, only tenants listed under treen titles.

The microfilms of the Manorial Rolls, *Liber Assed* (RB 595), show the Roll for the south in 1511 and the first couple of holdings are followed by the note: 'leased for seven years this being the sixth'. This statement ties in with the Derby Survey of 1506.

The 1511 'cottages of Castletown' show a slight increase in total rent as one would expect (2s 8d), but more interestingly the descriptions of the properties have begun to evolve, for example, 'No 79—by the burne'. Some of the sites for cottages now appear to have had buildings constructed on them, and sites are being amalgamated or separated.

Problems exist regarding the definitions of a house, a cottage, a tenement and a chamber. A possible indication of which people ran inns may come from the list of persons who paid rent for 'brew pans'!

Cottages of Castletown, 1506

Parish of Saint Lupus (Malew) from the Derby Paper reference 1715–2. List of the Cottages of Castletown in 1506.

1	James Lake, a cottage and a chamber, leased for 1 year	16d
2	Edmund Cowper, a cottage & garden leased for 7 years, 1st year	16d
3	John Lytherland, a chamber 12d, a cottage & two small gardens, 2 chambers and brewhouse, leased for 7 years, 1st year	6/-
4	William Goldsmythe, a cottage & garden, two chambers & brewhouse	7/-
5	Edmund Lake, a cottage 20d, a garden, cellar & one chamber 16d	3/-
6	William Hubart, 1 chamber near the Castle 8d, a cottage & garden 20d, a cottage & small garden 8d, a cottage, workshop & garden 18d	4/6
7	Thomas Norres, a chamber near the sea 12d, a cottage, 2 chambers and garden	6/6
8	William Vawse, one chamber	6d
9	William Bull, a cottage with Johanna Hayell	3/-
10	Johanna Hayell, another share of a cottage	12d

11 Huan Birche, a chamber near the sea 12d, with cottage & garden 4d, a cottage & garden 6/-, a croft with cottage & garden 12d temporally let to Gilbert Bredy. 8/4

12 John Clerke, a chamber near the sea 2/-

13 Richard Holte, a house, cottage, garden, & brewhouse, one site for a cottage and chamber 7/2

14 Thomas Clerke, 1 chamber near the Chapel 4d, a cottage, garden and brewhouse, 6/- 6/4

15 John Mc Quaken, 1 chamber 16d

16 Nicholas Buller, a cottage and garden 2/-

17 William Dycanson, a cottage, garden and two chambers 3/4

18 John Stephynson, two chambers 16d

19 Patric Slater, a cottage and garden 12d, one chamber 12d 2/-

20 Nicholas Duke, a cottage & garden, and a site for a cottage 4/-

21 Roger Flecher, a site for a house (Domus), chamber & garden 20d cottage, chamber and garden 2/6 4/2

22 Otnell Caterall, a cottage and garden 16d

23 Gilbert Mc Quyn, a cottage, chamber and garden 16d

24 The Servant of Patrike Ine Qullyam, one cottage 8d

25 William Norres, a cottage, chamber and garden 18d

26 Patrice Mc Conald, a cottage, chamber and garden 2/-

27 To pay for a garden and Hawkehouse,— Robert Caldcote (per annum) 12d

28 Michael Mc Kyineoke, a cottage and garden 16d

29 Robert Furbor, a cottage, chamber and garden 18d, with cottage, chamber and a moiety of garden 18d 3/-

30 Thomas Walsh, 1 House & garden with brewhouse & 4 chambers 6/-

31 Thomas Mc Cane, a cottage garden 2/-

32 Thomas Burscogh, a cottage, chamber & garden (Set to Thom. Mc Cane) 12d

33 Marion Gonnere, a cottage and garden 12d

34 John Mc Moleyne, a cottage and moiety of a garden 19d

35 Roger Gall, a cottage, chamber and a moiety of a garden 18d

36 Robert Abelson, a cottage, two chambers, brewhouse, garden 2/8

37 John Merceden, a chamber 12d, a cottage chamber & garden 2/8 3/8

38 John Wilkynson, a cottage, chamber and garden 3/-

39 Gilbert Mc Auley, a cottage and garden tenanted by Richard Brewer, another cottage, chamber and garden 5/-

40 William Hopper, a cottage, two chambers and garden 5/-

41 William Mc Quylly, a cottage and a small garden 8d

42 Alice More, a cottage and garden and two parts of a croft 2/-

43 More Ine Calne, a cottage and garden 8d

44 Robert Butteler, a cottage and garden 16d, a cottage 8d 2/-

45 Thomas Marshall, a cottage, garden and brewhouse 16d

46 A parcel of land near the Brewhouse of the said Thomas 2d

47 Mark Mc Quyll, a cottage and a moiety of a small garden 6d

48 Thomas Mc Kewne, a cottage and the fourth part of a croft 20d

49 John Mc Canell, a cottage 8d

50 John More, a tenement, chamber, brewhouse & garden. A small croft 2/-

51 Isabella Mc Jokyn, a cottage and garden 14d

52 James Mc Kelley, a small cottage & small parcel of land for a garden 8d

53 Marion Ine Cree, a moiety of a cottage, & a small parcel of land for a garden 12d

54 Richard Crekard, a cottage, chamber and garden — 12d

55 Jenkyn Baine, a cottage — 8d

56 Bartholomew Haydoke, site for a small cottage and garden — 6d

57 Rawlyn Smyth, a cottage and garden — 10d

58 The wife of Paton Mc Lucas, a cottage & a site for a cottage — 14d

59 Cristiana Ine Quorey, a cottage temporally occupied by Robert Picroft with a chamber and garden — 16d

60 John Mc Gegan, a cottage, chamber, garden & parcel of waste land to augement a garden — 12d

61 Agnet Wedall, a cottage, chamber and small garden — 12d

62 Thomas Hogell, a cottage and a parcel of garden — 12d

63 Armalpho Gomere, a cottage — 8d

64 Donald Mc Caren, a cottage — 6d

65 Finlo Mc Kelley, a cottage and garden — 12d

66 William Pyper, a cottage and a moiety of a garden — 8d

67 Cristian Ine How, a cottage and garden — 8d

68 John Farken, Abbot of Rushen, a chamber and small garden — 3/-

69 *To pay for a cottage, garden and chamber lately tenanted by Marchoke Blake, per year — 13d

70 *To pay for a tenement, two chambers and a brewhouse 2/7, a site for a cottage 6d lately tenented by Elene Corbet per year — 3/1

71 *To pay for a chamber and garden 14d, a cellar 2/- lately tenanted by William Parre, per year — 3/2

72 Robert Crayye, a chamber and a cellar — 4/6

73 *To pay for a chamber, Robert Corbet, per year — 6d

74 To pay for a cellar for the Lord's use, 6/8 per year — nil

75 To pay for two chambers, tenant Thomas Stephynson, leased for 7 years — 16d

76 Three cellars under one roof and a chamber, for the use of the Lord, Robert Calcote two cellars by the Castle burne 8/8, a tenement and loft re John Coole, and one cellar tenanted by William Goldsmyth 16d. — 10/-

77 John Ireland, soldier, and William Huble, One tenement—three chambers, brewhouse and garden. A cottage, 3 chambers and a garden tenanted by Cristian Corbet — 10/-

78 William Goldsmyth, a chamber near the sea tenanted by Cristian Corbet — 22d

79 *To pay for a cottage, chamber, brewhouse and moiety of a garden with five cellars tenanted by Marion Meser per year — 3/2

80 *To pay for a cellar, tenanted by Marion, per year — 2/-

81 *To pay for a chamber near the sea, Robert Ap Ethell, per year — 6d

82 William Lake, a chamber and a small garden — 12d

83 William Samlesbury, a cottage and a site for a cottage and garden — 2/8

84 Richard Brewer, a site for a cottage & moiety of a garden tenanted by Henry Lucas. — 12d

85 *To pay for a cottage & garden and small parcel of land augmenting the garden tenanted by Marion Corbet for 6d per year — 8d

86 *To pay for a broken cottage lately tenanted by Thomas Corbet previously at 12d year — nil

Sum total of Rent to Pay for Cottages, 9–16s-9d.

Note: Numbers followed by * have 'NO' noted against them in the left hand margin of the 'Derby Roll' and this is exactly repeated in the 'Composition Book'. This may indicate that these properties have not been leased for a term longer than one year. All the other properties are stated as having been (newly) leased for seven years, to the person specified in the Roll.

Extra information contained in the 1511 Roll

No 19 A chamber near DALHILL

No 69 Near the Burne

No 50 Johanne More, adjacent to the bog

No 30 One chamber in the hands of the Lord Abbot

No 44 Robert Butler with his partners

No 74 The Long House (of the Lord)

Summary

	Total
Cottage 9, 10, 24, 44, 48, 49, 55, 58, 63, 64, 83	11
Cottage and Chamber 1	1
Cottage and garden 2, 6, 6, 11, 11, 16, 19, 20, 22, 28, 31, 33, 34, 39, 41, 42, 43, 44, 47, 51, 52, 53, 57, 62, 65, 66, 67, 85	28
Cottage, chamber and garden 21, 23, 25, 26, 29, 32, 35, 37, 38, 39, 54, 59, 61, 69	14
Cottage, chamber, garden and parcel of wasteland 60	1
Cottage, garden, chamber and brewhouse 79	1
Cottage, garden and brewhouse 14, 45	2
Cottage, garden and two chambers 7, 17, 40	3
Cottage, garden, two chambers and brewhouse, 4, 36	2
Cottage, two gardens, two chambers and brewhouse 3	1
Cottage, cellar and chamber and garden 5	1
Part of a croft 42, 48	2
A croft, cottage and garden 11	1
Cottage, workshop and garden 6	1
A chamber 3, 6, 7, 8, 11, 12, 14, 15, 19, 37, 73, 78, 81	13
A chamber and garden 68, 71, 82	3
Two chambers 18, 75	2
A tenement, two chambers and a brewhouse 70	1
A chamber and a cellar 72	1
A cellar 71, 74, 80	3
House, cottage, garden and brewhouse 13	1
House, garden, brewhouse and four chambers 30	1
Tenement, chamber, brewhouse and garden 50	1
Tenement and loft 76	1
Cottage, three chambers, brewhouse and garden 77	1
Croft 50	1
Garden and Hawkehouse 27	1

Sites	Cottages 20, 58, 70	3
	Cottage and chamber 13	1
	Cottage and garden 56, 83, 84	3
	House, chamber and garden 21	1
	Total	8

An industrial site? Three cellars under one tenement, and a chamber, for the use of the Lord.

Tenants – Robert Calcote has two cellars by the Castle burne, John Coole has one tenement and a loft 76	1
William Goldsmyth has one cellar 76	1
Five cellars 79	1
A parcel of land 46	1
A broken cottage 86	1

Note With regard to 86, it is probable that the cottage had no roof and therefore paid no rent.

Appendix 2—Pottery thin-section analysis

J R Senior

An introduction to the material supplied by the Manx Museum

The pot sherds supplied by the Manx Museum were generally quite soft and rather difficult to prepare as thin sections, suggesting that relatively low firing temperatures may have been employed at the time of manufacture. Uneven firing conditions were indicated by differences in firing colours on some pots. The technical difficulties presented by the friable nature of the fabric of these sherds necessitated the use of special techniques for cutting and preparing the sections, using oil rather than water.

The pot sherds in thin section

The sherds received for examination had two components, the fine-grained clay bonding material, the 'matrix', and the coarse added fraction, the 'temper'.

The clay seems to be of a fine-grained iron-rich (reddish) variety, firing to 10YR dark greyish brown colours (Munsell 2.5YR 5/6–10YR 3/2), with Sample 1 (Castle Rushen) jet black in colour (Munsell 10YR 2/1). These clays may possibly be lacustrine or alluvial in origin. Some of the sherds show work features, the fabric being moulded and streaked out during manufacture.

The added coarse temper

The temper added to the clay fraction in the samples sectioned and examined seems to consist mainly of fresh granitoid fragments.

The granitoid material

This was undoubtedly obtained from sources immediately adjacent to the small patches of Caledonian granite found on the island at Dhoon, 7km south of Ramsey, and Foxdale, 6.5km south-east of Peel. Although there is some variety in the appearance and mineralogy within each granite mass, each does seem sufficiently different from the other to make it possible to attempt to locate the source of the temper. It would be useful to collect samples of material from specific sources for comparative purposes, rather than relying on existing thin-section collection material from poorly recorded sources or the descriptions made by Lamplugh (1903).

Composite metaquartzite clasts and individual quartz grains

Some of the sherds also contain contaminant material, including well-rounded quartz and composite metaquartzite grains (often from a low grade metamorphic source, indicated by strained crystal lattices).

The origin of this material is probably the Palaeozoic basement rocks (Manx Slate Formation).

Petrological descriptions of the sherd fragments

Sample 1. Castle Rushen (Manx Museum Accession No 2381)

A thoroughly reduced body sherd.

Clay matrix—jet black (Munsell 10YR 2/1) in colour, this is unique amongst this group of samples. It has a crude moulded fabric and is unusually friable.

Inclusions—numerous, all angular and very fresh in appearance, consisting of muscovite mica flakes up to 0.2mm × 1.4mm in size, quartz and quartz-alkali feldspar composite clasts up to 2.0mm × 2.2mm in size and subsidiary plagioclase (oligoclase in composition).

Diagnosis—the included temper, Foxdale-type granite, has been freshly broken up; no material from weathered soil profiles or river sources has been used.

Sample 2. Ronaldsway Village (Manx Museum Accession No 64.145/Y2)

The rim of a straight-sided vessel with external sooting.

Clay matrix—brown (Munsell 10YR 5/3) in centre, with weak red margins (Munsell 10YR 5/4). There is some evidence of working in the clay, with an alignment of flaky minerals parallel to the pot walls.

Inclusions—apart from a few rounded quartz grains, the majority of the temper inclusions are angular in appearance, with the mineral flakes and crystal grains very fresh indeed. Amongst the inclusions are very prominent muscovite mica flakes up to 0.1mm × 2.00mm in size, and angular composite grains of quartz and quartz with microline feldspar, with or without plagioclase (?oligoclase), up to 2.3mm × 3.3mm in size.

Diagnosis—the temper inclusions are freshly

broken from a granite source (probably the Foxdale granite). The very few well-rounded quartz grains may be accidental, or wind or water borne contaminants.

Sample 3. Ronaldsway Village (Manx Museum Accession No 64.145/Y3)

The base of a large probable cooking pot with external and internal sooting.

Clay matrix—light brownish grey to very dark grey (Munsell 10YR 6/2–10YR 3/1) on the exterior to light reddish brown on the interior of the pot (Munsell 2.5YR 6/4). The platy grains (particularly the highly visible muscovite mica flakes) can be seen oriented parallel to the pot walls.

Inclusions—all the inclusions are angular or naturally platy and very fresh, consisting of small fragments of muscovite mica, plagioclase and alkali feldspars with larger composite clasts of quartz, quartz with alkali feldspar, plagioclase feldspar (oligoclase), muscovite and biotite micas. The individual muscovite mica flakes range in size up to 1.0mm × 0.2mm, and the composite granite inclusions range from 0.05mm × 0.05mm to 2.25mm × 1.8mm in size. The quartz grains show strained lattices.

Diagnosis—a very fresh source of Foxdale granite has been crushed and used in this pottery, as witnessed by the presence of fresh biotite mica. This granite seems to have undergone slight regional structure deformation (the mineral components show stressed lattices). This seems to be a large piece of a well-made and well-fired pot; the degree of clay working is indicated by the mineral orientation within the clay fabric. The pot seems to have been well used, with the outside colour being due to fire burning (after manufacture?). The odd impressions on the inside of the pot seem to have been organic fragments (grass stems?) incorporated during wet clay manufacture, then carbonised and lost during firing.

Sample 4. Ronaldsway Smelt—Stenning Site (Manx Museum Accession No 66.388)

A small body sherd.

Clay matrix—reddish brown to red in colour (Munsell 2.5YR 5/4–5/6) with mica flakes parallel to the pot walls, indicating a high degree of clay working.

Inclusions—angular fragments of very fresh material with pronounced preferred orientation to the pot walls. Fragments include muscovite mica flakes (up to 0.55mm × 0.05mm in size); biotite mica flakes (up to 1.00mm × 0.30mm in size); quartz and composite quartz-microline feldspar; and quartz-microline feldspar-plagioclase (oligoclase) clasts up to 2.1mm × 2.0mm in size. Much of the quartz and feldspar shows slight strain features due minor deformation of the source rock.

Diagnosis—the included temper was obtained from a fresh granite source, definitely the Foxdale granite in this case. The presence of reasonably fresh biotite mica in this pot sherd not only indicates the freshly crushed nature of the temper, but also a relatively low firing temperature for the pot.

Sample 5. Castletown Grammar School (Manx Museum Accession No 65.60/136)

A small body sherd with external sooting

Clay matrix—very dusky red interior (Munsell 2.5YR 2.5/2) to red exterior (Munsell 2.5YR 5/6); this sherd shows some evidence of preferred inclusion (parallel to pot walls) due to clay working.

Inclusions—highly visible muscovite mica flakes up to 0.25mm × 0.1mm in dimension (largely parallel to the pot walls), rounded quartz clasts (with strained lattice fabric) up to 0.25mm × 0.3mm in dimension; one black opaque grain (?iron oxide), 1.8mm × 0.8mm in size; and angular quartz/muscovite mica/microline/plagioclase (oligoclase) clasts (occasionally composite) up to 2.1mm × 1.7mm in size.

Diagnosis—granite source (probably the Foxdale granite) is indicated for the inclusion material; the rock was freshly crushed: no altered or rotten material seems to have been used.

Conclusions

Although all the granite identified in the samples seems to be from the Foxdale source, it would be useful to collect accurately located samples of this rather variable granitoid intrusion in order to try and pinpoint the location source (and possible manufacture sites) for the pottery. At the same time the Dhoon granite intrusion should also be extensively sampled, in order to compare materials used in pot manufacture.

It might be an advantage to find out experimentally the temperatures of firing achieved by these pottery workshops. Inert granite temper should have allowed high firing temperatures, producing better quality pots. In addition, the systematic recording of similar chronological pottery finds from the Isle of Man on computerised base maps could eventually lead to the identification of the areas of manufacture.

The material used as temper in all the pot fragments examined seemed to have been deliberately manufactured, fresh rock having been crushed to form angular aggregates. The only water-rounded material seems to be a contaminant in the process.

Appendix 3—Technical Appendix

Numbering of trenches and contexts

Accession codes for the sites excavated are as follows:

Castle Rushen—89.159
Bank Street—89.160
Castle Rushen Stores (1991 excavations)—91.129
  Context numbers from Trial Trench 1 = 100s
  Context numbers from Trial Trench 2 = 200s
  Context numbers from Trial Trench 3 = 300s
Castle Rushen Stores (1992 excavations)
  Trench A—92.102
  Trench B—92.103
  Trench C—92.104

When it is clear from the text which trench is under discussion, contexts are given as simple numbers in brackets. When a number of trenches are being discussed, the appropriate accession code is given, followed by an oblique stroke and the context number. (Context 10 of Trench B from the 1992 Castle Rushen stores excavation would therefore be 92.103/10.)

Illustrations

The scale for each illustration is given in the figure caption. The key for the plans and sections is shown on page 14.

Not all the specialist reports have illustrations. Where illustrations are present they have been logically grouped and each group has been given a figure number (Fig XX). These figure numbers run in a continuous sequence through the monograph. Individual objects are numbered within each figure. Objects are referred to in the text by the figure number, followed by the individual number for each object. Item Number 2 of Figure 10, for example, would be given as Fig 10.2.

North points on illustrations indicate site north and are not an indication of true north.

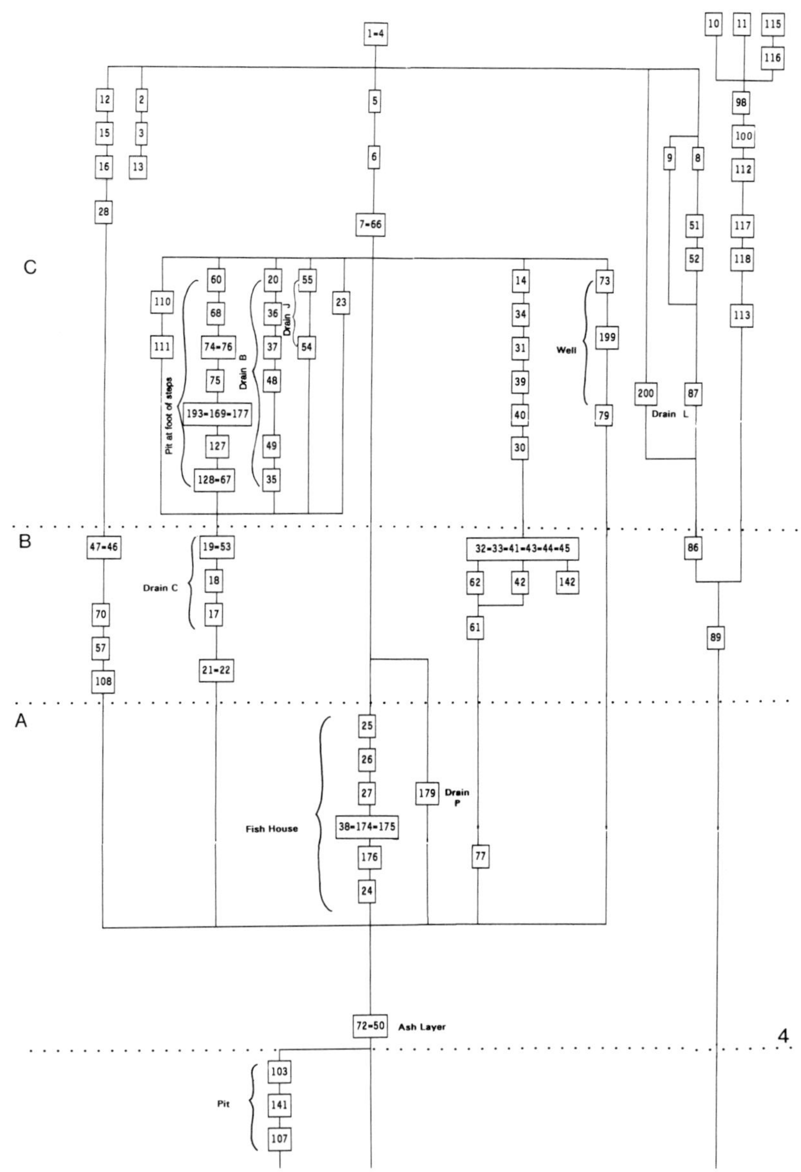

Fig 65   Castle Rushen, Site Matrix (upper)

Castle Rushen: context summary

001   Turf
002   Layer
003   Modern drain cut
004   Turf
005   Mixed layer, including turf-soil
006   Layer of disturbed subsoil
007   Fill of construction trench (38)
008   Layer of interstitial subsoil
009   Layer, similar to topsoil
010   Layer of topsoil
011   Layer; ?modern flower bed
012   Layer; gravel dump
013   Rigby drain trench
014   Fill of pit (upper)
015   Disturbed layer at foot of steps
016   Clay layer at foot of steps
017   Cut for Drain C
018   Fill of Drain C
019   Fill of Drain C
020   Layer sealing Drain B
021   Layer
022   Burnt layer
023   Fill within broken Drain C
024   Construction trench of 'fish-house'
025   Upper fill of construction trench for 'fish-house'
026   Fill of construction trench of 'fish-house'
027   Stony layer within construction trench of 'fish-house'
028   Mixed general layer

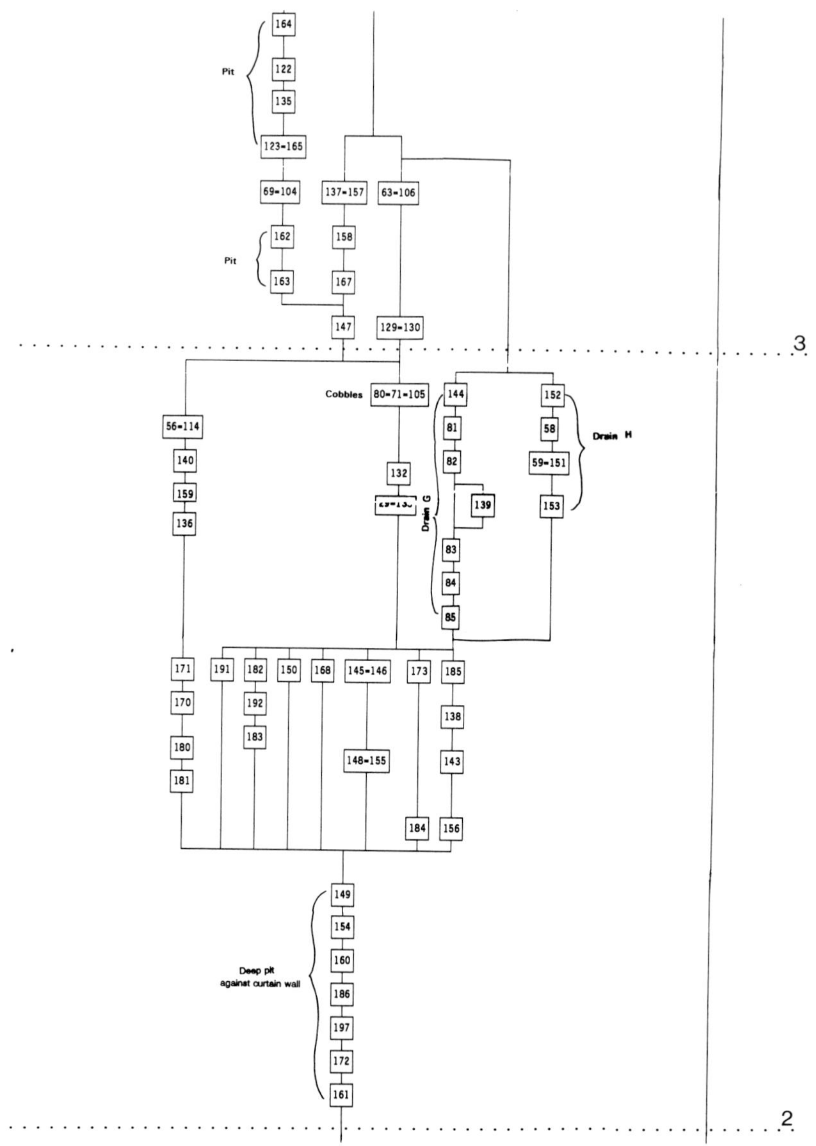

Fig 66   Castle Rushen, Site Matrix (middle)

029 Layer	044 Layer of hard-core; ? levelling
030 Cut of shallow pit	045 Layer of hard-core; ? levelling
031 Rubble fill of 30	046 Slaty layer
032 Layer, consisting of a scatter of cobbles	047 Stony layer
033 Layer of cobbles	048 Lower fill of Drain B
034 Cut for shallow scoop	049 Salt-glazed pipe in Drain B
035 Cut for Drain B	050 Layer of loose ash, same as 72
036 Clay upper fill of Drain B	051 Layer
037 Fill of cobbles in Drain B	052 Layer? sealing Drain L
038 Eastern wall of 'fish-house'	053 Upper fill of Drain C
039 Concrete repair of 40	054 Cut for Drain J
040 Square stone setting	055 Fill of Drain J
041 Irregular cobbled surface near curtain wall	056 Layer
042 Cut for an irregular shallow scoop, containing 41	057 Mixed layer
	058 Slate cover slabs for Drain H
043 Layer of hard-core; ? levelling	059 Side walls of Drain H

060   Mixed layer at foot of steps
061   Layer
062   Dump of large stones
063   Layer above cobbles
064   Upper layer of moat
065   Deep gravelly layer within moat
066   Layer
067   Cut for pit at foot of steps
068   Upper fill of pit at foot of steps
069   Mixed layer
070   Thin clay layer
071   Cobbled surface just outside door of chapel
072   Layer of loose ash, same as 50
073   Upper fill of well construction trench
074   Stony fill in pit at foot of steps
075   Mixed layer in pit at foot of steps
076   Stony fill in pit at foot of steps
077   Bone-rich layer below cobbles (62)
078   Cut for moat
079   Cut for well construction trench
080   Rough cobbled surface
081   Top slabs of Drain G (Pooilvaaish marble)
082   Side walls of Drain G
083   Bottom slabs of Drain G
084   Fill of construction trench for Drain G
085   Construction trench for Drain G
086   Layer
087   Top slabs of cess-pit chamber
088   Side walls of cess-pit
089   Top slabs of Drain E
090   Side walls of Drain D
091   Fill of construction trench for Drain D
092   Cut of construction trench for Drain D
093   Fill of construction trench for cess-pit
094   Cut for cess-pit walls
095   West wall of chapel
096   North wall of chapel
097   South wall of chapel
098   Floor slabs of chapel
099   East wall of chapel; west wall of drawbridge pit
100   Limestone wall
101   Context deleted
102   Context deleted
103   Cobble layer in pit (107)
104   Mixed layer
105   Cobbled surface
106   Stony layer above cobbles
107   Cut for shallow pit
108   Layer of shattered slate and stone
109   Side slabs of Drain E/F
110   Cut for small vertical pit
111   Fill of small vertical pit
112   Layer of bedding material
113   Layer
114   Gravelly layer
115   Fill of pit

116   Cut of pit (115)
117   Fill of construction trench
118   Cut for construction trench
119   Top slabs of Drain E/F
120   Cut for moat
121   Upper fill of moat
122   Fill of pit (123)
123   Cut for pit
124   Bottom slabs of Drain E/F
125   Fill of construction trench for Drain E/F
126   Cut for Drain E/F
127   Lower fill of pit at foot of steps
128   Cut for pit at foot of steps
129   Interstitial layer for cobbles (80)
130   Interstitial soil from cobbles (80)
131   South-west corner of gatehouse
132   Layer with crushed brick
133   Layer of loose cobbles
134   Mixed lower fill of moat
135   Fill of pit (123)
136   Gravelly layer
137   Layer near curtain wall
138   Layer
139   Contaminated fill of Drain G
140   Mixed slaty layer
141   Mixed clay layer
142   Dark layer adjacent to curtain wall
143   Mixed clayey layer

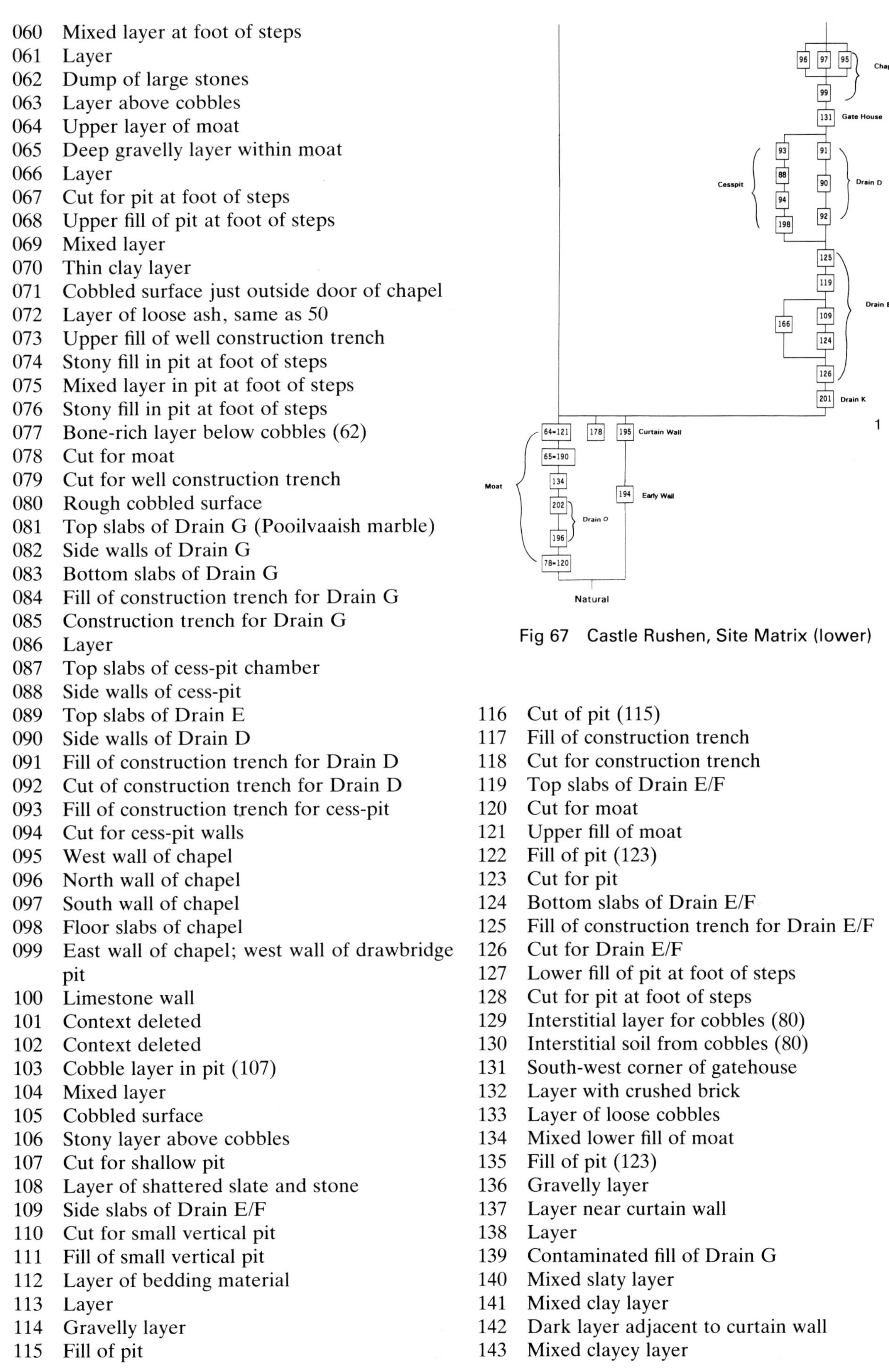

Fig 67   Castle Rushen, Site Matrix (lower)

144   Upper fill of Drain G
145   Area of stones north-east of well
146   Mixed stony layer, as 145
147   Structure of small subsidiary drain
148   Layer of mortary earth
149   Top fill of deep pit against curtain wall
150   Brick hearth
151   Side slabs of Drain H
152   Fill of Drain H
153   Bottom slabs of Drain H
154   Clay layer in deep pit against curtain wall
155   Layer of mortar
156   Mixed layer
157   Layer north of well, by curtain wall
158   Cobble layer near curtain wall, north of well
159   Stony, gravelly layer
160   Layer within deep pit against curtain wall
161   Cut for deep pit against curtain wall
162   Mixed clay fill in pit (163)
163   Steep-sided pit profile
164   Upper fill of pit (123)
165   Cut for pit, same as 123
166   ?Contaminated fill of Drain E/F
167   Layer adjacent to curtain wall
168   Layer
169   Silty fill of pit at foot of steps
170   Layer
171   Layer
172   Lower fill of deep pit against curtain wall
173   Mixed gravelly layer
174   North wall of 'fish-house'
175   South wall of 'fish-house'
176   Sandstone block in north wall of 'fish-house'
177   Clay fill of pit at foot of steps
178   Layer north-east of well
179   Structure of Drain P
180   Fill of shallow depression
181   Cut of shallow depression
182   Mixed fill of 183
183   Cut for feature at south-west corner of the site
184   Layer just south-east of well
185   Layer north of 'fish-house'
186   Peaty layer within deep pit against curtain wall
187   Deleted
188   Deleted
189   Deleted
190   Gravelly layer within moat
191   Mixed layer
192   Black, silty sand fill of 183
193   Clean clay fill of pit at foot of steps
194   Limestone wall
195   Curtain wall (limestone)
196   Lower fill of the moat
197   Wet peaty layer within deep pit against curtain wall
198   Limestone wall and slate top slabs of cess pit

199   Well head (limestone)
200   Drain L—not excavated
201   Drain K—not excavated
202   Drain O (limestone)

Castle Rushen Stores: context summary

Trench 92.102

001   Modern concrete floor
002   Cleaning layer, below 1
003   Cellar walls
004   Dry-stone wall holding back cellar fill
005   Fill between walls
006   Demolition layer
007   Demolition layer
008   Cellar fill
009   Fill of cellar steps
010   Trample etc. on steps and floor, same as 15
011   Cellar fill
012   Trampled surface
013   Cellar fill
014   Layer
015   Trample on floor of cellar passage, same as 10
016   Fill of cellar construction trench
017   Trampled surface
018   Surface
019   Post hole
020   Floor
021   Cellar floor bedding
022   Cellar floor bedding
023   Clay layer (?contemporary with 31)
024   Ash pit
025   Construction of front wall
026   Cobbles
027   Stone setting
028   Fill of cellar construction trench
029   ?Surface
030   Layer
031   Layer (?contemporary with 23)
032   Pit fill
033   Layer
034   Layer
035   Ditch
036   Post hole
037   Post hole
038   Post hole
039   Post hole
040   Layer
041   Clay layer
042   Post hole
043   Post hole
044   Layer
045   Pit

046　Layer
047　Layer
048　Natural
049　Pit with traces of bone
050　Large building stones

Trench 92.103

001　Fill of 2
002　Robber trench
003　Fill of 4
004　Robber trench
005　Garden Soil
006　Fill of 20
007　Fill of 21
008　Fill of 22
009　Fill of 23
010　Fill of 24
011　Fill of 25
012　Fill of 26
013　Fill of 27
014　Fill of 28
015　Fill of 29
016　Fill of 30
017　Fill of 31
018　Fill of 32
019　Fill of 33
020　Cut of garden feature, contains 6
021　Cut of garden feature, contains 7
022　Cut of garden feature, contains 8
023　Cut of garden feature, contains 9
024　Cut of garden feature, contains 10
025　Cut of garden feature, contains 11
026　Cut of garden feature, contains 12
027　Cut of garden feature, contains 13
028　Cut of garden feature, contains 14
029　Cut of garden feature, contains 15
030　Cut of garden feature, contains 16
031　Cut of garden feature, contains 17
032　Cut of garden feature, contains 18
033　Cut of garden feature, contains 19
034　Fill of 35
035　Cut of garden feature, contains 34
036　Fill of 37
037　Cut of garden feature, contains 36
038　Fill of 39
039　Cut of garden feature, contains 38
040　Fill of 41
041　Cut of modern pit, contains 40
042　Fill of 43
043　Cut of garden feature, contains 42
044　Fill of 45
045　Cut of garden feature, contains 44
046　Fill of 47
047　Cut of garden feature, contains 46
048　Fill of 49

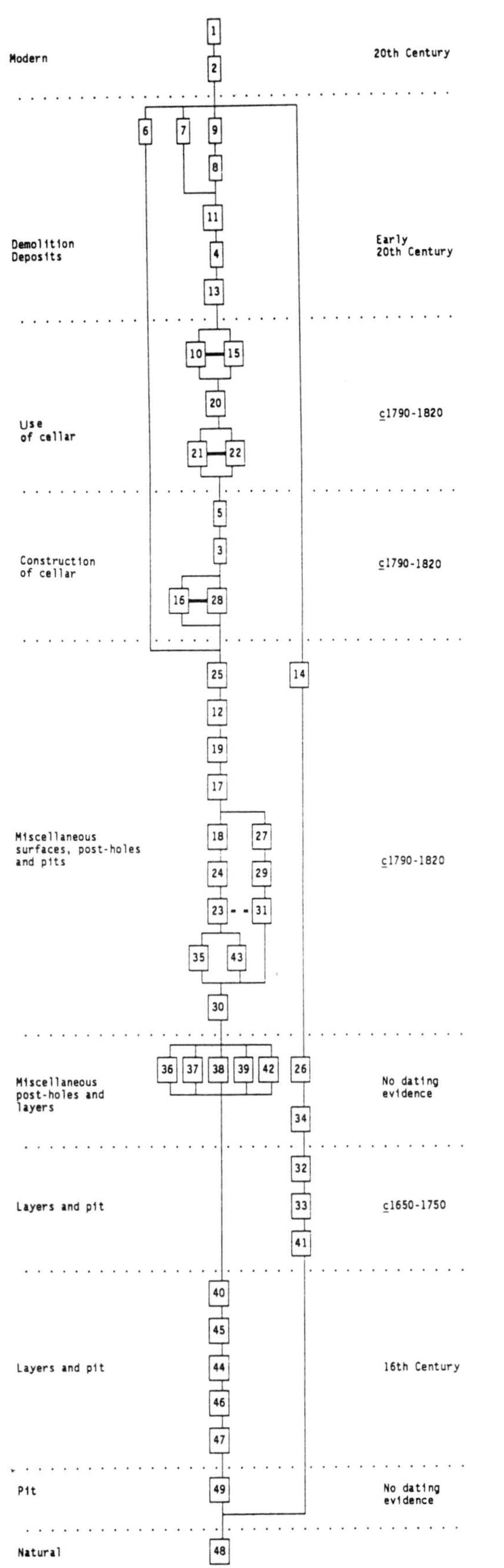

Fig 68　Castle Rushen Stores, Matrix for Trench 92.102

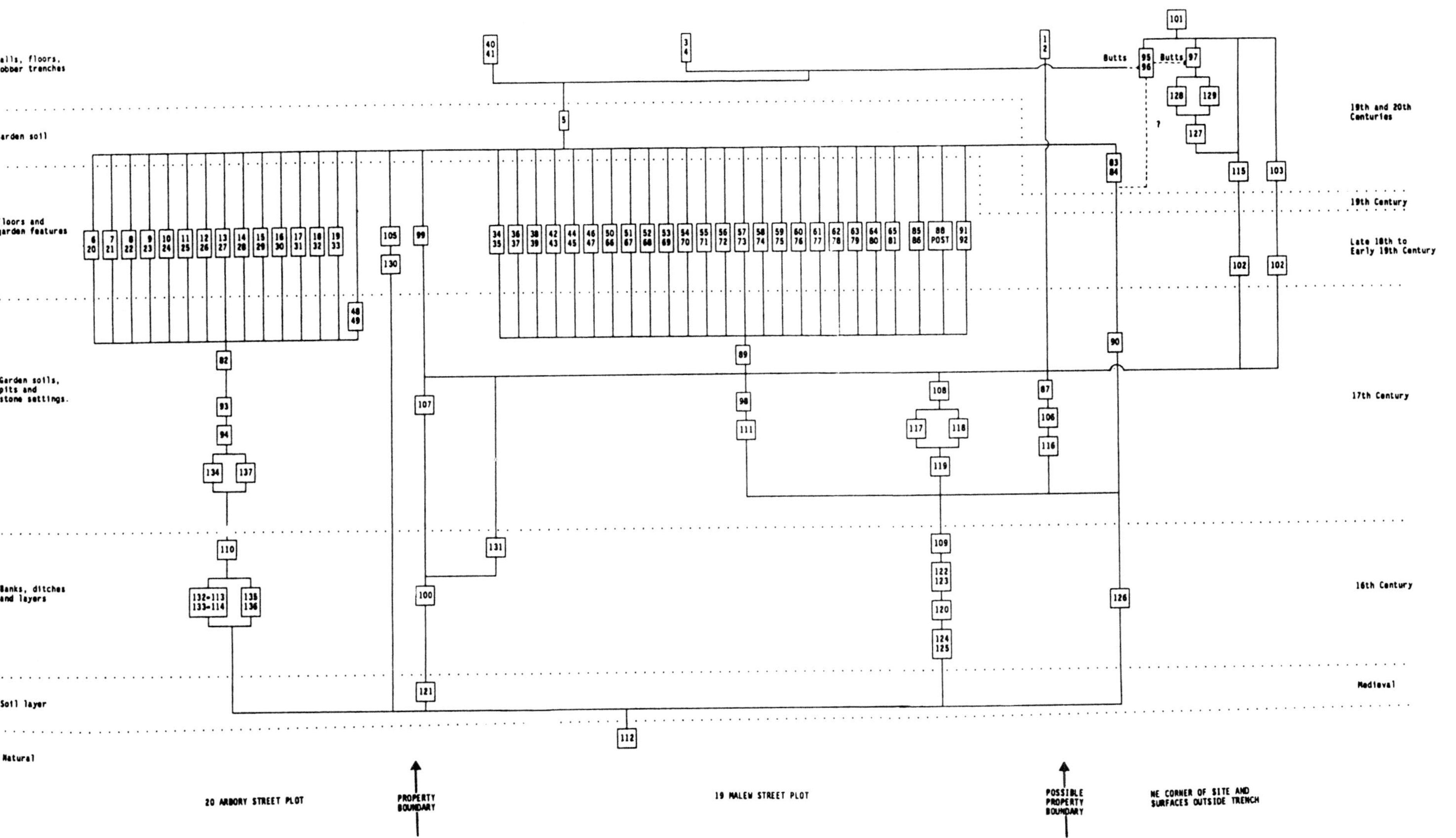

Fig 69 Castle Rushen Stores, Matrix for Trench 92.103

049 Cut of pit, contains 48
050 Fill of 66
051 Fill of 67
052 Fill of 68
053 Fill of 69
054 Fill of 70
055 Fill of 71
056 Fill of 72
057 Fill of 73
058 Fill of 74
059 Fill of 75
060 Fill of 76
061 Fill of 77
062 Fill of 78
063 Fill of 79
064 Fill of 80
065 Fill of 81
066 Cut of garden feature, contains 50
067 Cut of garden feature, contains 51
068 Cut of garden feature, contains 52
069 Cut of garden feature, contains 53
070 Cut of garden feature, contains 54
071 Cut of garden feature, contains 55
072 Cut of garden feature, contains 56
073 Cut of garden feature, contains 57
074 Cut of garden feature, contains 58
075 Cut of garden feature, contains 59
076 Cut of garden feature, contains 60
077 Cut of garden feature, contains 61
078 Cut of garden feature, contains 62
079 Cut of garden feature, contains 63
080 Cut of garden feature, contains 64
081 Cut of garden feature, contains 65
082 Garden soil
083 Fill of 84
084 Cut of small pit, contains 83
085 Fill of 86
086 Cut of garden feature, contains 85
087 ?Boundary bank
088 Wooden post
089 Garden soil
090 Soil
091 Fill of 92
092 Cut of garden feature, contains 91
093 Garden soil
094 Garden soil
095 Wall
096 Cut of construction of wall (95)
097 Step
098 Garden soil
099 Clay bank
100 Gravel boundary bank
101 Concrete floor
102 Cobble floor
103 Ash layer
104 Stone slab floor
105 Stone rubble

106 Rectangular stone stetting, contains 116
107 Small cobble patch
108 Demolition/dumping debris
109 Soil
110 Soil layer
111 Standing stones
112 Natural
113 Fill of 114, same as 132
114 Cut of ditch, same as 133, contains 113
115 Floor trample
116 Fill of 106
117 Wall
118 Wall
119 Cut containing 117, 118 and 108
120 Soil
121 Buried soil
122 Fill of 123
123 Cut of ditch, contains 122
124 Fill of 125
125 Cut of ditch, contains 124
126 Soil
127 Construction trench and fill
128 Post
129 Post
130 ?Wall footing
131 Clay strip
132 Fill of 133 (same as 113)
133 Cut of ditch (same as 114), contains 132
134 Single course wall
135 Fill of 136
136 Cut of ditch, contains 135
137 Single course wall

Trench 92.104

001 Modern garden soil
002 Modern garden soil
003 Fill of 11
004 Fill of 12
005 Fill of 13
006 Fill of 14
007 Fill of 15
008 Fill of 16
009 Fill of 17
010 Fill of 18
011 Cut of small pit
012 Cut of pit
013 Cut of small pit
014 Cut of pit
015 Cut of large circular ash pit
016 Cut of small pit
017 Cut of small pit
018 Cut of small pit
019 Arbitrary spit
020 Arbitrary spit below 19
021 Arbitrary spit below 20

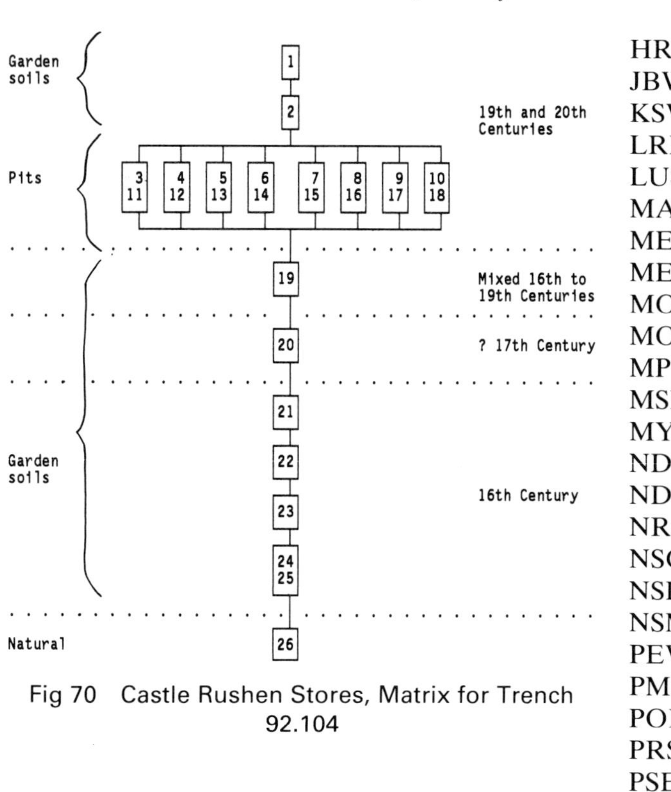

Fig 70   Castle Rushen Stores, Matrix for Trench
92.104

022   Arbitrary spit below 21
023   Arbitrary spit below 22
024   Fill of 25
025   Cut of linear feature
026   Natural

List of pottery codes

AGB	Agate bodied earthenware		HRS	Hollow reversed slipware
BGE	Bristol-type grey-bodied earthenware		JBW	Jackfield blackware
BSC	Beauvais sgraffito		KSW	Khaki-coloured stoneware
BSS	Brown salt-glazed stoneware		LRE	Lead-glazed red-bodied earthenware
BST	Beauvais stoneware		LUS	Lustreware
BSW	Brown stoneware		MAR	Martincamp flask
BTP	Blue transfer printed		MED	Medieval earthenware
CEW	Coarse gritty green-glazed earthenware		MER	Merida
CHP	Chinese porcelain		MOC	Mocha
CLP	Clay pipe		MOT	Mottled ware
CPW	Coarse purpleware		MPW	Midland purpleware
CRE	Creamware		MSM	Manx smoothware
CSW	Cologne stoneware		MYW	Midland yellow ware
DBB	Dark-glazed buff-bodied earthenware		NDG	North Devon gravel-tempered ware
DRB	Dark-glazed red-bodied earthenware		NDS	Nottingham/Derby stoneware
DRW	Drabware		NRG	Northern reduced greenware
ELW	Elersware		NSG	North Devon sgraffito
FSW	Frechen stoneware		NSL	North Devon slipware
GTW	Granite-tempered ware (Manx)		NSM	North Devon smoothware
HBS	Hollow buff-bodied slipware		PEW	Pearlware
HGT	Ham Green type earthenware		PMS	Press-moulded slipware
HMJ	Hartley marmalade jar type		POR	Porcelain
			PRS	Press-moulded reversed slipware
			PSE	Peasant enamel
			PTW	Prattware
			RBE	Red-bodied earthenware
			RMW	Red-bodied mottled ware
			RSC	Red-slip-coated buff-bodied earthenware
			RSO	Red-bodied overall yellow slip
			RSP	Red-bodied Rainford-type speckled ware
			RSR	Red-slip-coated red earthenware
			RST	Red-bodied trailed yellow slip
			RSW	Raeren stoneware
			RYW	Rainford-type yellow ware
			SAG	Saintonge 'all-over green'
			SBR	Brown Saintonge
			SCD	Saintonge chafing dish
			SEB	Shell-edged blue
			SMG	Saintonge mottled green earthenware
			SPA	Saintonge Palissy
			SPE	Speckled ware
			SPI	Pink Saintonge
			SPR	Red-bodied speckled ware
			SPY	Saintonge polychrome
			STW	Stoneware
			SUN	Unglazed Saintonge
			TGE	Tin-glazed earthenware
			TUD	Tudor green
			UCE	Unglazed coarse earthenware
			UCM	Unglazed clay marble
			UGS	Unglazed Saintonge earthenware
			URE	Unglazed red earthenware
			WBA	Wedgewood's basalt
			WDS	White dipped salt-glazed stoneware
			WES	Westerwald stoneware
			WHW	White ware
			WLN	Whieldan

WSB	White stoneware bottle		YST	Yellow-slip-coated slip-trailed red-bodied earthenware
WSE	White-bodied earthenware and stoneware		YSW	Yellow stoneware
WSS	White-bodied salt-glazed stoneware		YWA	Yellow ware
WSW	White stoneware			

BIBLIOGRAPHY

Maps

First Edition OS 25″, 1868, Sheet XVI.15

Trade Directories

The following Trade Directories in the Manx Museum Library have been consulted:
Bents 1902, 1907
Browns 1882, 1894
Pigots 1824, 1837
Pigot and Slaters 1843
Slaters 1846, 1852, 1857
Thwaites 1863

Books and Articles

Airne C W, 1949 *The Story of the Isle of Man 1, The earliest times to 1406*, privately published by C W Airne, Southport

Airne C W, 1964 *The Story of the Isle of Man 2, 1406 to modern times*, Norris Modern Press, Douglas, Isle of Man

Anon, 1931 Unpublished Documents in the Manx Museum, *J Manx Museum*, **II**, no 26, 9–14

Anon, 1987 'Alphabetical List of Pipemakers in Scotland', *The Archaeology of the Clay Tobacco Pipe X* (ed P J Davey), British Archaeological Reports, British Series, **178**, 337–50

Armstrong P, 1977 'Excavations in Sewer Lane, Hull, 1974', *East Riding Archaeologist*, **3**, Hull Old Town Report series 1

Baart J M *et al*, 1977 *Opgravingen in Amsterdam*, Amsterdam

Barrett J and Young C M, 1980 *Pocket Guide to the Sea Shore*, Collins, London

Bartlett K S, Brears P C D and Moorhouse S, 1971 'Excavations at Potovens, near Wakefield, 1968', *Post-medieval Archaeology*, **V**, 1–34

Bawden T A, Garrad L S, Qualtrough J K and Scatchard J W, 1972 *The Industrial Archaeology of the Isle of Man*, David and Charles, Newton Abbot

Bazin F (ed), 1984 *The Manx Loaghtan Sheep: The breed that refused to die*, The Manx Loaghtan Breed Society

Bearpark P J and Johnson B, 1977 'Lymn', in Davey (ed) 1977, 48–53

Bersu G, 1974 'Chapel Hill—A Prehistoric, Early Christian and Viking site at Balladoole, Kirk Arbory, Isle of Man', *Proc Isle of Man Nat Hist Antiq Soc*, **VII**, no 14, 632–65

Biddle M, 1990 *Object and Economy in Medieval Winchester* (2 vols), Winchester Studies, Oxford University Press, Oxford

Boessneck J, 1969 'Osteological Differences between Sheep and Goat', *Science in Archaeology* (eds D Brothwell and E Higgs), Thames and Hudson, London, 331–58

Boyd-Dawkins W, 1890 'Human, Animal and Marine Molluscan Identifications', in Swinnerton 1890

Brears P, 1967 'Excavations at Potovens, near Wakefield', *Post-medieval Archaeology*, **1**, 3–43

Brotherton-Ratcliffe E H, forthcoming *The Cheshire Tile Census*

Bruce J R, Colman J S and Jones N S (eds), 1963 *Marine Fauna of the Isle of Man and its Surrounding Seas*, Liverpool University Press, Liverpool

Buchanan, R and Stowell L, 1985 *Lorne House, Castletown*, Lorne House Trust Limited, Castletown, Isle of Man

Butler L, 1988 'The Cistercian Abbey of St Mary of Rushen Excavations 1978–79', *J Brit Archaeol Assoc*, **CXLI**, 90–94

Cable M, unpublished 'A History of Windows', public lecture, 23 May 1991, Society of Glass Technology North West Section, University of Sheffield

Campbell K, 1986 'Some Medieval Floor Tiles from Drogheda', *J Old Drogheda Soc*, **5**, 14–20

Charleston R J, 1984 *English Glass and the Glass Used in England, c400–1940*, George Allen and Unwin, London

Corlett D, c1974 *Castletown*, Castletown Press, Castletown, Isle of Man

Cornwall I W, 1974 'Animal Remains from Occupation Layer D', in Bersu 1974, 663–64

Coy J, 1981 'Animal Husbandry and Faunal Exploitation in Hampshire', in *The Archaeology of Hampshire* (eds S J Shennan and R T Schadla-Hall), Hampshire Field Club and Archaeol Soc Monograph, **1**, 95–103

Cramp S and Simmons K E L (eds), 1977 *Handbook of the Birds of Europe, the Middle East and North Africa Vol 1*, Oxford University Press, London

Cramp S and Simmons K E L (eds), 1980 *Handbook of the Birds of Europe, the Middle East and North Africa Vol 2*, Oxford University Press, London

Crellin M, 1969 'An early manorial roll', *J Manx Museum*, **VII**, no 85, 98–99, plates 28 and 29

Cubbon A M, 1971 'The Medieval Chapel of St Mary's, Castletown Later the Castletown Grammar School', *Proc Isle of Man Nat Hist and Antiq Soc*, **VII**, no 3, 1–36

Cullen J P and Slinn D J, 1983 *The Birds of the Isle of Man*, Manx Museum and National Trust, Douglas, Isle of Man

Cumming J G, 1848 *The Isle of Man: its History, Physical, Ecclesiastical, Civil and Legendary*, John van Voorst, London

Curphy R A, 1982 'Peel Castle', *Proc Isle of Man Nat Hist and Antiq Soc*, **IX**, no 1 (for 1980–1982), 59–94

Davey P J (ed), 1977 *Medieval Pottery from Excavations in the North West*, Institute of Extension Studies, University of Liverpool, Liverpool

Davey P J, 1989 'Pottery Production in Prescot', *J Merseyside Archaeol Soc*, **5** (for 1982–3), 103–06

Davey P J, 1991 'The Post-Roman Pottery', *J Merseyside Archaeol Soc*, **7** (for 1986–7), 121–42

Davey P J, 1992a 'Smoothwares', in Lewis 1992

Davey P J, 1992b 'The Pottery from the Peel Town Excavations', in Lewis 1992, 65–66

Davey P J, forthcoming 'The Ceramic Evidence from the Peel Castle Excavations 1982–87', in Freke, forthcoming

Davey P J and Rutter J A, 1977 'A Note on Continental Imports in the North West 800–1700 AD', *Medieval Ceramics*, **1**, 17–30

Davidson L S, and Davey P J, 1982 'Thin Section Analysis of Clay Used in Five British Clay Pipe Production Centres', *The Archaeology of the Clay Tobacco Pipe VII* (ed P J Davey), British Archaeological Reports, British Series **100**, 311–44

Davies W J, 1969 *The Nineteenth-Century Token Coinage*, 1904 reprint, B A Seaby Ltd, London

Duco D H, 1981 'De Kleipijp in de Zeventiende Eeuwse Nederlanden', *The Archaeology of the Clay Tobacco Pipe V* (ed P J Davey), British Archaeological Reports, International Series, **106 (ii)**, 111–468

Egan G, forthcoming a, in a report on post-medieval finds from London City sites

Egan G, forthcoming b *The Medieval Household* (Medieval finds from London Excavations Series), HMSO

Egan G and Pritchard F, 1991 'Dress Accessories', *Medieval Finds from London Excavations 3*, HMSO

Egan G *et al*, 1986 'Marks on Milled Window Leads', *Post-medieval Archaeol*, **20**, 303–09

Evans D H, 1979 'Gravel-Tempered Ware: A Survey of Published Forms', *Medieval and Later Pottery in Wales 2*, Welsh Medieval Pottery Research Group, Cardiff, 18–29

Evans J G, 1983 'Appendix 2: Molluscs and Other Invertebrates from Ardnave, Islay', in 'Excavations at Ardnave, Islay' (G Ritchie and H Welfare), *Proc Soc Antiq Scotland*, **113**, 350–58

Evans J and Evans V, 1987 'Marine Shells', in 'Excavations at the Ty Mawr Hut-Circles, Holyhead, Anglesey' (C Smith), *Archaeol Cambriensis*, **135**, 55–63

Evans J G and Spencer P, 1976–77 'The Mollusca and Environment, Buckquoy, Orkney', in 'Excavations of Pictish and Viking Age Farmsteads at Buckquoy, Orkney' (A Ritchie), *Proc Soc Antiq Scotland*, **108**, 215–17

Fenton A, 1976 'Traditional Elements in the Diet of the Northern Isles of Scotland', *Reports Second Internat Symp Ethnol Food Res*, Helsinki, 1–16

Fisher C T, forthcoming 'Report on the Bird Bones from the Peel Castle Excavations 1982–87', in Freke, forthcoming

Fisher J M Mc, 1966 *The Shell Bird Book*, Ebury Press and Michael Joseph, London

Fontecha y Sanchez R de, 1968 *La Moneda de Vellon y cobre de la Monarquia Española (años 1516–1931)*, Par Artef Gráficas SL, Madrid

Freke D, 1990 'History', in Robinson and McCarroll 1990, 103–22

Freke D, forthcoming *Excavations at Peel Castle 1982–1987*, Liverpool University Press, Liverpool

Gallagher D B, 1987 'The 1900 Price List of the Pipe Makers Society', *The Archaeology of the Clay Tobacco Pipe X* (ed P J Davey), British Archaeological Reports, British Series, **178**, 142–63

Gallagher D B and Price R, 1987a 'Thomas Davidson and Co, Glasgow', *The Archaeology of the Clay Tobacco Pipe X*, (ed P J Davey), British Archaeological Reports, British Series, **178**, 110–38

Gallagher D B and Price R, 1987b 'The Irish Price List of D McDougall', *The Archaeology of the Clay Tobacco Pipe X* (ed P J Davey), British Archaeological Reports, British Series, **178**, 139–41

Garrad L S, 1969 'Castletown Excavations', *Proc Isle of Man Nat Hist and Antiq Soc*, **VII**, no 2 (for 1966–68), 264–67

Garrad L S, 1972a 'Bird Remains, Including those of a Great Auk *Alca impennis* from a Midden Deposit in a Cave at Perwick Bay, Isle of Man', *Ibis*, **114**, 258–59

Garrad L S, 1972b *The Naturalist in the Isle of Man*, David and Charles, Newton Abbot

Garrad L S, 1977 'Was Pottery Made in the Isle of Man in Medieval Times?', in Davey (ed) 1977, 109–12

Garrad L S, 1978 'Medieval Pottery in the Isle of Man', in *Man and Environment in the Isle of Man* (ed P J Davey), British Archaeological Reports, British Series, **54 (ii)**, 357–65

Garrad L S, 1990 'Late Glacial and Postglacial Environment' in Robinson and McCarroll 1990, 55–76

Gawne J, 1944 'A Memory of the Great Auk?', *Peregrine*, **1 (2)**

Good G L and Russett V E J, 1987 'Common Types of Earthenware Found in the Bristol Area', *Bristol and Avon Archaeol*, **6**, 36–37

Goodall A R, 1983 'Non-Ferrous Metal Objects', in *Sandal Castle Excavations 1964–1973* (eds P Mayes and L A S Butler), Wakefield, 231–39

Goodall A R, 1985 'Copper Alloy Objects', in *Post-Medieval Sites and their Pottery: Moulsham Street, Chelmsford* (eds C M Cunningham and P J Drury), CBA Research Report **54**, Chelmsford Archaeological Trust Report **5**, 40–50

Grant A, 1975 'The Animal Bones', and 'Appendix B: the use of tooth wear as a guide to the age of domestic animals', in *Excavations at Portchester Castle, Vol 1: Roman* (ed B Cunliffe), Society of Antiquaries, London, 378–408 and 437–50

Grant A, 1983 *North Devon Pottery: The Seventeenth Century*, University of Exeter, Exeter

Grieve Symington, 1885 *The Great Auk, or Garefowl—Its History, Archaeology and Remains*, Thomas C Jack, London

Harrison H M and Davey P J, 1977 'Ewloe Kiln', in Davey 1977, 92–99

Higgins D A, 1992 'Speke Hall: Excavations in the West Range, 1981–82', *J Merseyside Archaeol Soc*, **8** (for 1988/9), 47–84

Hilton Price F G, 1908 *Old Base Metal Spoons*, Batsford, London

Hinton D A, 1990 'Hooked Tags', in *Object and Economy in Medieval Winchester* (ed M Biddle), Winchester Studies, 7, **II**, Oxford

Holling F, 1977 'Reflections on Tudor Green', *Post-medieval Archaeol*, **11**, 61–66

Hopstaken L, 1987 'Mantelhaker', in *Schatten uit de Schelde*, Markiezenhof Museum exhibition catalogue (H Bos *et al*), Bergen op Zoom (Netherlands), 44–48

Hume I N, 1961 'The Glass Wine Bottle in Colonial Virginia', *J Glass Studies*, **3**, 90–117

Hurst J G, Neal D S and Van Beuningen H J E, 1986 *Pottery Produced and Traded in North-West Europe 1350–1650*, Rotterdam Papers VI, Museum Boymans-van Beuningen, Rotterdam

Jewitt L, 1885 'Decorated Paving Tiles at Rushen Abbey', in *The Reliquary*, **XXV**, 167–69

Kermode P M C, 1924 'Balladoole Excursion Report', *Proc Isle of Man Nat Hist and Antiq Soc*, **II**, 174–77

Kermode P M C and Herdman W A, 1914 *Manks Antiquities*, Liverpool University Press, Liverpool

Lamplugh G W, 1903 'The Geology of the Isle of Man', *Mem Geol Surv UK*, **XIV**

Le Cheminant R, 1985 'The Development of the Pipeclay Hair Curler—A Preliminary Study', *The Archaeology of the Clay Tobacco Pipe VII*, British Archaeological Reports, British Series **100**, 345–54, Oxford

Lewis J (ed), 1992 *Peel Town: An Archaeological and Architectural Assessment*, Isle of Man Government and the University of Liverpool, Douglas

Llewellyn-Jones J and Pain C, 1980 'Oyster Shells', in 'Excavations at Billingsgate Buildings, Lower Thames Street, London, 1974' (eds D M Jones and M Rhodes), *London and Middlesex Archaeol Soc Special Paper*, **3**

Madoc H W, 1934 *Bird-life in the Isle of Man*, H F and G Witherby, London

Margeson S, 1993 *Norwich Households: the Medieval and Post-Medieval Finds from Norwich Survey Excavations 1971–78*, East Anglian Archaeol Rept, **58**

McCarroll D, Garrad L and Dackombe R, 1990 'Lateglacial and Postglacial Environmental History', in Robinson and McCarroll 1990, 55–76

McCarthy M, 1988 'Animals in the Economy of Medieval and Post Medieval Cork', unpublished MA thesis, University College Cork

Moore A W, 1900 *A History of the Isle of Man, I and II*, Fisher Unwin, London

Moorhouse S, 1971 'Finds from Basing House, Hampshire' (*c*1540–1645): Part Two in *Post-medieval Archaeol*, **5**, 35–76

Moorhouse S and Roberts I, 1992 'Wrenthorpe Potteries: Excavations of 16th and 17th-Century Potting Tenements near Wakefield, 1983', *Yorkshire Archaeol*, **2**

Murdoch T *et al*, 1991 *Treasures and Trinkets*, Museum of London, London

Noake P, 1993 'The Post-Medieval Pottery', in *Beeston Castle, Cheshire: A Report on the Excavations 1968–85 by Laurence Keen and Peter Hough* (ed P Ellis), Historic Buildings and Monuments Commission for England, London, 191–210

Noddle B, 1978 'Some Minor Skeletal Differences in Sheep', in 'Research Problems in Zooarchaeology' (eds D Brothwell, K D Thomas and J Clutton-Brock), *Inst Archaeol Occasional Publication*, **3**, 133–41

Nöel Hume I, 1970 *A Guide to Artifacts of Colonial America*, Knopf, New York

North J J, 1980 *English Hammered Coinage II*, 2nd edn, Spink and Son, London

North J J, 1994 *English Hammered Coinage I*, 3rd edn, Spink and Son, London

O'Neil B H St J, 1951 *Castle Rushen, Isle of Man*, Reprint from *Archaeologia*, **XCIV**, published by the Government Property Trustees, Isle of Man

Parkes C, 1992 'Micaceous Ware', in Lewis 1992, 62–63

Parslow J L F, 1967 'Changes in Status Among Breeding Birds in Britain and Ireland', *British Birds*, **60 (1)**, 2–47

Pearce J and Vince A, 1988 *A Dated Type-Series of London Medieval Pottery Part 4: Surrey White-wares*, London and Middlesex Archaeol Soc, London

Pennant T, 1776 *British Zoology*, **2**, Printed by W Eyres, Warrington for B White, London

Philpott R A, 1985a 'Mottled Ware', *J Merseyside Archaeol Soc*, **4** (for 1980–81), 50–62

Philpott R A, 1985b 'Wig-Curlers', *J Merseyside Archaeol Soc*, **4** (for 1980–81), 128–131

Philpott R A, 1989 'The Finds', in 'A Timber Framed Building at 21–23 Eccleston Street, Prescot (Site 30)' (eds R M Cowell and G Chitty), *J Merseyside Archaeol Soc*, **5** (for 1982–83), 27–33

Philpott R A and Davey P J, 1992 'Appendix 5: Peel Town Sampling Project 1985', in Lewis 1992, 55–73

Platt C and Coleman-Smith R, 1975 *Excavations in Medieval Southampton 1953–1969* (2 vols), Leicester University Press, Leicester

Ponsford M, 1983 'North European Pottery Imported into Bristol 1200–1500', in *Ceramics and Trade: The production and distribution of later medieval pottery in north-west Europe* (eds P J Davey and R Hodges), Department of Prehistory and Archaeology, University of Sheffield, Sheffield, 219–24

Prummel W and Frisch H J, 1986 'A Guide for the Distinction of Species, Sex and Body Size in Bones of Sheep and Goat', *J Archaeol Sci*, **13**, 567–77

Radcliffe C, 1989 *Shining by the Sea: a history of Ramsey 1800–1914*, privately published, Douglas

Radcliffe F J, 1991 *Manx Sea Fishing 1600–1990s*, Manx Heritage Foundation, Douglas, Isle of Man

Ralfe P G, 1905 *The Birds of the Isle of Man*, David Douglas, Edinburgh

Rigby A, 1927 *Castle Rushen: a historical and descriptive account*, Victoria Press, Douglas, Isle of Man

Robertson D, 1794 (1970 reprint) *A Tour Through The Isle of Man*, reprinted by Frank Graham, Newcastle-upon-Tyne

Robinson V and McCarroll D, 1990 *The Isle of Man: Celebrating a sense of place*, Liverpool University Press, Liverpool

Rutter J A, 1977 'Chester: Deanery Field Kiln No 2 (CHE/KIL)', in Davey 1977, 86–91

Rutter J A and Davey P J, 1980 'Clay Pipes from Chester', *The Archaeology of the Clay Tobacco Pipe III* (ed P J Davey), British Archaeological Reports, British Series, **78**, 41–272

Schmid E, 1972 *Atlas of Animal Bones for Prehistorians, Archaeologists and Quaternary Geologists*, Elsevier, Amsterdam

Schofield J, Palliser D and Harding C, 1981 *Recent Archaeological Research in English Towns*, Council for British Archaeology, London

Seaby Ltd B A, 1984 *Standard Catalogue of British Coins 2: Coins of Scotland, Ireland and the Islands*, London

Silver I A, 1971 'The Ageing of Domestic Animals', in *Science in Archaeology* (eds D Brothwell and E Higgs), Thames and Hudson, London, 230–68

Simon A L, 1944 *A Concise Encyclopaedia of Gastronomy*, Section 6 Birds and their Eggs, The Wine and Food Society, London

Somers Cocks A and Blair C, 1979 *Masterpieces of Cutlery and the Art of Eating*, Victoria and Albert Museum exhibition catalogue, London

Stenning E H, 1945 'Ancient Structures Uncovered at Derbyhaven, May 1935', *Proc Isle of Man Nat Hist and Antiq Soc*, **IV** (1932–42), 145–51

Stone L M, 1974 *Fort Michilimackinac 1715–1781*, Michigan State University Museum Anthropological Series, **2**, Mackinac Island State Park Commission, USA

Swinnerton F, 1890 'The Early Neolithic Cists and Refuse Heap at Port St Mary', *Proc Isle of Man Nat Hist and Antiq Soc*, **I**, no 5, 137–39

Swinnerton F, 1912 'Children's Rhymes in the Isle of Man', *Proc Isle of Man Nat Hist and Antiq Soc*, **II**, 41–2

Tait H, 1967 'Glass with Chequered Spiral-Trail Decoration: a group made in the Southern Netherlands in the 16th and 17th centuries', *J Glass Studies*, **9**, 94–112

Talbot T, 1924 *Manorial Roll of the Isle of Man, 1511–1515*, Oxford University Press, Oxford

Townley R, 1791 *A Journal Kept in the Isle of Man*, Volumes I and II, J Ware and Son, Whitehaven

Townsend M, 1967 'The Common Limpet (*Patella vulgata*) as a Source of Protein', *Folia Biologica*, **15 (3)**, 22–30

Von den Driesch A, 1976 *A Guide to the Measurement of Animal Bones from Archaeological Sites*, Bulletin 1, Peabody Museum, Harvard University

Watkins C M, 1960 'North Devon Pottery and its export to America in the 17th Century', *United States National Museum Bulletin*, **225**, 19–59

White A J, 1977 'Silverdale', in Davey (ed) 1977, 102–03

Williamson K, 1939 'The Great Auk in Man', *J Manx Museum*, **4**, 168–72

Woodfield C T P, 1966 'Yellow-Glazed Wares of the Seventeenth Century', *Birmingham Archaeol Soc Trans*, **81**, 78–88

Woodfield C, 1981 'Finds from the Free Grammar School at the Whitefriars, Coventry', *Post-medieval Archaeol*, **15**, 81–159

Woods H, 1982 'Excavations at Eltham Palace 1975–9', *Trans London and Middlesex Archaeol Soc*, **33**, 214–65

Wright M D, 1980–82 'Excavations at Peel Castle, 1947', *Proc Isle of Man Nat Hist and Antiq Soc*, **IX**, no 1, 21–57